The Encyclopedia of **SEA WARFARE**

from the first ironclads to the present day

a Salamander book

Published by
Thomas Y. Crowell Company
Established 1834
New York

The Encyclopedia of SEA WARFARE
from the first ironclads to the present day

A SALAMANDER BOOK

This edition published 1975 by
Thomas Y. Crowell Company
666 Fifth Avenue
New York, New York 10019
United States of America

ISBN 0 690 00769 8

Library of Congress Catalog Number:
74-02900

© Salamander Books Limited 1975
Hammer House
113 Wardour Street
London W.1
United Kingdom

This volume not to be sold outside
the United States of America or
Canada

Filmset by Photoprint Plates Ltd,
Rayleigh, Essex, England

Reproduced by
City Engraving Ltd, Hull
Yorkshire, England

Printed in Belgium by
Henri Proost, Turnhout,
Belgium

All correspondence concerning the
content of this volume should be
addressed to Salamander Books Limited.

CREDITS

**Captain Donald Macintyre, D.S.O.,
D.S.C. and Antony Preston**:
Consultants

Iain Parsons: Editor
Chris Steer: Design
Jonathan Moore: Photo research
Richard Natkiel: Maps
Profile Publications: Ship profiles in
colour
A & A Plans: Ship profiles in black line

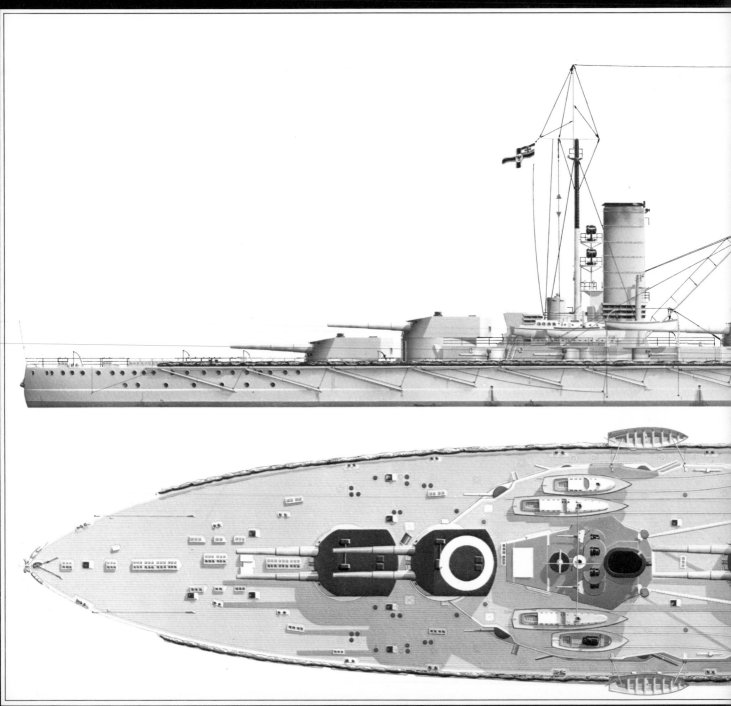

THE AUTHORS

Oliver Warner
Historian and author of numerous authoritative books on sea warfare and biographies of some of the great names of naval history, Vice-President of the Society for National Research, a member of the Council of the Navy Records Society, served in the Secretariat of the Admiralty in World War II.

Captain Geoffrey Bennett, D.S.C., R.N.
Author of many books on naval history and biography covering the last two hundred years, including both world wars, served as a signal communications specialist during World War II in the Home Fleet, in Force H in the Mediterranean, and in the South Atlantic.

Captain Donald Macintyre, D.S.O., D.S.C.
One of Britain's most respected naval historians and the author of numerous books on maritime history and the naval events of World War II, trained and served as a pilot with the Fleet Air Arm and during World War II became one of the most accomplished Escort Group Commanders in the Battle of the Atlantic.

Frank Uhlig, Jr.
United States Naval Institute senior editor, a veteran of the U.S. Navy, editor of the annual Naval Review, *a highly respected author on naval affairs and maritime history, and an authority on the nature of sea power and the roles of the Soviet and the United States navies.*

Desmond Wettern
Naval correspondent of the Sunday Telegraph, a frequent contributor to international specialist naval and defence journals, the author of a number of books on naval history, served in Britain's post-war Navy, former London editor of NATO Journal and an expert on the changing roles of the world's navies since World War II.

Antony Preston
Technical editor of Navy International, *a frequent contributor to authoritative international journals on naval affairs, formerly with the National Maritime Museum and the author of several books on the ships of both world wars.*

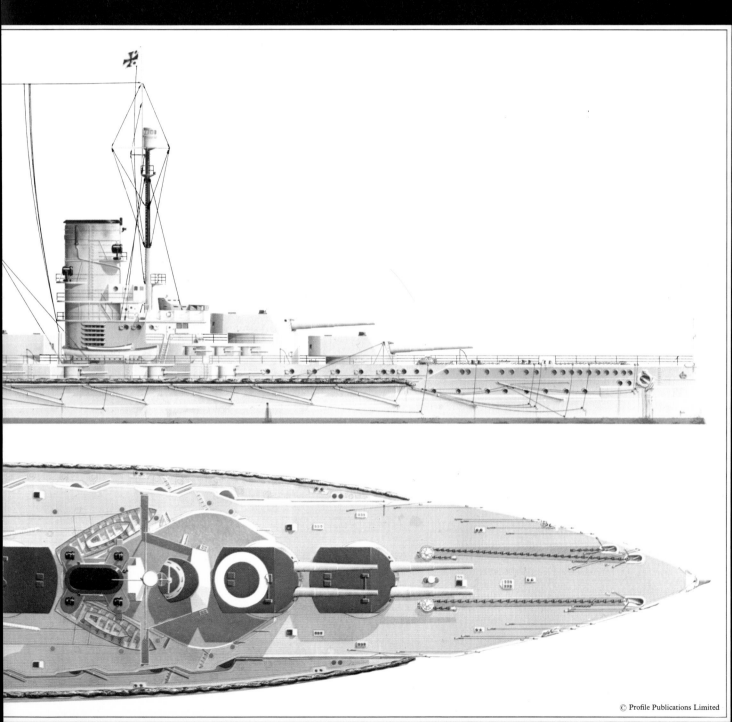

CONTENTS

HAMPTON ROADS TO TSUSHIMA

WORLD WAR I

FOREWORD

**By Admiral of the Fleet
the Earl Mountbatten of Burma, KG, PC,
GCB, OM, GCSI, GCIE, GCVO, DSO, FRS.**

At the time of my birth in 1900 my father, who had entered the Royal Navy as a Cadet in 1868, was a Captain. He belonged to the 'progressive' school of Naval Officers – headed at that time by Admiral Sir John Fisher who initiated the great Naval reforms then impending, and which really created the Navy which fought the First World War.

In 1902, whilst commanding the Battleship *Implacable*, he was made a Commodore and put in command of the 'X' Fleet for special joint manoeuvres. 'X' Fleet consisted of older, weaker and slower ships which were blockaded in the harbour of Argostoli by the combined might of the Mediterranean and Channel Fleets, with all their modern ships, but my father contrived to make a brilliant escape from the harbour under their very noses. This skilful performance signed the death-warrant of the Navy's traditional strategy of close blockade, which had been handed down from the days of Nelson.

In 1906 Admiral Fisher brought about a Naval revolution: the launching of HMS *Dreadnought*, the first all big-gun, turbine-driven, fast capital ship. This largely wiped out Britain's existing advantage in great numbers of pre-*Dreadnought* battleships and was a tremendous advance in Capital ship design.

But despite all Fisher's modernisations, the 'Agadir Crisis' in 1911 revealed a frightening gap in British preparations. There was no understanding between the War Office and the Admiralty over what

should be done in case of war, and it appeared that Lord Fisher had retired leaving the Navy with no written war plan at all. It was to clear up this mess that Winston Churchill first came to the Admiralty as First Lord in October 1911.

Two months later my father returned to the Admiralty as Second Sea Lord but it was a year later, in December 1912, when my father became First Sea Lord that the most fruitful period of his association with Churchill began. Together they started a Naval War Staff, they revised the war plans, this time taking the Army into account, and they decided on the strategy of distant blockade which was adopted from the moment war was declared.

But by far the most important thing they did together was their decision not to hold the normal annual manoeuvres in 1914 but instead to have, at my father's suggestion, a Test Mobilisation of the Reserve Fleet to find out just how effective the arrangements were for bringing the Navy quickly up to strength in time of war. This exercise took place in July 1914 and worked without a hitch. By this time I was in the Navy myself, having entered the Royal Naval College at Osborne the year before. We cadets were also mobilised and I was sent to my brother's ship, the battle-cruiser *New Zealand*.

After the Test Mobilisation the whole Fleet assembled at Spithead for the Royal Review – a sort of grand climax of two hundred years of British naval supremacy – which unbeknown to us at the time was soon going to be put to the ultimate test for all the time The King was reviewing his Fleet at Spithead the international situation was building up to the final crises which led to World War I.

As First Sea Lord my father was, of course, one of the first to know and it was on 26th July 1914 that he took the most momentous decision of his life. It was a Sunday and the First Lord and most of the Cabinet had gone away for the week-end. The next day all the men who had been called up for the Test Mobilisation were due to be paid off to go on holidays and the Fleet would be dispersed. Thus from a position of unparalleled naval strength and preparedness the country would pass overnight into a state of relative unpreparedness. On the other hand not to demobilise could well be construed as an act of war and might aggravate the international situation. It was a fearful decision to have to take and I remember my father telling me that he had had to take it absolutely alone. But there was no mistaking the meaning of the information coming in and he wrote out in his own hand the telegrams ordering the Fleet to stand fast. Churchill, when he heard what had been done, gave his immediate approval. And so, on 4th August 1914, when Britain found herself at war my father was able to report to the King "We have the drawn sword in our hand".

On 31st May 1916 259 British and German warships met and grappled in the North Sea at the Battle of Jutland. The British, in a series of unco-ordinated encounters, lost fourteen ships, the Germans eleven. The British failed to destroy the German Fleet which was their intention but the Germans also failed to cripple the British Fleet and the perils and losses they encountered at Jutland so discouraged them that they never sought battle again.

The battle-cruiser fleet was commanded by Vice Admiral Sir David Beatty, whose flagship was HMS *Lion*. I joined the *Lion* less than seven weeks after the Battle of Jutland. I was terribly disappointed to have missed the battle; my brother in the *New Zealand*, had been in the thick of it and of course everybody was talking about it. As a midshipman, just turned sixteen, I was tremendously excited to be in Beatty's Flagship. We thought the *Lion* was the greatest ship in the world, with the bravest men and the finest Admiral. When, a few months later, Beatty was appointed Commander-in-Chief of the Grand Fleet, I had the great fortune to be appointed to join his new flagship, the battleship *Queen Elizabeth*.

Britain had entered the war in August 1914 as the world's greatest sea-power and this received its acknowledgement on 21st November 1918 when the German High Seas Fleet made its last trip across the North Sea to surrender to the Royal Navy. This was a remarkable and ironic moment. Their Fleet undoubtedly played a significant part in building up the war fever and yet when war came this vast armada spent most of it in complete idleness. It only encountered its declared enemy – the British Grand Fleet, on one day, at Jutland, and it ended its existence in mutiny and abject surrender.

On the outbreak of the Second World War I was in command of the 5th Destroyer Flotilla. This was a wonderful command because they were all brand new ships of the 'J' and 'K' class, still building. My own ship, the Flotilla Leader, was HMS *Kelly*. For the first twenty-one months of the war I remained in command of this Destroyer Flotilla. Although this is often referred to as the period of the 'phoney war' for us at sea it was very real. My ship the *Kelly* was mined and later torpedoed in the North Sea, when I had to bring her home with her starboard gunwhale awash. She finally went down with her guns firing during the Battle of Crete.

In August 1941 I was appointed in command of the aircraft carrier *Illustrious* which had been severely damaged in Malta and was being repaired in the US Navy Yard at Norfolk. There was not a lot for me to do onboard while the *Illustrious* was refitting so I was delighted to be invited to visit the US Pacific Fleet and lecture to the officers about what the war at sea was like. The Fleet Base was Pearl Harbor and after two years of war I was appalled to see how unprepared the Americans were, and how vulnerable Pearl Harbor was to a surprise attack.

On my return from Pearl Harbor I received a telegram from Prime Minister Churchill ordering me to return home at once. I was put in charge of "Combined Operations" and given active part in planning the Normandy invasion. Before it took place, however, I was appointed in the Autumn of 1943 to be Supreme Allied Commander of the newly-formed South East Asia Command.

Victory in South East Asia on land and in the air was built on the firm foundation of the security of our sea communication for no combination of land and air forces could have succeeded if our merchant ships to, and within, the Command had ceased to run regularly and efficiently. It was the Navy which established superiority over the Japanese in preparation for the assault on Malaya, when the enemy's sea communications were cut as effectively as his land communications.

A number of Naval operations were carried out in the South East Asia Command but in particular I remember the sinking of the large Japanese 8 inch gun cruiser, *Haguro*, by the 26th Destroyer Flotilla.

On 15th May 1945 information was received in the early morning that a small Japanese convoy was in the Andaman Sea, steering south. The 26th Destroyer Flotilla was detached to intercept and was followed some hours later by the French Battleship *Richelieu* and a cruiser. About midday an enemy cruiser and destroyer (later identified as the *Haguro* and *Kamikaze* respectively) were sighted by aircraft. Just before midnight, after steaming 330 miles at 27 knots, the 26th Destroyer Flotilla obtained radar contact with the enemy at 78,000 yards and after manoeuvring for position, attacked with torpedoes and sank the cruiser *Haguro* without sustaining any serious damage themselves.

In July 1965 I retired from the post of Chief of the Defence Staff. I had been in uniform for fifty-two years and I had always been proud of that uniform. As a young midshipman I wept when I left my first ship, Admiral Beatty's flagship the *Lion*. I thought I would never love another ship so much – but of course I did. The Navy gave me great happiness.

This Encyclopedia of Sea Warfare covers naval history from the first Ironclads to the present day. It deals with a period of history during which sea warfare has undergone profound and far-reaching changes which I have found fascinating. I am sure readers will also be fascinated.

A.F.

HMS *Kelly*

The first clash of ironclads

The Dutch Buffel (1868), an early ironclad monitor built by the Glasgow firm of Robert Napier & Sons. She was typical of the coast defence ships built by all navies after the American Civil War. Unlike the original Monitor these later ships had more freeboard to allow them to fight their guns at sea.

During the American Civil War the historic Battle of Hampton Roads, the first between two ironclads, proved that either shells or armour would have to be transformed if the new protected ships were to decide a large scale naval battle. There were experiments with mines and spar torpedoes and highly dangerous submersibles. Then, in Europe the tactic of ramming earned an undeserved reputation at the Battle of Lissa. But by the 1870s revolving gun turrets were established and the advantages of doing away with sail rig had been convincingly demonstrated.

The last fleet action fought wholly under sail occurred in October 1827 at Navarino, where a squadron of British, French and Russian ships destroyed a Turkish-Egyptian force engaged in repressing the Greeks. Within the next thirty years, naval warfare was transformed by new inventions, or by the development of those as yet untried in operations.

During the Crimean War (1854–1856) the British and French were ranged against the Russians, though maritime activity was confined to the Baltic in the north and to the Black Sea in the south. The Russian navy was supine, presenting little opposition except in the shape of mines. This was strange, because in 1853, at Sinope on the Black Sea, Admiral Nakhimov had annihilated a Turkish force under Osman Pasha. The Russians had made devastating use of explosive shells devised by the Frenchman, Henri Paixhans.

The Anglo-French forces included ships of the line fitted with steam engines, much disliked by the deck officers. The French included iron-clad mobile batteries, for use against Russian forts.

The British followed suit in 1856 with this type of vessel, producing the *Thunderbolt*, *Aetna*, *Erebus* and *Terror*. The first and last of these ships had long lives, but they saw no testing service, and were not in commission until the war was over.

The French, ever inventive, were again ahead of their recent allies when in 1859 they produced the *Gloire*. She was of 5,617 tons displacement and was classed as a frigate. Her speed (13 knots) and her hull, which was of wood, but encased with iron, made her a formidable proposition. She had 34 guns,

and was originally rigged as a barquentine. Her designer was Dupuy de Lôme, generously described by a British contemporary as 'first among naval constructors of our time'.

As ironclads had become established as the warships of the immediate future, experts gave their attention to the problem of how best to arm them. The revolving turret seemed to be one answer. In Britain, Captain Cowper Coles, RN, who, during the Crimean War, had mounted a 32-pounder traversing gun on a raft, favoured this method, and he designed the turret ship *Rolfe Krake* for Denmark. John Ericsson, a Swede, designed the *Monitor*, the first ship to be conceived and built as an ironclad, for the Federal States of America, which had embarked on a civil war with the Confederates of the south. On her maiden voyage the *Monitor* took part, in March 1862, in a battle in Hampton Roads which, despite its unsatisfactory conclusion, attracted more attention from European Admiralties than almost any other event in the conflict. It was the first time that one ironclad fought another.

Devastating the blockaders

The Confederates, in Norfolk, Virginia, rebuilt a wooden steam frigate, the *Merrimack*, which the Federals had burnt, fitting her with a casemate of oak beams protected with iron rails and plating. The bow was reinforced and given an iron ram, and she proved devastating to the Federal blockaders.

The *Monitor* had an armour-plated hull and amidships was a rotating turret with two 11-inch guns, the largest calibre of the time.

USS Tecumseh

The *Tecumseh* and her sisters embodied all the basic features of Ericsson's original *Monitor*, the flat deck and single turret, but were larger and better armed. The Dahlgren smooth-bore guns fired spherical shells, effective at a range of up to 1,700 yards.

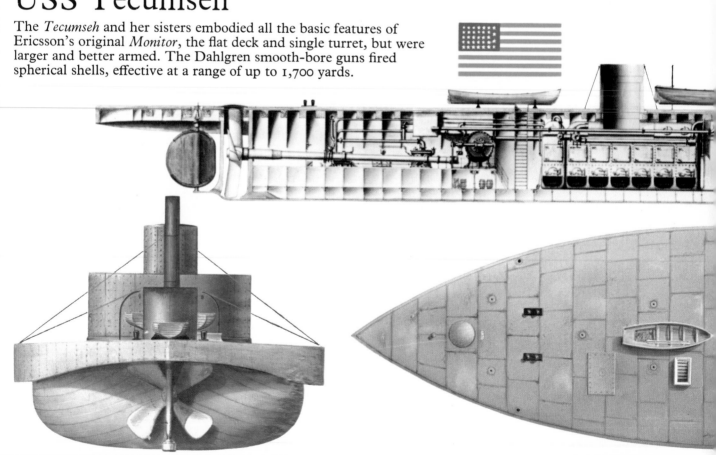

When in action, the deck was cleared except for the turret and a steering position forward. At sea, the vessel, with her low freeboard of little more than a foot, was no match for rough weather, which nearly sank her on her voyage from New York to Hampton Roads, where she arrived to find the *Merrimack*, now renamed *Virginia*, in process of destroying the five wooden Federal ships blockading the Chesapeake river.

The battle itself, fought on March 8, proved both sides right in thinking their ironclads were virtually unsinkable by gunfire, for, in a contest lasting about seven hours, they fired at one another until the *Monitor*'s ammunition was exhausted and the *Merrimack*'s gunnery officer, asked why he had ceased fire, answered—'I can do as much damage by snapping my fingers every three minutes.' Both ships were hit repeatedly—the marks of 41 hits were counted on the *Merrimack*—but neither was sunk. The *Merrimack* was scuttled the following year to avoid capture and the *Monitor*, predictably, foundered in a gale. They had convincingly demonstrated that shells would have to be improved if they were to decide a large-scale naval battle.

The broad strategy of the Federals was to blockade the southern ports, an attack on Charleston made in 1863 having failed. To achieve mastery at sea, David Farragut, their best commander, devoted all his remarkable energy and skill and his career was crowned with victory on August 4, 1864, at Mobile Bay. There, by his leadership, tactical ability

HMS Royal Oak *(1863), one of the Royal Navy's earliest ironclads.*

and disregard for loss, he won a decisive battle against ships and forts which marked the fulfilment of his work at sea.

The classic answer to blockade—evasion and raiding—was employed by the southern States, at first with much success. The most spectacular example was set by Captain Raphael Semmes in the *Alabama*. This ship was built in England and her crew came from ports of the British Isles, facts which later cost the British Government an indemnity totalling $15,500,000, to be paid in gold and on account of all such raiders. The *Alabama* cruised between 1862 and 1864 and inter-

The ram Affondatore, *the most powerful Italian ship at Lissa.*

cepted no fewer than 66 ships. The Federals at last caught up with the raider off Cherbourg. She was defeated by the USS *Kearsage* in a straight fight near the French port and within sight of spectators on June 19, 1864.

'Davids' sink the Goliaths

The American Civil War resulted in frequent experiments with mines, torpedoes mounted

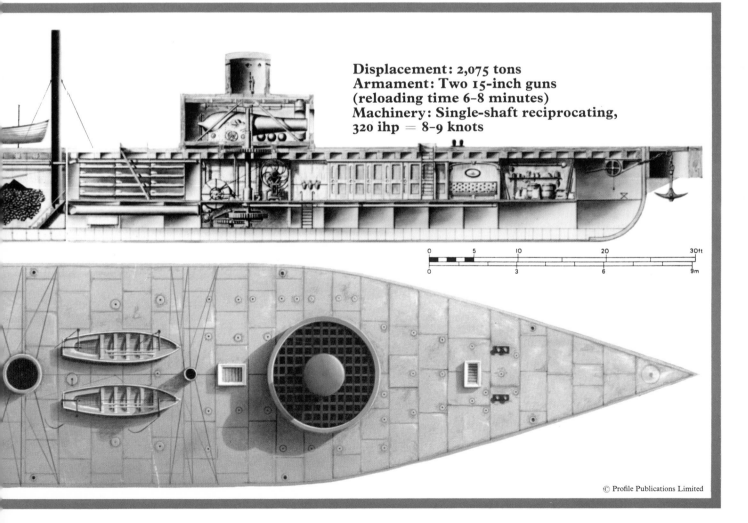

Displacement: 2,075 tons
Armament: Two 15-inch guns
(reloading time 6-8 minutes)
Machinery: Single-shaft reciprocating,
320 ihp = 8-9 knots

on spars, and craft, known as 'Davids', in which only funnel and hatches were above water. These submersible torpedo boats were called 'Davids' because of their attacks on the 'Goliaths' of the Federal fleet and because they recalled David Bushnell, who made attacks with a submersible in the 18th century.

The Confederates sunk the blockading USS *Housatonic* in 1864 off Charleston by such methods, the submersible herself being lost with all her crew of nine. And the Confederate Lieutenant Cushing ascended the Roanoke River, where he blew up the USS *Albemarle* as well as his own craft, he himself swimming to safety. Altogether, some 32 ships fell victim to mine or torpedo during the course of the conflict.

During the closing months of the war in America, much was happening in Europe, including efforts by Prussia and Austria to wrest the duchies of Schleswig and Holstein from Denmark. Prussia then had no fleet to speak of, and it was left to the Austrians under Admiral Wilhelm von Tegetthoff to sail a squadron to the North Sea to meet the Danes.

On May 6, 1864, Tegetthoff encountered a squadron under Commodore Suenson consisting of the *Niels Juel*, *Jylland* and *Heimdal* near Heligoland. Three German ships had joined the Austrians, who were in superior force, and Danish gunnery was good, and Tegetthoff, his flagship *Schwarzenberg* badly on fire, had to withdraw to the island of Heligoland, which was at that time held by the British. Honours were with Denmark, but the mere presence of the Austro-Prussian squadron raised a blockade which was not strong enough to be effective.

After having beaten Denmark and absorbed the Schleswig-Holstein duchies, Prussia turned on her Austrian ally, who also had an enemy in Italy, some of whose territory she had absorbed.

Tegetthoff, who was still under forty, was next called upon to lead a fleet against the Italians, who were set upon dominating the Adriatic. To that end, they planned to capture the island of Lissa as a base for operations against the Austrian ports of Pola and

Trieste. The Italian commander was Count Persano, a man of over sixty and the direct opposite of the active-minded Austrian.

The Italians refuse action

Tegetthoff, with a fleet including six ironclads, sailed to Ancona on June 27, 1866 and offered battle to Persano, who was in superior force. Persano refused action, and did not put to sea until July 8, when the Austrians had had to retire to coal ship. Persano then made for Lissa and began a bombardment of the fortifications. The defenders were in difficulties when news came that Tegetthoff, an ardent believer in ramming tactics, was coming. He had trained his fleet well. Despite the fact that no Austrian ship had a ram (at most there was the cutwater formed by the joining of the armour-plating), every captain knew his duty, and, as his ships were painted black, Tegetthoff ordered: 'Ram anything in grey'.

The fleets met on July 20, when the Italian warships with their projecting rams of over 6 feet were in a confused formation off Lissa. This was made worse by the decision of Persano to transfer his flag from the *Re d'Italia* to the brand-new, English-built *Affondatore* without telling his captains. For a time the Italians were leaderless, and the action turned into a mêlée.

Above: Turret ship HMS Devastation *(1873), the first seagoing battleship without sails. Her most useful feature was the positioning of the turrets forward and aft of the superstructure, giving clear arcs of fire for her 12-inch guns.*

Top right: HMS Glasgow *(1861), a good example of the last wooden steam frigates, superseded, first by corvettes and later by cruisers.*

During the fighting, the *Re d'Italia* was rammed by the *Erzherzog Ferdinand Max* and she went down, with most of her crew. Considerable damage was suffered by the Austrian ship *Kaiser*, but the size of Tegetthoff's victory is suggested by the respective losses. The Italians lost two ironclads and 612 officers and men. Austrian dead numbered only 38, most of whom were in the wooden *Kaiser*, which stayed afloat.

Tegetthoff did not long survive the battle, which did not save Austria from defeat at the hands of Prussia, but which did give a false idea of the potentiality of the ram. The ever-increasing range of naval artillery made it unlikely that it would see more than very limited use in the future.

The unstable *Captain*

Lissa did nothing to diminish a continuing argument between the adherents of the turret system and the central battery system. Captain Coles, always an advocate of the turret, was allowed a free hand in the design, for the Admiralty, of the turret ship *Captain* which proved unstable, capsizing in the Atlantic on September 7, 1870. The *Monarch*, of a somewhat similar Admiralty design, was stable and successful, though both ships suffered from the disadvantage of the sail rig with which they were fitted.

In 1873, HMS *Devastation* joined the British fleet. She had turrets but had no masts, and although officers of the old school viewed her with distaste, she proved highly successful and lasted until a few years before World War I.

Bottom right: HMS Agamemnon *(1883), one of a series of experimental freaks, with two turrets placed amidships on either side of the funnel but staggered to allow them to fire forward and aft.*

The Battle of Lissa, 1866

Austria		Italy	
1st Division (ironclads)	guns		guns
Ferdinand Max	18	Re d'Italia	36
Hapsburg	18	Re di Portogalla	28
Kaiser Max	30	Ancona	27
Prinz Eugen	30	Maria Pia	26
Don Juan de Austria	28	Castelfidaro	27
Drache	26	San Martino	26
Salamander	26	Principe de Carignano	22
Kaiserin Elisabeth	6	Affondatore	2
2nd Division (unarmoured ships)		Terribile	20
Kaiser	92	Formadabile	20
Novara	51	Palestro	5
Fürst Schwarzenberg	46	Varese	4
Graf Radetzky	31	Duca di Genova	50
Adria	31	Carlo Alberto	50
Donau	31	Vittorio Emanuele	50
Erzherzog Friedrich	22	Garibaldi	54
Greif	2	Principe Umberto	50
Stadium	—	Gaeta	54
3rd Division (minor vessels)		Maria Adelaide	32
10 misc. gunboats and steamers		15 unarmoured ships	

New power at sea

The last quarter of the nineteenth century saw enormous advances in the development of naval weapons and ships. Battles in South American, Far and Middle Eastern waters and in the Black Sea saw the proving of the locomotive torpedo, breech-loading guns, the cruiser, and the torpedo boat and the emergence of John Arbuthnot Fisher who was to revolutionise the Royal Navy. But perhaps the most significant development was not technical but political—the United States assumed the strategic obligations which would make her a sea power.

In 1877 Russia and Turkey began one of their recurrent wars. At that time Russia was at a disadvantage in that she had only a single ironclad in the Black Sea, where the Turks were in some strength, but the period was one in which much hope was placed in improved versions of the torpedo, and in that weapon Russia saw possibilities.

Initiative had originally come from Austria. Commander Johann Luppis of the Austrian navy had taken up the idea of a self-propelled torpedo such as had been envisaged in 1848 by a fellow countryman, Franz Pfeifer. Both men lacked the necessary expertise but this was supplied by an Englishman, Robert Whitehead, who worked for an engineering firm at Fiume. Whitehead tested a prototype successfully in 1869. It was powered by compressed air, ran submerged at 6 knots for 300 yards and carried an 18-pound charge in the nose. When developed, the device was to have a vast effect on all navies. Austrian share in the invention was enhanced when, at the suggestion of Ludwig Obry, a naval draughtsman, a gyroscope was added to

keep the missile on a set course, but the British were the first to purchase the weapon, in 1870.

The Russians, who were experts in mine warfare, had been experimenting at Kronstadt with launches carrying spar torpedoes. These were transported south by rail in May 1877 and on May 25, at the mouth of the Danube, a night attack was made against two Turkish gunboats, the *Seife* and the *Fethul Islam*, which were at moorings. The launches could only make 5 knots when armed, but an attack by four of them, led by Lieutenant Doubasoff, was startling in its effect. As the war-head had to be exploded against the enemy vessel herself, the launches inevitably came under very heavy fire. Nevertheless, the *Seife* was sunk, and the

Tsarvitch, the launch which had done the damage, suffered no casualties.

The first torpedo victim

At the far end of the Black Sea, at Batoum, the Russian admiral Makaroff was attempting to use a towed torpedo of a type known as the Harvey. This derived from Commander Harvey, RN, who invented a missile which, when launched from the deck of a steamer and towed by a wire, diverged from the track of the parent vessel and stood away at an angle of 45 degrees. It could be exploded either electrically or by contact.

Admiral Makaroff had no success with this weapon, which never proved useful, but it was another matter with the Whitehead locomotive torpedoes which he placed in two boats specially adapted for the purpose. On January 26, 1878, his officers, firing their missiles at 80 yards range, sank a 2,000-ton

The sail- and steam-powered gunvessel Condor *distracted the Egyptian gunners at the Bombardment of Alexandria in 1882. Her captain, Lord Charles Beresford became a controversial admiral.*

The Resurgam *was a submarine designed and built in 1879 by a Liverpool clergyman, the Reverend George Garrett. She was powered by steam stored in pressure tanks, and could move at 2 or 3 knots for ten miles. Her modest success led to a successful collaboration between Garrett and the Swedish armament tycoon Thorsten Nordenfelt.*

Turkish ship. This was the first success in war of the invention, and although the range had been very short, it had opened up extraordinary possibilities.

The torpedo was already in demand everywhere, not least by the navies of the South American countries of the Pacific coast. It was in Pacific waters that in 1877 the Peruvian monitor *Huascar* provided some lessons. Her captain turned piratical, and his ship was chased by the cruiser *Shah*. Both guns and locomotive torpedoes were employed in the action which resulted. This proved as indeterminate as that at Hampton Roads, for the torpedoes were ineffective, and the *Huascar* had strong enough armour to prevent damage from the shells of the *Shah*.

Returned to the service of her Government, the *Huascar* played an important part in the war between Chile and Peru (1879–1882) in which sea power was of great importance.

The *Huascar* fights on

Bolivia, backed by Peru, seized nitrate fields which were being worked by the Chilean Nitrate Company in the then Bolivian province of Atacama. Chile reacted by occupying the Bolivian ports of Cobija and Tocopilla and then proceeded to blockade Iquique, the most important southern port of Peru. This led to the first naval action of the war.

On April 21, 1879, the Chilean sloop *Esmeralda* and the gunboat *Covadonga* met the Peruvian *Huascar* and the ironclad *Independencia*. During the course of a sustained action, the *Independencia* was forced aground by the *Covadonga* and shelled into a wreck. The *Huascar*, redeeming her earlier piracy, sank the *Esmeralda*. The battle had the effect of lifting the Chilean blockade of Iquique, but not for long. The Chileans were determined to master the *Huascar*, renew the pressure on Iquique, and win the war.

Mastery at sea was achieved through an action on October 8, 1879, when the Peruvian monitor was attacked off Angamos Point by the Chilean ships *Blanco Encalada* and *Almirante Cochrane*. The *Huascar* fought as gamely as before, but by the end of the battle, when she surrendered, she had only one gun left in action, three-quarters of her crew were casualties, and her steering was useless. The Chileans made a remarkable job of repair, for in February 1880 she sailed to face the Peruvian monitor *Manco Capac*. The fight was indecisive, but the *Huascar* took no further important part in the war.

Peruvian resistance by land was protracted, but desperate. Dominant Chilean sea power proved at last decisive. The victors, by the terms of the peace, deprived Peru of Iquique, and took away Bolivia's entire outlet to the sea, which she has never since recovered.

Monster Italian guns

But the fact that the locomotive torpedo proved to be effective did not halt the development of guns, the paramount weapon of naval warfare ever since the Venetian galleasses proved so effective at Lepanto in 1571 against the Turks. Great efforts were made to increase both their size and their effectiveness.

Although breech-loading, especially for the lighter types of weapon, had been common in the 16th century, increasing technical difficulties led to its abandonment. In sailing ships with inboard broadside guns, muzzle-loading had been brought to a high standard of efficiency by the leading navies, but with turrets, armour, and the need for speed, loading by such a method was becoming an ever more difficult proceeding.

The French were the first to produce reasonably satisfactory breech-loaders. The British, despite constant experiment, were not, at the outset, so successful, and reverted to muzzle-loading for main armaments. The furthest point in the current arms race seemed to have been reached when the Italians laid down the mastless turret battleship *Duilio* in 1872, and the *Dandolo*, which was similar, a year later. They had engines by Penn and Maudsley, designed to achieve a maximum of 15 knots. The ships were armed with four enormous British-made guns weighing 100 tons apiece with a calibre of 17.7 inches. The designer, Benedetto Brin, who had absorbed the lessons of Lissa, abandoned vertical armour except for a thick belt to protect vital machinery and turrets.

Britain, whose gunfounders had been among the best in Europe since before the time of Elizabeth I, could not brook such rivals as these ships without an effort to surpass them. The *Inflexible*, of 11,000 tons displacement, was laid down in 1874. In her day she was the largest man-of-war ever built. She had four 16-inch muzzle-loaded guns weighing 80 tons each, and in due course these were actually fired in anger. Within the framework of her time, she was a sensational and impressive-looking ship, 320 feet in length and 75 feet broad at the water-line.

The Peruvian turret ship Huascar *sinks the Chilean sloop* Esmeralda *after a desperate action off Iquique, April 21, 1879.*

Tank experiments by William Froude on behalf of the Admiralty to determine the best form and action of propellers enabled her engines to achieve 15 knots at an economical expense of horsepower.

Vital lessons for Fisher

Novel features of the *Inflexible* included two 60-foot torpedo boats fitted with the first submerged tubes; anti-rolling tanks, and electric light. Her designer was Sir Nathaniel Barnaby, and her complexity was such that she was not in commission until July 1881. A year later, she was in action for the one and only time, and her captain was John Arbuthnot Fisher, who was to revolutionise the Royal Navy.

A military party in Egypt, led by Arabi Pasha, whose object was to overthrow Turkish rule, failed to prevent a massacre of Europeans at Alexandria, and as the French were unwilling to intervene to restore order, the task was left to the British, who sent a fleet under the command of Admiral Sir Frederick Seymour. This included seven powerful ironclads in addition to the *Inflexible*. They were the *Monarch*, *Invincible* and *Penelope*, which operated close inshore off Mex. The *Alexandria*, *Sultan* and *Superb* were stationed off Ras-el-Tin, the *Inflexible* and *Temeraire* being in a central position outside the harbour reef, halfway between Ras-el-Tin and Marabout, where there were gunboats under Lord Charles Beresford.

Arabi's naval force was negligible, but the fortifications of Alexandria were strong, and it had long been an axiom that ships were at a disadvantage in such circumstances. It proved so in the attack, which was made on July 11, 1882. Although the forts eventually

A Whitehead torpedo is fired from an above-water tube. First tested in 1868 it did not achieve real efficiency until 1914.

The Bombardment of Alexandria, 1882

The British Fleet

Inflexible	Alexandra	Temeraire	Superb
Monarch	Sultan	Invincible	Penelope
plus 6 small gunboats etc.			

Above: The Chilean gunboat Covadonga *drove the Peruvian ironclad* Independencia *ashore during the same action in which the* Esmeralda *fought her hopeless battle.*

Above: The Chilean torpedo gunboat Almirante Condell *torpedoed a rebel ironclad during the civil war of 1891.*

surrendered, the *Superb* blowing up the powder magazine in Fort Adda, this was not before the bombardment had revealed serious defects in the armament even of such ships as the *Inflexible*. This was stated by Fisher in a letter he composed within a few weeks of the event, though the full facts were not revealed to the general public.

'Our shooting,' he wrote, 'was not all that could be desired.' This was a staggeringly moderate pronouncement from Fisher, particularly when he gave details of dud shells, one of which landed harmlessly amidst 300 tons of gunpowder; bad fuses—'Shocking. I believe now the Ordnance Committee are to invent a fuse. Why not ask them to invent a new kind of perambulator!'; lack of big steel breech-loaders; and slow rate of fire.

This was a sad commentary on the naval armament of the era.

The cruiser of the sailing navy had been the ubiquitous, speedy and well-armed frigate. With the adoption of steam, it took some time for the most useful type of vessel for raiding, commerce protecting and secondary duties to evolve. The heaviest type of gun was ruled out, and so was more than the minimum of armour, in order to ensure the best possible endurance. The need seemed to be for quick-firing guns, which were being developed concurrently with sound breech-loading, speed, and a bare sufficiency of protection.

By the 1880's, two principal types of ship were being developed, known as Protected Cruisers and Armoured Cruisers. Protected Cruisers were without side armour, their vital under-water parts—engines, boilers and magazines—being shielded by steel decks with thicknesses which varied from three-quarters of an inch to 6 inches. Additional protection was afforded by arranging the coal bunkers at the sides of the ship and by watertight sub-divisions of the hull. The cruisers *Iris* and *Mercury*, dating from 1877, and the first British ships of war to be constructed entirely of steel, had these advantages. Armoured Cruisers relied mainly on side armour. The type had a comparatively long currency, although many thoughtful students of war held the view that, with cruising, superior speed and a high rate of fire were more advantageous than better protection and bigger guns when these had to be provided at a sacrifice of speed or endurance.

In the first main action in which cruisers were involved, which occurred in Chinese waters at Foochow in 1884, it was the smaller type, and torpedo boats equipped with the by then obsolescent towed weapon, which were mainly employed.

Trouble had arisen in Indo-China because of the encouragement given by the Chinese Imperial Government to Tu-Duc, the Annamite ruler, to break treaties made with France. The territory being remote, it was hard to induce the French Chamber of Deputies to take the matter with sufficient seriousness until a senior officer had been killed by mercenaries. Admiral André Courbet, who had originally been trained as an engineer, was then put in command of a miscellaneous force with which to bring the Chinese to reason. Courbet was to proceed to Tonkin to enforce the withdrawal of Chinese troops, and to ensure acknowledgement of French claims. Failing compliance,

he was to threaten the naval base at Foochow and occupy the port of Kelung in Formosa.

A daring sortie up-river

The Chinese proved obdurate, the first attack on Kelung failed, and so Courbet, determined not to 'lose face', planned an attack on Foochow. This lay some way up the Min River and could only be approached through two strongly fortified narrows. His armoured cruisers had too great a draught for the river, so Courbet transferred his flag to the smaller, 1,200 ton *Volta*. With five un-armoured cruisers, three gunboats and two torpedo craft, the admiral prepared to deal with a powerful arsenal and a Chinese fleet of eleven warships, six of more than 1,000 tons and the largest of 1,600 tons, and nine war junks with 47 old-fashioned, smooth-bore guns, including two 10-inch.

His attack, which began on August 23, 1884, was as successful as it was bold. Torpedo boat No. 46, commanded by Lieutenant Douzans, her approach well covered by fire from the larger French ships, set the Chinese admiral's flagship, the *Yanou*, on fire and caused confusion among his captains. Another success by the 32-ton, 90-foot torpedo boats was the destruction of the gunboat *Foo-Sing* by Lieutenant de Lapeyrère. This, said one account, 'went down sizzling and spluttering like a red-hot iron plunged into water.'

Having reduced the Chinese fleet to a shambles, Courbet made good his way back to the sea, destroying the forts in the narrows by clever warping of his ships. He then stood away for Kelung, hoping to avenge his

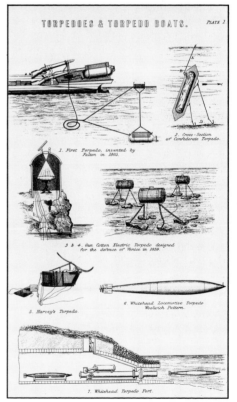

TORPEDOES & TORPEDO BOATS.   PLATE I

*The name 'torpedo' was given to any form
of underwater explosive device.*

*Left : The 16-inch 80-ton guns of HMS
Inflexible were the largest muzzle-loading
guns ever installed in a British ship, and also
the last. They were loaded from outside the
turret by depressing below an armoured
glacis.*

earlier repulse. Here again, he was successful. His mere presence in the area cut off the vital seaborne rice trade on which northern China depended, and this brought the Imperial Government to reason.

Courbet had shown himself a most able commander under extremely difficult circumstances, and it was a sadness to his fellow countrymen that he succumbed to cholera before he could return home to the acclaim he had earned. They paid him the deserved compliment of naming a battleship in his honour.

Another torpedo success

On the other side of the Pacific, and less than a year after her successes against Peru and Bolivia, Chile ran into serious internal troubles, in which her navy was heavily involved. Faction arose because of the unpopular and dictatorial rule of President Balmaceda, who succeeded in antagonising a high proportion of his armed forces, many officers supporting Congress in its opposition to the President.

By January 6, 1891, insurrection had reached a point when Captain Jorge Montt hoisted a broad pendant as commodore of a 'Congressional Squadron'. His newest vessel was the British-built protected cruiser *Esmeralda,* successor to the sloop which had been sunk in action by the Peruvians in 1879. He also had under his command the *Blanco Encalada,* an ironclad of 3,500 tons displacement which was to see much action in the brief but fierce civil war.

The President found that two fast torpedo gunboats, the *Almirante Condell* and the *Almirante Lynch,* remained faithful to him, and he also hoped to make use, when they were delivered, of three ships which were on order from European shipyards.

Ten days after declaring himself an adherent of Congress, Commodore Montt bombarded the fortifications at Valparaiso. Congress, indeed, retained the initiative throughout the struggle, through which it achieved its aims. But the President's forces (and the Whitehead torpedo) had at least one notable success. On April 23, 1891, an attack was made on the *Blanco Encalada* by one of the torpedo gunboats, and the ship was sunk with 14-inch locomotive torpedoes, the first major success of this weapon against a well-armed warship.

The success was followed up nearly a year later in Brazil, where, in the course of an insurrection against President Floriano Peixoto, the battleship *Aquidaban* was sunk by a single 16-inch torpedo fired from a torpedo boat on April 5, 1894. The torpedo, so long regarded as a weapon of potentialities, was fulfilling its promise in a resounding way.

Japan seizes her chance

In 1894 there began a fresh outbreak of the hostilities between China and Japan which had been a recurrent feature for centuries. Japan aspired to supremacy not merely in her own waters, but along the entire littoral of China.

The general disarray of the Ch'ing Dynasty, not least the manifest inefficiency of her navy, offered tempting opportunities to a zealous sea service which had been trained on British lines, and whose best ships had been built in British yards.

The core of the Japanese fleet mainly consisted of protected cruisers armed with quick-firing guns. During the course of the one and only fleet action, the highly disciplined and efficient Japanese were able to defeat their opponents, but they had not sufficient weight of artillery to sink either of the two old battleships which had put to sea, or more than one of the two armoured cruisers. The ships fought at speed, and it was this that, on their part, prevented the Chinese from scoring any success with torpedoes.

After the Chinese had retired upon Wei-Hai-Wei, the Japanese showed what they could achieve with Whitehead's weapon. Their torpedo boats twice attacked enemy ships in harbour, and sunk no fewer than five of them. It was a repetition of the success of Admiral Courbet at Foochow.

So far, the countries which had employed the newly evolving types of naval vessels and weapons had done so either on relatively unimportant missions, or against inferior opponents. Yet certain lessons had already been absorbed. The ram could be disregarded by wise tacticians, except under most unusual circumstances. The range and efficiency of guns had greatly increased, though there was huge scope for improvement. Armour had proved its value. So had the locomotive torpedo and the quick-firer, the former as a sinker of ships, the latter chiefly as protection.

Turning point for America

In 1898, for the first time in the history of the country, the United States of America, which was one day to possess the world's largest fleet, found herself engaged with a European power outside the framework of a world conflagration, yet on a two ocean basis. That power was Spain. In the distant past, Spain had been of paramount maritime importance, but her navy had long ceased to be regarded as of the first rank.

The war which followed had little of interest in a technical sense, for neither of the fleets engaged was as well equipped as the international status of the countries concerned might have suggested. Nonetheless, it was of great importance for the future, since it relegated Spain to an even lower status than before, and it forced the United States to consider re-organising her navy.

At the time, the greatest living writer on sea power, Captain Alfred Thayer Mahan, attached to the Navy Department in Washington, was at the height of his influence. His work had already made an immense impact abroad, and it was with natural gratification that, as the result of the clash with Spain, he observed that those who guided the destiny of his country were taking maritime and strategic problems as seriously as he himself had so long, though vainly, urged. Mahan, who had already held the post of Director of the War College, was appointed to the War Board, which supervised operational affairs at sea.

At the period at which the war opened, the once vast Spanish Empire overseas had shrunk prodigiously. Only Cuba and Puerto Rico in the Caribbean, the Philippines in the western Pacific, and territories in Africa were still in her possession. Even in what remained of her territories, revolt against her rule was almost endemic. The Philippine people had already appealed to the United States for protection. As for Cuba, it had taken extreme patience on the part of successive administrations not to intervene on the side of the rebels.

A dramatic explosion

The opening incident was highly dramatic. In February 1898, the US cruiser *Maine,* which was at Santiago in Cuba to protect United States interests, suddenly blew up,

The Battle of Tsushima, 1905

Russia			Japan			
Battleships & Coast defence ships	Armament		Battleships	Armament		
Kniaz Suvorov	4×12"	12×6"	Mikasa		4×12"	14×6"
Orel	4×12"	12×6"	Asahi		4×12"	14×6"
Borodino	4×12"	12×6"	Shikishima		4×12"	14×6"
Alexander III	4×12"	12×6"	Fuji		4×12"	10×6"
Osliabia	4×10"	11×6"	Armoured cruisers			
Sissoi Veliki	4×12"	6×6"	Nisshin		4× 8"	14×6"
Navarin	4×12"	8×6"	Kasuga	1×10"	2× 8"	14×6"
Nikolai I	2×12"	12×6"	Yakumo		4× 8"	12×6"
Gen. Adm. Graf Apraxin	3×10"	4×4.7"	Azuma		4× 8"	12×6"
Adm. Ushakov	4× 9"	4×4.7"	Tokiwa		4× 8"	14×6"
Adm. Seniavin	4× 9"	4×4.7"	Asama		4× 8"	14×6"
Armoured cruisers			Idzumo		4× 8"	14×6"
Dimitri Donskoi	6× 6"	10×4.7"	Iwate		4× 8"	14×6"
Vladimir Monomakh	5× 6"	6×4.7"	plus 7 light cruisers, 65 torpedo boats and destroyers			
Adm. Nakhimov	8× 6"	10×4.7"				
6 light cruisers 10 destroyers						

with the loss of 260 officers and men. Feeling against Spain had been mounting for some time and the outcry in the United States was universal. A Commission of Enquiry was set up to determine the cause of the loss, which was probably spontaneous combustion such as occurred not infrequently during the course of the next few years, due to the condition, or storage, of explosives, about which too little was then known.

The United States Government believed that the *Maine* had been mined and, without waiting for the result of the Commission's deliberations, declared war on April 25, 1898.

The first task of the War Board was to resist appeals to dissipate the Fleet in coast protection. Although hostilities were, in fact, to begin in the Pacific, the battleship *Oregon* was ordered out of that area to reinforce Admiral Sampson's Atlantic Squadron. The *Oregon* made the passage round Cape Horn in 66 days at an average speed of 12 knots, a considerable feat in itself. By the

Below : The Esmeralda *(1889) was the first in a series of fast and well-protected cruisers built for the Chilean Navy in British shipyards. In 1894 she was sold to Japan and became the* Izumi.

time she reached her *rendez-vous*, Sampson had a force of five armoured and two light cruisers, together with a few smaller ships. Wisely, he kept them concentrated.

Meanwhile, in the Pacific, Commodore George Dewey had hoisted his pendant in the cruiser *Olympia*, which, in December 1897, was at Nagasaki. Moving to Hong Kong, he began an intensive training programme with the four cruisers and two gunboats at his disposal. As soon as news of the outbreak of war reached him, he proceeded to Luzon, in the Philippines, which he reached on April 30. He found Subic Bay empty and continued towards Manila.

A Spanish squadron under Admiral Don Patricio Montojo was at anchor in the port, but the ships were in a state of unreadiness. At daybreak on May 1, 1898, Dewey was in sight of the enemy, and in two remarkable runs he put every Spanish ship out of action. It was a classic aggressive action of the best kind.

Blockade orders ignored

'The naval battle of Manila was won at Hong Kong', wrote Dewey afterwards. His ships scored 171 hits on Montojo's squadron. Only 15 Spanish shells found a target. The

Spaniards had 381 killed or wounded, the Americans only seven wounded. The way was open for troops to be sent from San Francisco, and, after the capitulation of Manila on August 13, the occupation of the Philippines was effected.

The orders of the senior Spanish admiral, Pasquale Cervera, were unrealistic. He was to leave Cadiz with six ships, on the outbreak of war, cross the Atlantic, destroy the American naval base at Key West, and then blockade the coast! Cervera knew his force to be inadequate for such a task, so he made for the Cape Verde Islands, there to await events. Then he moved to the Caribbean, the Dutch allowing him to refuel at Curaçao. He next proceeded to Santiago, on the southern side of Cuba, at which time Sampson was seeking him off Havana.

By May 28, Sampson had learnt of his opponent's movements, and when the Americans discovered the enemy, they were at anchor behind a minefield, with shore batteries ready to prevent attempts to sweep it. Sampson at first tried to bottle up the Spanish by sinking a cargo ship in the narrow entrance to the harbour. A shore battery destroyed the vessel's rudder, and she drifted away to sink clear of the channel.

The War Board then decided to send an expeditionary force to take the defences of Santiago by assault. They landed unopposed 15 miles from the port, but the general became alarmed at his isolated position and called for support from the fleet. Sampson sailed in the *New York*, leaving his second-in-command, Admiral Schley, to watch Cervera.

Breakout to destruction

The Spaniards had become convinced that the fall of Santiago would occur in a matter of days, and Cervera decided to force his way to sea. On the morning of July 3, he led his squadron in his flagship, the *Maria Theresa*, followed by three cruisers and two torpedo boats. Schley was waiting for him, and Sampson, learning of the sortie, at once reversed course to be present at the battle.

As at Manila, the encounter proved to be a massacre. The *Maria Theresa* came under the concentrated fire of the *Oregon* and four other ships. She was hit 30 times, her wooden decks caught fire, and she went aground, Cervera being made prisoner of war. Two of the three cruisers, the *Oquando* and the *Vizcaja*, also went aground, and the torpedo boats were an easy prey.

There remained the cruiser *Cristobal Colon*, the one vessel which succeeded in getting clear away to sea. She was pursued by the *Brooklyn* and the *Oregon*, and although she produced a remarkable burst of speed, she was caught, disabled, and beached.

Santiago capitulated a fortnight later, and, in effect, this was the end of the war. By the terms of the peace, the United States recognised Cuba as independent. Puerto Rico, Guam and the Philippines were taken under her protection. She had become a Power which had assumed strategic obligations which would call for a fleet larger than she had ever before possessed.

Fleets in conflict

In 1905 Russia and Japan were at war and a Russian armada of forty-five ships made an epic voyage from the Baltic to the Sea of Japan, only to be annihilated at the Battle of Tsushima. But a far more shattering event was the launching of the battleship *Dreadnought* which rendered all earlier battleships obsolete. Battlecruisers quickly followed in the subsequent rapid build-up of British and German fleets. By 1914 the shape of the major fleets was ominously settled.

At the turn of the century, all the principal Powers, and many smaller countries, were giving thought to the most advantageous composition of their navies. Britain had no close rival as the world's leading maritime nation, although this would soon change. The challenge would come not, as so often hitherto, from France, but from Germany. It was deliberate. The conquest of Schleswig and Holstein had ensured the security of the Kiel Canal, linking the North Sea and the Baltic. Heligoland had been acquired in 1890 in exchange for certain rights in Africa and had since been heavily fortified. Finally, a Navy Law of 1898, of which the inspiration was Admiral von Tirpitz who had the backing of the Kaiser, Wilhelm II, made it clear that within seven years Germany would possess a fleet of 19 modern battleships, six

large and 16 smaller cruisers, and appropriate flotillas of fast torpedo carriers, which had now become known as 'destroyers'.

Representatives of all the principal navies had a chance to size one another up during the course of the 'Boxer Rebellion' in China. This episode, which held grave menace for Europeans and their interests, was suppressed after much fighting in 1900. The principal operations, which took place on land, had to be based on squadrons which anchored in the Gulf of Taku. Here were gathered men-of-war from Britain, the United States, France, Russia, Germany, Austria, Italy and Japan, and here, over the mess tables, the more thoughtful officers could discuss the current shape of fleets and the trends in design and strategy which were becoming discernible in a fast-changing world.

There was by now some agreement as to how any fleet action in the near future would probably be fought. The battle line would consist of ships armed with high velocity guns, of a calibre of about 12 inches, mounted in turrets. These ships would have secondary batteries in casemates, largely for repelling attacks by destroyers. The armour belt would vary between 9 and 12 inches in thickness, and propulsion would be by triple-expansion reciprocating engines.

The main force would be supported, so it was thought, by armoured cruisers mounting guns of a calibre of between 7 and 9 inches, supplemented by smaller quick-firers. It was expected that battleships and cruisers would join action at ranges of only a few thousand yards.

East clashes with West

Within three years of the Boxer Rising, a situation arose which led to the first clash between a European and an Eastern Power in which the naval forces could be said to have been at all equally matched. This, the Russo-Japanese War of 1904–1905, was no side show. Not only did it give occasion for the biggest naval action since Lissa—it provided lessons which were studied by the leading navies.

When the war opened, the Russian and Japanese Far Eastern Fleets were not unequal. The Russians had the flagship *Petropavlosk* and six other battleships, supported by six cruisers and destroyer flotillas. Admiral Togo had six British-built 12-inch gun battleships, fourteen cruisers and attendant flotillas.

The Japanese, who needed to land troops on a defended coast in order to fulfil their aim of capturing Port Arthur, decided on a surprise attack without declaration of war. On the night of February 8, 1904, their flotillas attacked the Russians at anchor. Surprise was complete. Two battleships and a cruiser were damaged, though not sunk but Togo arrived late with his main force only to be repulsed by the port batteries.

The original Russian commander, Stark, was at once replaced by the energetic and popular Admiral Makaroff, who put in hand the repair of the damaged ships. Six weeks after his arrival, however, on April 10, 1904, Makaroff lost his life, as did 632 officers and men, when the *Petropavlosk* struck a mine as she was returning to harbour from a sortie.

Worse was to follow. By August, when the fleet anchorage came under fire from Japanese land forces, the Tsar ordered Admiral Witheft to sea. On August 10 the two fleets met at the Battle of the Yellow Sea, in which the Russian admiral lost his life, hit by a shell while on the bridge of the *Tzarevitch*.

The fate of Port Arthur was now sealed. Ships which had not already been disabled by shore artillery scuttled themselves, and by New Year's Day, 1905, the anchorage was in Japanese hands.

A Russian odyssey

If the Russians were not to end the war in humiliation, their Baltic Fleet would need to make an immense journey—three-quarters of the way round the world—to replace Far Eastern losses, and to face Togo. And in the 18,000 miles of sea between Kronstadt and his destination, Admiral Rojdestvensky, the expedition's commander, would not have the use of a single Russian base.

Orders had been issued for such an odyssey to begin in July 1904, long before the capitulation of Port Arthur, but there were delays. Five new battleships would form the core of the fighting force, including the *Borodino*, *Orel*, *Alexander III* and the flagship, *Suvaroff*, but even in October, when Rojdestvensky at last made a start, the fifth was months from completion. Altogether, 45 ships sailed, in-

cluding what would now be called the 'Fleet Train'. The smaller ships of the line, three cruisers and the destroyers were routed via Suez in charge of Admiral Felkersam. The rest went round the Cape, a *rendez-vous* being fixed at Madagascar.

The first incident was tragi-comic. Soon after the fleet had entered the North Sea, the supply ship *Kamtchatka*, which had fallen behind with engine trouble, signalled that she was being attacked under cover of darkness by torpedo boats! This was fantastic, though not quite as much so as it might now seem, since Britain and Japan were then in alliance, and the 'attackers' could possibly have been Japanese. Sporadic firing broke out on board the Russian ships, and in the aimless fracas a Hull trawler was sunk with her crew. The *Kamtchatka* had blundered into a fishing fleet! After that, Rojdestvensky was shepherded all the way to Gibraltar by a British cruiser squadron under Lord Charles Beresford.

Coaling, a laborious process, took place mainly at sea or from German colliers, and the *rendez-vous* was achieved at Madagascar in due course. The Russian Admiralty had decided to reinforce Rojdestvensky with the scrapings of the barrel, ancient vessels for which he was ordered to wait.

Togo 'crosses the T'

The 'Armada' was in Indo-Chinese waters early in May, and it was there that Rojdestvensky made his final dispositions for the run to Vladivostock. He weighed anchor on May 14, after which his force was not reported until the night of May 26, when the

Japanese auxiliary cruiser *Siano Maru* almost ran down one of the Russian transports. She signalled by wireless—'Enemy fleet in sight' at 5 am. Within two hours, Togo was at sea.

His patrols sighted the Russians at 7 am on a north-easterly course, 25 miles north-west of the island of Uku-Shima. They were shadowed by the cruiser *Idzumi*, which only turned away when the 12-inch guns of the flagship, the *Suvaroff*, were trained on her at a range of almost 9,000 yards. Further Japanese cruisers appeared but fire did not become general, as Rojdestvensky had to conserve ammunition and the Japanese cruiser captains knew that Togo was close at hand.

By mid-day on May 27 the main forces made contact near the southern point of Tsushima, after which island the battle became known. Action then became general, with the Russians in two columns, and Togo, with six battleships and six armoured cruisers, at first to starboard, but about to cross the enemy track. 'Crossing the T', as the manoeuvre was known, enabled complete broadsides to be fired at a time when an enemy could not reply effectively, except with his forward guns.

Togo's margin of superiority in speed was such that he was able to turn and re-cross the head of the Russian lines. He waited until he was within 6,000 yards of his opponent and

Rare visitors to Spithead. The French Fleet joined the British in a review at Spithead in 1905 to celebrate the Entente Cordiale. *It symbolized the end of 'splendid isolation' for Great Britain but also reflected the changing strategic requirements for the Royal Navy. Now the German Fleet was the principal adversary.*

then concentrated his fire on the flagships of the leading divisions, the *Suvaroff* and the *Osslyabia*. The latter, which was soon on fire and sinking, flew the flag of Admiral Felkersam, although he had died two days earlier. Rojdestvensky had wished the news to be kept from other ships.

The issue was decided within twenty minutes. After that, so a Japanese officer reported, 'the Russians seemed suddenly to go all to pieces, and their shooting became wild and almost harmless'.

The massacre of a fleet

Just before 3 o'clock, the *Suvaroff* swerved out of the line with her steering disabled, and from then onwards the fight became a massacre. One by one, the Russian battleships were put out of action, and by 5 o'clock the surviving remnant was being attacked by Togo's battleships from the east and from the south by his cruisers. Rojdestvensky had been twice wounded and his flag-captain killed. His flagship survived until next day when the admiral himself transferred to a destroyer, only to be captured by a Japanese flotilla.

Just three Russian ships survived to reach Vladivostock—two destroyers, and the light cruiser *Almaz*. Of the remainder of Rojdestvensky's fleet, two battleships which were not sunk were repaired, and added to the Japanese navy in the way which had been customary in the days of sail. Six smaller ships managed to reach neutral ports where they were interned. The rest were destroyed, beached or surrendered. Not one single major Japanese vessel had been lost although three torpedo boats were sunk. Three cruisers and six destroyers had damage in varying degree, but in respect of loss the victory was as decisive as Trafalgar. Japanese casualties were less than 600. Over ten times that number of Russians had died in the battle, 826 on the *Suvaroff* alone, and many more had become prisoners of war.

Although Tsushima did not hold many surprises for more advanced students of naval warfare, it emphasised certain trends. For instance, effective gun ranges were fast increasing. Most of Togo's effective fire had taken place at about 6,000 yards but it had been shown that heavy guns might be effective at three times that distance. Mixed armament in big ships had not proved satisfactory while the value of the armoured cruiser as supplementary to the battleship was in doubt and efficient fleet escort duties by destroyers was seen to be vital.

Advent of the *Dreadnought*

Shortly before the Russo-Japanese War broke out, the well-known Italian engineer Colonel Vittorio Cuniberti, outlined his ideas for 'An Ideal Battleship for the British Navy'. She would be of about 17,000 tons displacement, would be armed with twelve 12-inch guns for salvo firing, be protected by armour 12 inches thick in vital parts, and have a maximum speed of 24 knots.

The mind of Admiral Sir John Fisher, who became British First Sea Lord in October 1904, was moving swiftly in exactly the same direction. He had no use for mixed armaments or slow speeds, and his ideas were given immense impetus by the success of the turbine marine engine. This had been sensationally demonstrated by its inventor, Sir Charles Parsons, at the Naval Review of 1897. It had since proved its worth in many types of ship.

The turbine-propelled, all big gun *Dreadnought*, built in a year, was in service by 1906. She rendered all earlier battleships obsolete. Although she enabled rival navies to build up a fleet of modern ships from scratch, if they had the money and good designers, the *Dreadnought* gave Britain a flying start and she was the sensation of her era. Fisher's opponents proclaimed that it was a mistake to take such a leap ahead with such dramatic suddenness. This was the old wail of the opponents of steam, countered by the exclamation of Nelson's flag-captain, Thomas Masterman Hardy, when he said: 'Happen what will, England must take the lead!'

The *Dreadnought*, built at Portsmouth, followed most of Cuniberti's notions, and she had all the effect he intended. Her displacement was 17,900 tons. She mounted ten 12-inch guns, had an armour belt of 11 inches at its thickest, and was fitted with five submerged 18-inch torpedo tubes. Four screws enabled her to attain 21 knots, at which speed her engine rooms were a revelation to those accustomed to the appalling racket of a reciprocating engine driven at maximum revolutions.

One innovation, not generally followed (and not at all popular with those concerned), was that the officers' quarters were placed forward instead of aft. Sardonic bluejackets suggested that this was to save their officers from the vibration.

'The Superb Cat Class'

Two years later appeared the *Invincible*, first of the battlecruisers. This class was ill-fated, but its original purpose has sometimes been misunderstood. It was not considered by its designers as a fast, less well-armoured type of battleship so much as a type of cruiser so superior as to render all others obsolete. The *Invincible* had a 6-inch armour belt, much inferior to that of the *Dreadnought*, and eight instead of ten 12-inch guns. Her great asset was high speed. She could attain 26 knots and could sink any cruiser then afloat.

New types of Dreadnought battleship and battlecruiser followed in quick succession, the culmination being the *Queen Elizabeth* battleships, laid down in 1912/1913, and the *Lion*—'Superb Cat'—class of battlecruiser, huge for their time. The *Lion*, launched in 1910, was of 30,000 tons displacement and had to have a hull much larger than any capital ship built before her in order to carry her heavy armament at a speed of 28 knots.

The Germans were quick to follow the British lead and they had one great advantage. Whereas British capital ships could be called upon to operate in any part of the world, the Germans would operate largely in the North Sea and the Baltic. Thus no extended endurance or elaborate amenities for the crews were called for. The result was concentration on watertight sub-division so that German ships became very hard to sink. The apogee of this process was seen in the battle cruiser *Derfflinger* of 1914. This ship had a speed of over 26 knots, armour of between 12 and 10 inches, and eight 12-inch

Right: Togo's flagship at Tsushima, the battleship Mikasa. *The inscription is the famous signal, 'The fate of the Empire depends on this battle . . .'*

Above: The battleship Mikasa *seen in dock. Like the bulk of the Japanese fleet she had been built in Great Britain. She was similar in all major details to the very latest British ships.*

guns. In any other navy she would have been classed as a battleship for she had all the characteristics of such and could stand up to the heaviest of punishment.

In the United States, the most far-seeing of the younger gunnery experts, Commander William S. Sims, had come to the same conclusion as Fisher as to the paramount importance of a one calibre main armament and strong protection. The battleships *Michigan* and *South Carolina*, authorised in 1905 by Congress, embodied most of the attributes found in the *Dreadnought*, though they were not in commission until 1909. They mounted eight 12-inch guns, had a speed of 18.5 knots and their lattice masts made them among the most distinctive ships afloat. When Britain introduced the 13.5-inch gun into the *Lion*, the United States replied with the *New York* and the *Texas*, mounting 14-inch guns and so successful as to play their part in both world wars.

Unknown underwater quantity

By 1914, the shape of the major fleets was settled. Battleships would be preceded by a fast battlecruiser force, acting as an advance formation. Capital ship squadrons would be accompanied by fast light cruisers and destroyer flotillas.

The potentialities of all classes of surface ship were already known or could be guessed. What could not be gauged was the influence of the submarine. Every important navy possessed a submarine service by the opening of World War I. Every navy was anxious about the effect of submarine warfare. Events were to prove that there was every reason for this anxiety.

Right: The Russian battleship Orel *was badly battered at Tsushima, and was forced to surrender.*

26

皇國興廢在此一戰
各員一層奮勵努力
東郷平八郎
元帥伯爵東郷平八郎

Admiral Heihachiro Togo, victor of Tsushima. The inscription is his autograph.

'Commence Hostilities'

The aircraft carrier Furious epitomizes the advent and advance of naval air power in World War I. Begun in 1915 as a cruiser armed with 18-inch guns, the largest ever made, she finished the war as a carrier capable of launching an air strike.

Between 1900 and 1914 Germany became a major sea power. Britain reacted with a vigorous building programme and the two nations built up formidable surface fleets. But for the first time strategists had to evaluate the effectiveness of two new and potent weapons—the aircraft and the submarine. Developments and experiments went ahead and both sides were ready for the declaration of a war which was to bring their mighty navies into massive conflict.

Of all the reasons which led to the outbreak of World War I in August 1914, one is undisputed. Having unified Germany in 1871, Prince Otto von Bismarck was content to dominate continental Europe with the Armies of the Triple Alliance (Germany, Austria-Hungary, and Italy), and to rely on diplomacy to avoid a conflict with Britain. But after ascending the Imperial throne in 1888 and dismissing Bismarck two years later, Kaiser Wilhelm II determined to seize Neptune's trident. In this ambition he was aided and abetted by his Navy Minister, *Grosseadmiral* Alfred von Tirpitz. The Navy Laws which he pushed through the *Reichstag* in 1898 and 1900 authorised the transformation of Germany's small maritime coast defence force into a High Seas Fleet strong enough to challenge the Royal Navy.

Britain reacted with an alliance with Japan in 1902, with the *Entente Cordiale* with

Sopwith Camel fighter aircraft ranged on the forward deck of HMS Furious *in 1918.*

Right : This aerial view of the Furious *shows her slim cruiser-lines, with the flight deck which was built in 1917.*

France in 1904, and with a *rapprochement* with Russia in 1907. Equally importantly, First Sea Lord Admiral 'Jacky' Fisher transformed a Fleet riddled with Victorian complacency into a 20th-century fighting machine.

His memorial is HMS *Dreadnought*. Up to 1906 the 'standard' battleship displaced about 15,000 tons, was driven by coal fired reciprocating engines at 17–18 knots, and was armed with four 11-inch or 12-inch and twelve 6-inch guns. Examples are the British *Canopus* class and the German *Pommerns*. The latest British vessels had more mixed armaments, four 9.2-inch being added to the *King Edward VII* class and ten to the *Lord Nelsons*. The 17,900 tons *Dreadnought*, built in only fourteen months and completed in October 1906, was the first turbine driven all-big-gun battleship to be added to any navy. With a speed of 21 knots and mounting ten 12-inch guns she was clearly a match for any two of her predecessors, of which no more were built. Britain's determination to maintain the Royal Navy's supremacy and the capacity of her shipyards were enough to add to her 40 pre-Dreadnoughts by August 1914, as many as 22 Dreadnoughts of which the later ones displaced 25,000 tons and were armed with ten 13.5-inch guns.

Nor was this all. First Lord Winston Churchill requisitioned three which were building in Britain for Chile and Turkey. And on the stocks were ten more, to be completed in 1915–16, armed with eight 15-inch, including the five 27,000 tons *Queen Elizabeths* with a speed of 24 knots. Against this formidable armada Tirpitz managed by August 1914 to add to Germany's 20 pre-Dreadnoughts only fourteen Dreadnoughts of 19,000–25,000 tons armed with 11-inch or 12-inch guns, plus seven on the stocks, some belatedly armed with 15-inch on 28,000 tons, of which two were not destined to be completed.

Fisher's great mistake

But for all Fisher's greatness, he also made mistakes, and one was the all-big-gun armoured cruiser which he called a battle-cruiser. Armoured cruisers, such as the British *Warrior* class of 23 knots, armed with six 9.2-inch and four 7.5-inch guns on 13,550 tons, were protected against shells fired by weapons of these calibres. Fisher conceived a 25 knot, turbine driven version mounting eight 12-inch which, on 17,250 tons, was not adequately protected against shells of this size. He argued that 'speed is armour', a thesis which Jutland (and the destruction of the 'mighty' *Hood* in 1941) proved a tragic error. But in 1914 battlecruisers had all the supposed power and glamour of 'cavalry of the sea'. Britain had built ten, some armed with eight 13.5-inch guns on 29,700 tons, and was to finish five more during World War I with a speed of 31 knots, of which four (including the hybrid *Courageous* and *Glorious*) were armed with 15-inch guns and one, the freak *Furious*, with 18-inch. Across the North Sea Tirpitz completed only six battlecruisers by August 1914, armed with 11-inch or 12-inch guns,

HMS Hermes

This old cruiser was converted to a seaplane carrier, but after successful trials in the 1913 Manoeuvres the gear was removed. The platforms were reinstalled in August 1914 to allow her to ferry seaplanes across the Channel. While on this duty she was torpedoed.

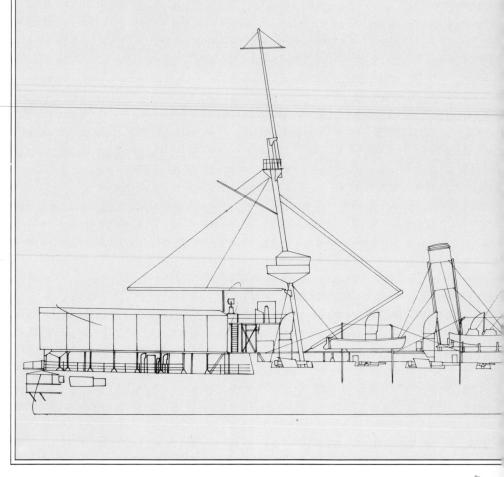

Above : The Italian Dreadnought battleship Conte di Cavour *was built just before the outbreak of war to counter the Austrian Navy's expansion.*

Left : The French destroyer Casque *was completed in 1911. She and her sisters were about the same size as British destroyers.*

Displacement: 5,650 tons
Armament: Eight 6-inch guns, nine 12-pdrs, two 18-in TT.
Machinery: Two shaft triple-expansion, 10,000 ihp = 20 knots

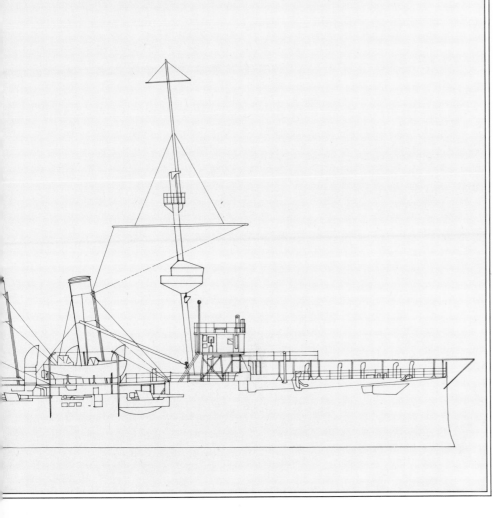

on 19,000–26,000 tons, except for the first, the 15,500 tons *Blücher* which, through faulty intelligence of Britain's building programme, was armed with twelve 8.2-inch. And during hostilities Germany managed to complete only two more of this new type.

Of the already-mentioned armoured cruisers, which the battlecruisers rendered obsolescent, Britain had in August 1914 as many as 32, Germany only six, including the 22-knot *Scharnhorst* and *Gneisenau* armed with eight 8.2-inch and six 5.9-inch guns on 11,600 tons. So, too, with smaller and likewise obsolescent protected cruisers of which Britain had 52, typified by the *Eclipse* Class with eleven 6-inch guns, and Germany only 25 much smaller ships armed with 4.1-inch weapons. But with the newer light cruisers—such as the British *Town* class of 25 knots armed with eight 6-inch guns on 5,250 tons, and the German *Kolberg* class of 27 knots armed with twelve 4.1-inch on 4,350 tons—Germany completed as many as 25 against Britain's 36 by August 1914. During hostilities, however, Britain built 32 more, including the 28 knot 'D' class armed with six 6-inch on 4,650 tons, against only 12 by Germany, including the *Bremse* class with the high speed of 34 knots but mounting only four 5.9-inch weapons on 4,000 tons.

Britain's destroyer force

In August 1914 Britain's destroyer force numbered as many as 270 of which the latest were the 35-knot 'M' class armed with three 4-inch guns and four 21-inch torpedo tubes on 1,000 tons. Germany counted only 140, which she classed as torpedoboats, of which the latest had the higher speed of 34 knots and were armed with three 3.5-inch guns and six 19.7-inch tubes on 812 tons. This disparity in strength was more than maintained during hostilities, when Britain completed 249, Germany only 92. The most numerous World War I British types were of the 36-knot 'S' class, armed with three 4-inch guns and four 21-inch torpedo tubes on 1,075 tons, and the larger 34-knot 'V & W' classes armed with four 4-inch guns (some with four 4.7-inch) and four or six 21-inch tubes on 1,272 tons. The Germans concentrated on 35-knot vessels armed with three 4.1-inch guns and six 19.7-inch tubes on 900–1,000 tons.

The few experimental 'submersibles' produced before 1900 were all failures, for lack of any suitable means of propulsion underwater. This was resolved at the turn of the century by the advent of the internal combustion engine linked with the electric motor. The Royal Navy acquired its first submarine in 1902, the Imperial German Navy its first U-boat four years later. By August 1914 Britain had as many as 80 in commission, of which the latest were the 660/800 tons 'E'

class of 15/10 knots armed with five 18-inch torpedo tubes. (*Note:* Where two figures are given the first is for on the surface, the second when submerged.) But Germany had built only 38, of which the latest were of the 685/844 tons *U31* class of 16/10 knots armed with four 19.7-inch tubes and one 3.4-inch gun.

During hostilities Britain built 250 submarines, the best known of which were the 890/1,070 tons 'L' class of 17/10 knots armed with six tubes and a 4-inch gun. But there were also the 1,883/2,565 tons 'K' class, steam driven at 24/9 knots and armed with eight tubes and a gun, which were intended to operate with the Grand Fleet, and the 1,600/1,950 tons 'M' class of 15/10 knots

armed with four tubes and a single 12-inch gun for surprise bombardments of the enemy's coast. Against this number Germany built nearly 300 U-boats, which fell into three main types. There were 'U-cruisers' of the 1,512/1,875 *U151* class of 12/5 knots, armed with two tubes and two guns; ocean-going boats such as the 712/902 tons *U51* class of 17/9 knots, armed with four tubes and a gun; and coastal boats such as the 508/639 tons *UBIII* class armed with five tubes and a gun.

Navies take to the air

Of the other types of warship developed in the decade before World War I, or during

HMS Dreadnought

This battleship had a heavier main armament than any previous ship and could in theory take on any two contemporaries. She was also the first battleship powered by the Parsons turbine, giving her increased speed with improved reliability and economy. Although other navies were contemplating 'super-battleships' the Royal Navy under the energetic leadership of Fisher took its competitors completely by surprise when the *Dreadnought* was built in fourteen months, a shipbuilding record which has never been surpassed. The *Dreadnought* never fired a shot in anger but she gave her name to an entire generation of capital ships. She made all existing battleships obsolete overnight and also proved conclusively the value of the steam turbine.

10   54   104

hostilities, only one need be mentioned. For aerial co-operation with the High Seas Fleet Germany employed Zeppelins—large rigid airships—chiefly for reconnaissance patrols over the North Sea. Britain preferred aeroplanes, floatplanes and flying-boats. To counter Zeppelins each battleship and battle-cruiser in the Grand Fleet was given a small, wheeled fighter which could be launched from a platform built on top of a gun turret. To carry machines for reconnaissance patrols ahead of the fleet, or for bombing raids on Germany's Zeppelin sheds, various merchant ships were converted into seaplane carriers by the addition of a hangar and cranes. One, the *Engadine,* was present at Jutland. But these innovations had clear dis-

advantages. A fighter flown off a battleship's turret could not be landed on again: it had to ditch and was lost, even though its pilot was picked up by a destroyer. And floatplanes could only take off and land in calm water, found all too seldom in the North Sea.

The solution, evolved in 1917–1918, was the aircraft-carrier: a ship with a clear deck from which wheeled aircraft—fighters, spotter reconnaissance machines, and torpedo-bombers—could fly off and subsequently land on, above a hangar in which they could be stowed. First of these was the *Campania,* a converted 18,000 tons liner with a speed of 22 knots which carried ten planes. Subsequent conversions were the 22,000 tons battle-cruiser *Furious* of 32 knots which

carried 20 planes, the 9,750 tons cruiser *Vindictive* of 29 knots which carried six, and the 15,775 tons liner *Argus* of 20 knots which carried 20. These were the first aircraft-carriers to join any Navy.

Some notable technical developments also occurred amongst weaponry and equipment —turbines, oil fuel, submarines and aircraft are the more obvious ones. But there were others. At the turn of the century it was supposed that battle fleets would engage at a range of around 4,000 yards, no more than twice that at which Nelson fought Villeneuve in 1805. When Captain Percy Scott demonstrated that accurate fire was possible at greater ranges and the range of torpedos was increased to as much as 15,000 yards, battle fleets were compelled to fight at distances of this order. To facilitate this British ships were equipped with director firing and the Dreyer fire-control table. The Germans preferred simpler fire-control gear, but gave their ships the advantage of stereoscopic rangefinders which were more accurate than the British coincidence type.

The wireless call to war

The depth charge was devised for attacking submarines—it was little more than a canister filled with explosive which, when dropped from the stern of a destroyer or other vessel, was detonated at a pre-set depth by a hydrostatic device. But their value was always limited by the difficulty of detecting a submerged submarine. Asdic, later Sonar, was still under development at the Armistice and the hydrophone was only of limited value.

Last, but not least, wireless, or, as it is now called, radio. The first warships were fitted with Marconi equipment shortly after the turn of the century. By 1914 all were equipped, so that World War I was the first in which ships and their commanders 'talked', using morse telegraphy, to each other, and with their Admiralties. But the range of W/T was measured in hundreds of miles and signals to and from vessels in the 'far seas' were normally routed through W/T stations or cabled to overseas Consuls.

Nonetheless, it was by wireless that the signal went out from Whitehall to all Britain's warships at home and overseas at 2300 on August 4, 1914: 'Commence hostilities against Germany'.

British battleships were visiting Kiel for the opening of the enlarged canal when the heir to the Austro-Hungarian throne was assassinated on June 28. Belgrade gave a conciliatory reply to Vienna's harsh protest, but this did not satisfy an aggressive Austria, who was backed by Germany. Russia reacted by mobilising in Serbia's support. This was enough for Tirpitz to recall the High Seas Fleet from its summer cruise and for First Sea Lord Admiral Prince Louis of Battenberg to order the British Home Fleet to Scapa Flow as the Kaiser answered the Tsar with a declaration of war and sent an ultimatum to her ally, France. The German Army's subsequent decision to advance through the Ardennes against France required Britain to fulfil her guarantee to uphold Belgium's neutrality. On August 4 the British Ambassador in Berlin delivered Britain's ultimatum, which received no answer before it expired at midnight, Central European Time.

Displacement: 17,900 tons
Armament: Ten 12-inch guns, twenty-seven 3-in, five TT.
Machinery: Four-shaft steam turbines, 23,000 shp = 21 knots

187   201

© Profile Publications Limited

Failure in the Med

Before a state of war existed Germany seized the initiative from Britain in the Eastern Mediterranean, a theatre in which the Allies were to gain precious little success for the duration of hostilities. The battlecruiser *Goeben* and the light cruiser *Breslau* succeeded in tieing up a vastly superior force for some time before finally succumbing to mines in 1918. The Royal Navy's other major aim in the area, the destruction of the Turkish forts protecting the Dardenelles, was also a costly failure.

The long line of battleships opens fire on the Turkish forts in the big bombardment at the Dardanelles on March 18, 1915. The damaged Inflexible *can be seen to the right with two French battleships.*

The battlecruiser Indefatigable *was unable to catch the German* Goeben.

HMS Inflexible *in dock after being mined at the Dardanelles in March 1915.*

Battlecruisers like Indomitable *were the fast spearhead of the battle fleet.*

By the summer of 1914 the Fleets of Germany's two Mediterranean allies, Austria–Hungary and Italy, were each headed by three Dreadnoughts. Against these France could deploy only one at Toulon, the other three being required at Brest. This obliged her ally, Britain, to reinforce Admiral Sir Berkeley Milne's Mediterranean Fleet, of four armoured cruisers and four light cruisers, with the battlecruisers *Inflexible*, *Indefatigable* and *Indomitable*. To counter their influence in the Eastern Mediterranean, where both Britain and Germany were wooing Turkey as a potential ally, the latter sent out the battlecruiser *Goeben,* flying the flag of *Konteradmiral* Wilhelm Souchon, and the light cruiser *Breslau.*

On July 30, as the war clouds gathered over Europe, the Admiralty cabled Milne that his prime task would be to help the French to protect their transports carrying their African army to Europe. He was also to shadow the *Goeben,* but was not to allow his ships to be drawn into action with a superior force. Knowing that the German warships had coaled recently at Brindisi, he sent the light cruiser *Chatham* to watch the Strait of Messina, and the *Indomitable* and *Indefatigable* with the armoured cruisers to the Strait of Otranto to prevent the German ships joining the Austrian Fleet at Pola. But when the *Chatham* reported Messina empty, the

Admiralty diverted these two battlecruisers to Gibraltar in the belief that Souchon was heading for the Atlantic. He was indeed steering west, but for a different purpose. At dawn on the 4th the *Goeben* bombarded Philippeville and the *Breslau* Bone, in French north Africa, to disrupt the embarkation of their troops. They then returned the way they had come because Berlin radioed that an alliance had been signed with Turkey and the two ships were to proceed to Constantinople.

When the *Indomitable* and *Indefatigable* chanced to sight them heading east, all four passed close to each other with guns trained fore and aft because their countries were not yet at war. The British battlecruisers then turned to shadow their likely opponents, but were unable to hold their quarry until Britain's ultimatum to Germany expired. By nightfall Souchon's force had outstripped them. The *Invincible* and *Indomitable* would have headed for the northern entrance to Messina had not Italy declared her neutrality. Instead they joined Milne in the *Inflexible* to the west of Sicily to prevent Souchon making a further attack on the French, while

the light cruiser *Gloucester*, Captain Howard Kelly, watched Messina.

A fatal debate

Souchon's ships arrived there early on August 5 and were allowed to replenish their bunkers. Kelly reported them as soon as they sailed in the evening of the 6th. Because they steered first for the Adriatic, Rear-Admiral E. C. Troubridge, commanding the British armoured cruisers, supposed they must be making for Pola, and went north to intercept. Not until midnight did he turn south, although Kelly had reported that the enemy had altered course for Cape Matapan shortly after dark.

Milne ordered the light cruiser *Dublin*, commanded by Howard Kelly's brother John, and two destroyers, which were *en route* from Malta to join Troubridge, to attack the *Goeben* during this moonlit night. Guided by the *Gloucester's* reports, John Kelly led his puny force to a position on the enemy's bow, expecting to sight them at 0330. But the *Breslau* glimpsed the *Dublin* without being seen herself, which allowed Souchon to turn away unseen.

Events on board Troubridge's flagship, the *Defence*, took a different turn. At 0245, her Captain, Fawcett Wray, asked his Admiral whether he intended to engage the *Goeben* with his four armoured cruisers. 'Yes,' replied Troubridge. Three-quarters of an hour later Wray said: 'The *Goeben* can circle around us within range of her guns but out-

side ours. It seems likely to be suicide for your squadron'. And this argument persuaded Troubridge to abandon the chase.

Meantime, Milne had taken his three battlecruisers into Malta for fuel, whence they sailed at 0030 on August 8. Fourteen hours later, half-way to Cape Matapan, the Admiralty signalled: 'Commence hostilities against Austria.' So Milne turned north to support Troubridge against a sortie by the Austrian Fleet. Not until 1230 next day did the Admiralty discover that this signal had been sent by a clerical error, and cancelled it.

This loss of 24 hours made all the difference. On the afternoon of the 8th Souchon's ships stopped at Denusa in the Aegean to replenish their bunkers. If there had been no false alarm over Austria, Milne could have caught the *Goeben* and *Breslau* as they left this island at 0545 on the 10th. As it was the British

HMS Mary Rose

The "M" Class destroyer was the latest type of fleet destroyer in the British Fleet in August 1914. Her powerful armament of three 4-inch guns was designed to sink German torpedo-boats, but her four 21-inch torpedo-tubes enabled her to attack the enemy battlefleet as well. The *Mary Rose* and another destroyer HMS *Strongbow* were sunk by German light cruisers in 1917 while gallantly defending a convoy to Norway.

Displacement: 1,025 tons
Armament: Three 4-inch guns, one 2-pdr pom-pom, four 21-in TT.
Machinery: Three-shaft steam turbines, 25,000 shp = 34 knots

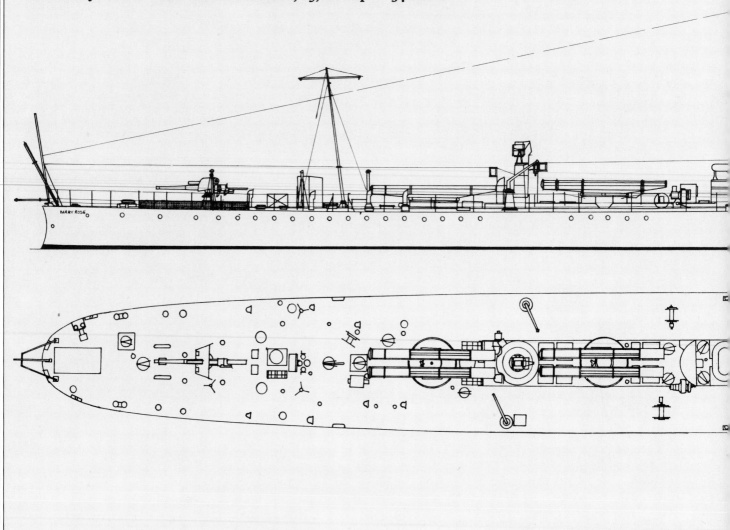

Above: The cruiser HMS Gloucester
which attempted to shadow the Goeben.
Left: The German battlecruiser Goeben.

ships were 40 miles north of Denusa on the 11th when they learned that Souchon had entered the Dardanelles the previous day. And when Turkey was reminded that belligerent vessels could remain in neutral waters for only 24 hours, German cunning was made clear: the *Goeben* and *Breslau* had been 'sold' to Turkey.

Britain's 'act of lunacy'

Milne and Troubridge suffered for allowing the German ships to elude them. Milne was recalled and received no further employment through the war. Troubridge was not only recalled but court martialled for failing to engage the *Goeben*. He was acquitted on the strength of the Admiralty's signal that he should not engage a superior force, but the verdict was not well received, and he was never again employed at sea. As Commodore Harwood showed at the battle of the Plate in 1939, four armoured cruisers could have inflicted substantial damage on the German battlecruiser. Flag Captain Wray was not penalised, but he was ostracized by many of his contemporaries in the Service.

Meantime, the Admiralty had signalled to Rear-Admiral S. H. Carden: 'Assume command of squadron off Dardanelles. Your sole duty is to sink *Goeben* and *Breslau* if they come out'. But Souchon was after bigger fish. He helped *General* Liman von Sanders to incite the Turks to join the war on Germany's side. To this end he led a squadron into the Black Sea, ostensibly for exercises, in reality for a dawn bombardment of Sevastopol and Novorossiisk on October 30.

The British reacted with what was later described as 'an act of lunacy'. On November 3 the outer forts protecting the Dardanelles were bombarded by the *Indefatigable*, *Indomitable* and two French Dreadnoughts. This warned the Turks to strengthen their defences. And they were given time to do this

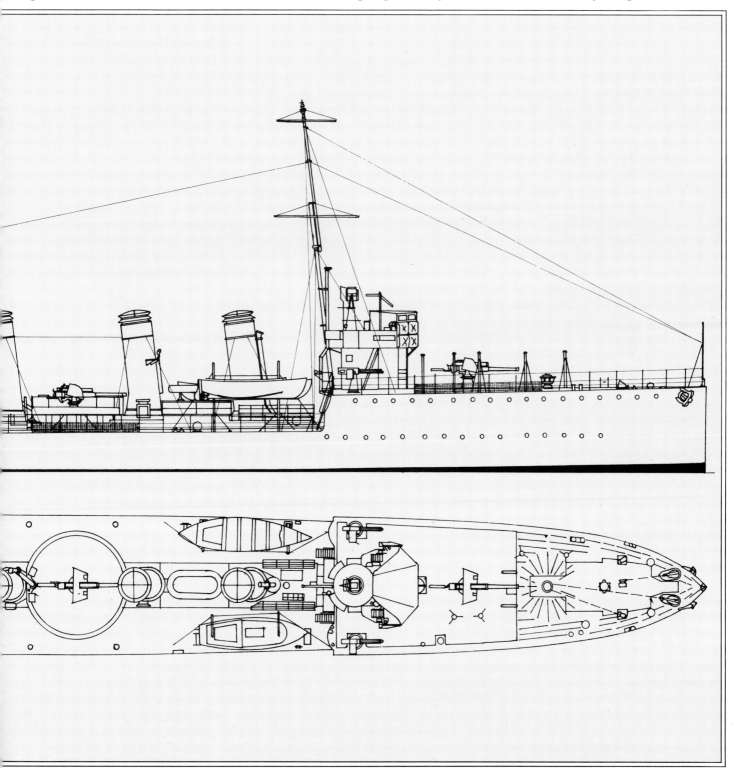

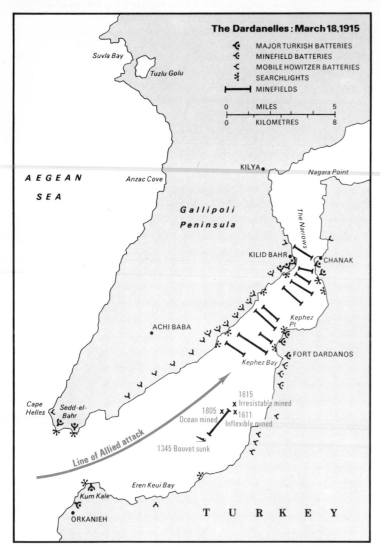

The Dardanelles: March 18, 1915

⚷	MAJOR TURKISH BATTERIES
⚷	MINEFIELD BATTERIES
⚵	MOBILE HOWITZER BATTERIES
⚶	SEARCHLIGHTS
⊢——⊣	MINEFIELDS

MILES 0 — 5
KILOMETRES 0 — 8

AEGEAN SEA

Suvla Bay
Tuzlu Golu
Anzac Cove
KILYA
Nagara Point
Gallipoli Peninsula
The Narrows
KILID BAHR
CHANAK
ACHI BABA
Kephez Pt
Kephez Bay
FORT DARDANOS
1615 Irresistible mined
1805 Ocean mined
1611 Inflexible mined
1345 Bouvet sunk
Line of Allied attack
Cape Helles
Sedd-el-Bahr
Eren Keui Bay
Kum Kale
ORKANIEH
TURKEY

because, not until Russia appealed for an Allied 'demonstration' to relieve their armies in the Caucasus in January 1915, did First Lord Winston Churchill signal Carden: 'Do you think it practicable to force the Dardanelles by ships alone?'

When Carden replied with a plan by which he expected to reach the Sea of Marmara in a month, he received Churchill's strong support. And Admiral 'Jacky' Fisher, who had been recalled as First Sea Lord, added the new Dreadnought *Queen Elizabeth* to the *Inflexible* and 16 French and British pre-Dreadnoughts with which Carden engaged the outer forts on February 19. Bad weather then intervened until the 25th when the Allied gunfire was more effective. On March 1 the outer defences were finally destroyed by demolition parties from Carden's ships.

But subsequent bombardments of the intermediate defences met considerable opposition from mobile howitzers. And when Carden began the reduction of the defences of the Narrows, not even the *Queen Elizabeth*'s guns could silence them. Consequently the British trawlers made little progress with clearing the Straits of Turkish minefields. On the 10th Churchill and Fisher ordered Carden to make 'a vigorous attempt to overwhelm the forts at decisive range'. He tried to do this, but again his minesweepers failed him and, near to a nervous breakdown, he resigned his command.

Pointless sacrifice of ships

His successor, Rear-Admiral John de Robeck, fixed the 18th for the 'big push'. At 1125 the *Queen Elizabeth, Inflexible,* and two pre-Dreadnoughts began bombarding forts mounting 75 guns of up to 14-inch calibre, whilst four more battleships engaged the mobile defences. By noon the latter were silent. Four French pre-Dreadnoughts then fired on the forts with such effect that these were nearly silenced. Six British pre-Dreadnoughts were moving up the Straits to continue their destruction when the retiring French *Bouvet* was struck by a shell that detonated a magazine. In spite of this, de Robeck ordered his trawlers to clear a way through the Kephez minefield. But, as had happened with Carden, when these came under fire their fishermen crews slipped their gear and retired.

Nor was this all. At 1611 the retiring *Inflexible* was damaged by a mine. Four minutes later the pre-Dreadnought *Irresistible* was trapped in the same field. And when de Robeck ordered all his ships to withdraw, the pre-Dreadnought *Ocean* was mined. For the price of six battleships and battlecruisers sunk or damaged, only two of the Turks' big guns had been destroyed.

With more pre-Dreadnoughts on their way out from England to restore his strength, de Robeck organised a destroyer minesweeping force for another all out attempt. But then he learned that Churchill had persuaded Kitchener to make 80,000 men available so that the Allies could force Turkey out of the war, remove the threat to the Suez Canal, and open a way for the supply of arms to Russia.

This changed de Robeck's mind. By March 22 he was 'quite clear he could not get through without the help of troops', just

The light cruiser Birmingham. *Cruisers scouted for the main fleet and backed up destroyers in defending against torpedo attack.*

when his attempt to force the Straits with ships alone was near success. For by now the Turkish defenders were demoralised and their ammunition nearly exhausted. If only Carden's attacks had been more vigorous; if only de Robeck had nerved himself to face further losses on the 19th, the defences might have been silenced by the 20th, when the British minesweepers would have had little difficulty in clearing a way into the Sea of Marmara. As it was, the Allies were com-

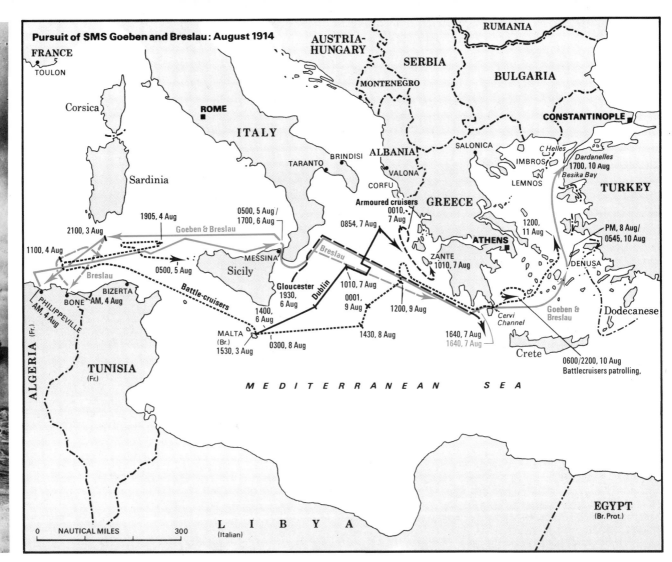

Pursuit of SMS Goeben and Breslau: August 1914

FRANCE

TOULON

Corsica

Sardinia

ROME

ITALY

2100, 3 Aug

1905, 4 Aug

1100, 4 Aug

0500, 5 Aug /
1700, 6 Aug

Goeben & Breslau

MESSINA

Breslau

BIZERTA

BONE AM, 4 Aug

PHILIPPEVILLE
AM, 4 Aug

0500, 5 Aug

Sicily

Battle-cruisers

ALGERIA (Fr.)

TUNISIA
(Fr.)

Gloucester
1930,
6 Aug

MALTA
(Br.)
1530, 3 Aug

1400,
6 Aug

Dublin

0300, 8 Aug

AUSTRIA-
HUNGARY

RUMANIA

SERBIA

MONTENEGRO

BULGARIA

CONSTANTINOPLE

ALBANIA

TARANTO

BRINDISI

VALONA

CORFU

SALONICA

C Helles

IMBROS

LEMNOS

Dardanelles
1700, 10 Aug
Besika Bay

TURKEY

Armoured cruisers
0010,
7 Aug

GREECE

0854, 7 Aug

ATHENS

ZANTE
1010, 7 Aug

1200,
11 Aug

PM, 8 Aug /
0545, 10 Aug

DENUSA

1010, 7 Aug

0001,
9 Aug

1200, 9 Aug

1430, 8 Aug

1640, 7 Aug
1640, 7 Aug

Cervi
Channel

Goeben &
Breslau

Dodecanese

Crete

0600/2200, 10 Aug
Battlecruisers patrolling,

MEDITERRANEAN SEA

EGYPT
(Br. Prot.)

LIBYA
(Italian)

0 NAUTICAL MILES 300

The old French battleship Bouvet *rolls over in a cloud of smoke and steam during the Allies' bombardment of the Dardanelles. A heavy shell had detonated her magazine.*

mitted to the Gallipoli campaign, for which their troops could not be ready until April 25.

Mines strike a blow

This further delay was fatal. When de Robeck's fleet landed 29,000 men on five beaches around Cape Helles and Gaba Tepe, the Turkish defenders were ready for them. And neither then, nor in the eight months that followed, did Allied troops gain more than a foothold on the peninsula. Three more pre-Dreadnoughts were lost while giving bombardment support; the *Goliath* to a torpedo from a Turkish destroyer, the *Triumph* and *Majestic* to torpedoes from the German submarine *U21*. Indeed, the British and Anzac divisions never advanced as far as Carden's small demolition parties had done in February. And all through the summer their casualties mounted as they failed to overcome the Turks' fierce resistance.

In November the British bowed to French pressure to open a new campaign in nearby Salonika. So, in December, the Royal Navy gave the British Army a final helping hand in Gallipoli. On the night of the 18th the last

Only the bow of the old battleship Majestic *can be seen after she has been torpedoed by* U21 *at the Dardanelles.*

Allied troops were withdrawn from Suvla Bay and Anzac Cove, and three weeks later from Cape Helles. Although this was done without the loss of a single man, it was small consolation for a bloody defeat.

At the end of April 1915, the *Goeben* emerged into the Sea of Marmara to attack Allied transports off Gallipoli, but on sighting the *Queen Elizabeth* quickly retired. Thenceforward Souchon preferred to operate against the Russian Fleet in the Black Sea, by whose mines the *Goeben* was damaged in December 1914, the *Breslau* in July 1915. Not until the threat to Constantinople was removed in 1917 did his successor, *Vizeadmiral* Rebeur Paschwitz, sortie into the Aegean. On January 19, 1918 the *Goeben* and *Breslau* sailed to bombard the allied base at Mudros. Ignoring the mine danger, they cleared Sedd-el-Bahr early on the 20th with only slight damage to the *Goeben*.

At 0740 they surprised the British monitors *Raglan* and *M28*, quickly sinking both. But an hour later the *Breslau* struck a mine off Cape Kephalo and, whilst manoeuvring to take her in tow, the *Goeben* struck another in the same British field. A few minutes later the drifting *Breslau* detonated four more mines and sank. The *Goeben* then headed back to the Straits, only to strike a third mine at 0948. Listing heavily, she ran aground off Nagara Point, but was towed off and back to Constantinople before the nearest Allied submarine could attempt a torpedo attack. The *Goeben* was, nonetheless, so severely damaged that she was not again ready for service until just before the end of hostilities in November 1918.

The fight in the far seas

At the outbreak of war Germany had eight cruisers outside Mediterranean and home waters. The *Emden* and the *Karlsruhe* won some fame before their destruction, sinking more than 100,000 tons of Allied shipping. The *Königsberg,* destroyed in an unusual action in the Rufigi Delta, was elusive but less successful. The other five, under Admiral von Spee, won a decisive victory at the Battle of Coronel only to be destroyed at the Battle of Falkland Islands. There remained only the Q-ships to hamper the Allied effort in the far seas.

The eight German cruisers outside home waters and the Mediterranean on August 4, 1914 had short lives. Five comprised *Vize-admiral* Graf von Spee's East Asiatic Squadron, the armoured cruisers *Scharnhorst* and *Gneisenau,* with the light cruisers *Emden, Leipzig* and *Nürnberg.* The others, also light cruisers, were the *Königsberg* off East Africa, and the *Dresden* and *Karlsruhe* in the Caribbean. All were so deployed because there were good reasons—colonies in Africa and the Pacific Islands, and substantial interests in China and Mexico—why Germany should be represented in peace by more than a handful of gunboats. Reinforced by armed liners in war, they would carry on cruiser warfare against enemy merchant vessels, bombard military establishments, and destroy cable and radio stations.

East of Suez Britain deployed three mixed squadrons, including the battlecruiser *Australia,* two pre-Dreadnoughts, and ten armoured and light cruisers, supported by four French and Russian cruisers and, when Japan joined the Allies on August 23, by her considerable Fleet. If all these had made von Spee's destruction their first aim, his career must have been short. But Rear-Admiral R. H. Peirse's East Indies Squadron was required to protect trade against attacks by the *Königsberg,* and Rear-Admiral Sir George Patey's Australian squadron to capture Germany's Pacific Islands, whilst a Japanese fleet, supported by HMS *Triumph,* invested Tsingtao.

This left little more than Vice-Admiral Sir Thomas Jerram's China Squadron to deal with von Spee's force which was widely dispersed, the *Scharnhorst, Gneisenau* and *Nürnberg* at Ponape, the *Emden* at Tsingtao, and the *Leipzig* off Mexico. And Jerram was not helped by the Admiralty's intervention; on July 28 he was ordered to concentrate at Hong Kong instead of watching Tsingtao, which allowed the *Emden* to escape and rejoin von Spee. And when the German Admiral left the Marianas on August 14 to attack trade off the west coast of South America, she was detached to the Indian Ocean.

The end of the *Emden*

Her *Kapitan zur See* von Müller struck with such effect in the Bay of Bengal and off Ceylon that he drew every available Allied warship in pursuit. Between September 10 and October 28 he sank or captured 23 merchant vessels. He also bombarded Madras and sank the Russian cruiser *Zemchug* at anchor off Penang. But on November 9, while raiding the Cocos Island cable station, the *Emden* was surprised by the Australian light cruiser *Sydney,* Captain John Glossop, and soon reduced to a battered wreck.

After futile raids on Apia and Tahiti, the *Scharnhorst* (flag), *Kapitan zur See* Schultz, *Gneisenau, Kapitan zur See* Maerker, and *Nürnberg, Kapitan zur See* von Schönberg,

The opening shots of the Battle of the Falklands, as the battlecruisers Invincible *and* Inflexible *open fire on the fleeing German cruisers. The clouds of coal-smoke and cordite fumes soon made firing difficult.*

reached Easter Island on October 12, where they were reinforced by the *Leipzig, Kapitan zur See* Haun, and *Dresden, Kapitan zur See* Lüdecke. The latter had been driven through the Magellan Straits by the cruisers which Britain and France deployed to protect their Atlantic trade. Rear-Admiral Sir Christopher Cradock's West Indies Squadron located the *Karlsruhe* in the Bahamas as early as August 6 but her speed enabled her to escape.

News that this ship and the *Dresden* were operating off Pernambuco drew Cradock south, well aware that they might be joined by von Spee's force. The Admiralty's reaction to this threat was belated and ineffective. Cradock was ordered to cover the Magellan Straits, but his armoured cruisers *Good Hope* (flag), Captain P. Francklin, and *Monmouth*, Captain F. Brandt, the light cruiser *Glasgow*, Captain J. Luce, and the armed merchant cruiser *Otranto* were reinforced only by the old pre-Dreadnought *Canopus*, Captain H. S. Grant. Her 12-inch guns *might* suffice to deal with von Spee. Unfortunately she developed engine defects. And Cradock's determination to protect British trade off the Chilean coast from an enemy of whom he had received no definite news for more than a month, impelled him to go north without this battleship's support.

On October 31, while the *Glasgow* was paying a call at Coronel, the British force intercepted radio transmissions from the *Leipzig*. Twenty-four hours later Cradock's four ships were spread 15 miles apart in the belief that they would soon encounter this single enemy vessel; and at 1620 Luce sighted her smoke on the *Glasgow*'s starboard bow. Von Spee was under a like delusion. Having received no news of Cradock's squadron since leaving Eastern Island until an agent reported the *Glasgow*'s arrival at Coronel, his force was also dispersed when Haun sighted her.

Cradock spurns flight

Twenty minutes later, however, the *Glasgow* reported the *Scharnhorst* and *Gneisenau* in company with the *Leipzig*. With their slight speed advantage the British might have escaped to the south; Cradock would have been complying with the Admiralty's instructions had he fallen back on the *Canopus*. But once he lost touch with von Spee, who could tell when he would be found again? Moreover, it was not essential to sink his ships; damage would compel them to seek internment in a neutral port. Moreover, as Cradock recorded in a letter which he had left with the Governor of the Falklands, he had no intention of being charged before a court martial as had happened to Troubridge.

Forty-five minutes later the *Good Hope*, *Monmouth*, *Glasgow* and *Otranto* were in single line ahead on a course that should bring them within range of the enemy, although this headed them into a sea that made it impossible to fight their main deck

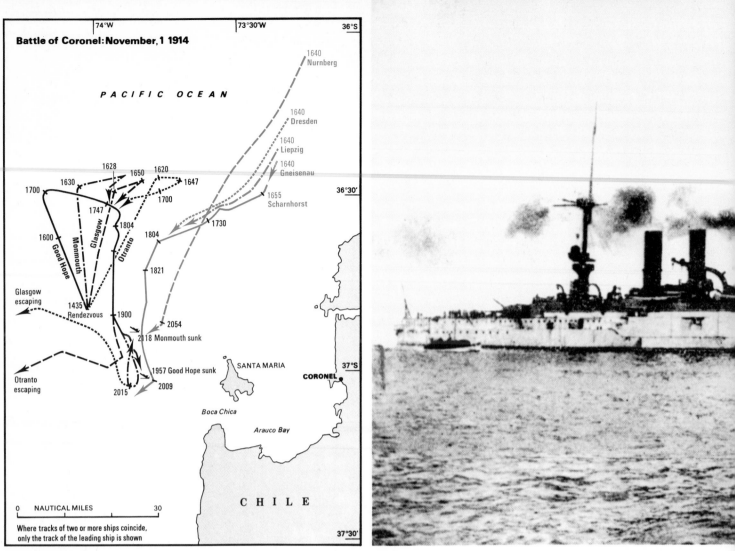

Battle of Coronel: November, 1 1914

74°W 73°30'W 36°S

PACIFIC OCEAN

1640 Nurnberg
1640 Dresden
1640 Liepzig
1640 Gneisenau

1628 1650 1620
1630 1647
1700 1700
1747 36°30'
1804 1730
1600 1804

Glasgow
Monmouth
Good Hope

1821

Glasgow escaping
1435 Rendezvous
1900
2054
2118 Monmouth sunk

Otranto escaping
1957 Good Hope sunk
2015 2009

SANTA MARIA
37°S
CORONEL

Boca Chica
Arauco Bay

CHILE

0 NAUTICAL MILES 30

Where tracks of two or more ships coincide,
only the track of the leading ship is shown

37°30'

guns. At 1818 Cradock radioed the *Canopus*: 'I am now going to attack the enemy'.

Von Spee had already identified his opponent, and was in full pursuit until 'the sun dipped below the horizon shortly before 1900 when, wrote one of the *Glasgow*'s officers, 'we were silhouetted against the afterglow with a clear horizon behind us to show up splashes from falling shells while the [German] ships were smudged into low black shapes scarcely discernible against the background of gathering darkness. The enemy were no longer avoiding action'. When the range was down to 12,300 yards, von Spee signalled his ships to open fire. 'And, to quote a German witness, 'with that [order] disaster broke over Admiral Cradock's squadron. Barely three seconds afterwards the air quivered under the crash of the *Scharnhorst*'s first salvo.'

According to the *Scharnhorst*'s spotting officer: 'The *Good Hope* received serious hits in the fore part of the ship, on the upper bridge, on the mast, and on the foretop. She was also hit repeatedly amidships, most of these causing fires. The after battery was hit several times and fires broke out. The flames in the interior could be seen through the port holes. The *Monmouth* was hit on her fore turret. The shell blew off the roof. A terrific explosion must then have blown the whole turret off the forecastle for it disappeared. Many shells struck the ship amidships. A huge column of fire shot up on the starboard side. At times three or four fires were burning simultaneously.'

An officer aboard the *Glasgow* noted that 'by 1945, by which time it was quite dark, *Good*

Hope and *Monmouth* were obviously in distress. *Monmouth* yawed off to starboard burning furiously, *Good Hope* was firing only a few of her guns. The fires onboard were increasing. At 1950 there was a terrible explosion between her mainmast and her after funnel. She lay between the lines a low black hull lighted only by a dull glow. No one onboard the *Glasgow* actually saw her founder'—with all hands, including Sir Christopher Cradock, around 2000. But Luce could guess her fate. He turned his ship to succour the stricken *Monmouth*, signalling her at 2015: 'Can you steer north-east?'

'There was no answer,' wrote one of the *Glasgow*'s officers. 'The *Monmouth* could neither fight nor fly. She was badly down by the bows, listing to port with the glow of her ignited interior brightening the portholes.' To divert the *Canopus* before she, too, was sunk, the *Glasgow* increased to full speed and left the enemy astern. The weakly armed *Otranto* had been ordered to seek safety to the south half-an-hour before.

Von Spee signalled his light cruisers to search for the surviving British ships. They found the wreck of the *Monmouth* and, at 2118, sent her to the bottom, her flag still flying. As with the *Good Hope,* no rescue attempt was possible; the sea was too rough for boats to be launched. The *Canopus,* despite achieving as much as a knot less than her designed speed, was still 200 miles from the scene when the *Glasgow*'s radio warned her of Cradock's fate. Because the maximum range of her heavy guns was less than that of the German armoured cruisers, Grant decided that she would be best employed

covering the *Glasgow*'s and *Otranto*'s retreat to the Falkland Islands. But for fear of meeting this battleship, von Spee called off his pursuit and turned north, well content with a victory which had given him command of the south-west Pacific.

Winston Churchill's successor as First Lord, Arthur Balfour, gave this verdict: 'The German Admiral was far from any port where he could have refitted. If he suffered damage even though he inflicted greater damage than he received, his power might suddenly be destroyed. He would be in great peril as long as his squadron remained inefficient, and if Admiral Cradock judged that he himself, and those under him, were well sacrificed if they destroyed the power of this hostile fleet, then there is no man but would say that he showed the highest courage. We shall never know his thoughts when it became evident that success was an impossibility. He and his gallant comrades lie far from the pleasant homes of England. Yet they have their reward; theirs is an immortal place in the great role of naval heroes.'

Churchill's fighting response

Berlin reacted to the news of von Spee's victory with a warning that cruiser warfare now offered few prospects of success, and advised him to try to break through with all his ships and return home. The German Admiral agreed, but made two fatal mistakes. He delayed a full month before taking his five cruisers round Cape Horn, and he decided to interrupt his Atlantic voyage with a raid on the Falkland Islands.

Battle of the Falkland Islands: December 8, 1914

Scharnhorst, Nurnberg, Gneisenau
Liepzig and Dresden

SOUTH ATLANTIC OCEAN

Invincible

1617 Scharnhorst sunk

1800 Gneisenau sunk

Cornwall   Kent

1927 Nurnberg sunk

1700 Dresden escaping

2035 Leipzig sunk

0   NAUTICAL MILES   40

Where tracks of two or more ships coincide, only the track of the leading ship is shown

Above : The armoured cruiser Scharnhorst *was completed in 1907. Like her sister* Gneisenau *she had a powerful armament of eight 8.2-inch guns, but the type was totally outclassed by the battlecruiser, as the Battle of the Falklands proved.*

Right : The Emden *was caught at Cocos Keeling Island by HMAS* Sydney.

Below : The Scharnhorst *at Valparaiso after the Battle of Coronel.*

The Admiralty had responded to Cradock's defeat by sending strong reinforcements to every area to which von Spee might go. In particular, Churchill and Fisher sent the battlecruiser *Princess Royal* to the Caribbean in case von Spee should pass through the recently opened Panama Canal, and the *Invincible* (flag), Captain P. T. H. Beamish, and *Inflexible,* Captain R. F. Phillimore, to the South Atlantic. Sailing secretly from Devonport on November 11 under Vice-Admiral Sir Frederick Sturdee's command, these two ships reached the Falklands on December 7 to form a squadron that included the armoured cruisers *Carnarvon,* Captain H. L. d'E. Skipwith, flag of Rear-Admiral A. P. Stoddart, *Kent,* Captain J. D. Allen, and *Cornwall,* Captain W. M. Ellerton, and the light cruisers *Glasgow* and *Bristol*, Captain B. H. Fanshawe.

Sturdee intended to go through the Magellan Straits in search of von Spee off the Chilean coast as soon as his ships had coaled, leaving the *Canopus* to defend the Falklands. But at 0800 on December 8 he received the startling news that the German squadron was approaching the islands. Unperturbed at being caught whilst coaling, he ordered steam to be raised for full speed. The *Kent* cleared the harbour at 0845 and most of the others an hour later. By 1000 the *Invincible* was at sea flying the exhilarating signal, 'Chase!'

A 12-inch salvo from the *Canopus*, and a sighting report of two Dreadnoughts in Stanley harbour, decided von Spee to seek safety in flight to the south-east. Not until 1100 did he learn the fateful truth, that his

43

SMS Scharnhorst, *flagship of Admiral Spee, the first ship sunk at the Battle of the Falklands.* Gneisenau *fought on alone to enable the smaller cruisers to scatter.*

squadron was being overhauled by two battlecruisers. At 1245 these great ships opened deliberate fire at a range of more than 16,000 yards. When they scored their first hit half an hour later, von Spee signalled his light cruisers to leave the line and try to escape. In accordance with Sturdee's *Fighting Instructions*, the *Kent*, *Cornwall* and *Glasgow* went in pursuit.

Annihilation in revenge

This divided the battle into a number of separate actions. That of the battlecruisers and the *Carnarvon* against von Spee's armoured cruisers was prolonged by Sturdee's decision to avoid damage to his own vessels when they were so far from any dockyard. The British ships' heavier shells easily penetrated the decks of the German armoured cruisers and played havoc below. The damage increased continually, especially in the centre of the *Gneisenau*. No. 1 boiler room was flooded and had to be abandoned. No. 3 boiler room also began to fill. Fires broke out fore and aft. The *Scharnhorst* suffered as severely. Badly holed both forward and aft below the waterline, she could be seen to be on fire in several places, and by 1530 her third funnel had been shot away and her gunfire had slackened perceptibly, whereas the hits which had been obtained on the battlecruisers had done nothing to reduce their fighting value.

The *Scharnhorst* went to the bottom at 1617 with von Spee and all her crew. The *Gneisenau* survived until 1750 when the British ships stopped to rescue 190 of her officers and men.

The *Kent* went after the *Nürnberg*, from which there were only seven survivors when she sank at 1926, two and a half hours after opening fire. The *Leipzig* was pursued by the *Glasgow* and *Cornwall* until 2030 when she, too, was sunk, darkness and icy seas preventing the rescue of more than eighteen of her crew. The *Dresden* eluded pursuit, to disappear round Cape Horn under the cover of darkness. And only one of von Spee's supply ships escaped destruction; the others were caught and sunk by the *Bristol*.

There was no doubting this British victory: by skilful tactics Sturdee had annihilated von Spee's squadron at negligible cost to his own force. Cradock's defeat had been decisively avenged. That evening Sturdee signalled to Commander Pochhammer, the senior surviving German officer: 'The Commander-in-Chief is very gratified that your life has been spared, and we all feel that the *Gneisenau* fought in a most plucky manner to the end. We sympathise with you in the loss of your Admiral and so many officers and men. Unfortunately the two countries are at war; the officers of both Navies, who can count friends in the other, have to carry out their country's duties which your Admiral, Captain and officers worthily maintained to the end.'

Sturdee received the equally chivalrous reply: 'In the name of all our officers and men saved I thank your Excellency for your kind

SMS Emden

The *Emden* and her sister *Dresden* were typical of the small light cruisers built for the German Navy between 1905 and 1914. They were designed to scout for the main fleets and to attack British shipping on the high seas, a task for which they were well suited. Like all German light cruisers of the period the *Emden* was armed with the 10.5-cm (4.1-inch) gun as the German Navy preferred rate of fire and high velocity to hitting power.

**Displacement: 3,650 tons
Armament: Ten 10.5-cm guns, four 8-mm, two 18-in TT.
Machinery: Two-shaft triple-expansion, 16,000 ihp = 24 knots**

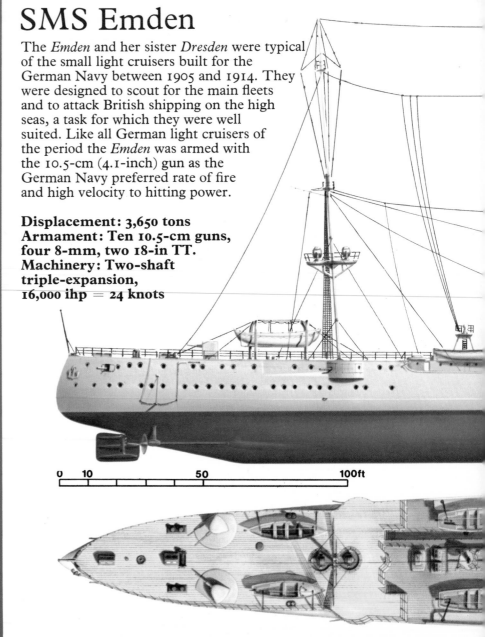

Above : The Dresden, *the only German ship to escape from the Falklands.*

Top right : Sailors from HMAS Sydney *come ashore after the battle with the* Emden.

words. We regret, as you, the course of the fight, as we have personally learned to know during peace time the English Navy and her officers. We are all most thankful for our good reception.'

The *Dresden* eluded searching British cruisers for nearly three months, during which she did negligible damage to Allied shipping. Then the Admiralty intercepted a cable disclosing her intention to rendezvous with a collier 300 miles west of Coronel. The *Kent* sighted her there on March 7, too late to catch her before dark. Prevented from coaling, the *Dresden* was compelled to anchor off Mas a Fuera. The *Kent* and *Glasgow* found her there on the morning of the 9th. And in an action lasting less than five minutes she suffered enough damage for Lüdecke to hoist a white flag, whereby he gained the time to scuttle his ship after her crew had sought safety ashore.

The Admiralty had already solved the mystery of why they had received no reports of the *Karlsruhe* for so long. After capturing or sinking 76,500 tons of Allied shipping by the end of October 1914, she had headed for Barbados to raid the island's defenceless capital. But fate, in the guise of unstable cordite, intervened. The *Karlsruhe* was rent by the spontaneous explosion of her magazines. Her two tenders saved 140 of her officers and men and slipped through the British blockade to reach Germany early in December.

Since the few German armed merchant cruisers which escaped from neutral ports had soon been sunk by Allied warships, or had been compelled to seek internment, only the light cruiser *Königsberg* remained to be accounted for. Deprived of her base by the cruiser *Astraea*'s attack on Dar-es-Salaam at the outset of the war, she first harried trade off Aden for a week, then found a haven in the delta of the Rufigi river, whence she emerged to sink the small cruiser *Pegasus* at Zanzibar on September 20. But by the end of the month she had been located by the light cruisers *Dartmouth* and *Weymouth*, after which she was confined to her Rufigi

HMS Invincible

The battlecruiser was originally designed as an armoured cruiser equivalent of the *Dreadnought*, with a heavy main armament and steam turbines to produce high speed. Their purpose was to hunt down cruisers on the trade-routes and to scout for the battlefleet but they came to be thought of as fast battleships. In recognition of this they were re-rated as battlecruisers in 1913 but the Battle of Jutland showed that they could not withstand punishment.

The *Invincible* and her sisters were nearly as well armed as the *Dreadnought* but had much thinner armour to allow them a margin of speed. The Battle of the Falklands was the high-point in the battlecruisers' story, whereas, only eighteen months later, Jutland proved their weakness; three of the British ships, including the *Invincible* blew up with heavy loss of life.

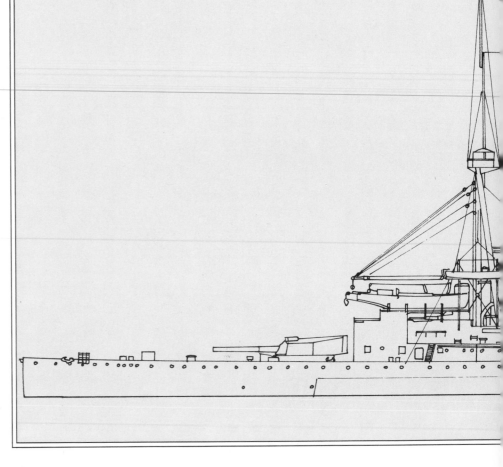

The Battle of Falkland Islands, 1914

Great Britain	Armament		Germany	Armament	
Invincible	8×12"		Scharnhorst	8×8.2"	6×6"
Inflexible	8×12"		Gneisenau	8×8.2"	6×6"
Kent	14× 6"		Leipzig	10×4.1"	
Cornwall	14× 6"		Nürnberg	10×4.1"	
Caernarvon	4× 7.5"	6×6"	Dresden	10×4.1"	
Glasgow	2× 6"	10×4"			

hide-out until July 1915, when two shallow-draft monitors, the *Severn* and *Mersey*, arrived from Britain. These penetrated the mangrove swamps and reduced the *Königsberg* to a stranded wreck.

Her destruction brought down the curtain on the war in the far seas. No other warship left Germany to raid the trade routes. A number of merchant ships were, however, armed with guns, torpedoes, and mines concealed beneath their peacetime trappings. The *Möwe* left Hamburg in December 1915, for a four months' cruise in the South Atlantic, which

was followed by another in November 1916, from which she returned with a total bag of 34 Allied merchant ships and the pre-Dreadnought *King Edward VII* sunk by a mine laid off Cape Wrath.

Her record was, however, exceptional. The *Greif* was sunk in February 1916, only two days after leaving Germany for her first cruise. The *Wolf* sailed in December 1916 to lay mines off the Cape of Good Hope, and to land ammunition to enable *General* von Lettow-Vorbeck's beleaguered garrison to hold out in South-East Africa until the end of

the war; but during her subsequent cruise in the Indian Ocean she sank only twelve Allied ships. The *Leopard* was sunk by the cruiser *Achilles* as she tried to break out of the North Sea in March 1917. And although the *Seeadler* passed the Allied blockade under Norwegian colours to operate first in the South Atlantic, then in the Pacific, proving an armed sailing vessel's ability to avoid detection, she also showed how small were her chances of achieving much. She was wrecked in the Fiji Islands in August 1917 after sinking only ten Allied ships.

Displacement: 17,250 tons
Armament: Eight 12-inch guns, sixteen 4-in, four 18-in TT.
Machinery: Four-shaft steam turbines, 41,000 shp = 25½ knots

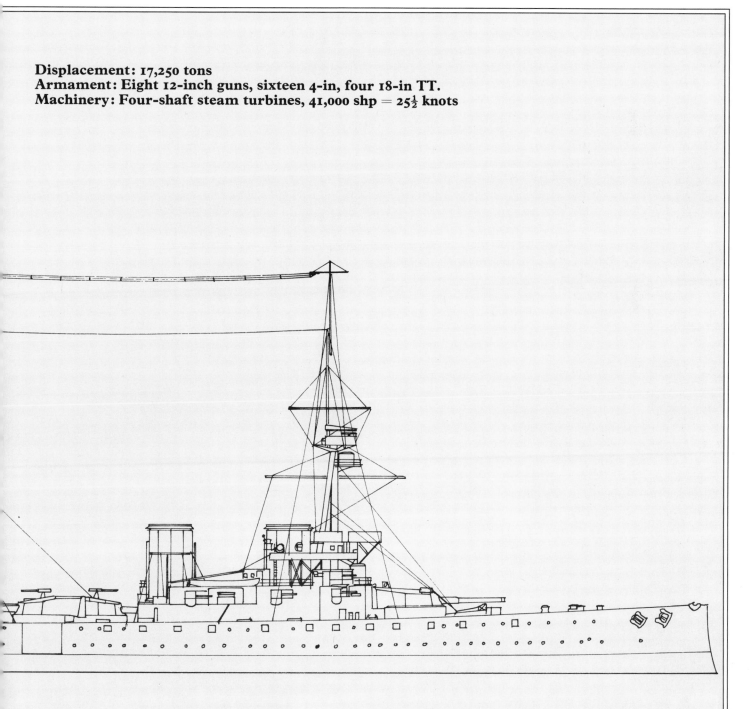

Skirmishes in the North Sea

Throughout the first 21 months of the war the strategy of the Grand Fleet was to confine Germany's High Seas Fleet in the North Sea until it could be brought to action. The Kaiser sought to weaken the Royal Navy by waging seaborne guerilla war. The result was a series of fierce skirmishes and near disasters for both sides. In the meantime all-out submarine warfare, in defiance of international conventions, cost Britain 900,000 tons of shipping before the weight of world opinion brought it to a halt. Both sides were manoeuvring for the advantage in the inevitable meeting of the two massively powerful battle fleets.

Although in August 1914 the Grand Fleet, of which Admiral Sir John Jellicoe became Commander-in-Chief on the day before hostilities began, was much stronger than Germany's High Seas Fleet, it could not adopt the traditional close blockade; coal-fired boilers, mines, and submarines had made this impossible. The Admiralty conceived the alternative of distant blockade—the High Seas Fleet was to be confined to the North Sea by a fleet based on Scapa Flow until it could be brought to action.

Again and again during August Jellicoe swept south in the hope that the Germans would come out, but *Admiral* von Ingenohl's Dreadnoughts did not leave the Jade. Persuaded that Paris would quickly fall to his Army, the Kaiser had ordained that his ships were only to wage 'guerrilla' war until the British Fleet had been so weakened that the two could meet on equal terms.

The Admiralty countered by ordering Commodore Reginald Tyrwhitt's Harwich Force of two light cruisers, the *Arethusa* and *Fearless,* and 16 destroyers to raid the Heligoland Bight at dawn on August 28. This might draw German ships out of the Jade

to where submarines, controlled by Commodore Roger Keyes, were waiting. Rear-Admiral David Beatty's five battlecruisers and Commodore W. E. Goodenough's six light cruisers came south from Scapa Flow in support.

Tyrwhitt sighted enemy torpedoboats shortly before 0700 and gave chase until he was within range of two light cruisers, the *Stettin* and *Frauenlob*, with whom the *Arethusa* and *Fearless* had a brief engagement. Tyrwhitt then swept west to meet further torpedoboats, which likewise fled after their leader had been sunk. At 1100 the *Arethusa* encountered the light cruiser *Strassburg* and drove her off into the mist. Next, the light cruiser *Mainz* was pursued to the north where she ran into Goodenough's squadron which sunk her at 1310.

Before this, Tyrwhitt was again engaged by

the *Strassburg*, supported by the light cruiser *Köln*. Both were driven off, but the appearance of three more German light cruisers, the *Stralsund*, *Danzig* and *Ariadne*, together with the *Stettin*, alerted the waiting Beatty to the possibility that Tyrwhitt's force, in which the *Arethusa* and two destroyers had suffered damage, might be overwhelmed. By 1135 the British battlecruisers were heading to the rescue, and soon after 1230 their 13.5-

inch salvoes sent the *Köln* and *Ariadne* to the bottom. But though Beatty's boldness had achieved a victory, the raid had come too near disaster for the Admiralty to repeat it.

Caution not in tradition

In November the German submarine *U18* penetrated Scapa Flow. Though rammed and damaged by a trawler before she could find targets for her torpedoes, Jellicoe moved his base, first to Loch Ewe, then to Loch Swilly, until Scapa's defences could be strengthened. Although he now had 30 Dreadnoughts and battlecruisers under his command, six were away refitting, the *Audacious* had been sunk by a mine, and Cradock's defeat had brought Admiralty orders to send three battlecruisers out into the Atlantic. So for the time being the High

The First Battle Squadron of the British Grand Fleet. The Revenge *(leading),* Resolution *and* Royal Sovereign *joined the Fleet in 1916. The completion of a further two with 15-inch guns offset the loss of three battlecruisers at Jutland.*

Above: The heavily damaged Seydlitz *in dock after Jutland, with a Kaiser Class battleship behind her.*

Seas Fleet was numerically as strong. As important, Jellicoe knew that ship for ship the German Dreadnoughts were tougher than the British. In these circumstances he decided that he would only fight a fleet action in the northern half of the North Sea where the Germans could not rely on submarines and minelayers to help them. Although such caution did not accord with tradition, the Admiralty assured Jellicoe of their confidence in his determination thus to maintain the Allied blockade.

Coupled with the Kaiser's restrictions on his ships, this delayed a major clash between the two Fleets for another eighteen months. Meantime there were lesser engagements. On November 3, *Konteradmiral* Franz Hipper's battlecruisers bombarded Yarmouth, which was too far south for the Grand Fleet to reach the scene in time. Thereafter, copies of the German Navy's codes, salvaged from the wrecked cruiser *Magdeburg,* enabled the Admiralty to decipher enough German radio signals to give warning of their future plans. They learned that von Ingenohl had ordered a further raid on the British east coast on December 16, but not that it was to be supported by the whole High Seas Fleet.

British destroyers encountered von Ingenohl's advanced screen at dawn. Convinced that he was running into the whole Grand Fleet, the German C-in-C hurried his battleships back to the Jade, leaving his bombarding battlecruisers to their fate. By the time the *Derfflinger* and *Von der Tann* had fired on Scarborough and Whitby, and the *Seydlitz, Moltke* and *Blücher* had inflicted damage on Hartlepool, their escape routes through the east coast minefield had been cut. Hipper chose the centre gap where Beatty's

SMS Stettin

This German light cruiser was sistership of the *Nürnberg*, which was sunk at the Battle of the Falklands. She herself missed destruction at the hands of British battlecruisers during the Heligoland Bight action in August 1914.

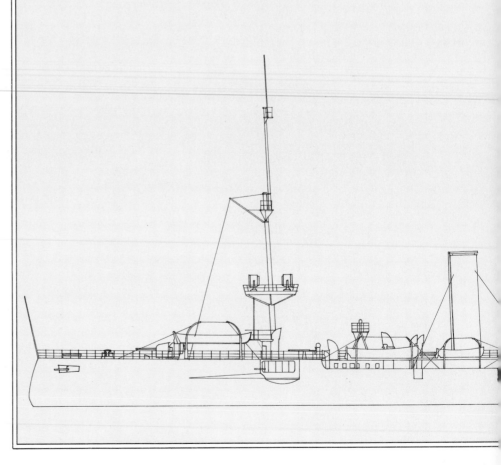

Above: The last photograph of the doomed Cunard liner Lusitania *as she left New York. Her sinking was to strain diplomatic relations between Germany and America to breaking point.*

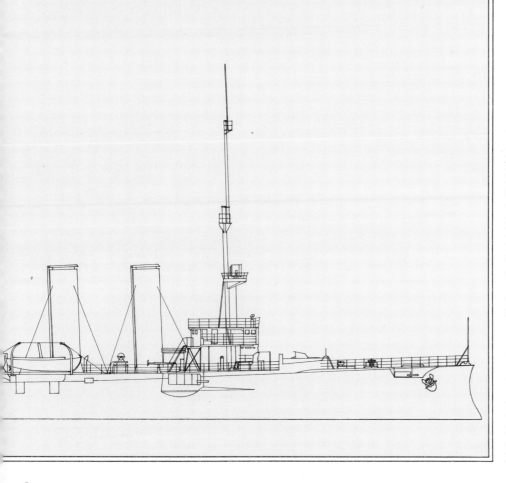

Displacement: 3,550 tons
Armament: Ten 4.1-inch guns, two 18-in TT.
Machinery: Four-shaft steam turbines, 21,000 shp = 25 knots

four battlecruisers, with eight Dreadnoughts under Vice-Admiral Sir George Warrender, were waiting. His advanced cruisers were sighted by Goodenough's light cruisers, but an unfortunate signal error by the *Lion*, Beatty's flagship, misled them into losing touch. Hipper's force was able to haul away to the north before Warrender's squadron could sight them.

Signal error allows escape

On January 23, 1915 Hipper again left the Jade with four battlecruisers to raid the British Dogger Bank patrol. The Admiralty had enough warning to order Beatty's five battlecruisers, accompanied by Goodenough's light cruisers, to rendezvous with Tyrwhitt's force at 0700 on the 24th between the Germans and their base. As Beatty's ships met Tyrwhitt's north-east of the Dogger Bank, they sighted Hipper's which promptly turned for home. They were, however, steadily overhauled until, at 0900, the *Lion* opened fire on the *Blücher*.

As the chase continued, Beatty's battl-cruisers engaged their opposite numbers, and at 0930 the *Lion* scored a hit on the *Seydlitz*'s after turret, whose flash passed down the trunk of the magazine and into the adjacent turret, killing both their crews. Only prompt flooding saved the ship from destruction.

By 0950 the *Blücher* was badly battered, whereas the British ships went unscathed until shortly after 1000, when the *Lion* was hit by three shells from the *Derfflinger*, one of which reduced her speed. Fifteen minutes later Hipper decided to leave the *Blücher* to

The armoured cruiser Blücher *was built in 1908 before full details of the British battlecruisers became known. She is seen here in 1910 before being refitted with a tripod foremast.*

The German battleship Bayern *leaving Wilhelmshaven. She and the* Baden *were the only German battleships completed after August 1914.*

SMS Seydlitz

German battlecruisers built in reply to the British *Invincible* Class carried heavier protection at the expense of gunpower. No ship justified this approach more than the *Seydlitz*, the most heavily damaged of all Jutland survivors.

Displacement: 24,610 tons
Armament: Ten 11-inch guns, twelve 5.9-in, four 20-in TT.
Machinery: Four-shaft steam turbines,
89,700 shp = 27 knots

The Battle of Dogger Bank, 1915

Great Britain	Armament	Germany	Armament
Lion	8 × 13.5"	Seydlitz	8 × 12"
Tiger	8 × 13.5"	Derfflinger	8 × 12"
Princess Royal	8 × 13.5"	Moltke	10 × 11"
New Zealand	8 × 12"	Blücher	12 × 8.2"
Indomitable	8 × 12"	plus 4 light cruisers, 19 destroyers	
plus 7 light cruisers, 35 destroyers			

The German submarine U29 seen from a ship she would shortly torpedo.

her fate. With the *Indomitable* ordered to finish her off and his other ships closing the rest of the enemy, an annihilating victory was within Beatty's grasp. Unfortunately, at 1100 he thought he saw a submarine's periscope on the *Lion*'s starboard bow. Suspecting a U-boat trap, he signalled his squadron to turn 90 degrees to port, then hoisted, 'Course NE'. With the *Lion* lagging astern,

Beatty gave the further order: 'Attack the enemy's rear'. And because the flags for 'Course NE' were still flying, both were read together as: 'Attack enemy bearing NE'. This being the *Blücher*'s bearing, Rear-Admiral Sir Archibald Moor allowed the *Tiger, Princess Royal* and *New Zealand* to swing round and join the *Indomitable* in completing the destruction of the German lame duck. By the time Beatty could rehoist his flag in the *Princess Royal*, Hipper had vanished over the horizon.

'The sinking of the *Blücher* and the flight of the other German ships was a solid and indisputable result,' wrote Churchill. But it would have been more decisive if Moore had pursued the main enemy force instead of concentrating on the destruction of one crippled vessel. As important, the British Navy remained in ignorance of a serious defect in the turret design of its Dreadnoughts, while the Germans profited from the near loss of the *Seydlitz*. to correct theirs.

Indiscriminate destruction

The Kaiser vented his anger at the loss of the *Blücher* on von Ingenohl and he was super-

seded by the cautious von Pohl who never allowed his ships beyond the Horns Reef. But his U-boats were authorised to begin a new campaign. As soon as September 22, 1914, *U9* had sent the armoured cruisers *Aboukir, Cressy* and *Hogue* to the bottom of the North Sea. The *Hawke* followed them on October 15, and the pre-Dreadnought *Formidable* early on January 1, 1915. Germany was not, however, content with operations which only hampered the Grand Fleet's blockade. When the Kaiser's dream of a swift victory on land dissolved into the nightmare of trench warfare, the *Admiralstab* realised the potency of the U-boat as a weapon for attacking merchant shipping.

Against unleashing unrestricted U-boat warfare there was, however, one obstacle—submarines as well as surface ships were required to board a merchant vessel to check whether she was carrying contraband and ensure the safety of her passengers and crew before sinking her. This exposed a U-boat to destruction by British light craft. The solution was to defy international law. Germany declared a 'war-zone' round the British Isles on February 16, 1915, in which 'every merchant vessel will be destroyed without it

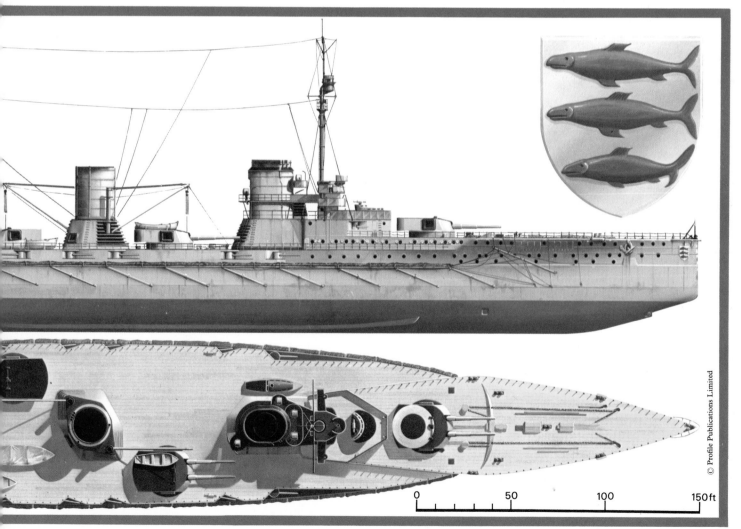

0 50 100 150ft

being possible to avoid damage to the crew and passengers, it being impossible to avoid attacks being made on neutral ships in mistake for those of the enemy'.

In spite of the many steps taken by the Admiralty to counter this campaign, including an Auxiliary Patrol of more than 1,000 small ships, and the innovation of Q-ships, it achieved considerable success. But initial neutral protests were as nothing to the outcry that followed *U20*'s attack on the *Lusitania* on May 7, 1915, which cost the lives of 1,198 of her passengers and crew. The world raised its voice in such scandalised horror that the Kaiser banned further attacks on passenger liners. But this restriction did not prevent another serious incident: on August 19 *U24* sent the liner *Arabic* to the bottom. This time the USA protested so strongly that on October 5, by which time Britain had lost 900,000 tons of shipping, the Kaiser issued orders to cease all forms of submarine warfare on the west coast of Great Britain and in the Channel.

Confrontations avoided

In the first month of 1916 von Pohl was found to be mortally ill and was succeeded by *Vizeadmiral* Reinhardt Scheer, who was not slow to pursue a more forward strategy. In February a British minesweeping flotilla was overwhelmed by German light forces on the Dogger Bank before Beatty or Tyrwhitt could reach the scene. Further operations were planned to trap weaker elements of the Grand Fleet. The first attempt, in March, failed because the Admiralty learned of it too late to order any units of the Grand Fleet out. Ten days later, when the Harwich Force attacked the Zeppelin sheds at Tondern, Scheer left the Jade intent on Tyrwhitt's destruction. Beatty sped south to his rescue, and early on the 26th it seemed likely that the British battlecruisers would meet the High Seas Fleet without Jellicoe's support. Perhaps fortunately for them, a rising gale decided Scheer against risking action in a storm.

The German fleet put to sea again on April 21, to bombard Lowestoft. The Admiralty learned of this when the *Seydlitz* was damaged by a mine. The Grand Fleet and the Harwich Force were immediately ordered out, Tyrwhitt in time to sight four German battlecruisers at first light on the 25th. Although not deflected from their first objective, the Germans were obliged to answer a call for help from their light cruisers before they could bombard Yarmouth. Even so, they made no attempt to destroy Tyrwhitt's small force; instead they retired eastwards at high speed towards Scheer's battle fleet, which had already reversed course for home. Tyrwhitt took the Harwich Force after them but the Admiralty, fearing the outcome, called off the chase. Beatty's battlecruisers, coming south at full speed, also turned for home, not knowing that the enemy was less than 50 miles away.

German pre-Dreadnought battleships on manoeuvres in the days of peace before 1914. The vessel in the centre of the picture is the minelayer Albatross, *which was designed to lay mines in the path of an advancing enemy fleet.*

Jutland-the clash of fleets

At the end of May 1916 the Grand Fleet and the High Seas Fleet finally met in the massive showdown that had been threatened since the war began. Jutland, with its fascinating possibilities of total, crushing victory for one side, was the last fearsome conflict of two mighty battle fleets. Both sides claimed to have won. But while Jutland may have been inconclusive it was not indecisive. After it Britain's powerful Grand Fleet, which had so keenly sought the action, was still on the offensive. The High Seas Fleet was not eager for conflict on such a scale.

From the bombardment of Lowestoft Scheer learned that the High Seas Fleet had crossed the North Sea too far south to trap part of Jellicoe's fleet. So he designated Sunderland as the next target for Hipper's battlecruisers, with U-boats stationed off the British bases to cause losses as the Grand Fleet emerged. Extensive, careful Zeppelin reconnaissance would make certain that Jellicoe was not already at sea. However, defects in several German Dreadnoughts compelled postponement of this operation from mid-May 1916 to the end of the month, when the weather was unsuitable for airships. So Scheer chose the less risky alternative of showing his fleet off Norway as a means of drawing the British out.

Hipper, in the *Lützow*, led his battlecruisers to sea at 0200 on May 31, accompanied by four light cruisers and three torpedoboat flotillas. Fifty miles astern, up the swept channel to the Horns Reef, followed Scheer's battle fleet; seven Dreadnoughts of the 3rd Battle Squadron under *Konteradmiral* P. Behncke; the fleet flagship *Friedrich der Grosse* leading eight Dreadnoughts of the 1st BS under *Vizeadmiral* E. Schmidt, and six pre-Dreadnoughts of the 2nd BS, *Konteradmiral* F. Mauve, with five light cruisers and four torpedoboat flotillas.

The Admiralty received sufficient warning of this sortie from intercepted radio messages to order the Grand Fleet out on the evening of the 30th. The *Lion* led Beatty's 1st Battlecruiser Squadron, Rear-Admiral O. de B. Brock, of four ships and 2nd BCS, Rear-Admiral W. C. Pakenham, of two ships to sea from the Forth, supported by the 5th BS of four *Queen Elizabeth* class Dreadnoughts, Rear-Admiral H. Evan-Thomas, 12 light cruisers, and three destroyer flotillas. Jellicoe's battle fleet sailed from Scapa and Cromarty; 24 Dreadnoughts, divided into the 1st BS, Vice-Admiral Cecil Burney, 2nd BS, Vice-Admiral Sir Thomas Jerram, and 4th BS, Vice Admiral Sturdee, with the 3rd BCS of three 'Invincible' class ships, Rear-Admiral the Hon. H. Hood, eight armoured cruisers, 12 light cruisers, and three flotillas of destroyers. The two forces are best tabulated for comparison:

	Grand Fleet	High Seas Fleet
Battleships:		
Dreadnoughts	28	16
pre-Dreadnoughts	–	6
Battlecruisers	9	5
Armoured cruisers	8	–
Light cruisers	26	11
Destroyers/		
Torpedoboats	77	61

Around noon on the 31st the Admiralty misinterpreted its intelligence to the extent of telling Jellicoe and Beatty that Scheer was still in the Jade. At 1415, having reached a position 100 miles to the north of the Horns Reef without sighting the enemy, Beatty swung his force round to meet Jellicoe's, 65 miles to the north. Since some 50 miles then seperated the *Lion* from Hipper's force on its course for Norway, Beatty would have missed making contact but for the chance that the light cruiser *Galatea* moved east to investigate a neutral steamer and sighted the light cruiser *Elbing*, of Hipper's screen, doing likewise. Beatty reacted to her enemy report with an order swinging his force back to SSE at 22 knots. But the 5th BS was too far to the north to read the *Lion's* flag signal: by the time Evan-Thomas received it by searchlight his powerful Dreadnoughts were ten miles astern of the battlecruisers—a 'failure' (Jellicoe's word) to concentrate that was to have considerable consequences. Beatty was,

The British battlecruiser flagship Lion *reels under the impact of heavy shells. The plume of smoke rising vertically between her funnels is from a near-fatal hit on a turret which caused a cordite fire.*

however, chiefly concerned to ensure that Hipper did not again find safety in flight.

Beatty's 'bloody ships'

The German Admiral held his course in the hope of destroying the British light cruiser squadron; not until he sighted Beatty's battlecruisers at 1530 did Hipper swing round to SSE to lead his opponent towards Scheer's battle fleet. This allowed Beatty to close the range to 15,000 yards by 1545, when both sides opened fire. The Germans did the greater damage. The *Lion* was only saved from destruction by the rapid flooding of her midship turret magazine. The *Indefatigable* was stuck by a salvo from

the *Von der Tann* soon after 1600, and rent by an explosion that left only two survivors. Not until Evan-Thomas managed to bring his 5th BS into action was the *Von der Tann* damaged and two of the *Seydlitz's* turrets put out of action.

The British did not, however, keep their margin of nine ships over the enemy's five: at 1626 the *Queen Mary* met the same fate as the *Indefatigable*. But Beatty remained unperturbed: 'There seems to be something wrong with our bloody ships today', was his now legendary comment as he ordered his force to close the range; and whilst the 5th BS smote the *Moltke* and *Von der Tann* again and again, a destroyer's torpedo flooded the *Seydlitz*.

At 1638 Goodenough, in the light cruiser *Southampton*, dispelled Jellicoe's and Beatty's illusion that Scheer's Dreadnoughts were still in the Jade with an electrifying report: 'Have sighted enemy battle fleet bearing SE course N'. In spite of the loss of two battlecruisers, Beatty had been confident that his eight remaining heavy ships could destroy Hipper's five. Now he had to escape from overwhelming strength and lead Scheer north into the maw of Jellicoe's battle fleet. With the enemy's Dreadnoughts only eleven miles away, he ordered his ships to reverse course. But again there was a delay in passing this signal to Evan-Thomas; by the time the 5th BS turned, it was within range of Scheer's battle fleet. Fortunately the *Queen*

1 *The decisive battle in the war at sea.*

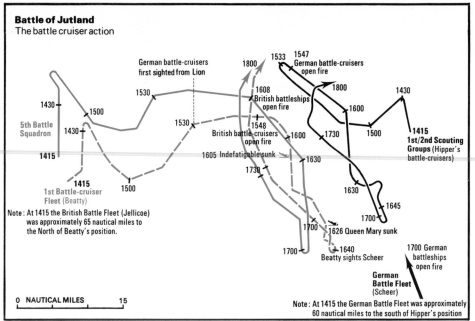

2 *The battle started with a chance encounter between the battlecruiser fleets.*

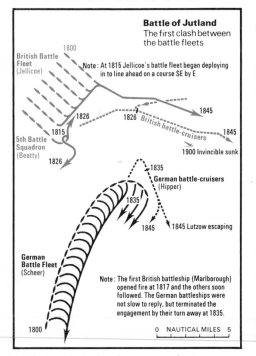

3 *The two fleets closed at some 40 knots.*

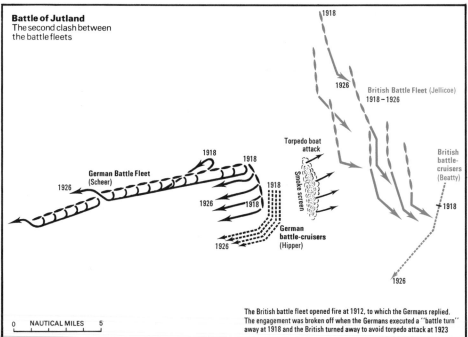

4 *The Germans turned away in a 'battle turn', the British to avoid a torpedo attack.*

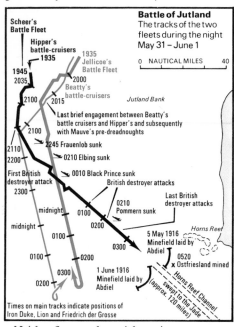

5 *Neither fleet sought a night action.*

Elizabeth class were stoutly armoured; they not only withstood this onslaught but inflicted further damage on Hipper's battle-cruisers, and on the head of Scheer's line. Goodenough held on until he could report the details of Scheer's battle fleet from a range inside seven miles.

Jellicoe had reacted to the *Galatea's* sighting report by increasing his battle fleet's speed to 20 knots, and sending the 3rd BCS on ahead. By the time the *Iron Duke* received Goodenough's report, Scheer's battle fleet was only 50 miles away. Nonetheless, Beatty realised that if his C-in-C was to make contact he must prevent Hipper giving warning of the British battle fleet's approach. To this end he maintained a speed of 25 knots after turning to NNW, whereby his battlecruisers drew out of range by 1710, leaving the 5th BS to continue their effective engagement for another quarter of an hour. Beatty then swung round to the north-east to prevent the pursuing Hipper from sighting Jellicoe, and the eight British heavy ships inflicted so much further damage on their opponents

that by 1800 Hipper was in full flight to the east.

Much of consequence happened around this time. Jellicoe's battle fleet was approaching Scheer's in six columns of four ships in line ahead disposed abeam. To deploy into single line the C-in-C depended on his advanced forces for news of an enemy beyond the horizon. But his admirals and captains failed him: although the two fleets were closing at a speed of 40 knots, none gave him the bearing and distance of Scheer's flagship. Moreover, when the *Marlborough*, leading his western column, sighted Beatty's flagship, Jellicoe learned the disturbing fact that the *Lion* was 11 miles nearer the *Iron Duke* than he had supposed. He would sight Scheer's battle fleet 20 minutes earlier than expected; he had that much less time in which to deploy before the two battle fleets came within range.

The 3rd BCS, pressing ahead since 1510, could not help him because Hood had steered SSE to prevent the enemy escaping through the Skaggerak. This took him to the eastward of Hipper, contact being made

The Battle of Jutland, 1916

Great Britain

Grand Fleet

1st Battle Squadron	Armament	
Marlborough	10×13.5″	12×6″
Revenge	8×15″	12×6″
Hercules	10×12″	
Agincourt	14×12″	
Colossus	10×12″	
Collingwood	10×12″	
Neptune	10×12″	
St. Vincent	10×12″	

2nd Battle Squadron		
King George V	10×13.5″	
Ajax	10×13.5″	
Centurion	10×13.5″	
Orion	10×13.5″	
Monarch	10×13.5″	
Conqueror	10×13.5″	
Thunderer	10×13.5″	

1st Cruiser Squadron		
Defence	4× 9.2″	10×7.5″
Warrior	6× 9.2″	4×7.5″
Duke of Edinburgh	6× 9.2″	10×6″
Black Prince	6× 9.2″	10×6″

2nd Cruiser Squadron		
Minotaur	4× 9.2″	10×7.5″
Cochrane	6× 9.2″	4×7.5″
Shannon	4× 9.2″	10×7.5″
Hampshire	4× 7.5″	6×6″

3rd Battle Cruiser Squadron (on Loan from BCF)		
Invincible	8×12″	
Indomitable	8×12″	
Inflexible	8×12″	
plus 12 light cruisers, 52 destroyers		

Battle Cruiser Force

1st Battle Cruiser Squadron		
Lion	8×13.5″	
Princess Royal	8×13.5″	
Queen Mary	8×13.5″	
Tiger	8×13.5″	

2nd Battle Cruiser Squadron		
New Zealand	8×12″	
Indefatigable	8×12″	

5th Battle Squadron (on loan from GF)		
Barham	8×15″	12×6″
Valiant	8×15″	12×6″
Warspite	8×15″	12×6″
Malaya	8×15″	12×6″
plus 14 light cruisers, 27 destroyers, 1 seaplane carrier		

Germany

High Seas Fleet

1st Squadron	Armament	
Ostfriesland	12×12″	14×5.9″
Thüringen	12×12″	14×5.9″
Helgoland	12×12″	14×5.9″
Oldenburg	12×12″	14×5.9″
Posen	12×11″	12×5.9″
Rheinland	12×11″	12×5.9″
Nassau	12×11″	12×5.9″
Westfalen	12×11″	12×5.9″

2nd Squadron		
Deutschland	4×11″	14×6.7″
Pommern	4×11″	14×6.7″
Schlesien	4×11″	14×6.7″
Schleswig-Holstein	4×11″	14×6.7″
Hannover	4×11″	14×6.7″
Hessen	4×11″	14×6.7″

3rd Squadron		
König	10×12″	14×5.9″
Grosser Kurfurst	10×12″	14×5.9″
Markgraf	10×12″	14×5.9″
Kronprinz	10×12″	14×5.9″
Kaiser	10×12″	14×5.9″
Prinzregent Luitpold	10×12″	14×5.9″
Kaiserin	10×12″	14×5.9″
Friedrich der Grosse	10×12″	14×5.9″

1st Scouting Group		
Lützow	8×12″	12×5.9″
Derfflinger	8×12″	14×5.9″
Seydlitz	10×11″	12×5.9″
Moltke	10×11″	12×5.9″
von der Tann	8×11″	10×5.9″
plus 11 light cruisers, 61 destroyers		

when his light cruiser *Chester* encountered the 2nd SG. Speeding to her rescue, Hood's battlecruisers reduced the *Wiesbaden* to a smoking wreck, and left the *Frankfurt* and *Pillau* in little better condition. The German light cruisers were saved from annihilation by the appearance of Hipper's battlecruisers.

But none of this was reported to Jellicoe. He was left in doubt over the position of Scheer's battle fleet until 1801, when the *Lion* appeared out of the mist on the *Iron Duke*'s starboard bow and signalled: 'Enemy battle fleet bearing SSW'. This was just in time for Jellicoe to make the vital decision on which the future course of the action depended. At 1815 the Grand Fleet began to deploy on the port wing column, steering SE by E, whereby he not only crossed the enemy's 'T' but put the Grand Fleet between the High Seas Fleet and its base.

Shortly before 1800 the 1st Cruiser Squadron of armoured cruisers sighted the 2nd SG, turned in pursuit, and met disaster. Hipper's 1st SG and Scheer's 3rd BS loomed out of the haze only 7,000 yards away. Arbuthnot's flagship, the *Defence*, was destroyed with all her crew; the *Warrior* was so crippled that she had to be taken in tow, only to sink early next morning; the *Black Prince*, likewise seriously damaged, blundered into Scheer's battle fleet during the night and was sunk. The visibility round this aptly-named 'Windy Corner' was so bad that Evan-Thomas did not sight Jellicoe's flagship until it was too late to take the 5th BS into its proper station ahead of the battle fleet, and when turning towards the rear, the *Warspite*'s helm jammed. By the time her Captain had extricated his ship from turning two involuntary circles under fire, she had suffered so much damage that she had to return to Rosyth.

The German C-in-C, with his battleships already in single line ahead, remained unaware of the approach of the British battle fleet until 1817. With Jellicoe's deployment cloaked by a pall of smoke, Scheer's illusion was not shattered until the *Marlborough*, *Agincourt* and *Revenge* opened fire, followed by many more. At last, after nearly two years of waiting, Jellicoe had brought the High Seas Fleet to action. The *König*, *Grosser Kurfürst* and *Markgraf* suffered hits, whilst Scheer's gunners were unable to score. But Hipper's force gained one more dramatic success. Beatty's four surviving battlecruisers, reinforced by Hood's 3rd BCS, were speeding to the van of their battle fleet when they were heavily engaged with Hipper's ships. And at 1829 a shell from the *Derfflinger* struck the midship turret of Hood's flagship, the *Invincible*, which blew up.

But Hipper's ships were in a worse state than the surviving British ones. The *Derfflinger* had 180 killed and wounded, all the *Von der Tann*'s turrets were out of action, and the *Lützow*'s speed was so much reduced that Hipper had to transfer his flag to the *Moltke*. Scheer's van would have suffered as badly had he not ordered his battle fleet to reverse course, so that by 1845 the whole of the High Seas Fleet was heading westward into the mist.

Nothing exemplifies Jellicoe's difficulties more than the brevity of this first clash between the battle fleets. In spite of the skill with which he had trapped the High Seas Fleet, poor visibility had allowed Scheer to extricate his ships after the *Iron Duke* had fired only nine salvoes. The effective counter to Scheer's turn was a resolute chase, but the British C-in-C would not risk his battleships by following closely after an enemy whom he believed would cover his retreat with torpedo attacks and by sowing mines in his wake. This possibility gained support when a torpedo from the crippled *Wiesbaden* struck the *Marlborough,* flooding a boiler room. Because this might be a mine, Jellicoe waited half an hour after Scheer's 'battle turn' before altering as far as SW by S.

However, at 1855, Scheer reversed course to steer straight for Jellicoe's line. As soon as

HMS Furious

The light cruiser *Furious* was converted into an aircraft carrier in 1917–18 to provide the British Grand Fleet with better aerial reconnaissance and to combat the constant snooping by Zeppelins. Although not ideal she showed that it was possible not only to fly off a carrier but also to land on the deck. The greatest achievement of the *Furious* was to fly off aircraft for a raid on the Zeppelin sheds at Tondern in 1918. After World War I she was completely rebuilt and served with distinction until 1945. She was also famous as the only British warship designed to be armed with 18-inch guns.

Displacement: 19,513 tons
Armament: Ten 5.5-inch guns, four 3-in AA.
Machinery: Four-shaft steam turbines, 90,000 shp = 31½ knots

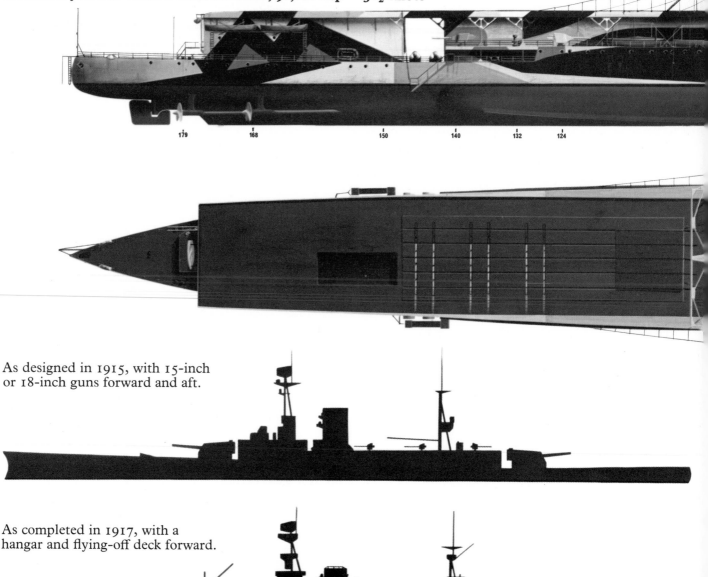

As designed in 1915, with 15-inch or 18-inch guns forward and aft.

As completed in 1917, with a hangar and flying-off deck forward.

Goodenough reported that the enemy was again steering east, Jellicoe swung his ships back to south. And by 1910, when Hipper's battlecruisers and leading German battleships appeared out of the mist to starboard, the British C-in-C knew that he was again crossing his opponent's 'T'.

The *Marlborough* sighted three ships of the *König* class and opened fire at 10,750 yards.

The *Lützow* and *Wiesbaden* suffered so much that they sank during the night. Beatty's ships joined in at 1920, 'making splendid practice'. The Germans replied to little effect: only the *Colossus* was hit, her damage slight. To save his fleet from destruction, Scheer signalled his battlecruisers to 'close the enemy and ram'. The 1st SG 'hurled themselves against the enemy', but they

were not required to complete their death-ride: at 1917 Scheer changed his order to 'operate against the enemy's van', while he extricated his stricken fleet by a second 'battle turn' of 16 points. By 1935, after an engagement of just 15 minutes, compared with 25 on the first occasion, the German heavy ships were again heading west into the mist.

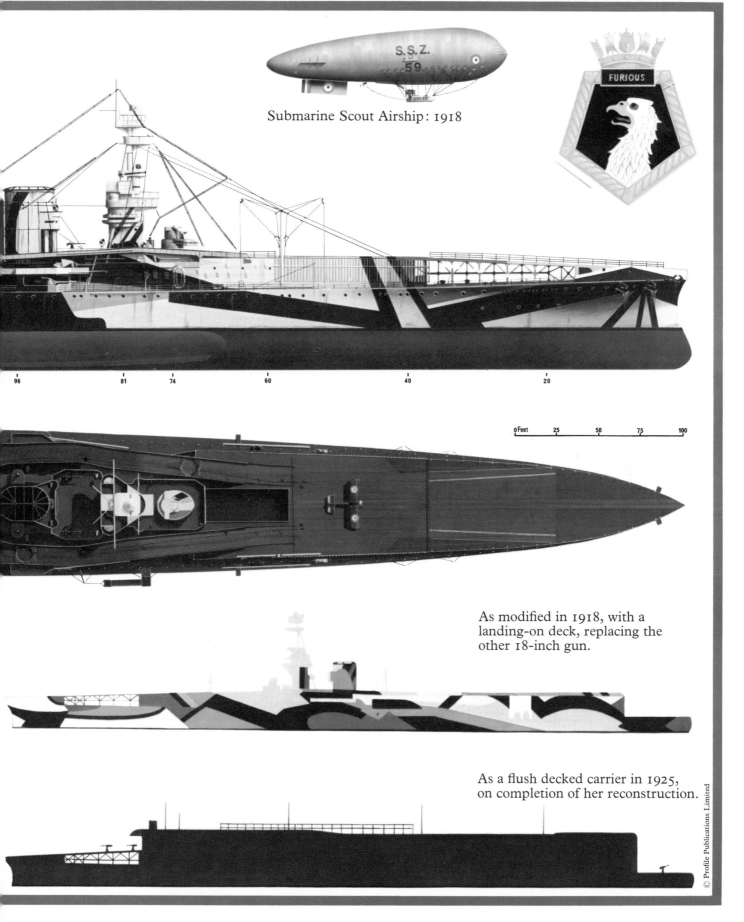

Submarine Scout Airship: 1918

As modified in 1918, with a landing-on deck, replacing the other 18-inch gun.

As a flush decked carrier in 1925, on completion of her reconstruction.

61

HMS Royal Sovereign *and ships of the First Battle Squadron train their 15-inch guns to starboard.*

HMS Lion

Beatty's flagship at Jutland was nearly sunk by cordite flash, the cause of the other battlecruisers' loss.

Displacement: 26,350 tons
Armament: Eight 13.5-inch guns, sixteen 4-in, two 21-in TT.
Machinery: Four-shaft steam turbines, 70,000 shp = 28 knots

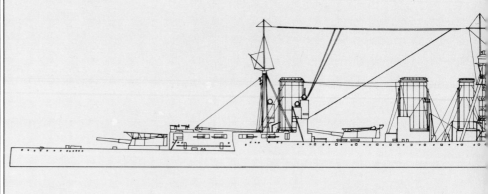

HMS Iron Duke

Although a contemporary of the *Lion*, Jellicoe's flagship showed the difference in protection afforded to a battleship. She was protected by a 13-inch armour belt as against a 9-inch belt in the *Lion*, but with less than half the power her speed was seven knots slower. Her sistership *Marlborough* was hit by a torpedo at Jutland but kept her place in the battle line. The *Iron Duke* was the first battleship to be armed with anti-aircraft guns, and she also reintroduced heavy secondary guns, a feature which had been dropped in the original *Dreadnought* and her successors. She was the flagship of the Grand Fleet from 1914 to 1916 and distinguished herself at Jutland by her very accurate shooting. Although partially disarmed to comply with international treaties she survived to serve in World War II as a depot ship.

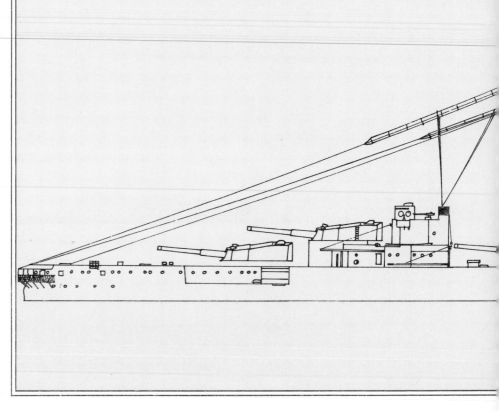

Scheer's torpedoboats covered this retirement, closing to 8,000 yards and firing 31 torpedoes, of which ten reached the British line. But Jellicoe believed his battle fleet to be threatened by many more, of which he expected 30 per cent to score hits unless he turned away. Not until years later did he acknowledge that when such a turn would result in losing contact, the more risky alternative of turning towards might be justified. As it was, he supposed the enemy's disappearance to be due to the mist thickening; when the torpedo threat was over, he turned only to the parallel course of south-west. Not until 2000, when Scheer was some 15 miles away, did the British C-in-C turn his battle fleet to west.

Concerned at being headed so far from his base, Scheer had altered to south at 1945. The *Iron Duke* was then only 12 miles to the east, and the two fleets were soon in contact again. Around 2025, the German battlecruisers came under heavy fire from Beatty's force, before the latter turned their guns on Mauve's squadron which was now leading Scheer's battle fleet. The light cruisers *Caroline* and *Royalist*, stationed in the van of Jellicoe's line, sighted Scheer's battle fleet, but Jerram believed them to be British battlecruisers and continued to lead the battle fleet on a parallel course.

These were the last encounters between the two fleets before nightfall. But since Scheer had twice fled from the guns of a force which now stretched for ten miles between the High Seas Fleet and its harbour, Jellicoe had high hopes of another 'Glorious First of June' when the sun rose in five hours' time.

Scheer was so determined to gain the sanctuary of the Horns Reef that he accepted the hazards of an engagement during the night. Jellicoe rejected such an action as leading to possible disaster, owing to the presence of torpedo craft in large numbers and to the difficulty of distinguishing friend from foe. Knowing that there were two other swept channels to the Jade as well as the Horns Reef, he decided to steer to the southward where he should be in a position to renew the engagement at daylight. At 2117 he closed his battle fleet into its night cruis-

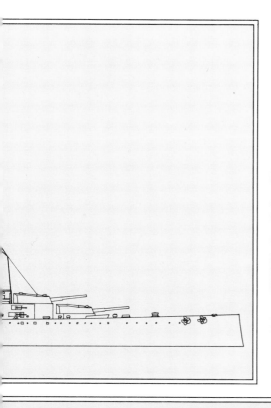

A German battle squadron on manoeuvres in the Baltic.

ing order of four columns. He did not ignore the Horns Reef route; his destroyers were stationed five miles astern where they would be in a good position for attacking the enemy should they try to regain their base that way during the night.

Scheer forces his way home

Such news as Jellicoe had gleaned from his ships around this time led him to believe that the High Seas Fleet was well to the north-west. In reality it was only eight miles away because, at 2114, Scheer had altered to SSE. Two hours earlier he had decided to assist his fleet's escape by sending all available destroyers to attack the Grand Fleet. But the 2nd Flotilla approached when there was still enough light for it to be driven off, and was too far astern to achieve anything when it tried again half an hour later. Joined by the 3rd Flotilla it set course for the Skaw and returned to Kiel. The 5th and 7th Flotillas fired four torpedoes at one of the British flotillas at 2150 without result, and then passed astern of the Grand Fleet on a course for the Horns Reef.

Displacement: 25,000 tons
Armament: Ten 13.5-inch guns, twelve 6-in, two 3-in AA, four 21-in TT.
Machinery: Four-shaft steam turbines, 29,000 shp = 21 knots

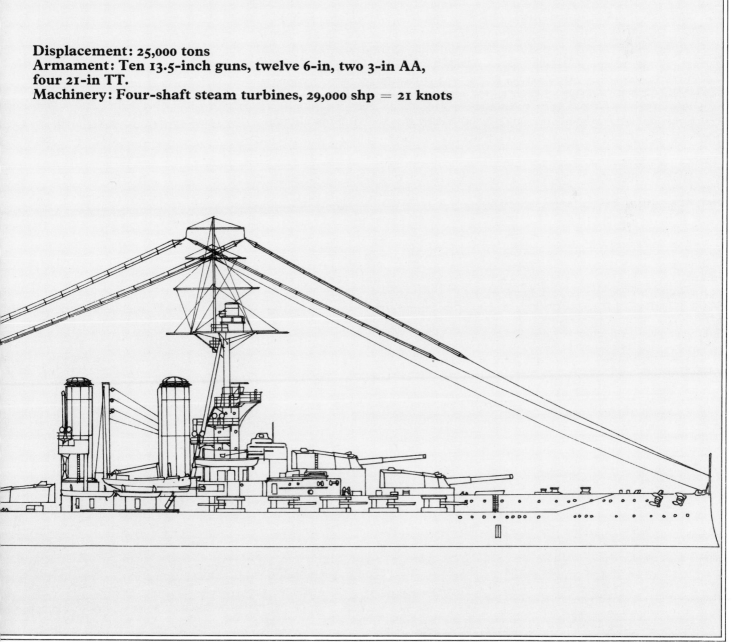

Throughout the night there was a series of clashes with the British destroyers as Scheer forced his way past the rear of Jellicoe's battle fleet. Both sides lost ships, the Germans one pre-Dreadnought, three light cruisers, and two torpedoboats; the British one armoured cruiser and five destroyers. Nonetheless, the Germans gained their objective: by dawn, their whole battle fleet was safe inside its own minefields.

Although the fighting during the night had been severe no British ship had signalled Jellicoe that the enemy fleet was breaking through. Even more extraordinary, some of the battleships in the rear of Jellicoe's battle fleet, notably the 5th BS, actually sighted German battleships, but neither reported them nor engaged them.

A German Dreadnought battleship fires a broadside from her main armament.

SMS König

This ship was the German equivalent of the British *Iron Duke*, the latest class of battleship in service at the outbreak of World War I. As with the battlecruiser designs, the German Navy chose armour in preference to gunpower in its battleships; the *König* had 14-inch belt armour and 12-inch guns. This proved a great asset in action at Jutland, when she was hit several times by the *Iron Duke* without being disabled. The *König* is depicted as she appeared at Jutland in May 1916, before she received a heavy foremast. The circles painted on the turret-tops were for aircraft-recognition. Like the *Iron Duke* she had anti-aircraft guns on the after superstructure, but she and other German capital ships retained torpedo-nets long after the British had abandoned them as cumbersome and dangerous in action.

HMS Hardy, *steaming at speed in the early days of the war. Destroyers on both sides were painted black to avoid detection at night, a practice not dropped until the Battle of Jutland.*

The Admiralty was also far from blameless. During the night several vital signals from Scheer were intercepted and deciphered, all indicating that the High Seas Fleet was making for the Horns Reef. But none was passed to Jellicoe. Had he received even one of them he could have altered course and brought Scheer to action in the early morning of June 1.

Such was Jutland's unsatisfactory ending. For two years the Grand Fleet had been praying for a full-scale meeting with the High Seas Fleet. Now victory had been denied them, partly by the North Sea mist, partly by a series of signal failures at critical moments, partly by mistakes in the Admiralty, and partly by a lack of decisive action by the captains of the battleships which sighted Scheer's ships as they made their way through the wake of the Grand Fleet during the night.

By four o'clock on the morning of June 1, Jellicoe received a signal from the Admiralty which made it clear that Scheer was in the swept channel beyond Horns Reef. Sadly, he swept northward with his fleet in the vain hope of finding damaged ships or stragglers. During the morning of June 2 Beatty's battlecruisers reached their base at Rosyth; in the afternoon the battle fleet was anchored in Scapa Flow. At 2145 that evening Jellicoe informed the Admiralty that the Grand Fleet was again ready for sea and action at four hours' notice.

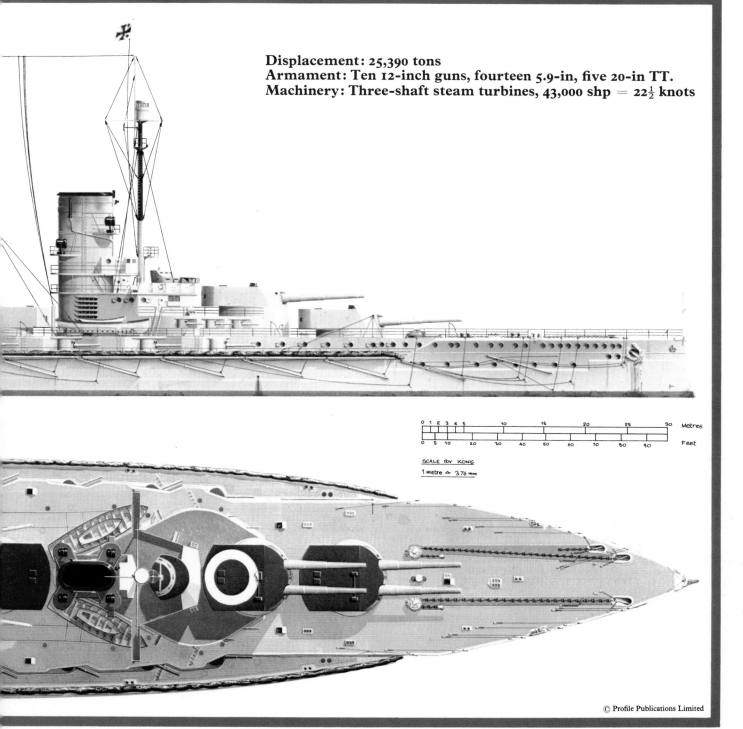

Displacement: 25,390 tons
Armament: Ten 12-inch guns, fourteen 5.9-in, five 20-in TT.
Machinery: Three-shaft steam turbines, 43,000 shp = 22½ knots

SCALE for KÖNIG
1 metre ≈ 3.76 mm

Sea power ends the war

After Jutland Germany concentrated her main naval efforts on U-boats and the cutting of Britain's vital sea links. In the first eight months of 1917 Britain lost almost 3,000,000 tons of merchant shipping. The convoy system finally reduced losses to acceptable limits and two raids on Zeebrugge in 1918 struck bravely but unsuccessfully at this important U-boat base. But in the end it was the Grand Fleet's blockade that brought Germany to starvation, her navy to mutiny and the war to an end.

Although Britain and Germany both claimed a victory at Jutland, Scheer was quick to realise that, whatever the German people might be led to believe, his officers and men were not so gullible. To restore morale he took the High Seas Fleet to sea again in the middle of August for a dawn bombardment of Sunderland by Hipper's battlecruisers. The Grand Fleet sailed to intercept, and by 1400 on the 19th its ships were cleared for action. But chance denied Jellicoe the battle he so much desired.

Zeppelin *L13* sighted Tyrwhitt's light cruisers and destroyers north-east of Cromer and reported them as battleships. Believing he had a detachment of the British battle fleet within his grasp, Scheer turned towards them. By the time he realised that he was chasing phantoms, *U53* had sighted Jellicoe's fleet and revealed how near the High Seas Fleet had been to being trapped by overwhelming force. Nor did it return to Germany without damage; submarine *E23* put a torpedo into the *Westfalen* as she was hurrying back to the Jade.

The 24 U-boats which Scheer deployed for this abortive operation scored two successes; they sank the light cruisers *Nottingham* and *Falmouth*. The Admiralty reacted by endorsing Jellicoe's cautious strategy. The Grand Fleet, in which it would take a year to remedy the deficiencies revealed at Jutland, notably in the design of the Dreadnoughts' magazines and of their armour-piercing shells, was still the keystone of the Allied blockade of Germany. When next warned, on October 18, that Scheer intended a sortie the Grand Fleet was not immediately ordered out; it was brought only to short notice for steam. Nor was it required to sail. A few hours after the High Seas Fleet left the Jade *E38* torpedoed the light cruiser *München* and Scheer, fearing a submarine trap, hurried back to harbour.

The German C-in-C had a further setback in November. Sailing the *Moltke* and a division of Dreadnoughts to cover the rescue of *U20* and *U30* which had stranded on the Danish coast, he nearly lost the *Grosser Kurfürst* and *Kronprinz* to torpedoes from the British *J1*. Two raids on the Straits of Dover were, however, more successful. On

The German pre-Dreadnought Schlesien *fires her 11-inch guns during a battle practice. Constant drill was needed to familiarize the turret-crews in their complex drills to ensure good shooting in battle.*

October 28 German torpedoboats sank a
British destroyer and six drifters; a month
later they bombarded Margate. The latter
sortie revived the public criticism that had
followed earlier bombardments of the British
east coast so that the Government decided to
appoint a more vigorous First Sea Lord. At
the end of November Jellicoe was called to
the Admiralty and Beatty took over command
of the Grand Fleet.

Massive U-boat programme

Jellicoe was also needed in London for a more
important reason. In 1916 the German Navy
began to reap the harvest of a building
programme which would augment its underwater fleet by more by than 300 submarines.
With the German Army's growing demand
for a naval offensive that would help to
achieve a breakthrough on the Western
Front, came a note from the USA to all
belligerents which seemed to provide the
Kaiser with a solution to the contradictory
advice of his civilian and Service advisers.

This was a proposal that merchant ships
should no longer be armed. And when the
British Government rejected the idea, Berlin
supposed that Washington would attempt to
compel London's compliance. It was therefore construed that it would be safe to renew
U-boat warfare against merchant shipping,
provided that passenger ships were exempt
from attack. But when on March 24, 1916,
UB29 torpedoed the cross-Channel steamer
Sussex, which was carrying a number of
American passengers, Washington threatened to sever diplomatic relations unless
Germany at once abandoned submarine
warfare against all merchant ships. This was
enough for U-boats to be restricted to legit-
imate targets for the next nine months.

But Britain's strategic victory at Jutland,
and the failure of Scheer's subsequent sorties, persuaded the Kaiser to change his

HMS Swift

Originally designed merely as a "super-destroyer" under the inspiration of Admiral Fisher, the *Swift* became a flotilla-leader shortly before the outbreak of World War I. Leaders were large destroyers with extra accommodation for the administrative staff and signalmen needed to control a flotilla of sixteen destroyers. Despite her size the *Swift* proved too frail for Northern waters and had to be sent South to join the Dover Patrol. One night in 1917, while in company with HMS *Broke*, she encountered a group of German destroyers returning from a raid. In the ensuing melee two German destroyers were sunk by gunfire and ramming without loss. At the time the *Swift* mounted a 6-inch gun on the forecastle, as shown in this drawing, the heaviest calibre of gun ever used in a destroyer. After the action in 1917 it was removed and replaced by two 4-in. guns.

Displacement: 2,170 tons
Armament: One 6-inch gun, two 4-in, one 57-mm AA, one pom-pom, two 18-in. TT.
Machinery: Four-shaft steam turbines, 30,000 shp = 35 knots

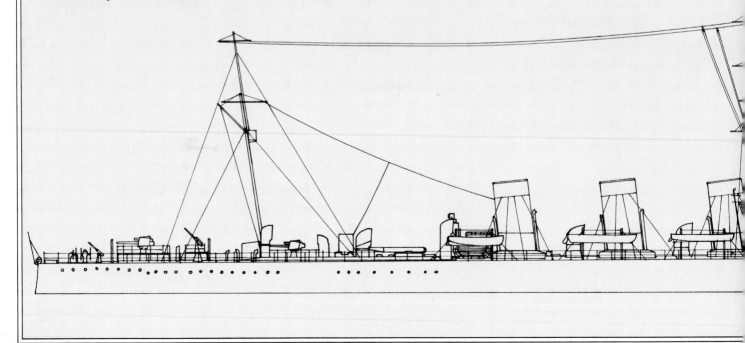

German torpedo-boats and U-Boats with the repair ship Vulkan *at Kiel.*

mind once more. Accepting Scheer's contention that victory could only be attained by destroying the economic existence of Great Britain, he ordered unrestricted U-boat warfare to begin on February 1, 1917. The Admiralty reacted by intensifying its anti-submarine measures, only to find that it was fighting a losing battle against this new form of blockade. In the first four months of 1917, 1,250,000 tons of British merchant shipping were sunk, a figure which rose by a further 1,500,000 tons in the next four. This was a rate which Britain's shipbuilding resources could not hope to match. In spite of the belated introduction of stringent rationing, the country's reserves of essential foods dropped to six weeks' supply. So, too, with the sinews of war; for shortage of oil the Grand Fleet's exercises had to be curtailed.

Lack of escort destroyers

Rear-Admiral A. A. M. Duff, whom Jellicoe

had appointed to head a new Anti-Submarine Division of the Naval Staff, suggested adopting the traditional, proven method of protecting seaborne trade by sailing merchant ships in escorted convoys. Jellicoe contended that this was not possible; that in any case Britain lacked the destroyers to provide the necessary escorts. Not until May, a month after the entry of the USA into the war removed this objection, did Jellicoe allow a trial convoy to be run. And it needed another three months before he agreed to all shipping being escorted through the war zone. So it was not until the last four months of 1917 that the convoy system became effective and the rising graph of merchant shipping losses was reversed. This, together with the merchant shipbuilding and repair programme, considerably improved the supply problem.

By then, the end of 1917, Jellicoe had been dismissed as First Sea Lord and replaced by Admiral Sir Rosslyn Wemyss. And under him, by May 1918, the convoy system was so effective that the tonnage of newly built British ships exceeded the tonnage lost by enemy action. As important,

because U-boats were forced to seek their prey around the convoys where the Allied anti-submarine forces were concentrated, the number of submarines sunk in 1917–18 was as high as 132, a rate of loss in both craft and crews that Germany could ill afford.

Up in Scapa Flow and Rosyth Beatty made no change in the Grand Fleet's strategy. However, as an anti-U-boat measure he began running the Scandinavian trade in convoy. He realised that this would provide attractive targets for tip-and-run raids by German surface warships but believed the risk to be acceptable; and when six months elapsed without incident, it seemed that he was justified. In truth, Scheer was otherwise occupied. In the summer of 1917 the High Seas Fleet was convulsed by mutinies caused by inactivity, short rations, callous officers, and subversive propaganda. The Allies might

Below : A U-boat's torpedo strikes home. In the spring of 1917 one in every four merchant ships heading for Britain was sunk, reducing the country to six weeks' rations at the worst moment.

be powerless to break the German Army's stranglehold in Flanders, but the British Navy's blockade was sapping the German people's will for war. It was October before Scheer suppressed this revolt and was free to operate against the Scandinavian convoys.

British convoys destroyed

On October 16 he sailed the two new light cruisers *Brummer* and *Bremse* for a foray against the Lerwick-Bergen route. Evading detection by Beatty's patrols the two ships reached a position 60 miles to the east of the Shetlands at dawn on the 17th where they sighted an east-bound convoy escorted by the destroyers *Strongbow* and *Mary Rose*. Both were quickly sunk, and nine out of twelve merchant ships followed them to the bottom before the cruisers returned unscathed to Germany. Six weeks later eight German torpedoboats made a similar raid. Four went west, to sink two stragglers from a south-bound convoy off Berwick on December 11. The other four reached the latitude of Bergen on the 12th where they sighted six merchant ships, escorted by the destroyers *Partridge* and *Pellew*. The *Partridge* was sunk and the *Pellew* so disabled that she could do nothing to prevent the enemy sinking the whole convoy.

German minesweeping activities in the Heligoland Bight provided the next opportunity for action. After Tyrwhitt's Harwich Force had had a successful encounter with German torpedoboats protecting the minesweepers, radio intelligence revealed to the Admiralty that Scheer intended to provide them with battleship cover. Since the Grand Fleet had been strengthened by Rear-Admiral H. Rodman's 6th BS of five US Dreadnoughts, and the Battlecruiser Force had been augmented by the *Repulse*, *Renown*, *Courageous* and *Glorious*, he could afford to risk a surprise attack to gain a rich prize. On November 16 Scheer's minesweepers were escorted out by two torpedoboat flotillas supported by *Konteradmiral* von Reuter's 2nd SG and the Dreadnoughts *Kaiserin* and *Kaiser*. Forewarned, Beatty sailed his battlecruisers, now commanded by Vice-Admiral Pakenham, accompanied by Admiral Sir Charles Madden's 1st BS.

Shortly after 0800 next day the minesweepers were surprised by British light cruisers. They retired homewards at full speed as von Reuter hurried to their rescue, only to come under fire from the *Courageous* and *Repulse*. The German Admiral reversed course and headed for the protection of his battleships. A running fight ensued until 0930 in which neither side scored more than an occasional hit. By then Rear-Admiral T. D. W. Napier in the *Courageous* judged that the minefield risk was too great for the larger British ships to advance and hoisted the recall. The *Repulse* ignored it and, with the 1st LCS, pressed on and was rewarded by sighting the *Kaiser* and *Kaiserin*. The British ships swung away to the north-west to lead their opponents to where Pakenham and Madden's squadrons were waiting. But to no avail; the German battleships would not leave the safety of their minefields even though the *Hindenburg* and *Moltke* were hurrying to their support. So the action came to an inconclusive end with no significant losses or damage on either side.

In January 1918, the British Government concluded that the failure of the previous autumn's offensive in Flanders was of such consequence that the Grand Fleet should do nothing to provoke a fleet action, even though it now had 43 Dreadnoughts to Scheer's 24. Subject to maintaining the blockade, the Navy's overriding task was to defeat the U-boats. The rest of the nation's effort must be devoted to enabling its Army to hold back the Germans, who were now being reinforced from their eastern front following Russia's collapse, until the full weight of the US Army could be put into the line in 1919. A fleet action was, nonetheless, possible. The Scandinavian convoy *débâcles* obliged Beatty to cover the Lerwick-Bergen trade with a division of Dreadnoughts which might yet draw the High Seas Fleet. And although the British C-in-C welcomed such a chance to avenge Jutland, he feared that the Admiralty might fail to give him enough warning for the Grand Fleet to reach the scene before this covering force was overwhelmed.

April 1918 showed that this fear was not groundless. The Admiralty gleaned no news of the High Seas Fleet's sortie from the Jade on the 22nd, its quarry a homeward-bound convoy covered by battlecruisers and light cruisers. Beatty remained ignorant of the crucial fact that the German battle fleet was moving as far north as Stavanger. Fortunately, Scheer's intelligence was 24 hours in error: the convoy for which he was looking had already crossed the North Sea. And when he ordered Hipper's battlecruisers to search for it, the *Moltke* lost a propeller, an accident which obliged Scheer and Hipper to break radio silence. This was enough for the Admiralty to order Beatty to sea. But the High Seas Fleet was already retiring to the south, with the *Moltke* in tow of the *Oldenburg*. By nightfall it had crossed ahead of the Grand Fleet's line of advance, to reach the Jade without incident except for the near-loss of the *Moltke* to a torpedo fired by *E42*.

The British Navy throughout the war laid numerous minefields in the Heligoland Bight at a depth where they were a danger to U-boats leaving and returning to German ports submerged; but channels could be swept through these fields too easily for them to be a completely effective deterrent. Mine barriers at a greater distance from Germany were needed if U-boats were to be prevented from reaching the shipping lanes off the west

HMS General Wolfe

The Royal Navy built specialized shore bombardment craft in 1915–16 to enable them to bombard the exposed flank of the German Army on the Belgian coast. These monitors (named after the original type) were at first armed with guns removed from obsolete battleships and then with the latest weapons. HMS *General Wolfe* was first armed with a twin 12-inch gun turret from an old battleship and in 1918 she received one of the 18-inch guns removed from the light cruiser *Furious*. This gun can be seen mounted aft, and could fire a 3000-lb shell nearly thirty miles. Because of the size of the mounting and the gun it could only fire to starboard on a fixed bearing, although the gun elevated to 40°.

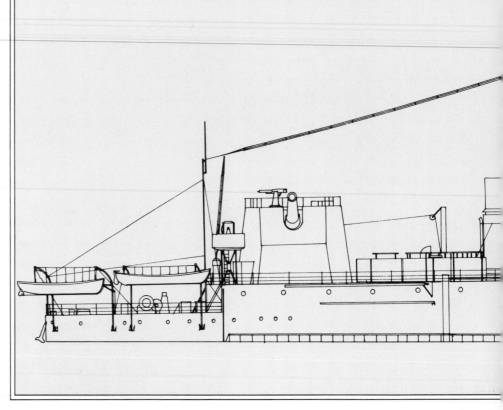

Above: A dazzle-painted Cunard liner, the Ausonia sinks after being torpedoed by U62 in May 1918.

Left: The Royal Navy used mines against the U-boats, planting thousands of them in their exit routes into the North Sea.

coast of the British Isles. The northern barrage, from the Orkneys to Norway, was a project of such magnitude that it had to await the USA's entry into the war, and was not completed before hostilities ended. Indicator nets were laid across the Dover Straits as early as January 1915; when fouled by a U-boat they ignited warning flares as a signal to patrol craft. U32's near-destruction in the nets on April 6, 1915 alarmed Berlin into denying their U-boats this route through the Channel, which lengthened their journey to and from the Irish Sea by 1,400 miles, and cut their time on patrol by seven days.

The war's 'finest feat of arms'

The Admiralty was, however, unaware of this ban; they noted only that the nets accounted for few U-boats. Vice-Admiral Sir Reginald Bacon, commanding the Dover Patrol, tried to lay nets sufficiently heavy to be a physical obstruction, but the difficulties of doing this across 20 miles of tide-swept water proved insurmountable. This failure was not, however, of importance until December 1916 when, shortly before beginning the third unrestricted U-boat campaign, Berlin not only withdrew their ban on the Channel

Displacement: 5,900 tons
Armament: One 18-inch gun, two 12-in, two 6-in.
Machinery: Two-shaft triple-expansion, 2,300 ihp = 6½ knots

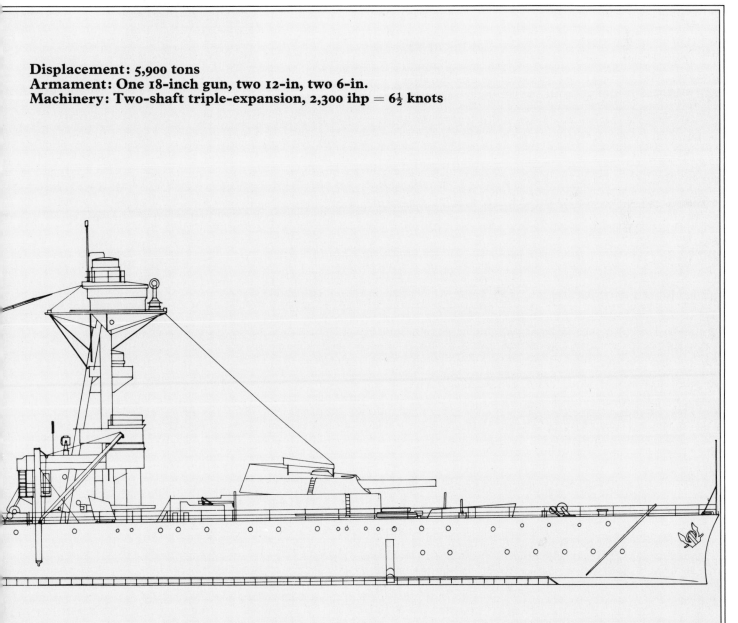

passage but sent large torpedoboats to wreak havoc among British patrol craft. Bacon reinforced these with destroyers, which led to several spirited actions, notably one in which the *Broke* rammed and sank *G42*. Such fights were, however, only a prelude to an exploit aptly described by Churchill as 'the finest feat of arms in the Great War and unsurpassed in the history of the Royal Navy'.

Germany had put Bruges, in occupied Belgium, to good use as a U-boat and torpedoboat base. Six miles inland, and connected to the North Sea by canals, nothing could attack this port except aircraft, against whose bombs the U-boats were given concrete shelters. The British Government recognised the vital importance of the ports at which the two Bruges canals entered the sea, Ostend and Zeebrugge, as early as November 1916; and Jellicoe's pessimistic declaration in June 1917 that, unless these were denied to the enemy the Allies would lose the war, was enough for Prime Minister Lloyd George to accept the heavy casualties expected of an advance by the British Army through Flanders designed to capture them. When this was a near-disastrous failure, Bacon proposed a blocking attack on Zeebrugge and Ostend from the sea, but showed too little enthusiasm for such a venture to satisfy the First Sea Lord, now Admiral Rosslyn Wemyss, who sent Rear-Admiral Roger Keyes to relieve him early in 1918.

Keyes quickly produced his own plans. A landing force of 1,300 volunteers was given special training and a small armada of vessels assembled in the Thames estuary. Many of these were specially adapted for their role. The old cruiser *Vindictive*, Captain A.F. Carpenter, was equipped with flame-throwers, mortars, and a dozen long-hinged brows along her port side. The cruisers, *Brilliant, Iphigenia, Intrepid, Sirius* and *Thetis* were each filled with 1,500 tons of concrete, and provided with scuttling charges. Submarine *C3* carried explosives in her forward compartments. The upper works of the Liverpool ferries *Iris II* and *Daffodil* were protected with bullet-proof plating.

Suddenly, out of the smoke

After two starts had been aborted by winds that prevented coastal-motorboats laying the heavy smokescreens required to cloak its final approach, this force left the Swin on the eve of St. George's Day, 1918. Shortly after 2300 Commodore H. Lynes turned one part of it away to the south towards Ostend, whilst Keyes, in the destroyer *Warwick*, led the remainder towards Zeebrugge. Here the thick smoke-screen and heavy bombardment by monitors and aircraft proved their worth. The German defences were not alerted until shortly before 2350, when the *Vindictive* suddenly appeared out of the darkness only 1500 yards from the end of the mile-long mole. One minute after midnight Carpenter placed his ship alongside amidst a hail of shot and shell that decimated the waiting storming parties, their commanders, Captain H. C. Halahan, RN, and Lieutenant-Colonel B. N. Elliott, RM, being among the killed.

While the *Daffodil*, Lieutenant H. G. Campbell, held her there, Lieutenant-Commander A. L. Harrison's naval storming party crossed the *Vindictive's* brows. Their objective was the 5.9-inch battery at the mole's seaward end, where they encountered strong opposition. Major B. G. Waller's Royal Marine storming party and Lieutenant C. C. Dickenson's naval demolition party followed, to destroy as much material on the mole as time would allow. Their task was facilitated by submarine *C3* which Lieutenant R.D. Sandford rammed into the girders supporting the viaduct which joined the mole to the shore. Her detonation by a time-fuse, after her crew had been taken off by a picket-boat under the command of Sandford's older brother, breached the viaduct and prevented the arrival of German reinforcements.

Coincident with Sandford's exploit, HMS *Thetis*, Commander R. S. Sneyd, emerged from the smokescreen and steamed past the head of the mole, only to be stopped by a net obstruction. She then grounded at the entrance of the dredged channel. While the Germans concentrated their fire on her, the *Intrepid*, Lieutenant S. Bonham-Carter, and *Iphigenia*, Lieutenant E. W. Billyard-Leake, were taken inside the canal entrance. As soon as both these cruisers had been sunk, Carpenter recalled his storming parties. By 0115 the *Vindictive* had re-embarked the survivors and was on course for home.

An inspiring attack

Keyes believed the Zeebrugge raid, which cost the British 214 killed and 383 wounded, with the destroyer *North Star* sunk, had blocked the canal to Bruges. But Lynes's attempt to do the same at Ostend failed because the Germans had moved the buoy marking the entrance. The blockships *Brilliant*, Commander A. E. Godsal and *Sirius*, Commander H. N. Hardy, stranded a mile to the east, where they had to be sunk after their crews had been rescued.

Keyes quickly prepared another raid on this port. On May 9 the *Vindictive*, now converted into a blockship under Godsal's command, reached the entrance to this canal. But there, at the crucial moment, Godsal was killed, and before Lieutenant Victor Crutchley could take his place the ship had run hard aground and had to be abandoned. To add to Keyes's chagrin at this second failure, his own flagship, the *Warwick*, was mined and had to be towed home to Dover.

With characteristic determination he planned a third attempt on Ostend. But the Admiralty withheld approval when they learned that another attempt to block Zeebrugge would also be needed. The Germans had been able to dredge a channel round the blockships in time for four small torpedoboats to clear this canal as soon as April 24, and by May 14 it was being freely used by both torpedoboats and U-boats. But if in this respect unsuccessful, Zeebrugge was not attacked in vain. The news that the Royal Navy had carried out this direct assault on an enemy-held port came shortly after German troops had broken through the British line at St. Quentin, and proved an inspiration that upheld the Allies' flagging spirits until their armies were able to launch a successful counter-attack at Chateau-Thierry on June 18. In Germany, where the Grand Fleet's blockade had brought morale to a low ebb, the news came as a stunning

Germany became a naval power so swiftly that pre-war manoeuvres were vital to attain fighting efficiency.

blow heralding final defeat.

By June 1918 the convoy system had won the long-drawn battle against the U-boats. Germany had no other weapon with which to disrupt the flow of supplies across the Channel and Atlantic, nor to prevent the Allied armies being reinforced by a million fresh US troops. The German spring offensive was halted short of Paris, and was followed with a crushing Allied riposte on the Marne. On August 8 the British armies advanced nine miles; four weeks later the Germans were in full retreat all along the Western front.

Germany near starvation

By the end of September, when Bulgaria and Turkey sought an armistice to save Sofia and Constantinople, Germany was menaced by a danger greater than defeat on land. Brought near to starvation by the Grand Fleet's blockade, the people were raising the Red Flag of revolution. To avert a tragedy such as that to which Russia had succumbed, the German Chancellor appealed to President Wilson, who replied that no negotiations were possible so long as U-boats continued sinking passenger ships. Scheer responded by abandoning unrestricted submarine warfare on October 21.

This freed his U-boats to support a planned sortie by the High Seas Fleet. Led by Hipper, two groups of light cruisers and torpedoboats were to raid the Flanders coast and the Thames Estuary, which was expected

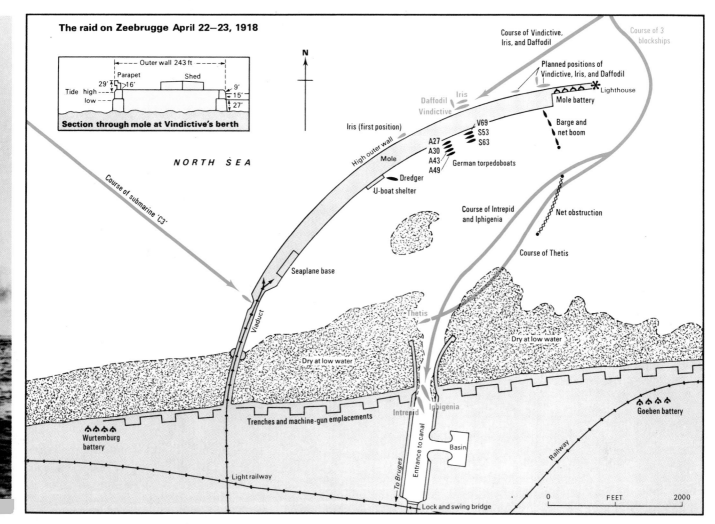

The raid on Zeebrugge April 22–23, 1918

Section through mole at Vindictive's berth
- Outer wall 243 ft
- Parapet
- Shed
- 29' · 16' · 9' · 15' · 27'
- Tide high low

NORTH SEA

N

Course of submarine 'C3'

Course of Vindictive, Iris, and Daffodil

Course of 3 blockships

Planned positions of Vindictive, Iris, and Daffodil

Daffodil
Iris
Vindictive

Iris (first position)

High outer wall

Mole

Lighthouse
Mole battery

V69
S53
S63

A27
A30
A43
A49

German torpedoboats

Barge and net boom

Dredger
U-boat shelter

Net obstruction

Course of Intrepid and Iphigenia

Course of Thetis

Seaplane base

Viaduct

Thetis

Dry at low water

Dry at low water

Trenches and machine-gun emplacements

Intrepid
Iphigenia

Goeben battery

Wurtemburg battery

To Bruges

Entrance to canal

Basin

Railway

Light railway

Lock and swing bridge

0 · FEET · 2000

to draw the Grand Fleet south against a main body of 18 battleships, 5 battlecruisers, and 6 torpedoboat flotillas.

The Admiralty had already warned Beatty that an attempt to draw the Grand Fleet was being planned. But he was not required to sail. When Hipper ordered his ships to raise steam late on October 29, their crews refused to obey their officers. They had no wish to be sacrificed in battle when they knew that the end of the war was near.

On November 11, before Hipper could restore discipline, Britain, France, Italy, and the USA granted Germany's request for an armistice, and at 1100 hostilities ceased on all fronts. The armistice terms required Germany to surrender all her U-boats, and to send her High Seas Fleet to an Allied port for internment. On November 20 Tyrwhitt's Harwich Force began receiving 150 U-boats to await scrapping. Next day the Grand Fleet sailed for the last time, to meet and escort five battlecruisers, 11 Dreadnoughts, 10 light cruisers, and 50 torpedoboats into captivity. They were brought into Rosyth and eventually taken to Scapa Flow where they rusted at their anchors in those gale-swept waters whilst the Allies wrangled over a peace treaty, until they were finally scuttled in June 1919.

The vindication of sea power

This might not be the annihilating victory to which the Royal Navy had looked forward since August 1914, and for which the Grand Fleet never ceased to hope in spite of the disappointing results of Jutland. But, as Captain Richmond wrote in his diary for 1916: 'It is absolutely necessary to look at the war as a whole; to avoid keeping our eyes only on the German Fleet. What we have to do is to starve and cripple Germany, to destroy Germany.' And this the Royal Navy undoubtedly achieved. Many a good vessel has struck its flag in battle; many another has faced destruction rather than surrender; but the annals of naval warfare held no parallel to November 21, 1918. As the Admiralty rightly signalled: 'The surrender of the German Fleet, accomplished without shock of battle, will remain for all time the example of the wonderful silence and sureness with which sea power attains its ends.'

Above: Another British merchantman is torpedoed, but by mid-1917 the use of convoying had reduced the losses.

Left: The scene at Zeebrugge after the British raid. In the canal mouth the old cruisers Iphigenia *and* Intrepid *lie blocking the channel, with the* Thetis *further out. The* Mole *can be seen in the background.*

Europe's navies prepare for war

Before World War I had even been brought to a conclusion a naval arms race was already underway. Two unsuccessful treaties failed to halt the world-wide build-up. France took the initiative in the building of fast battleships; Germany built submarines in secret and Hitler pushed ahead with his infamous Plan 'Z'; Italy secured the advantage in the Mediterranean; Britain's powerful surface fleet was dangerously stretched by global commitments. In reality no European navy was ready for the savage war that was to be fought first in the seas closest to their homelands.

When the German High Seas Fleet steamed into captivity between the long, watchful lines of the Grand Fleet on November 21, 1918, the British Royal Navy, with 41 Dreadnought battleships or battlecruisers, was, even though many of these were nearing the end of their useful life, incomparably the most numerous and powerful in the world. Only for the time being, however: for, in 1916 both the United States and Japan had announced huge programmes of naval expansion, the former firmly stating that it wanted to acquire a 'navy second to none'.

In response to Japan's programme of building and maintaining a fleet of eight battleships and eight battlecruisers, none of which would exceed eight years of age, the United States decided to lay down ten battleships and six battlecruisers over the next five years, as well as ten cruisers and more than 80 destroyers.

Great Britain, with her world-wide imperial responsibilities, could not at first accept even equality of naval strength with any other single power; she felt bound to compete and her naval estimates for 1921 provided for four new battlecruisers and a number of battleships.

The prospect of such an economically crippling armaments race was so daunting, however, that a hint was conveyed to the United States Government that a limitation agreement would be acceptable. President Harding called a conference at Washington of the major naval powers. A Four-Power Treaty in December 1921 terminated the Anglo-Japanese Treaty to which America objected; and on February 6, 1922 a naval limitations treaty was signed. This established a ratio of 5:5:3:1.75:1.75 between the overall naval strength of Britain, USA, Japan, France and Italy respectively. Further

limitations within individual types of ship, both by tonnage and gun calibre, were also laid down. Cruisers, for instance, were limited to 10,000 tons displacement and guns of no more than 8-inches.

Aircraft carriers were similarly limited in total and individually. Britain had the *Argus* and *Eagle* in commission, the *Hermes* nearing completion and the *Furious* under conversion. She now took the *Furious*'s sister-ships *Courageous* and *Glorious* under conversion also. This left her sufficient tonnage for one more carrier; but not until 1935 did she lay down the *Ark Royal*. Neither the French nor the Italians had any carriers but the French were now to start conversion of the Dreadnought *Béarn*, completed in 1927.

Germany's secret build-up

Meanwhile Germany, in eclipse as a naval

As soon as Hitler repudiated the Treaty of Versailles the construction of U-boats began once more. This is Krupp's yard before World War II.

Japan modernised and reconstructed her battleships between the wars. Here the Fuso *is running trials in 1933, with her new 'pagoda' mast.*

power and restricted by the Versailles Treaty to warships of not more than 10,000 tons, but unaffected by the Washington Treaty, had made a modest revival with a few light cruisers and then gone on to produce the 12,000-ton 'pocket battleships', ingeniously designed with an eye to commerce raiding. Since 1934, also, following Hitler's rise to power, Germany had been secretly evading the clause of the Versailles Treaty which forbade her to build submarines.

A major change had been taking place in the characteristics of the battleship at this time. It had begun to be appreciated that with aircraft carriers capable of and needing to steam at speeds of 30 knots, battleships would require a similar capability. The French had implemented the idea with the *Dunkerque* and *Strasbourg*. It was in response to these ships that in 1934 the Germans laid down in secret two 31,800 ton battlecruisers, *Scharnhorst* and *Gneisenau*; so that when Britain and Germany signed a naval agreement on June 18, 1935, permitting the latter to build up to 35 per cent of the former's surface naval strength and 45 per cent of her submarine strength, this merely brought into

the open a situation which already existed *sub rosa*.

Also in reply to the *Dunkerque* and her sister, the Italian battleships *Littorio* and *Vittorio Veneto* were laid down in 1934, though these made little pretence of keeping to treaty limitations, having a displacement of 41,167 tons, an armament of nine 15-inch guns and a speed of 30 knots.

These various fast battleships made all existing battleships obsolete just as the *Dreadnought* had done 30 years earlier. When the Washington Treaty and the London Naval Treaty of 1930 lapsed at the end of 1936, therefore, America and Britain both embarked upon a programme of fast battleships. The latter having already designed 14-inch mountings, installed ten of these guns in the *King George V* class.

Raeder's vengeful Plan 'Z'

The Germans had already laid down the fast battleships *Bismarck* and *Tirpitz* of 42,500 tons displacement which were to mount eight 15-inch guns. These and the five 14,475-ton cruisers of the *Admiral Hipper* class, laid down between 1935 and 1937, were but the first units of the long term building plan—Plan 'Z'—by which, following abrogation of the Anglo-German agreement at a suitable moment, it was intended to build up the German fleet to a force of eight battleships, five battlecruisers, four aircraft carr-

HMS Sussex

The County Class heavy cruisers were built under the Washington Treaty limitations on tonnage and gunpower. Their purpose was the protection of trade, for which their large fuel stowage and high speed made them admirable.

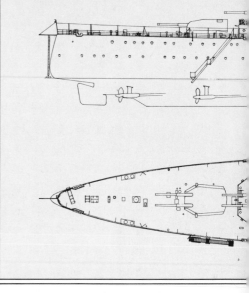

Above : The German pocket-battleship Lützow, *one of three armoured cruisers built to evade the restrictive clauses of the Versailes Treaty. They were the first large warships to be driven by diesel engines.*

Left : The battlecruiser Gneisenau *was named after the old cruiser of Falklands and Coronel fame.*

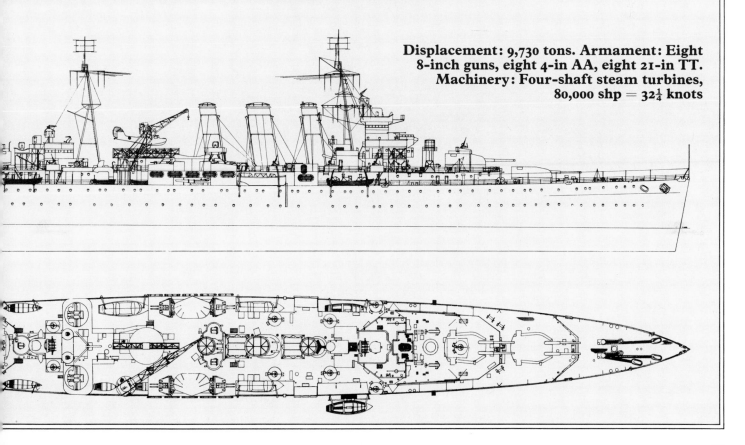

Displacement: 9,730 tons. Armament: Eight 8-inch guns, eight 4-in AA, eight 21-in TT. Machinery: Four-shaft steam turbines, 80,000 shp = 32¼ knots

HMS Rodney

Much criticised when they first appeared in 1928, the *Rodney* and her sistership *Nelson* were the most powerful battleships in service in any navy at the start of World War II.

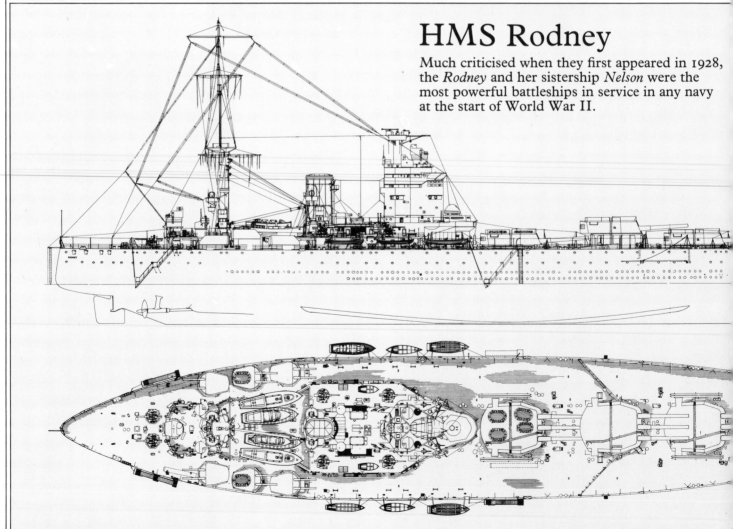

Left : The new battleship Bismarck on her first trials. She was the first instalment of the German Navy's Plan 'Z'.

iers, over 200 submarines, and a large number of cruisers and destroyers in time for the aggressive war Hitler was to launch to avenge 1918.

Fortunately for Germany's enemies, Plan 'Z' was geared to an opening date of 1944 or 1945 for that war; so that when it began on September 3, 1939, of the major surface ships only the two battleships, the five cruisers and the aircraft carrier *Graf Zeppelin* were under construction; and of the U-boat arm only 57 were in commission, of which 27 were ocean-going types, the remainder coastal.

Even more than in World War I, therefore, the German surface fleet would not be able directly to challenge the British and, as will be seen, it was deployed instead on commerce raiding operations except for the brief interlude of the Norwegian Campaign. In the Mediterranean, on the other hand, the Italian fleet, centred on four modernised Dreadnought battleships and including a powerful force of armoured 8-inch cruisers, would in theory be superior to any fleet the British could deploy there, and distinctly so when the *Littorio* and *Vittorio Veneto* commissioned in 1940.

An imponderable in the situation was the relative effectiveness of the naval air element on either side. The Germans and Italians had each developed an independent Air

**Displacement: 33,900 tons
Armament: Nine 16-inch
guns, twelve 6-in, six 4.7-in
AA, two TT. Machinery:
Two-shaft geared turbines
45,000 shp = 23 knots**

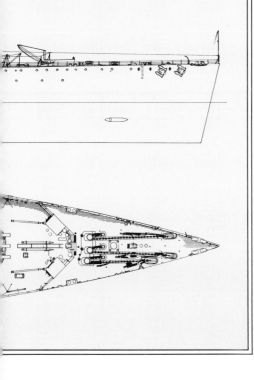

Above : The new Japanese cruiser Magami *running trials in 1935. Her fighting qualities astonished Western observers, but she was poorly designed.*

Force upon which their navies had to rely entirely for air support, ship-borne or shore-based, with the emphasis on the latter. The Italians had taken no steps to acquire an aircraft carrier; the Germans were, in the event, never to complete any of those projected by them.

British sense—and folly!

The British, though they, too, had absorbed their naval and military air services into a single, independent Royal Air Force in 1918, had come to realise that ship-borne naval aviation at least was most effective when under naval organisation, command and control; and in 1937 these had reverted to the Admiralty—too late for all the defects and neglects to be remedied, but in time, as events were to show, to give the Royal Navy an advantage in this respect. Their seven carriers had come to be recognised as an integral and essential part of any naval force. The comparative efficiency of the opposing systems makes an interesting feature of the naval operations which were about to begin in European waters.

As regards submarine warfare, the British were enjoying a false sense of security. The invention of the 'Asdic' sonar-ranging system of detecting and directing the attack on a submerged submarine had been accepted as banishing for ever the threat posed by those sinster craft. Unfortunately the 'Asdic' was very far from being the infallible system it was made out to be. Again, plans had been

made to put all merchant shipping into convoy; but no steps had been taken to provide the necessary escort vessels or escort aircraft.

The radar revolution

Technical advances during the years between the wars had taken place chiefly in the fields of electronics and marine engineering. In the former, besides the considerable advances made in wireless telegraphy and telephony, the introduction of what was to come to be known as 'radar' (radio detection and ranging) was by far the most consequential, enabling approaching aircraft to be detected far beyond their visible range. Ship-borne radar to detect surface ships was still in its infancy at the beginning of the war, with the Germans further advanced in that direction and already using radar to control ships' guns. The use of radar in that way was, indeed, to revolutionise the capabilities of naval gunfire; but otherwise neither surface nor anti-aircraft gunnery had progressed greatly since the end of World War I.

In the field of marine engineering the use of high pressure steam had made the greatest impact. A typical consequence of such a development was the reduction of the number of boilers in the battleship *Queen Elizabeth* during modernisation from twenty-four to eight, a saving in weight of 50 per cent and in space of 33 per cent while her endurance at 10 knots was trebled. Diesel engines had been greatly improved also, as may be seen from the 26 knots achieved with them by the German pocket battleships.

Such, in the briefest terms, was the opposing 'line-up' for the war which broke out on September 3, 1939.

A sea war in earnest

The war at sea began in grim fashion with the sinking of the liner *Athenia*. Ominously, the U-boats gained more successes. The Allies struck their first real blow at the Battle of the River Plate and further victories were gained during the battle for Norway. Then the Royal Navy became involved in the costly and disheartening evacuations of defeated troops from the mainland of Europe as Churchill's 'Twilight War' came to a violent end and Britain was left in isolation.

When Britain and France declared war on Germany on September 3, 1939 to honour their promise to go to the aid of Poland if she were attacked, they were still too unprepared and ill-equipped to launch any offensive action. By standing on the defensive, therefore, they hoped to be given more time to remedy defects and deficiencies.

The consequent absence of activity on land and in the air during the autumn and winter led to references to the 'Phoney War' —or in Winston Churchill's less contemptuous phrase, the 'Twilight War'. It was far from either at sea, however, where, on the first day the Donaldson liner *Athenia*, the first of 41 merchant ships to be destroyed in that month, was torpedoed without warning and sunk by *U30*. In the same month, too, the Royal Navy suffered its first loss of a major unit, the aircraft carrier *Courageous*, unwisely deployed on anti-submarine patrol in the Western Approaches where she was torpedoed by *U29*. Three days earlier the *Ark Royal* had narrowly escaped the same fate. Although a convoy system had been initiated, the old lesson that it was by escorting the convoys, not 'patrolling the sea lanes' that the submarine attack would be defeated, had still to be re-learned.

One of the vessels that went to the aid of *Courageous* was the destroyer *Kelly*. Under the command of Captain Lord Louis Mountbatten this ship came to epitomize the fighting spirit of Britain's navy. In the first eight months of the war *Kelly* steamed thousands of miles protecting convoys and hunting submarines and powerful surface raiders. Like all destroyers she was overworked but she suffered more than most, being torpedoed, mined and damaged by heavy seas and collision.

Another demonstration that the war at sea was far from 'phoney' was provided by *U47*, commanded by Günther Prien, who skilfully penetrated the unfinished blockship barrier of an entrance to Scapa Flow on October 14, to sink the battleship *Royal Oak* with 833 of her crew, before escaping by the same route. Mines had also been taking their toll, including air-laid magnetic types which were first encountered on September 16. An important victim was the new cruiser *Belfast* which suffered a broken back when mined in the Firth of Forth in October. Then on December 4 the Home Fleet flagship *Nelson* was damaged by a magnetic mine off Loch Ewe where the fleet had transfered its base while the defences of Scapa Flow were being perfected.

On November 23 the P. & O. Liner *Rawalpindi*, converted to an armed merchant cruiser at the outbreak of war and deployed as one of the Northern Patrol stretched between Iceland and the Faeroes, sighted the battlecruiser *Scharnhorst* making the German surface fleet's first tentative sortie into the Atlantic with her sister, the *Gneisenau*. It took just fourteen minutes for the *Scharnhorst* to sink her greatly inferior opponent before the two battlecruisers steered for home.

Pocket battleship successes

Further afield, merchant ships were falling one by one into the hands of the pocket battleship *Admiral Graf Spee* which, with her sister-ship *Deutschland* (soon to be renamed *Lützow*) had been secretly sailed, before the war began, to the South and North Atlantic, respectively. The *Deutschland* had been largely neutralised by the convoy system which replaced the stream of transatlantic shipping by a few widely separated,

escorted groups. After capturing one ship and sinking another she had been recalled to Germany.

The *Graf Spee*, on the other hand, had been finding easy pickings. By December 7 she had sunk nine ships totalling 50,000 tons. She might have been able to continue her profitable cruise for a long while, in spite of the several hunting groups formed to run her to earth, just as her sister-ship *Admiral Scheer* was to do later in the war; but Captain Langsdorff of the *Graf Spee* was tempted by

the expectation of a rich harvest amongst the shipping off the River Plate. And there, at 0608 on December 13, 1939, a calm, blue summer day with visibility extreme, he was intercepted by a British squadron composed of the 8-inch cruiser *Exeter* and the light-cruisers *Achilles* of the Royal New Zealand Navy, and HMS *Ajax*, flagship of Commodore Henry Harwood.

A running fight ensued with the *Exeter* engaging from one side, the two light-cruisers from the other. The *Graf Spee*, aided by the surface warning radar with which she was equipped, quickly found the *Exeter*'s range and within 35 minutes had put her out of effective action. She had also suffered damage and casualties, however, both from the *Exeter*'s 8-inch guns and from the light cruisers' 5.9-inch; and by 0730 Langsdorff had settled on a course for neutral Montevideo for repairs. The *Ajax* and *Achilles* hung on to *Graf Spee*'s tail until she entered harbour.

A scuttling and a suicide

During the next few days diplomatic manoeuvres by the British to delay the *Graf Spee*'s departure until a force adequate to

The British destroyer Hotspur *at Liverpool, headquarters of Western Approaches Command. Her decks are crowded with anti-submarine weapons and detection gear.*

engage her was assembled, combined with false reports that this had, in fact, been achieved, led Langsdorff to the conclusion that internment or scuttling were the only choices open to him. He chose the latter and on the evening of December 17 the *Graf Spee* steamed slowly out of harbour and was blown up in the estuary after her crew had been taken off. Three days later Langsdorff shot himself.

To a nation engaged in what seemed to many a 'phoney' war, the skirmish off the River Plate made a sensation greater perhaps than history would evaluate it in the context of the world-wide struggle which was soon to develop. Already plans were being made both by the Allies and by Germany to widen the scope of the war by carrying hostilities to Scandinavia.

Those of the Allies developed originally out of a desire to go to the aid of Finland which had been brutally invaded by Russia. When Finland capitulated, plans were adapted to embrace the idea of halting the traffic in Swedish iron ore via the Norwegian port of Narvik by mining a portion of the route through Norwegian territorial waters. Against the likelihood of a German seizure of Norwegian ports in retaliation, an expedition to forestall this was prepared.

The plans were ill-conceived, amateur affairs; the military force allocated was

Left: German torpedo-boats on a sweep in the North Sea. These small destroyers proved useful in the English Channel and North Sea, thus releasing fleet destroyers for the Arctic and Bay of Biscay.

HMS Royal Oak

This veteran of the Battle of Jutland underwent modernization in 1934-35, but in 1939 was not fit for front-line duties with the battle fleet. Despite this her loss, the first of a capital ship, in Scapa Flow in October 1939 was a bad blow to British prestige. Other ships of the Revenge Class saw extensive service in World War II.

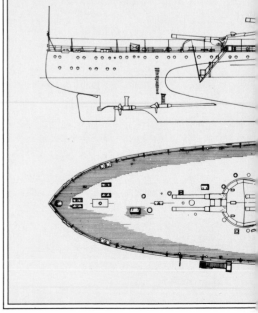

neither equipped nor trained for the rigours of the Arctic climate of north Norway; it was naively believed that it would be welcomed by the Norwegians; the expedition would be devoid of any air support other than a handful of low-performance naval aircraft. On April 7, 1940, however, the day before the first move of the British plan was made, it was pre-empted by the launching of a German plan, long prepared, to take by ruthless treachery all the principal ports of Norway.

For this almost the entire German surface fleet was employed, divided into six groups. If they were to avoid interception by the superior forces of the British Home Fleet, secrecy was essential. Group I comprised ten destroyers carrying 2,000 troops to capture Narvik, supported by the *Gneisenau* (flagship of Vice-Admiral Lütjens) and *Scharnhorst* which were to make a diversionary cruise in the Artic after escorting the destroyers to Vestfiord. Group II, to start out in company with Group I, was composed of the heavy cruiser *Hipper* and four destroyers carrying 1,700 troops to occupy Trondheim. They sailed early on April 7. The secrecy on which the German plan relied was broken by the aerial detection of Groups I and II soon after sailing; but hesitation, followed by faulty deployment of the Home Fleet, prevented their interception or that of Group III

Left : The pocket-battleship Graf Spee *lies off Montevideo after her crew had scuttled her. Believing that she was trapped, Hitler gave the order to scuttle to avoid the disgrace of a surrender.*

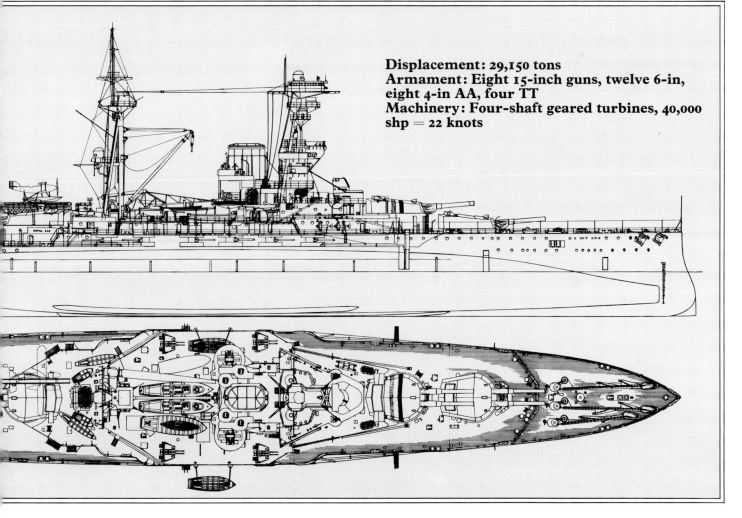

Displacement: 29,150 tons
Armament: Eight 15-inch guns, twelve 6-in, eight 4-in AA, four TT
Machinery: Four-shaft geared turbines, 40,000 shp = 22 knots

centred on the light cruisers *Köln* and *Königsberg* making for Bergen.

One fortuitous encounter there was during the 8th, however. The *Glowworm*, one of the destroyer screen of the battlecruiser *Renown* covering the British mine-laying destroyers, had fallen behind during the 6th while searching for a man swept overboard; in the thick and stormy weather prevailing she never rejoined and so was alone when at first light she sighted and engaged two destroyers of the *Hipper*'s screen. The cruiser, looming out of the smother at short range, severely damaged the *Glowworm* but not before she was able to radio her enemy report. Then, unable to escape the destroyers, she was steered to launch her torpedoes and, when those were avoided, to charge suicidally into

The German destroyer Georg Thiele *lies wrecked in Rombaksfiord.*

HMS Hardy

The leader of the destroyers which attacked the German destroyers in the First Battle of Narvik in April 1940.

Displacement: 1,455 tons
Armament: Five 4.7-inch guns, eight 0.5-in AA machine guns, eight 21-in torpedo tubes
Machinery: Two-shaft geared turbines, 38,000 shp = 36 knots

HMS Kelly

This famous ship was the first of a new class of destroyers which had stronger hulls and, because of more efficient boilers, only one funnel. The damage sustained early in the war by *Kelly* would have sunk any previously-built destroyer, and so all later destroyers were built on similar lines. Under her captain, Lord Louis Mountbatten, she earned a fighting reputation second to none and was finally sunk by German bombers during the Battle for Crete in 1941.

Displacement: 1,760 tons
Armament: Six 4.7-inch guns, one quad pompom AA, ten 21-in torpedo tubes
Machinery: Two-shaft geared turbines, 40,000 shp = 36 knots

her over-powering opponent. This despairing effort before she blew up and sank caused considerable damage to the *Hipper* though not enough to put her out of action. A posthumous Victoria Cross was awarded to Lieutenant Commander Roope of the *Glowworm* in acknowledgment of his gallantry.

In response to the destroyer's report, the C-in-C Home Fleet detached part of his force to try to catch the *Hipper* but in vain, and at dawn on the 9th the six German invasion groups arrived unhindered at their objectives. Besides the three groups mentioned above there was Group IV for Kristiansand centred on the light-cruiser *Karlsruhe*, a small group VI for Egersund to occupy the cable station there, and Group V composed of the heavy cruiser *Blücher*, the pocket-battleship *Lützow* (ex-*Deutschland*), the light-cruiser *Emden* and some smaller craft, carrying 2,000 troops for the occupation of Oslo.

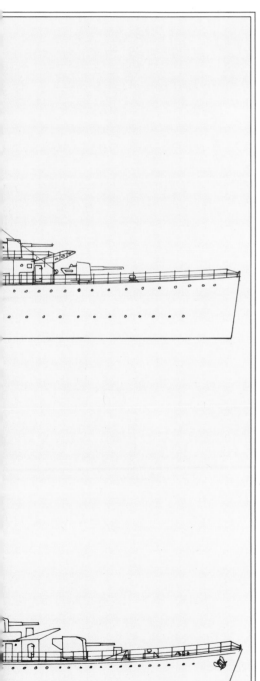

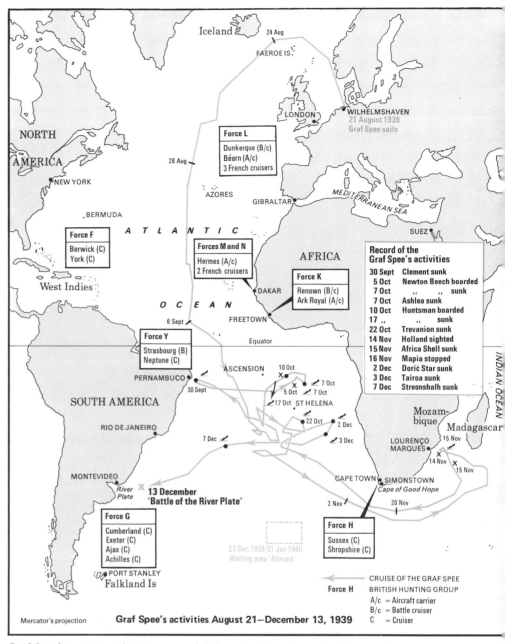

Record of the Graf Spee's activities

30 Sept	Clement sunk
5 Oct	Newton Beech boarded
7 Oct	,, ,, sunk
7 Oct	Ashlea sunk
10 Oct	Huntsman boarded
17 ,,	,, ,, sunk
22 Oct	Trevanion sunk
14 Nov	Holland sighted
15 Nov	Africa Shell sunk
16 Nov	Mapia stopped
2 Dec	Doric Star sunk
3 Dec	Tairoa sunk
7 Dec	Streonshalh sunk

Graf Spee's activities August 21—December 13, 1939

Mercator's projection

CRUISE OF THE GRAF SPEE
Force H BRITISH HUNTING GROUP
A/c = Aircraft carrier
B/c = Battle cruiser
C = Cruiser

Graf Spee's success against commerce tied down the ships of seven hunting groups.

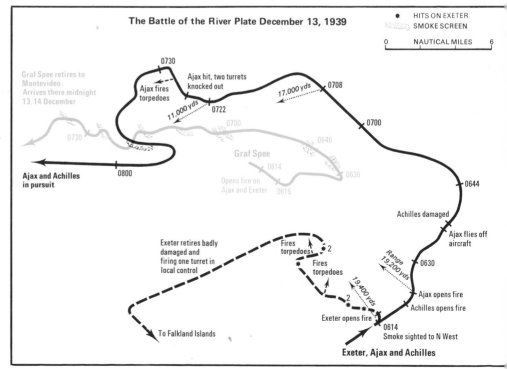

The Battle of the River Plate December 13, 1939

* HITS ON EXETER
SMOKE SCREEN

0 NAUTICAL MILES 6

Graf Spee outgunned the three British cruisers but was unable to escape from them.

The First Battle of Narvik, 1940

Great Britain	Germany	
Destroyers	*Destroyers*	
Hardy	*Wilhelm Heidkamp*	*Diether von Roder*
Hotspur	*Anton Schmidt*	*Woldgang Zenker*
Havock	*George Thiele*	*Erich Giese*
Hunter	*Hans Ludemann*	*Erich Koellner*
Hostile	*Hermann Kunne*	*Bernd von Arnim*

Scharnhorst flees in a gale

The last of these was the only Group to meet any determined and effective opposition, suffering the loss of the *Blücher* to the guns and torpedoes of the shore defences of Oslo fiord. Nevertheless, by noon the Norwegian capital was in German hands as were all the other principal ports.

Far to the north, Admiral Lütjens, having parted company with the destroyers of Group I off Vestfiord on the previous evening, had taken the *Gneisenau* and *Scharnhorst* northwards in a mounting northerly gale. At dawn on the 9th he was surprised by the *Renown* and, having suffered considerable damage from three 15-inch hits on his flagship, he fled northwards at high speed, accepting further damage from the huge seas into which his ships were forced to escape. The *Renown* had received two hits which did little damage.

Other surface forces of the Home Fleet, having failed to intercept any of the German groups on their way to their objectives, now found themselves driven off the Norwegian coast by the lack of any fighter cover against attacks by high-level bombers and dive-bombers of the German Air Force able now to operate from Norwegian airfields. In spite of an extravagant and unproductive expenditure of the limited anti-aircraft ammunition, the battleship *Rodney* was hit and damaged, the destroyer *Gurkha* was sunk. British submarines, however, in the Kattegat and Skagerrak had been taking a toll of enemy supply ships; and, on the evening of the 9th, the *Truant* intercepted and sank the *Karlsruhe* as she was returning home from Kristiansand.

The German warships' return voyage was, indeed, their moment of greatest peril with the Home Fleet mobilised against them. The *Gneisenau* and *Scharnhorst*, the *Hipper* and the *Köln*, aided by the wild weather and low visibility were to evade all search and get safely home. But at Bergen, the *Königsberg*, damaged by the Norwegian shore defences, was attacked early on the 10th by naval dive-bombers from Katston air station on Orkney and sunk at her berth, the first major warship ever to be sunk during hostilities by air attack. Late on that same day the *Lützow*, returning from Oslo to Kiel, was torpedoed by the submarine *Sunfish* and so damaged that she was to be out of action for a year.

A brave destroyer attack

The German Navy was thus already paying a painful price for their treacherous rape of neutral Norway. And at snow-covered Narvik the ten German destroyers had to delay their departure because of the tankers from which they were to refuel. The danger of their being trapped had been increasing every hour. Since noon on the 9th four

destroyers of the British Second Flotilla under Captain Warburton-Lee in the *Hardy*, followed by the *Hotspur*, *Havock* and *Hunter*, had been steering up Vestfiord with orders to proceed to Narvik to sink or capture the single German ship reported to have arrived there.

While seeking further information from the pilot station inside the fiord, Warburton-Lee had been joined by a fifth ship of his flotilla, the *Hostile*. He now learned that at

Right : A deck scene on board a German S-boat or minesweeper, with marker buoys ready for laying.

Far right : In happier days Graf Spee's sailors celebrate the ceremony of Crossing the Line.

Admiral Graf Spee

The pocket-battleship is shown as she appeared at the Battle of the River Plate. The false high-speed bow and midships waves were to produce a false estimation of her speed at first sighting. She had six 11-inch guns and 10,000 miles endurance but was slower than any foreign cruiser and no better armoured.

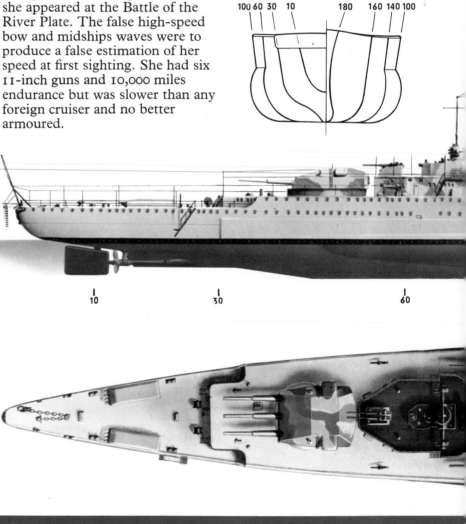

Arado – 196 spotter-
reconnaissance sea-plane.

100   140   160   180

5 10   25   50   75   100
FEET

© Profile Publications Limited

least six German warships larger than his own were at Narvik. But relying upon the effect of surprise and in spite of some uninspired messages from the Admiralty, he signalled his intention of attacking at dawn. And as the curtain of snow-fall and mist parted in the first light, he saw three of the German destroyers at anchor off the town of Narvik, two more alongside the tanker.

The explosion of one of the *Hardy*'s torpedoes which wrecked the *Wilhelm Heidkamp*, flagship of Commodore Bonte, who was killed, and two more which sank the *Anton Schmitt*, were the first indications to the Germans that they were under attack. The *Diether von Roeder* and the *Hans Lüdemann* were heavily damaged by gunfire; merchant ships in the harbour were sunk at their moorings. This action occupied the best part of an hour, after which Warburton-Lee turned to retire seawards with his flotilla.

Unknown to him, the remaining German ships were berthed in inlets off the main fiord, and they now arrived on the scene to take the British force between two fires. The *Hardy* was quickly shattered and set on fire, her captain killed, and the ship herself beached in a sinking condition. The *Hunter* was next to be crippled and sunk, while the *Hotspur* was severely damaged. In reply two of the new arrivals had taken considerable damage from the British gunfire and fortunately the other German destroyers were too short of fuel to chase the *Hotspur* as she limped away, covered by the *Havock* and *Hostile* which had escaped serious damage. Thus for the loss of the *Hardy* and *Hunter* and the crippling of the *Hotspur*, all but four of the German flotilla had been destroyed or so damaged as greatly to reduce their battle-worthiness.

Air attacks take their toll

Warburton-Lee's incisive leadership compared very favourably with the uninspired and vacillating behaviour of some other British commanders in the area, as a result of which it was not until the afternoon of the 13th that a force of nine destroyers and the battleship *Warspite* moved into the Narvik fiord. In the interval the German destroyers were given time to make repairs and the action which followed was by no means the one-sided affair it might otherwise have been. The entire German force was destroyed, it is true; but in reply the destroyers *Punjabi*, *Cossack* and *Eskimo* were seriously damaged. Further delays in following up with a military landing force were now also to give the German occupying troops, who had fled into the hills, time to regain their morale and return. The capture of Narvik was thus to be delayed for six weeks.

Elsewhere, British and French naval units had been engaged in landing and supporting two military expeditions at Namsos and Aandalsnes, north and south respectively of Trondheim—two arms of a pincer movement aimed at the re-capture of that important port. Both the warships and transports were repeatedly bombed during the landings as were the warships throughout subsequent daylight hours as they lay in the little harbours to give anti-aircraft gun support. Most suffered damage but, incredibly, only one of those stationary targets, the sloop *Bittern*, became a total loss.

HMS Ajax

This light cruiser and her sister *Achilles* were both involved in the Battle of the River Plate and *Ajax* is drawn as she appeared after repairs to the damage received from the *Graf Spee*. Both were unusual in having only one funnel, the result of having all boilers together to economise on weight.

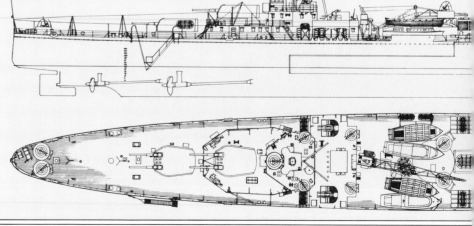

With no air support and exposed to unhindered dive-bombing attacks by German Stukas based on nearby airfields, the military expeditions were doomed from the start. Some two weeks after being landed, the decision was taken to re-embark them by night between April 30 and May 2. The operation was brilliantly and successfully carried out; casualties amongst the ships engaged were avoided until the morning of May 2 when the full fury of the disappointed *Luftwaffe* descended upon the destroyers carrying the rearguard of the Namsos force. Nearly two hours of continuous attack had achieved nothing when a hit was at last obtained on the French *Bison* which caught fire and was abandoned. The British *Afridi* which had picked up many of the French crew was then caught by three Stukas which sent her to the bottom.

Heroism averts a tragedy

All Norway other than the extreme north had now been abandoned by the Allies. And when the Germans launched their great offensive into France and Belgium on May

Above : Evacuated soldiers watch blazing oil tanks in Dunkirk as their transport pulls away from the harbour.

Left : A petrol tanker is set ablaze during a German air raid in the Norwegian campaign, 1940.

10, it soon became clear that allied resources would be far too meagre for even a foothold to be retained on the continent. Although on the 28th British, French and Polish troops at last captured Narvik, it had already been decided, three days earlier, to evacuate the whole of Norway. Once again the British navy found itself committed to the disheartening experience of withdrawal of the army. A series of convoys of fast troopships or slow supply transports was organised, beginning on June 4.

Although these were given a close escort, a certain complacency bred by the absence of any surface threat by the German Navy over the past two months, and a paucity of resources available to the C-in-C Home Fleet at the time, led to a lack of any adequate heavy covering force. So that when the *Scharnhorst*, *Gneisenau* and *Hipper* and four destroyers arrived on the convoy route on the night of June 7/8, there were all the elements of impending tragedy. Tragedy there was, indeed, to be; but a fortuitous chain of circumstances and a heroic deed were greatly to reduce its scope.

During the forenoon of the 8th the German squadron intercepted a tanker and its trawler escort and an unescorted empty troopship which were all sent to the bottom. The *Hipper* and the destroyers, short of fuel, were now ordered away to Trondheim. The two battlecruisers remained in position to intercept a troop convoy carrying 10,000 troops, an encounter which must have resulted in a heavy loss of life if it had taken place. But instead, at 1545 that afternoon the carrier *Glorious* with the destroyers *Ardent* and *Acasta* loomed up over the horizon.

The *Glorious* had been employed during the closing period of the Narvik campaign in transporting RAF Gladiator and Hurricane fighters to operate from Norwegian airfields. When the time came for evacuation the pilots appealed to be allowed to land their planes on board rather than destroy them,

although none had ever landed on a deck before and they had no arrester hooks. This was permitted and performed with great skill and without loss. The carrier, short of fuel and hampered by all these extra aircraft from operating her own scouts had now been caught by surprise with steam only for moderate speed available. She was quickly overwhelmed by the Germans' 11-inch guns and at 1740 she sank.

Acasta strikes a vital blow

The *Ardent* and *Acasta*, after trying to screen the carrier with smoke, steamed gallantly for the enemy to attack with torpedoes. The *Ardent*'s attack failed and she was quickly torn apart and sunk. The *Acasta*, however, shortly before her end, succeeded in hitting the *Scharnhorst* aft, the explosion killing 48 of her crew, putting her after turret out of action and flooding two of her engine rooms which reduced her speed to 20 knots. The German admiral at once shaped course for Trondheim with both ships. The damage to the Allied troop convoys had been thus dramatically removed by a deed of gallantry successful far beyond what could have been expected of it.

So ended a campaign notable on the one side for the ruthless efficiency of the forcible occupation of a strictly neutral country and the bold acceptance of a calculated risk of disaster to a fleet in the face of greatly superior force; on the other for an amateurish lack of understanding of the effect of aerial domination upon an amphibious expedition and the failure through vacillation to use the sea power available to make an enemy pay the full price for his defiance of it.

The Twilight War had in the meantime ended in a blazing German dawn as Hitler's panzers rolled across France and Belgium, driving most of the British Army and a portion of the French into a coastal bridgehead at Dunkirk by May 26. There every available

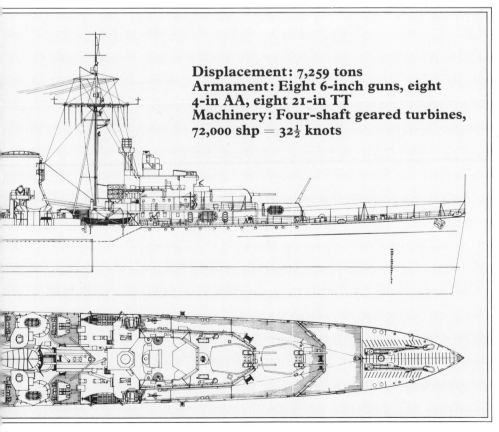

Displacement: 7,259 tons
Armament: Eight 6-inch guns, eight 4-in AA, eight 21-in TT
Machinery: Four-shaft geared turbines, 72,000 shp = 32½ knots

French transports lying in an English port after the evacuation from Dunkirk. Many Frenchmen were repatriated to France but their ships were not allowed to return.

destroyer of the Royal Navy (for the most
part veterans of World War I brought
out from reserve), a few French and Polish
destroyers and a swarm of civilian craft ranging from cross-Channel packets to motor-
boats, gathered to evacuate them.

British destroyers had been already engaged since the beginning of the German
blitzkrieg in evacuating the Netherlands
Government and Royal Family and carrying
out demolition of Dutch port facilities; in
bringing refugees home through Ostend and
taking reinforcements to the British troops
holding Calais and Boulogne. This had cost
three destroyers sunk and others damaged by
German dive-bombers. Now, between May
26 and June 4 when the 'miracle' of Dunkirk
came to an end, six British destroyers and
three French, and eight personnel ships were
to be sunk, a further 19 British destroyers
and nine personnel ships put out of action.
But 338,126 troops, including 26,175 French
had been brought off.

The cost of Germany's gamble

It is of interest to consider how much of
this could have been achieved, and at what
cost, if the Germans had not had to pay in
ships lost and damaged for their Norwegian
gamble.

Dunkirk was the largest and most specac-
ular evacuation of Allied troops of the great
withdrawal from Europe. There were a
number of others. One, sadly, was a failure
when the rescue of the Highland Division,
cut off under French command at St. Valery-
en-Caux, was frustrated by the descent of
fog at the crucial moment. But at Le Havre
11,059 British troops were lifted for the loss
of one personnel ship and damage to three
destroyers. From Cherbourg 30,630 were
embarked; from St. Malo 21,474; from
Brest 32,584; from St. Nazaire and Nantes
57,175; from La Pallice 2,303 British and
more than 4,000 Polish; from Bordeaux and
Bayonne more than 15,000 Poles. In all,
including the figures for Dunkirk, a total of
368,491 British and 189,541 Allied troops
were brought away to resume the fight at a
later date.

Battle in the Atlantic

The first stage of the Battle of the Atlantic was fought in the dark days when Britain stood virtually alone, dependent on convoys fighting their way through with vital supplies. At first the U-boats, operating in 'wolf-packs', had the upper hand. Then the 'Happy Days' when under-protected convoys were almost annihilated were brought to an end. Slowly the escorts wrested the initiative. In the surface war the loss of the *Hood* was offset by the sinking of the *Bismarck* and, at the time of America's entry into the war, the stage seemed set for a decision.

Light flak guns on the forward turrets and forecastle of the heavy cruiser Prinz Eugen *firing off Gdynia in 1945. The German Navy covered the withdrawal of the Army as the Russians advanced.*

Unlike the early days of World War I, the need for merchant ships to be gathered in convoys was accepted by the Allies in September 1939 and they were soon operating a regular cycle across the Atlantic, the outward-bound being given a close escort to points about 100 miles west of Ireland where they were dispersed. The escorts then picked up a homeward-bound convoy which, having assembled at Halifax, Nova Scotia, would have had up to then the escort of an armed merchant cruiser or perhaps a solitary sloop.

The number of escort vessels available would be ludicrously inadequate until the large building programme of 'Flower'-class corvettes, put in hand in July and August of 1939, could begin to bear fruit; furthermore too many destroyers were employed fruitlessly patrolling the empty ocean wastes. Nevertheless the system was largely effective in giving the ships in convoy protection during the first nine months of the war against the handful of U-boats that could be kept on patrol. The system however was not complete. Ships of over 15 knots or less than nine were sailed independently and it was these which the submarines naturally preferred to attack, sinking 102 of them by the end of 1939. There was a lull even in this activity when all U-boats were recalled in March 1940 to take part in the invasion of Norway.

At the end of March 1940 the disguised merchant commerce raider *Atlantis* sailed from Germany, the first of seven to operate in the distant oceans between this time and the end of 1941. She was the most successful, accounting for 22 ships of 145,697 tons before she was caught and sunk in November 1941. Another, the *Pinguin,* was to sink 17 freighters and 11 whalers to a total of 136,551 tons before she, too, was run to earth. The remainder were much less successful, though one of them, the *Kormoran,* intercepted by the Australian cruiser *Sydney* on November 19, 1941, succeeded in sinking the man-of-war before going down herself. Though these raiders were a thorn in the flesh and tied up a considerable British naval force involved in hunting for them, they were never to constitute any such mortal threat as did the U-boats at the height of their campaign.

Deadly 'wolf-packs' form

The conclusion of the Norwegian Campaign released the German U-boat fleet to prey again upon Allied shipping in the North Atlantic. And when the collapse of France enabled a U-boat base to be established at Lorient in July 1940 the submarines were able to probe farther out into the ocean and to keep a larger proportion of their total number on patrol. The number of U-boats was increasing, also, while the number of escorts available to combat them was so reduced by the casualties during the withdrawal from Europe that convoys were often sailed under the illusory protection of a single destroyer or sloop. Nor could Coastal Command of the RAF obtain what they considered a fair share of the long-range aircraft they needed to fulfil their dual function of reconnaissance for the Home Fleet and convoy escort. As for their ability to play an offensive role, not until 1941 were they to develop an effective air-borne depth-charge.

At the same time the German Air Force was brought into the campaign by the establishment of a squadron of four-engine, long-range Focke-Wulf Condor aircraft at Bordeaux to reconnoitre for the U-boats as well as to attack ships with bombs. As the summer wore on, the U-boats roamed ever further westward to attack ships from outward bound convoys after they had dispersed. Escort was therefore extended to 17 degrees west. But it was on the more valuable homeward bound, deep laden convoys that the attack was mainly concentrated; and a new tactic of massed attack by groups of submarines—which came to be known as 'wolf-packs'—was developed.

Aided by the German ability to decypher British naval signals these groups of six or more surfaced U-boats were spread across the expected track of a convoy. The first to sight it signalled the necessary information by high frequency wireless to U-boat head-quarters. This was then re-broadcast to the others who steered to intercept towards dusk. The Germans had discovered two fatal flaws in the submarine detection capabilities of their opponents—the Asdic could not detect a surfaced submarine; and a surfaced submarine was almost invisible by night from the bridge of an escort. No ship-borne radar was yet available to the escorts. Attacking by night, therefore, the U-boats could evade the sparsely spread convoy-screen to loose their torpedoes at close range at the target of massed merchant ships. One or two of their most skilful commanders—such as the top-scoring 'ace', Otto Kretschmer of *U99*—took advantage of this to the extent of penetrating between the convoy columns where they could pick off their victims at their leisure.

'Aces' slaughter a slow convoy

Using these methods, U-boats made a number of successful attacks and got away unscathed. In October 1940 they achieved results amounting to massacre on two homeward-bound convoys. The first of these, the slow convoy SC7 of 34 ships, under the solitary escort of the old, 14-knot sloop *Scarborough*, reduced to 30 owing to severe

Right : U-boat escape training.

Far right : The Bismarck, *battered into a wreck by British battleships.*

Bismarck

Built as part of Admiral Raider's 'Plan Z', the *Bismarck* and her sister *Tirpitz* were larger than international naval treaties allowed. *Bismarck* was fast, well protected, heavily armed and carried enough fuel to allow her to act as a commerce-raider in the Atlantic. Although credited with great ingenuity of design the *Bismarck* was very conservative in conception, having an armour arrangement considerably inferior to current British and American ideas, and a cumbersome arrangement of low-angle secondary guns for surface work and a separate anti-aircraft armament. Her deck armour was badly placed to deal with either bomb-damage or plunging

shellfire, and in her last action she was very quickly silenced by British shells. The *Bismarck* is seen here as she looked before her last sortie in May 1941. For that sortie the false bow and stern waves and camouflage to reduce her apparent length were painted out with the normal grey of German warships.

**Displacement: 41,700 tons
Armament: Eight 15-inch guns, twelve 5.9-in, sixteen 4.1-in AA.
Machinery: Three-shaft geared turbines, 138,000 shp = 29 knots**

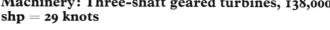

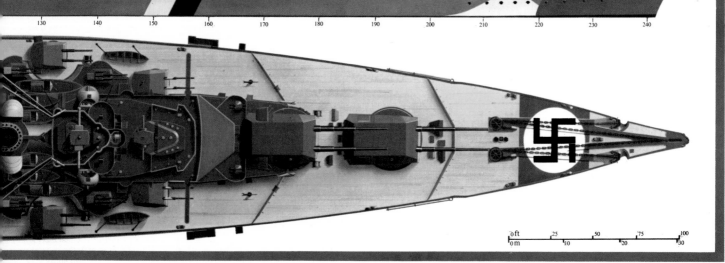

gales in which four ships had lost company, three of them to meet the common fate of stragglers from U-boat torpedoes, reached 21° 30′ west longitude on the 16th. There the escort was reinforced by another sloop, *Fowey*, and the corvette *Bluebell*. There, too, the convoy was intercepted by a U-boat and a wolf-pack, which included Kretschmer's *U99* and *U100* commanded by another leading 'ace' Joachim Schepke, was directed on to it.

In preliminary attacks by single submarines during the next two nights two merchant ships were sunk, a third crippled by torpedo. On the third night, Ocober 18/19, the wolf-pack moved in and, in spite of the addition of two more escorts, sank 15 ships and damaged another; they themselves suffered no loss or damage from the overwhelmed escort which was fully occupied picking up survivors.

By the morning of the 19th the remnants of SC7 were nearing the North Channel and their tormentors drew off; those who had any torpedoes left were diverted to the fast (10 knot) convoy HX79 which had been located and reported by Günther Prien, hero of Scapa Flow, in *U47*.

The escort of HX79 was numerically large, two destroyers, a minesweeper, four corvettes and three trawlers. But they were a force hastily gathered, most of them newly commissioned or manned by inexperienced crews. The result was that they were swamped by the massed attack which developed during the night October 19/20. By daylight 12 ships had been sunk and two more damaged. Not one U-boat had been attacked in reply.

The massacre of these two convoys was a painful shock to the British Defence Committee which was induced by it to release a number of destroyers from other duties to join the escort force. This was promptly rewarded by the destruction of three U-boats. In September the Prime Minister had negotiated the transfer of 50 over-age destroyers from the reserve of the US Navy and these would in due course become available. Nevertheless the problem of combatting the

night attack by the surfaced submarine remained insoluble and it was fortunate that, with less than 30 operational U-boats in commission, pack operations like those in October were followed by a lull. Not until early December was there another when four U-boats sank 11 ships from HX90 including the armed merchant cruiser *Forfar*.

A new and powerful menace

Meanwhile a new threat to Allied shipping had been posed by the German surface fleet. On November 5 the pocket-battleship *Admiral Scheer*, having passed undetected through the Denmark Strait into the Atlantic intercepted Convoy HX84. Its solitary escort, the armed merchant cruiser HMS *Jervis Bay* boldly steamed out to engage her vastly more powerful opponent. The outcome was inevitable; the *Jervis Bay* was sent to the bottom, but the gallant defiance of the AMC's Captain Fegen imposed a delay sufficient to enable his convoy to scatter so widely that only five of its 37 ships were rounded up and sunk

The *Scheer* then made for the South Atlantic and Indian Ocean where over the next five months she accounted for 11 more independently sailing ships before returning to Germany. Attacking escorted convoys was not the tactics for surface raiders which could not risk being damaged far from dockyard support. When the cruiser *Hipper* similarly broke out into the Atlantic on December 7 and, later that month encountered a troop convoy, she was driven off by the cruiser escort and forced to make for Brest for repairs. Emerging again in Februruary, however, she was fortunate to find an unescorted convoy from which she sank seven ships before ending her brief cruise.

On February 4, a potentially much more serious threat developed when the powerful battlecruisers *Scharnhorst* and *Gneisenau* also broke out into the Atlantic. But they, too, on two occasions sheered off from convoys at the sight of a single veteran battleship escort; it was only when they got amongst ships recently dispersed from outward-bound con-

Above : Survivors from the Bismarck *scramble to safety. The battleship carried a crew of 1962 men, only 118 were rescued, 25 by the destroyer* Maori, *85 by the cruiser* Dorsetshire *and eight by German ships.*

Right : The Bismarck *seen over the guns of the* Prinz Eugen *at Bergen, just before she sailed on her breakout through the Denmark Straits to take on the* Hood *and the* Prince of Wales *before being overwhelmed.*

HMS King George V

The latest design of British battleship, the *King George V* was smaller than the *Bismarck* and slower. To compensate she had much thicker armour on the belt and decks and, because she embodied practical experience gained in World War I and from tests on surrendered German battleships, the arrangement of armour and underwater protection was greatly improved. This showed to good advantage in battle when her sistership *Prince of Wales* suffered only slight damage from the *Bismarck* and *Prinz Eugen*. Interesting features of the *King George V* were the quadruple 14-inch gun turrets and the dual-purpose surface/anti-aircraft secondary armament. She was also the first battleship designed to carry aircraft on board, in hangars on either side of the forward funnel.

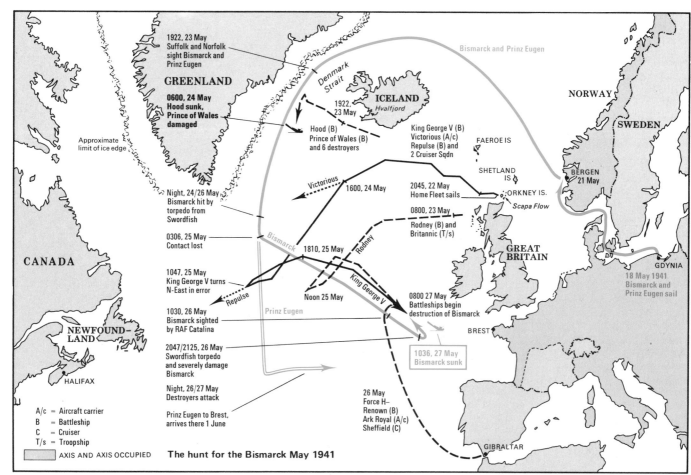

1922, 23 May
Suffolk and Norfolk
sight Bismarck and
Prinz Eugen

GREENLAND

Denmark
Strait

ICELAND
Hvalfjord

NORWAY

SWEDEN

**0600, 24 May
Hood sunk,
Prince of Wales
damaged**

1922,
23 May

Hood (B)
Prince of Wales (B)
and 6 destroyers

King George V (B)
Victorious (A/c)
Repulse (B) and
2 Cruiser Sqdn

FAEROE IS

SHETLAND
IS

BERGEN
21 May

Approximate
limit of ice edge

Victorious

1600, 24 May

2045, 22 May
Home Fleet sails

ORKNEY IS.

Scapa Flow

Night, 24/26 May
Bismarck hit by
torpedo from
Swordfish

0800, 23 May
Rodney (B) and
Britannic (T/s)

0306, 25 May
Contact lost

Bismarck

1810, 25 May

Rodney

**GREAT
BRITAIN**

CANADA

1047, 25 May
King George V turns
N-East in error

King George V

GDYNIA

18 May 1941
Bismarck and
Prinz Eugen sail

Repulse

Noon 25 May

Prinz Eugen

**NEWFOUND-
LAND**

1030, 26 May
Bismarck sighted
by RAF Catalina

0800 27 May
Battleships begin
destruction of Bismarck

BREST

1036, 27 May
Bismarck sunk

2047/2125, 26 May
Swordfish torpedo
and severely damage
Bismarck

Night, 26/27 May
Destroyers attack

26 May
Force H–
Renown (B)
Ark Royal (A/c)
Sheffield (C)

HALIFAX

Prinz Eugen to Brest,
arrives there 1 June

GIBRALTAR

A/c = Aircraft carrier
B = Battleship
C = Cruiser
T/s = Troopship

AXIS AND AXIS OCCUPIED   **The hunt for the Bismarck May 1941**

voys that they scored any success—five ships on February 22, 16 on March 15–16. They then returned to Brest where they were to await the planned sortie of the splendid battleship *Bismarck* and the heavy cruiser *Prinz Eugen* which were nearing completion. Together they were expected to form a combination most deadly to the vital trans-atlantic traffic.

But this would not be until May and, while waiting, the battlecruisers became the object of repeated bomb and torpedo attacks by aircraft of the RAF which damaged one or the other; or they were penned in harbour by mines laid by aircraft or the minelayer *Abdiel*. Meanwhile it was the U-boat force, now increasing in numbers, which kept up the attack.

The 'Happy Time' ends in death

Their opponents, too, were now more numerous and were beginning to be better equipped and trained. Regular groups were being organised; the crews of individual escorts were becoming experienced; radio-telephone communication between escorts greatly improved cohesion; a primitive radar set, adapted from the air-borne set (ASV), with a fixed aerial was being fitted in escort

Displacement: 36,830 tons
Armament: Ten 14-inch guns, sixteen 5.25-in DP
Machinery: Four-shaft geared turbines, 112,000 shp = $29\frac{1}{4}$ knots

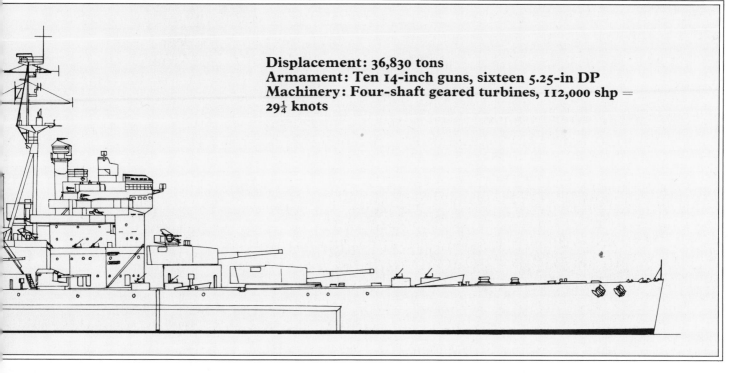

destroyers, though it was of very limited performance. Another device intended to remove the cloak of darkness during night attacks was the 'Snowflake' illuminating rocket provided to merchant ships as well as escorts. This was not to prove a success, however.

When the 'wolf-pack' containing the experienced 'aces' Kretschmer, Prien and Schepke was concentrated in March against convoys south of Iceland, they discovered that the 'Happy Time' they had been enjoying was over. Prien's *U47* was surprised on the surface and hunted to destruction by the destroyer *Wolverine*. *U70* was sunk by the corvettes *Camellia* and *Arbutus*. And in the same week *U100* was rammed and sunk by the *Vanoc*; Kretschmer and his crew were captured when *U99* was sunk by the *Walker*.

The shock of this disastrous week led the U-boat Command to shift their concentration further westward. They at once met success when a convoy not yet joined by its escort was intercepted and lost ten ships out of the 22 of which it was composed. In response the Admiralty based aircraft and ships in Iceland which escorted convoys between 35 and 18 degrees west. By May 1941 the expansion of the Royal Canadian Navy enabled them to give some degree of escort between the Canadian coast and 35 degrees west.

There now came a shock which for five days threatened the whole convoy system with dislocation and disruption. The 42,000 ton battleship *Bismarck* and the battlecruiser *Prince Eugen* broke out through the Denmark Strait. Intercepted by the battlecruiser *Hood* and the 36,750 ton battleship *Prince of Wales* on May 24 they sank the former and damaged the latter and, having survived the attack by a handful of torpedo planes from the carrier *Victorious*, shook off the shadowing cruisers to disappear. The *Bismarck* had not escaped unscathed, however. Damage from hits by the *Prince of Wales's* 14-inch guns and a consequent loss of a thousand tons of oil fuel forced Admiral Lütjens to order her to make for Brest. And though she was lost to view for 32 agonising hours, she was re-located in the nick of time before she could gain the cover of shore-based air power, by an aircraft of Coastal Command. She was crippled by a torpedo from an aircraft of the *Ark Royal* and finally overwhelmed and sunk by the guns and torpedoes of the British Home Fleet.

The threat to Atlantic shipping remained primarily that of the U-boats. The battle spread ever wider; convoys were escorted right across the Atlantic; U-boat concentrations shifted their ground, seeking weak links in the chain, and from time to time were to inflict painful losses when a convoy with a weak or inexperienced escort was intercepted. But many convoys were getting through without loss. The U-boat strength was increasing; at the end of August there were 198 in commission, with 80 operational, and there were not many lost that summer; but their achievements also decreased.

In September 1941, however, the U-boat chief, Admiral Dönitz, found the soft spot he had been looking for, the western section of the convoy route where inexperienced ships of the Royal Canadian Navy formed the escort. Convoy SC42 lost 16 ships out of 65 with which it started. Dönitz prepared to take advantage of this. But before he could do so, to his bitter chagrin, he was ordered by Hitler to send U-boats to the Mediterranean; in November he received orders to send the entire force of operational U-boats to that sea or the approaches to the Straits of Gibraltar. The British were thus given a welcome respite to replace the weak link in the transatlantic chain.

Air power to the rescue

One group of Atlantic convoys now came under a very heavy threat by this deployment of the U-boats—those running between Gibraltar and the UK. They had always been a favourite target for the Focke-Wulf Condors, to combat which fighter-catapult ships and catapult-merchant ships (CAM ships) carrying Hurricane fighters had been fitted out, achieving a moderate success. It was primarily against these aerial attackers that the first escort carrier, HMS *Audacity* had been equipped to operate six Grumman 'Martlet' fighters; but in the event her aircraft were to demonstrate their value in combating U-boats also, even though they carried no weapon lethal to a submarine.

This new form of defence against U-boat and air attack was convincingly demonstrated in December 1941 when the *Audacity* was attached to the 36th Escort Group commanded by Commander F. J. Walker who was to become the most successful destroyer

HMS Hood

Rightly described as the most beautiful warship in the world when she appeared in 1920, the *Hood* combined the speed of a battle-cruiser with heavy armour. Unfortunately much of the armour was wasted in places which did not need it, whereas later designs concentrated thick armour over the vital areas of machinery and magazines. She was nevertheless a heavily armoured ship, and recent research suggests that her tragic loss may have been caused by an ammunition fire rather than penetration of her armour by a shell. The *Hood* is shown as she appeared in May 1941. She carried

384   372   366   356   346   332   320   310   300   290   257   221

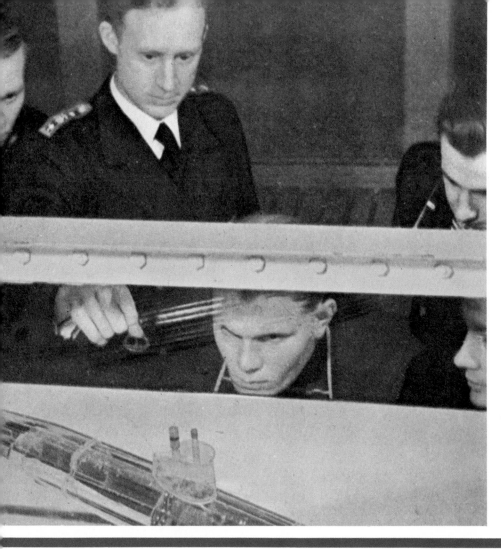

of U-boats of the war. Walker's Group of two sloops and seven corvettes had been carefully and thoroughly trained by their commander, a dedicated specialist in the art of U-boat hunting. It was strengthened by the addition of three destroyers as well as the *Audacity* to escort the homeward-bound convoy HG76 which left Gibraltar on December 14. In a running fight extending from the night of the 16th, when the first of a U-boat pack arrived on the scene, until the morning of the 22nd when Dönitz called the survivors off, four U-boats were sunk and only two ships of the convoy torpedoed. The *Audacity*, whose aircraft had played an important part in the destruction of the submarines as well as shooting down two of the Condors and driving off several others, was torpedoed and sunk, as was the ex-American destroyer *Stanley*.

But in spite of these painful losses the action was judged by both sides to be a notable victory for the escorts. New skills and a new confidence was inspiring them and the stage seemed set for a decision in the Battle of the Atlantic during 1942. It was not to be. For on December 7 Germany declared war on the United States. A whole new complex of trade routes from the Caribbean to Canada, hitherto the US Security Zone forbidden to Dönitz's sea wolves, was thrown open to devastating attack. Until these routes were made secure the U-boats would continue to wreak havoc.

Left : U-boat trainees study a model U-boat.

anti-aircraft rocket-projectors in 'B' turret and the shelter deck, and ammunition for these was set on fire during the action with the *Bismarck* and *Prinz Eugen*. She had radar control for her 15-inch guns and by 1940 her original secondary guns had been entirely replaced by anti-aircraft guns.

Displacement: 42,100 tons
Armaments: Eight 15-inch guns, ten 4-in AA, four 21-in TT
Machinery: Four-shaft steam turbines, 144,000 shp = 31 knots

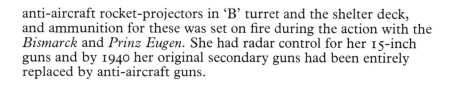

Fluctuating fortunes in the Med

When Italy entered the war in June 1940 her powerful navy gave her superiority in the Mediterranean. Britain reversed the situation with the brave raid on Taranto only for Hitler to deploy devastating aerial forces and regain control. The Battle of Matapan was a decisive Allied victory, Crete a disastrous loss. British submarines struck powerful blows only for U-boats to make an overwhelming response and Italian chariots to strike at Alexandria. By the end of 1941 Britain's fortunes in the Mediterranean were at their absolute nadir and Malta's cause seemed lost.

When Italy entered the war at the side of Germany on June 11, 1940, and France collapsed, French control of the western half of the Mediterranean, which had been the agreed allied strategy, disintegrated. The British Mediterranean Fleet under Admiral Sir Andrew Cunningham, was based on Alexandria. It consisted of four old battleships, of which only one, the *Warspite*, was modernised, six light cruisers, 20 destroyers, and the old aircraft carrier *Eagle*. It could not hope to dominate other than the eastern half in the face of Italian strength of three old, but modernised battleships, seven heavy and

11 light cruisers, as well as more than 100 submarines.

A fleet to be known as Force 'H' was hastily assembled at Gibraltar on the 28th, therefore, the battlecruiser *Hood*, flagship of Admiral Sir James Somerville, the old battleships *Valiant* and *Resolution*, the *Ark Royal*, two light cruisers and 11 destroyers. Sadly, the first duty put upon it was that of persuading the French fleet at Mers-el-Kebir to demilitarise itself and, when this failed, to put it out of action by bombardment—a tragic event which took place on July 3.

The basic situation that developed, and

which was to persist for the next two years and ten months, was one in which the rival naval and air forces fought around two main convoy routes. These were the 2,000-mile route east-west of the British convoys between Gibraltar and Alexandria and the 500-mile north-south route of the Axis convoys supplying their armies in Libya.

The first clash in this long campaign occurred on July 9 when a greatly superior Italian fleet fled after their flagship had received one hit from the *Warspite's* 15-inch guns at extreme range. The British fleet was subjected during the next four days to

repeated massed air attacks by high-level bombers. Although these failed to achieve concrete results, it was clear that British air strength would have to be greatly increased if Cunningham was to operate in the central basin with any confidence.

The new carrier, *Illustrious*, operating 12 Fulmar two-seater fighters and 22 Swordfish torpedo-reconnaissance planes, was sent out to him on September 1, therefore as well as the modernised and radar-equipped battleship *Valiant* and two small anti-aircraft cruisers. In the previous month, too, the *Argus* had flown off 12 Hurricane fighters to Malta from a position south of Sardinia to join the three old Gladiator biplane fighters and the nine Swordfish which had been the island's total air strength until then. This was the first of a long series of deliveries of fighters by carriers over the next two and a half years which was to play a decisive part in the island's successful defence.

A brave and decisive raid

With the air support provided by the *Illustrious*, comparatively meagre as it was, Cunningham sought opportunities to bring the Italian fleet to action while covering convoy operations, which included supply convoys to Greece which had been invaded by the Italians in October. But although the Italian Admiral Campioni had by now been reinforced by the fast, powerful new battleships *Vittorio Veneto* and *Littorio*, he was under orders to follow the strategy of not accepting battle without an important ulterior object. It was decided, therefore, that he must be attacked in his lair. And during the night November 11/12, 1940 a force of 21 Swordfish from the *Illustrious* raided the Italian fleet at Taranto, putting out of action the *Littorio*, *Caio Duilio* and *Conte di Cavour* —the last of these permanently, the others for five and six months respectively. Italian ability to dispute the control of the central basin was temporarily at an end and this was made evident when their fleet refused action with Force 'H', now reduced to the *Renown*, *Ark Royal*, two cruisers and five destroyers, covering a convoy to Malta at the end of November while Cunningham's fleet, simultaneously covering a convoy from Alexandria, was not even threatened.

Taking advantage of the improved situation, another convoy was run in January 1941 from Gibraltar for Malta and Greece covered by Force 'H' simultaneously with another from Alexandria under cover of the Mediterannean Fleet. The improvement was already being reversed, however, by the German decision to go to the aid of their ally by deploying *Fliegerkorps X*, some 300 aircraft of all types, including JU87 Stukas, which had received special training in shipping attack. When the Mediterranean Fleet moved into the Sicilian Narrows it was the *Illustrious* upon which this formidable force concentrated, unopposed even by the carrier's handful of low-performance Fulmar fighters which were caught off-guard. The armoured flight-deck which was a design feature of British carriers saved her from destruction but seven bomb hits sent her limping away to Malta. There she survived further prolonged attacks before escaping to Alexandria and thence to the USA for repairs. Other attacks sank the cruiser *Southampton* and damaged the *Gloucester*.

Heavy Italian losses

When the fleet retired from the area, *Fliegerkorps X* and Italian bombers turned their full attention to Malta in a first attempt to neutralise the island. This they failed to do and RAF Wellingtons from the island's airfields continued to retaliate against their Sicilian bases while the naval Swordfish took a steady toll from the Libyan convoys. Furthermore, a submarine base was set up whence, from February onwards, the convoys carrying the Afrika Korps to Tripoli were attacked. An early victim was the light cruiser *Armando Diaz* sunk by the *Upright*.

On March 27, at the impatient urging of their German ally, the Italians ordered their fleet to sea—the *Vittorio Veneto*, flagship of Admiral Angelo Iachino, six 8-inch cruisers, two 6-inch and accompanying destroyers— to intercept supply ships running between Egypt and Greece, to whose aid Britain had gone in anticipation of a German invasion. It was located and reported by an RAF Sunderland flying-boat south of Messina the following morning.

Admiral Cunningham in the *Warspite*, with the *Barham* and *Valiant* and the carrier

The aircraft carriers Furious *(left) and* Ark Royal *(centre), escorted by the battle-cruiser* Renown *in 1941. The 'Ark' with* Renown *and the cruiser* Sheffield *formed the backbone of Force 'H', the striking force based on Gibraltar which featured in so many Mediterranean actions.*

The Battle of Cape Matapan, 1941

Great Britain		Italy	
Aircraft Carrier		**Battleships**	
Formidable		*Vittorio Veneto*	
Battleships		**Cruisers**	
Warspite	*Barham*	*Zara*	*Trento*
Valiant		*Fiume*	*Trieste*
Cruisers		*Pola*	*Bolzano*
Orion	*Ajax*	*G. Garibaldi*	
Perth	*Gloucester*	*Abruzzi*	

Formidable (which had been sent to replace the *Illustrious*) sailed from Alexandria that evening, steering for a rendezvous at dawn off Gavdo Island with a squadron of four 6-inch cruisers which had been operating in the Aegean. In the Battle of Matapan which followed, the *Vittorio Veneto* and the cruiser *Pola* were both damaged by torpedoes launched by the *Formidable's* Swordfish aircraft; the cruisers *Zara* and *Fiume* sent to stand by the immobilised *Pola* stumbled into Cunningham's fleet during the night. All three cruisers and two of their accompanying destroyers were sunk.

The pendulum of fortune now began a swing towards the Axis as General Rommel went over successfully to the offensive in Libya and the British army, depleted through the despatch of aid to Greece, was soon in full retreat. In Greece the German 12th Army had crossed the frontier from Bulgaria and was overcoming all resistance. Malta's offensive air strength had already been reduced by *Fliegerkorps X*'s assaults to a handful of surviving Swordfish, though a total of 82 Hurricanes flown off to the island from the *Ark Royal* in March, April and May prevented its complete neutralisation. As a result the British submarines continued to operate and a division of four destroyers based on Malta succeeded in intercepting and annihilating a convoy of five transports and its escort of three Italian destroyers during the night of April 13.

This was the last notable offensive success by the Mediterranean Fleet for some time,

HMS Furious

HMS Furious was completely rebuilt between 1922 and 1925. Despite lacking an island she proved highly successful in her new guise. Just before World War II she was given new AA guns and a small island on the starboard side of the flight deck, but the funnel-smoke was still emitted through the long series of vents under the flight deck aft. *Furious*, depicted here as she looked in August 1941 and with a Seafire 1B on her flight deck, saw constant action.

Flycatcher, No 405 Flight HMS Furious 1928/9.

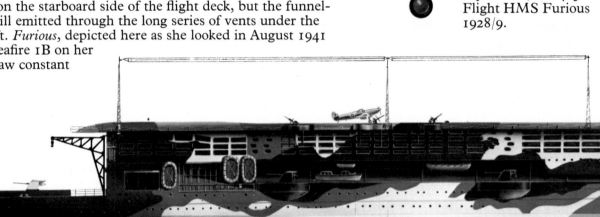

Displacement: 22,450 tons
Armament: Twelve 4-inch AA guns, thirty-three aircraft
Machinery: Four-shaft geared turbines, 90,000 shp = 29½ knots

1939. With small island and improved HP armament. Twelve 4-in AA three multiple pompoms. Aircraft complement 30.

however; for, during the last week in April, it was forced to turn its whole attention to the evacuation of the army from Greece. Though 50,732 troops were safely embarked, it was at a cost of four troopships and two destroyers sunk by dive-bombers.

The fleet was next called upon, in conjunction with Force 'H', to cover the passage through the Mediterranean of the 'Tiger' convoy carrying desperately needed tank reinforcements to Wavell's army in Egypt; at the same time supplies for beleaguered Malta were to be run through from Alexandria. The operation went off with unexpected smoothness. The Italian surface fleet did not venture to intervene. Air attacks on Force 'H'

The Ark Royal photographed from one of her own Swordfish torpedo-bombers.

and the convoy to the westward of Malta were successfully driven off by the *Ark Royal*'s little force of Fulmars until they came under the umbrella of Beaufighters specially deployed on Malta for this operation. One transport was lost through being mined in the Skerki Channel and another was slightly damaged. Beyond Malta and through the channel between Crete and Cyrenaica the *Formidable*'s Fulmars were similarly successful and on May 12, 238 tanks and 43 crated Hurricanes were safely delivered at Alexandria.

Destruction of a fleet

There was little time or incentive for celebration of this success, however. For it had been decided by the British government that Crete was to be held, although the air

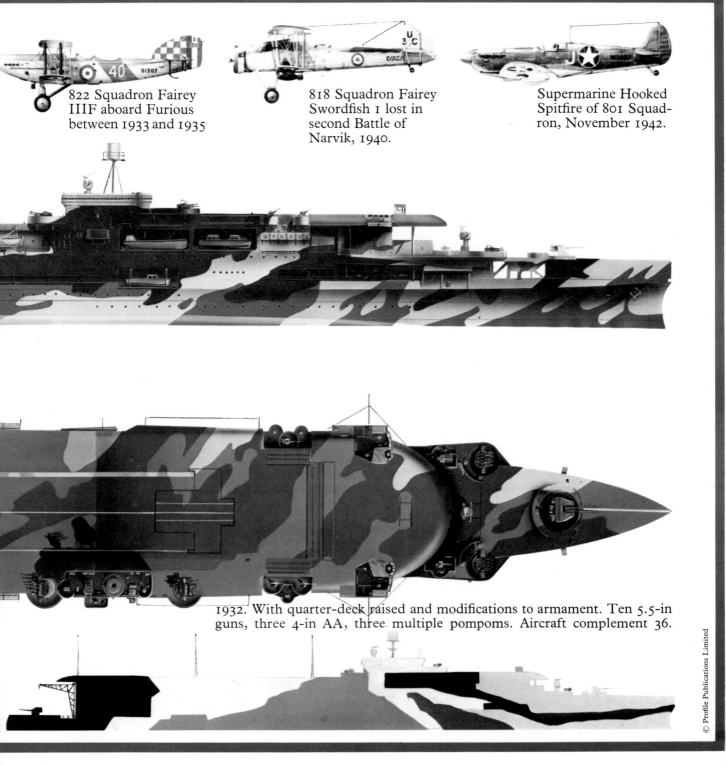

822 Squadron Fairey IIIF aboard Furious between 1933 and 1935

818 Squadron Fairey Swordfish I lost in second Battle of Narvik, 1940.

Supermarine Hooked Spitfire of 801 Squadron, November 1942.

1932. With quarter-deck raised and modifications to armament. Ten 5.5-in guns, three 4-in AA, three multiple pompoms. Aircraft complement 36.

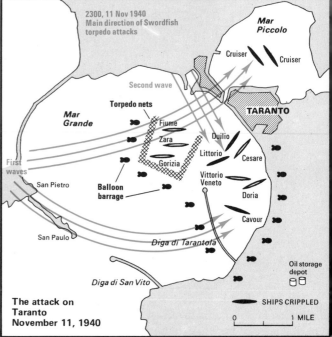

2300, 11 Nov 1940
Main direction of Swordfish
torpedo attacks

*Mar
Piccolo*

Cruiser — Cruiser

Second wave

Torpedo nets

*Mar
Grande*

TARANTO

Fiume

Zara

Duilio

Gorizia

Littorio

Cesare

First
waves

San Pietro

**Balloon
barrage**

Vittorio
Veneto

Doria

San Paulo

Cavour

Diga di Tarantola

Oil storage
depot

Diga di San Vito

**The attack on
Taranto
November 11, 1940**

SHIPS CRIPPLED

0   1 MILE

strength available for its defence had
dwindled by the end of April to half a dozen
Hurricanes and a dozen obsolete Gladiators.
Opposed to this remnant was a German air
strength in Greece of *Fliegerkorps VIII* and
part of *Fliegerkorps X* as well as *Fliegerkorps
XI* of parachute and airborne troop carriers.
When the German attack began in earnest on
May 20, fighter defence had been almost
eliminated during softening-up attacks.

It was clear from the start that naval
participation in defence of the island and the
inevitable evacuation to follow would involve
heavy losses to the enemy's unopposed air
power. And so it proved: the cost to the fleet
was three cruisers and six destroyers sunk,
(amongst them the gallant *Kelly* and her
sister *Kashmir* which were set upon by two
dozen Ju 87s on the morning of May 23),
two battleships, the only aircraft carrier, two
cruisers and two destroyers damaged beyond
local repair, three cruisers and six destroyers
less seriously damaged.

The main strategic consequence of the loss
of Crete was the acquisition by the German
Air Force of the island's airfields whence
shipping passing between Egypt and Malta
could be attacked, giving to the route the
grimly-earned title of 'Bomb Alley'. Since the
arrival of *Fliegerkorps X* in Sicily and the
consequent cessation of supply convoys for
Malta from the west, the island had been
kept going in austere conditions by the
despatch of single ships, notably the naval
auxiliary HMS *Breconshire* which made
numerous trips from Egypt. Now, however,
this became increasingly difficult. As a stop-
gap the larger types of submarine of the
Alexandria flotilla were pressed into service
as transports bringing aviation spirit, kero-
sene, medical stores, etc.

On the other hand, for the attack on
Russia which Hitler launched on June 22,
Fliegerkorps VIII and part of *Fliegerkorps X*

*Taranto Harbour before and after the
torpedo attack. Left: Warships at anchor.
Right: Four large ships surrounded by oil fuel.*

Lower left: Destroyers at Malta, 1941.

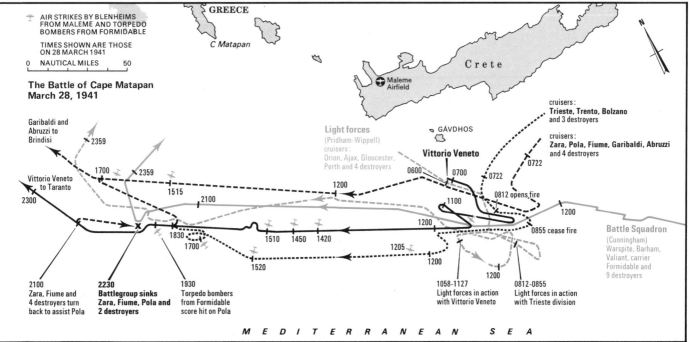

AIR STRIKES BY BLENHEIMS
FROM MALEME AND TORPEDO
BOMBERS FROM FORMIDABLE

TIMES SHOWN ARE THOSE
ON 28 MARCH 1941

0   NAUTICAL MILES   50

**The Battle of Cape Matapan
March 28, 1941**

GREECE

C Matapan

Crete

Maleme
Airfield

GÁVDHOS

Garibaldi and
Abruzzi to
Brindisi   2359

Light forces
(Pridham-Wippell)
cruisers:
Orion, Ajax, Gloucester,
Perth and 4 destroyers

Vittorio Veneto

cruisers:
Trieste, Trento, Bolzano
and 3 destroyers

cruisers:
Zara, Pola, Fiume, Garibaldi, Abruzzi
and 4 destroyers

1700   2359

Vittorio Veneto
to Taranto
2300

1515
2100   1200

0600   0700   0722
0722

0812 opens fire

1100

1200

0855 cease fire

Battle Squadron
(Cunningham)
Warspite, Barham,
Valiant, carrier
Formidable and
9 destroyers

1830
1700

1510 1450 1420

1205

1200

1200

1520

2100
Zara, Fiume and
4 destroyers turn
back to assist Pola

**2230
Battlegroup sinks
Zara, Fiume, Pola and
2 destroyers**

1930
Torpedo bombers
from Formidable
score hit on Pola

1058-1127
Light forces in action
with Vittorio Veneto

0812-0855
Light forces in action
with Trieste division

M E D I T E R R A N E A N   S E A

to sink the strongly-escorted troopship *Conte Rosso*. In September he sank two other big, escorted liners carrying troops to Libya, the *Oceania* and *Neptunia*; while yet another, the *Esperia* fell a victim to Lieutenant A. R. Hezlet's *Unique*. These were but the highlights of one part of the campaign of steady attrition of Italian shipping on the Libyan convoy route.

The old Greek battleship Kilkis *lies on the bottom of the harbour at Salamis after being sunk by Stuka divebombers during the invasion of Greece. She was the former USS* Mississippi, *a pre-Dreadnought which had been bought from the United States in 1914. Her sistership* Lemnos *(ex-USS* Idaho*) was also sunk in this attack.*

With the relaxation of the air assault on Malta, two squadrons of Blenheim bombers could also be deployed on the island. These aircraft gallantly bombed at masthead height by daylight at a fearful casualty rate, while the naval Swordfish took up the attack by night. The pendulum of fortune had swung back again in favour of Britain.

By July, however, the problem of keeping Malta supplied had become acute. It was decided that a convoy from the west must be fought through at all costs; so a convoy of six store ships—Operation 'Substance'—left Gibraltar on the 21st under the cover of Force 'H'—*Renown* (Admiral Somerville's flagship), *Nelson*, *Ark Royal*, the cruiser *Hermione* and six destroyers—as far as the Sicilian Narrows—with a close escort of three cruisers, the fast minelayer *Manxman* and eleven destroyers to go through to Malta. Opposition to this force was confined to

were transferred, leaving the remainder of the latter to cover the whole eastern Mediterranean. The neutralising of Malta was thus left to the Italian Air Force—a task they were unable to fulfil and so the island's air offensive capability recovered to complement the activities of the Tenth Submarine Flotilla based on Valetta.

British submarines strike back

The latter indeed had been performing brilliantly throughout the year, the most successful of an impressive team being the *Upholder*, whose captain, Lieutenant-Commander M. D. Wanklyn was to earn the Victoria Cross following a successful attack

HMS Upholder

This famous submarine sank three U-boats and a destroyer, damaged a cruiser and destroyer and sank or damaged 119,000 tons of shipping in less than eighteen months. She and her sisters of the Malta submarine squadron waged a ruthless war on the German and Italian supply-lines between Italy and North Africa in a classic submarine campaign. The "U" Class was originally designed for training but proved ideal for the Mediterranean. The *Upholder* was lost in April 1942, probably after being depth-charged by an Italian escort vessel.

aircraft of the Italian Air Force, which succeeded in sinking the destroyer *Fearless* and torpedoing the cruiser *Manchester* which was able to get back to Gibraltar, and a few MTB's in the narrow waters of the Skerki Channel. They torpedoed and damaged one of the transports but the remainder got through to make Malta viable for the next two months.

The lack of enterprise of the Italian surface fleet makes more conspicuous the suicidally gallant but unsuccessful attempt at this time to attack Valetta's Grand Harbour by means of explosive motor-boats and 'human torpedoes'.

By September it had again become urgent

HMS Illustrious *on fire and surrounded by bomb bursts January 10, 1941.*

to re-supply Malta. Operation 'Halberd', similar to 'Substance', was mounted. On this occasion the Italian fleet put to sea to pose a threat but Admiral Iachino, bound by orders not to join action unless he had a clear superiority of strength, kept his distance. A succession of aerial torpedo attacks was beaten off by the *Ark Royal*'s fighters and the guns of the escort, though one of these aircraft attacking in the moonlight sank one of the nine supply ships. The remainder reached Malta safely and the island was now stocked and victualled until the following spring.

This success was followed by the arrival at Malta on October 21, 1941 of Force 'K'—the cruisers *Aurora* and *Penelope* and two destroyers—under the command of Captain W. G. Agnew of the *Aurora*. During the night November 8/9 they intercepted an Italian convoy of seven merchant ships and, without loss to themselves, destroyed them all as well

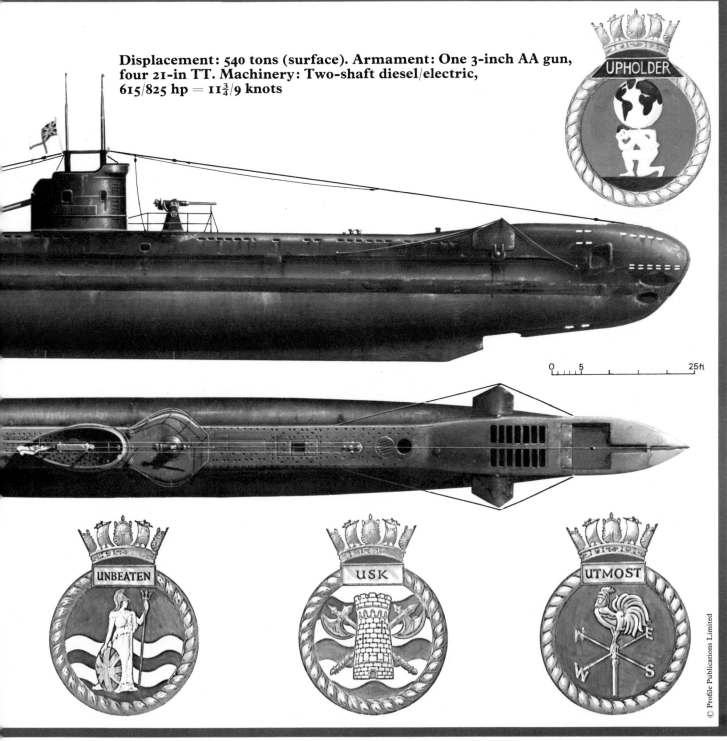

Displacement: 540 tons (surface). Armament: One 3-inch AA gun, four 21-in TT. Machinery: Two-shaft diesel/electric, 615/825 hp = 11¾/9 knots

0 5 25ft

as one of the destroyers of the escort of two cruisers and ten destroyers.

Already, however, the pendulum swing towards British success had been reversed and was gathering speed towards disastrous setbacks. Dismayed by the defeats being suffered by his Italian ally at sea, Hitler had ordered Dönitz, against the latter's protests, to deploy six U-boats in the Mediterranean in September and now a further four. They quickly achieved two resounding successes. On November 13, the *Ark Royal*, returning from a Hurricane-delivery to Malta, was torpedoed and sunk by *U81* off Gibraltar. Twelve days later, at the other end of the Mediterranean. *U331* attacked the fleet as it returned from a sweep and with three torpedoes blew up the *Barham* in a cataclsmic explosion. At the same time, at Hitler's orders, *Fliegerkorps II* was moving to Sicilian airfields to take up once again the task of neutralising Malta. By the end of the year the renewed 'Blitz' would be well under way.

Before the pendulum completed its swing there was one final success for the allied navies when a force of three British destroyers, *Sikh*, *Maori* and *Legion* and the Netherlands *Isaac Sweers*, under Commander G. H. Stokes in the *Sikh*, intercepted the Italian cruisers *Da Barbiano* and *Di Giussano* off Cape Bon. Both cruisers were torpedoed and sunk; Stokes' force was unscathed. At the same time, the *Vittorio Veneto* was torpedoed by the *Urge* and put out of action for several months.

Britain's squadron of two

But from this time onward the way was downhill for the Mediterranean Fleet for the remainder of 1941. Rear Admiral Vian's flagship *Galatea* was torpedoed and sunk off Alexandria by *U557*, reducing his squadron to two. In spite of this, when Vian's two ships and eight destroyers were joined by the *Aurora* and *Penelope* and four destroyers

from Malta to cover the passage of the *Breconshire* with urgent supplies of oil fuel for Force 'K', only to encounter the Italian fleet composed of the *Littorio, Andrea Doria, Giulio Cesare*, two heavy cruisers and ten destroyers in the Gulf of Sirte, on December 17, it was the Italians who turned away under threat of a torpedo attack by Vian's destroyers.

Disaster struck, however, when Force 'K' —*Neptune, Aurora* and *Penelope*—racing through the night in an effort to catch the convoy for which the Italian fleet had been the cover, ran into a minefield. The *Neptune* was lost with all hands; *Aurora* and *Penelope* were both damaged and put out of action; the destroyer *Kandahar*, also mined, had to be scuttled.

And while this calamity was occurring, three Italian chariots transported to the spot in the submarine *Sciré*, were penetrating Alexandria harbour to attach their explosive charges undetected to the battleships *Queen Elizabeth* and *Valiant*. This brilliantly executed feat resulted in both ships sinking on to the shallow harbour bottom. In a few disastrous days, Cunningham's fleet had been reduced, apart from destroyers, to three light cruisers, the old anti-aircraft cruiser *Carlisle* and the light cruiser *Ajax* at Malta.

Not yet, however, had British seapower in the Mediterranean reached its nadir. For in the last days of 1941, the Axis armies had been driven once again out of Cyrenaica by the British Eighth Army. While the Cyrenaican airfields remained in British hands, it would be possible to run supply ships from Egypt to Malta under fighter cover. The time was coming, however, when this would no longer be the case and the time of Malta's greatest suffering was then to come.

The destroyer Legion *goes alongside the sinking* Ark Royal *to take off her crew. The carrier had been torpedoed by a U-boat.*

Conti di Cavour

This battleship served in World War I but was completely rebuilt between 1933 and 1937. This involved removal of a midships triple 12-inch gun turret, lengthening the hull, and complete rebuilding of the upperworks. The weight saved was devoted principally to higher speed and better underwater protection, and she was four or five knots faster than she had been in 1915. The *Conti di Cavour* was sunk at Taranto in November 1940 during the British torpedo attack by carrier aircraft. Although salvaged she was still under repair when Italy surrendered in 1943. She was then seized by the Germans but was sunk once more by Allied bombing in 1945.

Displacement: 26,140 tons
Armament: Ten 12.6-inch guns, twelve 4.7-in, eight 3.9-in AA.
Machinery: Two-shaft geared turbines, 75,000 shp = 27 knots

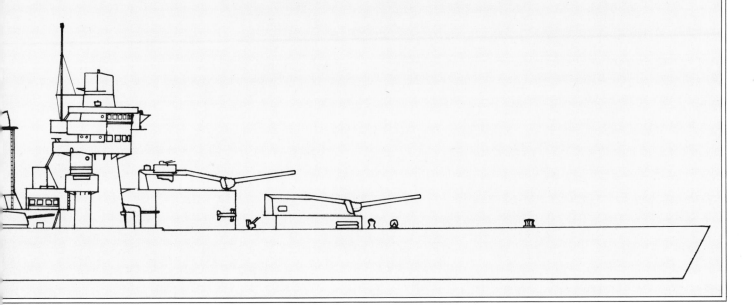

Action in Arctic waters

America's entry into the war stretched Allied escort forces beyond capacity and the U-boats enjoyed a second 'Happy Time' in the western Atlantic. However, new ships, new techniques and intensive training restored the balance. But in Arctic waters U-boats and land-based aircraft exacted a terrible toll on the ships of the Russian convoys. Consolation for the Allies came at the end of 1942 in a courageous small ship action against vastly superior forces which all but ended the effective contribution of German surface units to the Axis war effort.

Russian destroyers of the Gnevnyi Class on patrol in the Barents Sea in 1942. Although the Red Fleet maintained strong forces in the Arctic they showed little initiative or inclination to support the Allied convoys to Murmansk.

The United States had been giving the Allies actual aid, though not openly admitted, in the defence of shipping in the Atlantic since July 1941 when American troops relieved the British garrison in Iceland and Allied ships were permitted to join convoys sailing between the USA and Iceland under protection of the US Navy. On September 1, 1941 the US Navy had begun taking a share in escorting transatlantic convoys in the western half of the ocean on the grounds that they contained ships for Iceland. When, three days later, the US destroyer *Greer* hunted and was, in turn, attacked unsuccessfully by

a U-boat, an undeclared state of local war between the USA and Germany had begun, leading to the USS *Kearney* being torpedoed and severely damaged with a number of casualties on October 15; fourteen days later the USS *Reuben James*, escorting convoy HX156, was sunk, 115 of her crew being lost.

In spite of this state of affairs, Hitler had been anxious to avoid a full-scale war with the United States; German submarines had not been allowed to operate against the shipping thronging the sea routes between the Caribbean and New York. And, in spite of full access to British experience to date, no steps towards the preparation of a convoy system there had been made by the Americans.

When Germany declared war on the United States on December 9, 1941, Admiral Dönitz saw the great opportunity being presented. He was allowed at first to divert only five long-range, 1,000-ton U-boats from the 'primary area', the Mediterranean, a number later increased and maintained at

between 12 and 18 by the use of 'milch-cow' submarines supplying fuel, stores and torpedoes. They inflicted a holocaust on shipping during the next six months. Not until May did the Americans bestir themselves to organise a convoy system along their coasts. Losses there immediately ceased; but the U-boats were then transferred to the Gulf of Mexico and the Caribbean where the massacre continued until the system was extended to that area in July. This brought the second 'Happy Time' for the U-boats to an end. The Battle of the Atlantic swung back to mid-ocean and this time it was to be decisive.

Scharnhorst breaks out

That it was to be waged on the German side primarily by the U-boats had been ensured when, on February 12, the *Scharnhorst*, *Gneisenau* and *Prinz Eugen* sailed from Brest and boldly dashed through the English Channel under the umbrella of a swarm of fighter planes from French and Netherlands

Right: A German warship sinks an Allied merchantman by gunfire.

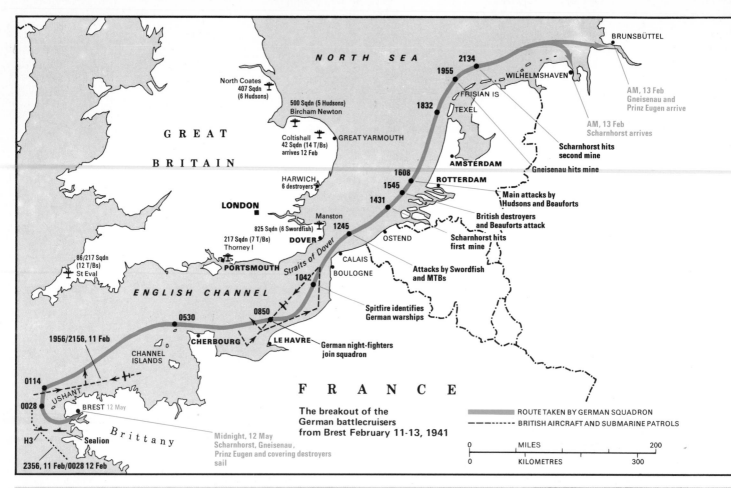

NORTH SEA

BRUNSBÜTTEL

2134
1955
WILHELMSHAVEN
1832
FRISIAN IS
TEXEL

GREAT
BRITAIN

North Coates
407 Sqdn
(6 Hudsons)

500 Sqdn (5 Hudsons)
Bircham Newton

Coltishall
42 Sqdn (14 T/Bs)
arrives 12 Feb

GREAT YARMOUTH

AMSTERDAM

AM, 13 Feb
Gneisenau and
Prinz Eugen arrive

AM, 13 Feb
Scharnhorst arrives

**Scharnhorst hits
second mine**

Gneisenau hits mine

HARWICH
6 destroyers

1608
1545
1431

ROTTERDAM

**Main attacks by
Hudsons and Beauforts**

LONDON

Manston
825 Sqdn (6 Swordfish)
217 Sqdn (7 T/Bs)
Thorney I

DOVER
1245

OSTEND

**British destroyers
and Beauforts attack**

**Scharnhorst hits
first mine**

86/217 Sqdn
(12 T/Bs)
St Eval

PORTSMOUTH

Straits of Dover

CALAIS

BOULOGNE

1042

**Attacks by Swordfish
and MTBs**

ENGLISH CHANNEL

0530

0850

**Spitfire identifies
German warships**

1956/2156, 11 Feb

CHANNEL
ISLANDS

CHERBOURG

LE HAVRE

**German night-fighters
join squadron**

0114

USHANT

F R A N C E

The breakout of the
German battlecruisers
from Brest February 11-13, 1941

0028

BREST 12 May

Brittany

H3

Sealion

Midnight, 12 May
Scharnhorst, Gneisenau,
Prinz Eugen and covering destroyers
sail

2356, 11 Feb/0028 12 Feb

━━━━━ ROUTE TAKEN BY GERMAN SQUADRON
━·━·━ BRITISH AIRCRAFT AND SUBMARINE PATROLS

0   MILES   200
0   KILOMETRES   300

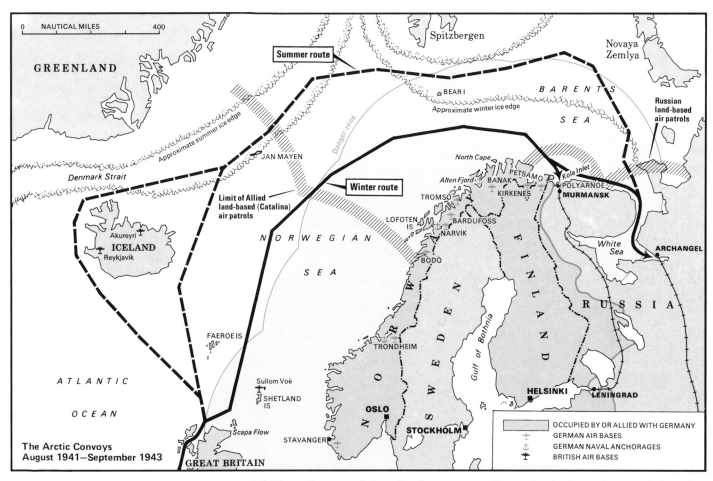

The Arctic Convoys
August 1941–September 1943

Above: The British destroyer Velox *making a smoke screen.*

Left: Convoy PQ-17 on its way to North Russia, photographed by a German aircraft. Only ten ships reached Murmansk.

airfields and escorted by six destroyers. Breakdown of the radar of the RAF scouting aircraft kept aloft especially to watch for such a break-out, permitted the German squadron to reach the Straits of Dover before being detected. A lamentable failure of the torpedo plane squadrons of RAF Coastal Command to react swiftly or efficiently enough and of a large force of aircraft of Bomber Command to attack effectively thereafter, permitted them to pass the Straits unscathed. 'Forlorn hopes' in the shape of a partially-trained squadron of six slow Swordfish torpedo-planes, which earned its leader, Lieutenant-Commander Eugene Esmonde a posthumous Victoria Cross, and another by the squadron of veteran World War I destroyers based on Harwich, achieved nothing. Both the German battle-cruisers were mined off the Dutch coast, however. The *Gneisenau* was never to go to sea again.

Meanwhile, in the Atlantic, U-boat strength had reached a new high level and was rapidly increasing. By July there were 140 operational boats out of a total of 331; groups of up to 20 could be deployed, improving the chances of intercepting convoys and then of swamping the defence. The Black Gap in mid-Atlantic where air cover could not be given to the convoys was appreciated and advantage taken of it.

On the other hand the force available for convoy escort had increased numerically and the equipment and training very much improved. Equipment included 10-centimetre ship-borne radar, enabling surfaced U-boats to be detected at a range of several miles; ship-borne High Frequency Direction Finders with which U-boats could be pin-pointed if they transmitted on radio; methods of hunting deep-diving submarines and depth-charges with which to attack them; aircraft, too, were being provided with a new, more

effective depth-charge. To enable fast (destroyer) escorts to remain with convoys throughout their voyages, tankers from which they could refuel were provided. To enable escorts to concentrate on U-boat hunting when an attack developed, special rescue ships were equipped and provided to pick up survivors. Furthermore, many of the escort commanders and group leaders had by now gained an experience and expertise which made them more dangerous opponents.

The Arctic convoys begin

Nevertheless the number of escorts available was still less than adequate; not all the escort groups had yet received the latest equipment, nor had they acquired the efficiency of the more experienced. Thus in the Atlantic fortunes in the battle swung from one side to the other; some convoys lost many of their number, but more reached their destinations unassailed.

A new convoy route had meanwhile been growing in importance, through the Arctic to Archangel or Murmansk. The first convoy had sailed on August 22, 1941, less than two months after Russia had become a reluctant ally of Britain through Hitler's treacherous attack. The first 11 convoys suffered only trifling loss and it was not until March 1942 that a serious threat to them developed through the deployment in northern Norway of the battleship *Tirpitz* and the *Admiral Scheer*, of eight U-boats and bomber squadrons of the German Air Force.

On March 6 the *Tirpitz* and three destroyers narrowly missed intercepting the outward-bound convoy PQ12 and the homeward QP8. In her turn the battleship was located and unsuccessfully attacked by torpedo planes from the *Victorious*, which narrow escape led to a ban on the *Tirpitz*'s employ-

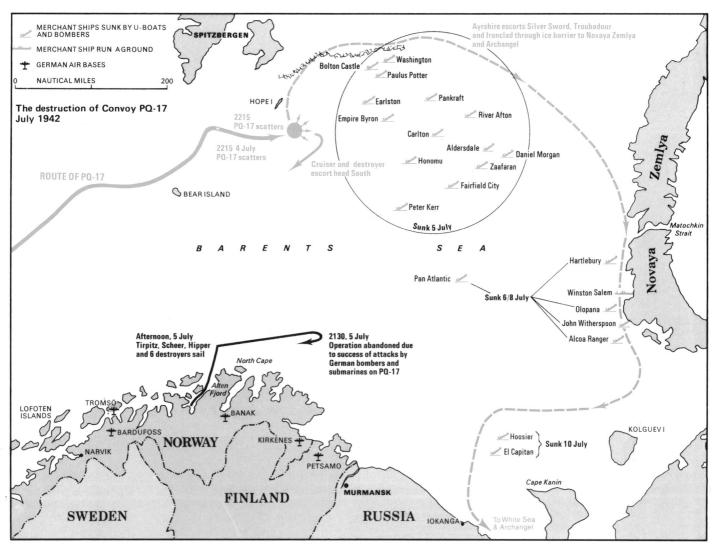

The destruction of Convoy PQ-17 July 1942

SPITZBERGEN

Ayrshire escorts Silver Sword, Troubadour and Ironclad through ice barrier to Novaya Zemlya and Archangel

Washington
Bolton Castle
Paulus Potter
Earlston
Pankraft
Empire Byron
River Afton
Carlton
Aldersdale
Daniel Morgan
Honomu
Zaafaran
Fairfield City
Peter Kerr

HOPE I

2215 PQ-17 scatters
2215 4 July PQ-17 scatters

Cruiser and destroyer escort head South

ROUTE OF PQ-17

BEAR ISLAND

Sunk 5 July

B A R E N T S   S E A

Pan Atlantic

Sunk 6/8 July

Hartlebury
Winston Salem
Olopana
John Witherspoon
Alcoa Ranger

Matochkin Strait

Novaya Zemlya

Afternoon, 5 July Tirpitz, Scheer, Hipper and 6 destroyers sail

North Cape

Alten Fjord

2130, 5 July Operation abandoned due to success of attacks by German bombers and submarines on PQ-17

TROMSÖ
BANAK
LOFOTEN ISLANDS
BARDUFOSS
NARVIK
NORWAY
KIRKENES
PETSAMO

Hoosier
El Capitan
Sunk 10 July

KOLGUEV I

Cape Kanin

SWEDEN
FINLAND
MURMANSK
RUSSIA
IOKANGA
To White Sea & Archangel

---

was sunk by air attack two months later on her way back to England.

Round QP11, homeward bound at the beginning of May, a surface action developed; firstly the covering cruiser *Edinburgh* was torpedoed and so crippled that she had to turn back for Murmansk, barely under control, screened by the destroyers *Forester* and *Foresight*. This left four elderly destroyers to defend the convoy against three powerful German Z-class destroyers which intercepted it on May 1; but so skilfully and with such bold bravado did the escort leader, Commander M. Richmond, repeatedly interpose his ships between the enemy and the convoy that the Germans eventually gave up and steered for easier prey, the limping *Edinburgh*. There in a series of confused fights the *Hermann Schoemann* was sunk by the cruiser and both the British destroyers damaged. A German torpedo at the end of its run hit and finally immobilized the *Edinburgh* which had to be scuttled. The Germans then withdrew.

PQ17 sails to destruction

On May 3 the first torpedo attack by He 111 aircraft sank three ships of PQ15. The attack on PQ16 was mainly by aircraft which sank six ships, though another was sunk by a U-boat. The further running of Arctic convoys during the summer period of continuous daylight had become 'an unsound operation with the dice loaded against us in every direction', in the words of Admiral Sir Dudley Pound, First Sea Lord. Nevertheless Churchill and Roosevelt decided that to aid

their hard-pressed Russian ally, they were to continue. On June 27, PQ17, comprising 34 freighters and tankers, the majority American, sailed from Iceland. At the same time the German High Command had decided that an all-out effort by air, surface and submarine forces should be made to destroy it.

The air force available comprised 103 Ju 88 and 30 Ju 87 dive-bombers, 15 He 115 torpedo seaplanes, 42 He 111 torpedo landplanes and 74 reconnaissance aircraft. Ten U-boats would be concentrated against the convoy. To be moved to Altenfiord, near the North Cape, in time to sortie and intervene were the *Tirpitz*, *Lützow*, *Admiral Scheer*, *Admiral Hipper* and ten destroyers.

The close escort of PQ17 under Commander J. E. Broome in the old destroyer *Keppel* was numerically impressive, but they were either old destroyers adapted primarily for hunting submarines, corvettes, minesweepers, trawlers or little anti-aircraft ships. Such a force could not be expected on its own to do more than delay the German surface squadron if it attacked; a supporting escort of two British and two American cruisers under Rear Admiral Louis Hamilton in the *London* was not to be risked far into the Barents Sea; the covering squadron, centred on two battleships (one British, one American) and the aircraft carrier *Victorious*, hovered distantly far to the westward.

Between the evening of July 2 and that of the 4th, Broome's close escorts defeated every effort of the U-boats to get at their convoy; and they kept the casualties from air attack down to three ships lost and one

Above: The boats of the American SS Carlton come alongside the U-boat which has torpedoed her, to allow the Germans to interrogate her captain.

Above left: A U-boat scores a hit on one of the defenceless stragglers from the tragically scattered PQ-17.

Left: As a torpedoed merchantman sinks, her captive balloon can be seen above her stern. This was a simple but effective defence against low-level strafing runs.

ment against the convoys. But U-boats, destroyers, torpedo planes and bombers steadily increased their attacks. Thus PQ13 lost five of its 19 ships. The German destroyer *Z26* was sunk by the escort but in reply the destroyer *Eclipse* was damaged while the cruiser *Trinidad* was hit by one of her own torpedoes which malfunctioned in the bitter cold. She reached Murmansk damaged but

German aircraft fly over a torpedo-boat during the 'Channel Dash' in February 1942.

damaged for which they exacted a stiff toll of aircraft shot down. But then, from the Admiralty, where information of the *Tirpitz*'s arrival at Alterfiord had been received, came orders for the withdrawal of the cruiser squadron and for the convoy to scatter. These signals delivered the erstwhile compact and well-defended convoy piece-meal and defenceless into the hands of the U-boats and aircraft. Twenty-one ships were sunk during the next five days. The *Tirpitz*, *Scheer*, *Hipper* and seven destroyers put to sea on the afternoon of July 5, but returned to harbour the same day. The massacre of PQ17 was both a major naval disaster and a stain on the reputation and honour of the Royal Navy, Controversy about apportionment of the blame has continued ever since.

Special *Luftwaffe* effort for PQ18

The fact remained, however, that the operation had been undertaken in the face of apparently impossible odds. Nevertheless it was to be repeated in September. No battle squadron or aircraft carrier support was to be given inside the Barents Sea. Instead, on the correct assumption that the Germans would not face a powerful torpedo threat to their few large surface units, a strong 'Fighting Destroyer Escort'—16 destroyers—was provided. The close escort of A/S vessels was reinforced by the A/A cruiser *Scylla*, two converted A/A ships and—most significantly—the escort carrier *Avenger*, operating three A/S Swordfish and 12 Hurricane MKI fighters, with her personal escort of two destroyers.

As with PQ17 there was a Cruiser Covering Force of three cruisers and a Distant Covering Force centring on the battleships *Anson* and *Duke of York*. But as, in the event, the Germans did not send their surface ships against PQ18, neither of these forces played any significant part. Instead,

U107

The fourteen boats of the IXB type built between 1938 and 1940 between them sank more than 1.4 million tons of shipping in the Battle of the Atlantic. This was ten percent of the total tonnage sunk by U-boats and gives some idea of how near the Allies came to defeat at sea. *U107* was commissioned in October 1940 and operated in the North Atlantic and off Freetown at various times. After sinking 38 ships totalling 217,751 tons she was finally depth-charged by a Sunderland flying boat of RAF Coastal Command in August 1944. The Type IX U-boat was 251 feet long and was armed with four 21-inch torpedo-tubes forward and two aft. She carried twenty-two torpedoes and enough fuel to take her 8,700 miles on the surface. Like other U-Boats *U107* had her anti-aircraft guns increased in 1943 to meet the growing threat from aircraft. She is depicted here as she appeared in 1941.

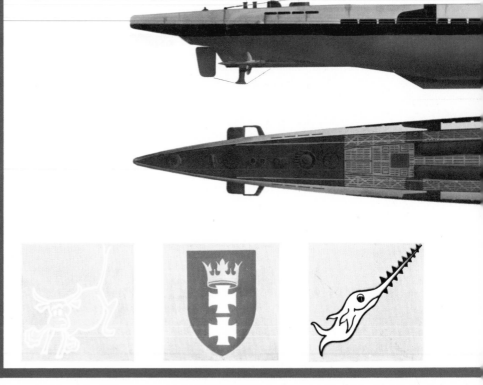

the German Air Force in northern Norway more than 220 bombers and torpedo planes—and the U-boat arm were enjoined to make a special effort. U-boats succeeded in sinking three of the convoy but they lost three of their own number in the process.

The massed air attacks which began on September 13 were initially far more effective. The guns of the escorts took a certain toll of the first swarm of torpedo planes as they sped in low over the water. The *Avenger*, however, inexperienced as yet in convoy defence, had used all her fighters against a number of Ju 88 bombers which had been attacking far less dangerously; none were now available. The surviving majority of the torpedo planes, therefore, were able to launch scores of torpedoes at close range to sink eight ships. Profiting from lessons learned by all the defenders from this attack, later efforts found the Hurricanes ready for them and the A/A ships deployed where they could bring their guns most effectively into action. The morale of the airmen did not survive this welcome and the heavy losses they suffered. Later attacks

The battleship Tirpitz *on one of her rare sorties in Norwegian waters.*

were far less boldly delivered. PQ18 lost only two more ships; some forty German aircraft were destroyed.

The homeward bound QP14, to which the majority of the escorts transferred, was attacked only by U-boats which, in the absence of the *Avenger* and her Swordfish, and in water conditions which made the Asdic ineffective, succeeded in sinking the destroyer *Somali*, the minesweeper *Leda* and four of the convoy.

The biggest convoy yet

PQ18 was the last of the summer convoys to Russia, chiefly because escorts could not be spared from the more vital operation to be launched in the autumn—Operation 'Torch', the Anglo-American landings in North Africa. This was in itself the greatest convoy operation ever mounted up to that time and it was surprisingly uneventful. The many troop and supply convoys which set out during October 1942 from the United States or the United Kingdom completed their Atlantic voyages undisturbed and almost totally unseen by the enemy.

Credit for this must go largely to the fact that the U-boats were fully occupied attack-

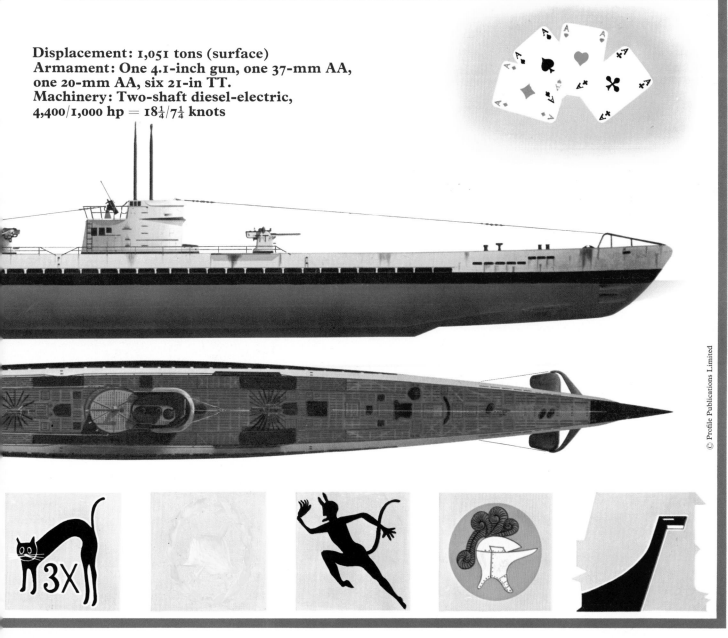

Displacement: 1,051 tons (surface)
Armament: One 4.1-inch gun, one 37-mm AA, one 20-mm AA, six 21-in TT.
Machinery: Two-shaft diesel-electric, 4,400/1,000 hp = 18¼/7¼ knots

© Profile Publications Limited

ing the trade convoys, both trans-atlantic and on the route between Sierra Leone and the UK. Several of the former suffered heavy losses in September and October. In the south, ten U-boats were concentrated against the north-bound SL125 from which, over seven days, thirteen ships were sunk; but this it was that principally enabled the first military convoys for North Africa to pass unsighted and unscathed.

Too late, Dönitz re-deployed his U-boats only to lose seven of them in a week to obtain meagre success against the numerous escorts. Then, against his earnest protests, he was ordered to send more boats to the Mediterranean and the approaches to Gibraltar. Thus the heavy loss-rate amongst Atlantic shipping in November had been sharply cut by the end of the year, aided by the seasonal tempestuous weather. Nevertheless the U-boats were employing, in the words of an Admiralty report, 'a bolder and more reckless strategy'. It was clear that 1943 would see the battle reach its point of decision.

Meanwhile, on the last day of 1942 the German surface fleet was to suffer a moral

In defence of Convoy JW51B the escorts fought a classic destroyer action.

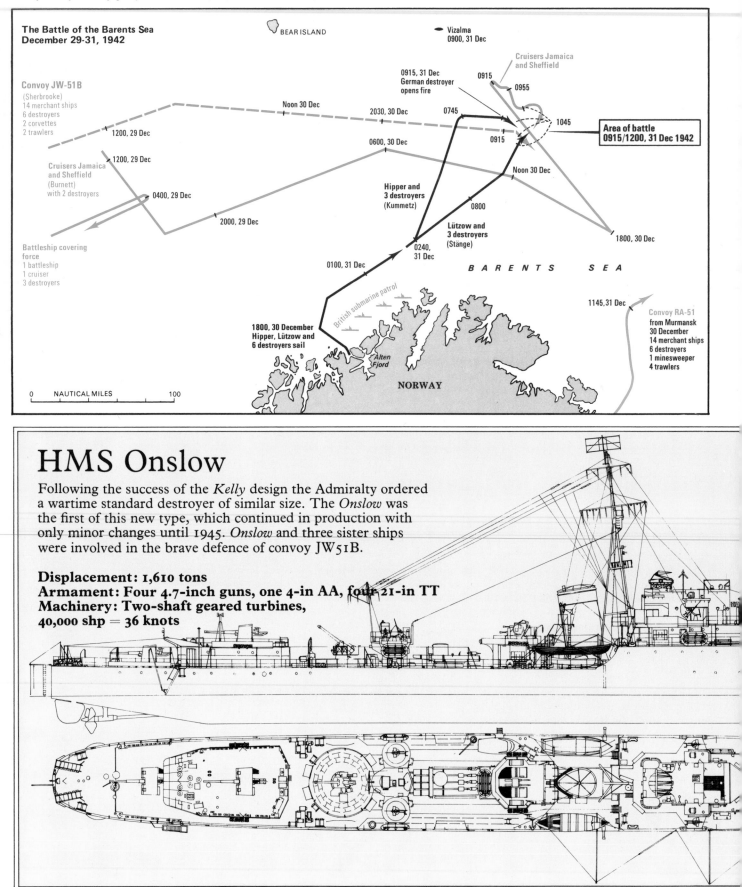

HMS Onslow

Following the success of the *Kelly* design the Admiralty ordered a wartime standard destroyer of similar size. The *Onslow* was the first of this new type, which continued in production with only minor changes until 1945. *Onslow* and three sister ships were involved in the brave defence of convoy JW51B.

Displacement: 1,610 tons
Armament: Four 4.7-inch guns, one 4-in AA, four 21-in TT
Machinery: Two-shaft geared turbines, 40,000 shp = 36 knots

defeat which was to have fatal consequences for it. The Artic Convoys to Russia had been resumed in December. The first was left undisturbed by the German squadron— *Admiral Hipper, Lützow* and six destroyers assembled in Altenfiord—and arrived at Murmansk unscathed. Admiral Schniewind, commanding in the north, determined that this should not happen to the next which, from the reports of shadowing U-boats, would be off the North Cape early on the 31st. Late on the 30th, therefore, the squadron sailed to intercept at dawn.

The convoy JW51B had been reduced from 14 to 12 by the straggling of two ships during a fierce gale with driving snow. The close escort, commanded by Captain R. St. V. Sherbrooke in the destroyer *Onslow*, consisted of four of that class, mounting a puny armament of four 4-inch guns each, the old destroyer *Achates*, two corvettes and a trawler. Another trawler was escorting one of the stragglers; the minesweeper *Bramble* had also been detached to search for the other. Some 30 miles to the north at dawn on the 31st was Rear Admiral Burnett's covering force of two 6-inch cruisers— *Sheffield* and *Jamaica*. Of this force, Admiral Kummetz in the *Hipper*, had no knowledge.

The situation was apparently one in which the German squadron would be able to brush aside the meagre opposition of the close escort and massacre the convoy. And as the Arctic night slowly gave way to a misty greyness interspersed with the black of drifting snow storms, the interception was duly made at 0820 on the 31st.

During the next three hours the *Hipper* and three destroyers were held off by the threat of torpedo attack by Sherbrooke's little ships. During that time the *Achates*, screening the convoy with smoke, was fatally

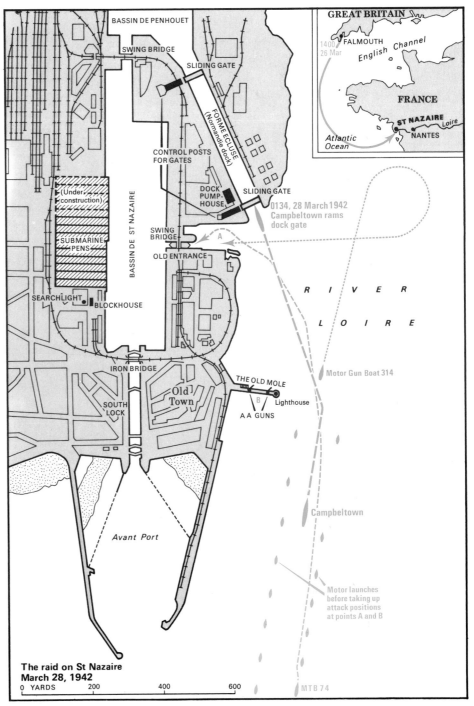

The raid on St Nazaire
March 28, 1942

0 YARDS   200   400   600

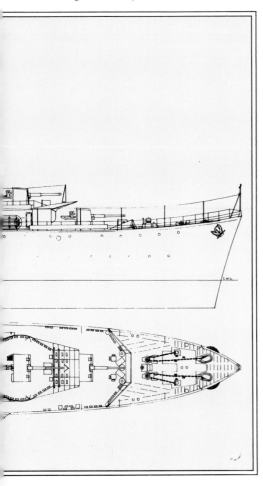

damaged, eventually to sink; the little *Bramble*, stumbling out of the snow smother on to the scene, was blown out of the water; and the *Onslow* was heavily damaged. But the convoy was unharmed. And when, at 1130 the *Sheffield* and *Jamaica* arrived, the *Hipper*, hit and damaged, at once fled, while one of her destroyers was sunk.

Similarly when the *Lützow* and her three destroyers arrived according to plan at the far side of the convoy at 1045, her captain was too timid to risk an attack until the weather cleared at 1140, by which time his admiral was calling for a general withdrawal, which he obeyed, having achieved nothing.

The futile performance by the German surface fleet, induced though it was by Hitler's own injunctions against taking any risks with it, infuriated the German leader. Grand Admiral Raeder was ordered to decommission all the big warships; when he objected and resigned, Dönitz was appointed in his place. The war at sea was in the future to revolve mainly round the activities of his U-boats.

In 1942 one of the bravest combined operations of the war was mounted to destroy the dry dock at St Nazaire and thereby force the withdrawal of the Tirpitz, Germany's only remaining battleship, to home ports. To confuse the port's defenders the destroyer HMS Campbeltown was converted to resemble a German Möwe class torpedo boat, then operating west of Biscay ports. She was given thin armour plating and her armament was modified for close-range attack. On March 28, after some fine seamanship and navigation in the darkness and after braving withering enemy fire, the Campbeltown rammed the dock gates at 0134 hours. Ten hours later the four tons of TNT on board exploded and destroyed the dock gates. Success was gained at a cost of 250 men and all but four of the 20 smaller support craft.

Decision in the Atlantic

As the Battle of the Atlantic entered its third phase at the beginning of 1943 it was clear that it would be decisive. The U-boats enjoyed some spectacular success in the 'Black Gap' in mid-Atlantic, however, scientists, statisticians and air power swung the battle the Allies' way. But despite the new technology the fight still had to be fought to the end at sea, often in appalling conditions and always against a ruthless and determined enemy. Even in victory there were heavy penalties to pay.

The year 1943 opened with operations in the North Atlantic proceeding at a modest tempo. Each side in the battle was girding itself for a decisive encounter. As long ago as August 1942 Dönitz had written in his War Diary that 'difficulties which confront us in the conduct of the war can only lead, in the normal course of events, to high, and indeed intolerable losses.'

The fact was that Allied scientists were winning the technical war, particularly in the introduction of short wave radar and shipborne H/F D/F, about neither of which the Germans were aware. German scientists had not been able to provide their U-boats with radar of their own. The 'Metox' search receiver being fitted in U-boats to detect enemy radar transmissions was designed for the early $1\frac{1}{2}$ metre wave length and was useless against the 10 centimetre sets now being fitted in escorting ships and aircraft. Urgent measures to improve the U-boats' equipment were in hand, such as a torpedo to home acoustically on the noise of a ship's propellers, a 'schnorchel' breathing tube to enable bat-

A convoy makes an emergency turn. This picture gives some idea of the discipline and training required to make the convoy system workable—such turns had to be executed immediately and in unison or else there could be multiple collisions. A convoy looked a tempting target but the formation proved to be the only way of beating the U-boats as it forced them to come within range of the escorts.

teries to be re-charged while submerged, and new types of boat with a very high submerged speed. But none of these would emerge in time to affect the decision in the Battle of the Atlantic.

On the Allied side, much improved technical equipment was being provided. The escorts were becoming more and more expert as a result of experience and the thorough training provided. In addition the number of escorts available had at last become adequate. This had come about partly as a result of operational research under the leadership of Professor P. M. S. Blackett (later Lord Blackett) which was able to demonstrate statistically that by increasing the size of convoys open to attack at any one time, losses could be enormously reduced.

Fewer convoys meant either larger surface escorts or a surplus of escorts. Initially the latter was accepted and converted into groups which could reinforce the regular escort of a convoy under threat. Some of these groups were centred on escort carriers which, after having been first used in the North African landings to provide fighter cover until Air Force squadrons could get themselves established ashore, were now given the employment for which they had been designed. The first to operate in the Atlantic had been the USS *Bogue* in March, but by the end of that month HMS *Biter* had become the centre of a British Support Group shepherding convoys through the 'Black Gap'.

Furthermore, the fewer convoys could more easily be given continuous escort by the shore-based VLR Liberators. Professor Blackett had forecast that with continuous air escort a 64 per-cent reduction of losses in convoy could be expected. This and his calculations to show how much more useful results an aircraft could achieve on escort duty compared to bombing operations over Germany, resulted in the number allocated to Coastal Command being raised from ten to 40, allowing about 13 to be operational at any one time.

Another factor giving the defence improved prospects was the remarkable accuracy with which the Tracking Team in the Admiralty was able to plot the positions of U-boats from the various intelligence sources available to them by this time. Convoys could, and often were able to successfully, divert away from the patrol lines spread to catch them.

So it was that Allied prospects in the Battle of the Atlantic at the beginning of March 1943 were brighter than they had ever been. Yet it was in that month that three homeward-bound convoys suffered such appalling losses, with the U-boats concerned apparently remaining unscathed, that, in the Admiralty, despairing voices were raised to cast doubt upon the convoy system. The first of these convoys, SC121, was disorganised by mountainous seas with snow, followed by fog as the winds took off.

A lookout keeps a watch for targets or hostile ships and aircraft from the conning-tower of a U-boat in the Atlantic.

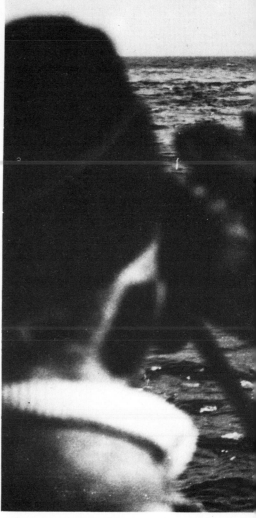

A Short Sunderland presses home a depth charge attack on a U-boat. Over 700 Sunderlands were built and their long range of 2,980 miles made them ideal for anti-submarine patrol duties.

Seventeen U-boats which pursued through the storm picked off stragglers and then pressed on to get amongst the main body of the convoy and sink a total of 13 ships without loss to themselves.

That an efficient escort could beat off such an attack, was, in the same week, demonstrated by the escort of HX228 where the mixed British, Free French and Polish Group led by Commander A. A. Tait in the destroyer *Harvester* kept losses down to four of the convoy while destroying two U-boats, and seriously damaging others. Unfortunately the *Harvester*, immobilized through ramming one of these, was also torpedoed and sunk, her captain being lost with her.

But when the next convoy HX229 was set upon ten days later, again in the 'Black Gap' by 38 U-boats, the escort was overwhelmed and 13 ships were sent to the bottom in the first two days. The same wolf-pack then attacked SC122 from which eight ships were sunk. Not until Liberators from Iceland were able to join the escort was one U-boat destroyed. Although Dönitz's War Diary recorded that 'nearly all the other boats suffered from depth-charges or bombs and two were severely damaged', this was not known by the defenders. And though the total of 34 ships lost out of three convoys was calamitous, it had to be seen in conjunction with the several other convoys which, around

HMS Warspite

The most famous British battleship, with possibly the finest fighting record of any ship in World War II, *Warspite* suffered bomb damage at Crete, was hit by glider bombs at Salerno and was finally mined in the Channel, but still survived.

A U-boat officer surveys the wreckage of an American merchant ship. In March 1943 U-boats sank 627,000 tons of shipping; by June the total had been reduced to 18,000 tons for the month.

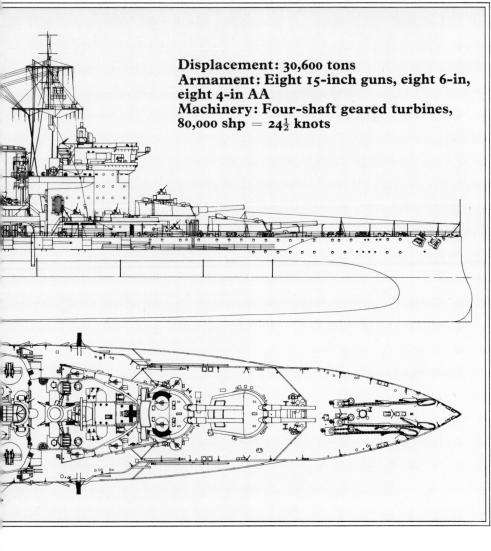

Displacement: 30,600 tons
Armament: Eight 15-inch guns, eight 6-in, eight 4-in AA
Machinery: Four-shaft geared turbines, 80,000 shp = 24½ knots

this time were being got safely through to their destinations.

The climax of the battle

Toward the end of March a lull occurred in the battle round the convoys. This was partly owing to the succession of storms of hurricane force which swept the routes and partly owing to the necessity for those U-boats which were not in need of repair to return to base for replenishment and rearmament. Fresh boats from Germany and from the Biscay bases streamed forth to take their places—no less than 98 during April. But to Dönitz's chagrin they had, according to his War Diary: 'Meagre success, achieved generally at the cost of heavy losses'; and in fact during the last week in April, five U-boats were destroyed round the convoys and many others damaged for an almost negligible loss of merchant ships. A supreme effort by a concentration of the huge number of U-boats on patrol was organised.

Their target was the small, slow, outward-bound Convoy ONS5 of 40 ships escorted by Group B7, led by Commander Peter Gretton, one of the most successful and well-trained groups, comprising the old destroyer *Duncan* (Gretton's own ship), another old destroyer *Vidette*, the frigate *Tay* and four corvettes. After a week of appalling weather the gath-

123

ering of elderly freighters had battled their way through mountainous seas to a position south of Iceland on April 28 where it was intercepted and reported by the first of the swarm of U-boats spread in waiting for it. That night the wolves began to close in; but though they made repeated efforts to penetrate the screen, they were radar-detected each time and driven off. Only one, waiting submerged ahead of the convoy managed to sink one ship on the next morning and escape.

The foul weather then returned in full fury. Over the next five days the convoy became disorganised; a Support Group of five destroyers had joined in the interval but three of them as well as the *Duncan*, unable to refuel from the escort tanker, had by May 3 been forced to return to harbour to do so, leaving Lieutenant Commander R. E. Sherwood, RNR of the *Tay* as Senior Officer of the Escort. During the 4th the massed attack which was to begin that evening and continue for the next 24 hours, was foreshadowed by the sighting and chasing of a number of U-boats (one of them caught and destroyed by a flying-boat of the RCAF) and the cluttering of the radio waves with their excited signals. Eleven ships were sunk; one U-boat was depth-charged to destruction by

the corvette *Pink* during the 5th, a rate of exchange that seemed to foretell the annihilation of the convoy.

Offensive from out of the fog

But at dusk that day the convoy slipped under the shroud of dense fog which often followed in the wake of an Atlantic cyclone. The advantage of invisibility was suddenly transferred to the radar-equipped defenders: through the night that followed the groping U-boats were surprised again and again. The corvette *Loosestrife*, the *Vidette*, the destroyer *Oribi* and the frigate *Pelican* of a Group arriving to give support, each sank a U-boat. Not a ship of the convoy was touched. At daybreak the defeated wolf packs were called off. The final grim score—12 merchantmen lost against five attackers destroyed by surface escorts and two more by associated air patrols, while another two, pounding through stormy seas, had collided and gone to the bottom—was recognised by Dönitz as a clear defeat for the U-boats.

Right: Operating the controls of a U-boat while diving, the most tense moment of all for submariners in peace and war.

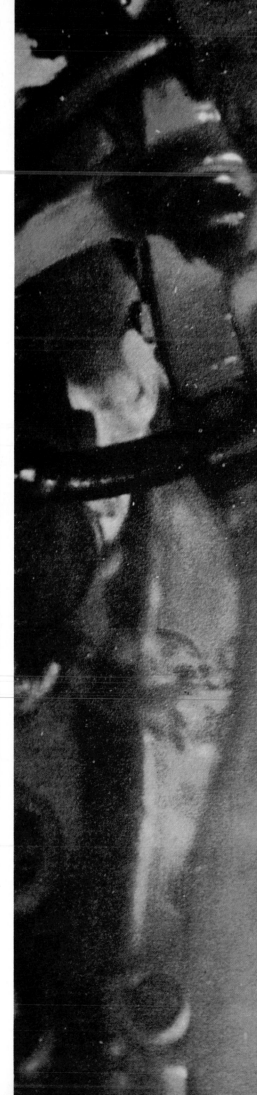

Above: The end of a captured U-boat. Although decided by mid-1943, the Battle of the Atlantic continued until the end of the war when 156 U-boats surrendered and another 221 were destroyed or scuttled by their crews.

Left: A Catalina flying boat drops a depth-charge. The need for an air-dropped depth-charge had not been foreseen pre-war and it took time to produce.

HMS Biter

Built on a merchant ship hull, *Biter* was one of the first escort carriers brought into service to bridge the 'Black Gap' in land-based air cover.

Displacement: 8,200 tons. Armament: Three 4-inch AA guns, ten 20-mm AA guns, 16 aircraft.

The passage of this convoy battle has been generally recognised as the grand climax and moment of decision in the Battle of the Atlantic. Around the convoys which followed the U-boats gathered again; but knowledge of the recent losses of their comrades and of the many hair-breadth escapes from destruction of the survivors had eroded the morale of the U-boat commanders. Even when not prevented from reaching attacking positions by the ubiquitous escort planes, either shore-based Liberators or the carrier planes, they shrank from closing into the attack. Those which did were pounced upon and sunk or severely damaged before they could achieve anything.

During May the U-boat fleet suffered the appalling losses of 41 of their number, of which 25 were sunk by convoy escorts, sea or air. Dönitz, who had lost his son in one of them, threw in the sponge and withdrew the survivors from the North Atlantic.

Donitz's costly tactical error

Six of the sunk U-boats had been destroyed on passage to and from their bases by aircraft on Biscay patrol. It had come about as a result of a costly tactical mistake by Dönitz.

The Bay patrols had up to now been markedly unprofitable, accounting for only an average of one U-boat a month at a cost in flying hours 25 times greater than each 'kill' by aircraft round the convoys. But now the aircraft were being increasingly fitted with 10 centimetre radar. When evidence came to hand of the failure of the 'Metox' to detect the aircrafts' transmissions, Dönitz had ordered his U-boats to dive by night and surface long enough to charge batteries by day, diving if attacked. When this led to four losses during the first half of May, Dönitz ordered his commanders to stay on the surface and fight it out with the aircraft. It was a fatal policy costing 27 U-boats between then and the end of July when the earlier tactics were resumed and sinkings reverted to the one-a-month average.

From May to September 1943, operating in the South Atlantic, the Gibraltar approaches and the Arctic, the U-boats sank just nine ships in convoy at a cost of 33 of their own number sunk by the escorts. From June 1943 onwards the number of merchant ships emerging from Allied shipyards greatly exceeded the losses from all causes: U-boats led an increasingly harried existence with an average life of $1\frac{1}{2}$ patrols before being de-

stroyed. As time went on it was no longer only in the vicinity of convoys that they were in dire peril. Increasingly their movements were effectively tracked and they fell victims to hunting groups, such as that led by Captain Walker which accounted for six U-boats in a single patrol in February 1944, or to groups centred on escort carriers, the majority American, which had a rich harvest of them between March and July of that year.

By September 1943 the acoustic homing torpedo was in production and the U-boats returned with renewed hope to the North Atlantic. After a brief success with the new weapon they were again totally defeated.

In 1944, U-boats began to be fitted with the Schnorchel breathing tube which was to give them greater immunity from air attack and enable them to operate in coastal waters of the British Isles. But this did not affect the issue and their loss-rate remained agonising, particularly when they were deployed against the Allied invasion forces in the Channel. Nor did the new fast U-boats under development become operational before the end of the war.

With a discipline and courage which their enemies were forced to admire, U-boat crews continued to operate widely-spread over the

Legionario

The big destroyers of the Soldati Class were built between 1937 and 1942 and were the last destroyers completed for the Italian Navy in World War II. Eleven out of nineteen were sunk and most of the remainder were taken over by the Allies in 1943. Some units, including the *Legionario*, had a fifth gun and all had two sets of triple torpedo-tubes.

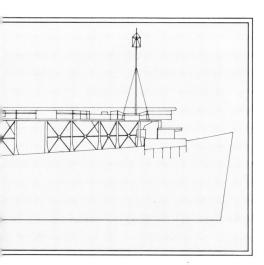

Above : The submarine U570 *surrenders to the Royal Navy south of Iceland in August 1941. She went into service as HMS* Graph *and was used against her former masters.*

Left : The sloop Wild Goose, *part of the 2nd Support Group, commanded by Captain F. J. Walker, the outstanding anti-submarine officer of the war. In February of 1944 this group sunk 6 U-boats in one trip, all in the area 200–400 miles south-west of Ireland where Admiral Dönitz had concentrated his forces to attack convoys bound for the Mediterranean and the Atlantic convoys which were routed well to the south at that time of year.*

oceans to the last, tying down vast forces of the Allies. As Dönitz put it in his Memoirs: 'We came again and again to the same conclusion: the U-boat campaign must be continued with the forces available. Losses, which bear no relation to the success achieved, must be accepted, bitter though they were.'

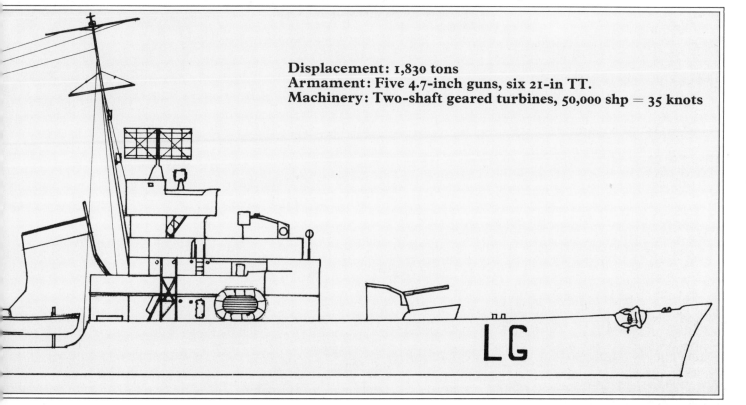

Displacement: 1,830 tons
Armament: Five 4.7-inch guns, six 21-in TT.
Machinery: Two-shaft geared turbines, 50,000 shp = 35 knots

Victory in the Med

At the beginning of 1942 the Axis powers were winning the war in the Mediterranean and North Africa. Malta was under constant siege and Rommel's supply ships were crossing the Mediterranean almost unopposed. Determined efforts, at a great cost in men and ships, saved Malta and hard won Allied sea power was the underlying cause of victory at El Alamein. The landing of forces in North Africa, Sicily, Italy—under savage air attack—and finally the South of France virtually completed the Allied naval effort in the Mediterranean.

The battleship Nelson *fires her 16-inch guns. The blast has created an area of disturbed water for some yards away from the ship's side and the noise was audible ten miles away.*

The safe passage of three supply ships from Alexandria to Malta in a convoy covered by the meagre remnant of the Mediterranean Fleet—Vian's four light cruisers—in the second half of January 1942 was made possible by the British possession of the Cyrenaican airfields whence fighter cover could be supplied over the whole route. It was to be Malta's last substantial relief for many months; and in the meantime the island was suffering the most devastating of the several air assaults she endured, as *Fliegerkorps II*'s count of raids rose in January to 262, opposed by Hurricanes whose number had fallen to eleven by the middle of February.

This 'blitz' was reducing Malta's offensive capabilities, aerial and submarine, to negligible proportions—the submarine base would eventually be closed down at the end of April. The British naval objective was now confined to attempting to keep Malta sup-plied. Force 'H', deprived of the *Ark Royal*'s air support, could no longer bring in convoys from the west. It was able, however, to cover the old carriers *Eagle* and *Argus* when they sortied on three occasions during March to fly off a total of 45 Spitfires for the first time to the island. A first attempt to run a convoy from Alexandria in mid-February resulted in two of the three escorted transports being sunk by air attack in 'Bomb Alley' between Crete and Cyrenaica; the third was damaged and sent into Tobruk. A further convoy of three fast merchantmen and the supply ship HMS *Breconshire* set out on March 20 with a close escort of the AA cruiser *Carlisle* and seven destroyers and covered by Rear Admiral Vian's three cruisers, *Cleopatra* (flagship), *Dido* and *Euryalus* and four more destroyers. From Malta the cruiser *Penelope* and a destroyer came out to meet them. Although bold and brilliant tactics by Vian's force fended off a much superior Italian squadron under Admiral Iachino in the Gulf of Sirté to allow two of the freighters and the *Breconshire* to reach Malta, the German dive-bombers sank the latter before she could be unloaded and only 5,000 tons from the remainder were saved.

Axis consider Malta defeated

The enemy's bomber sorties against Malta during April totalled 9,599 with 6,700 tons of bombs. In spite of further deliveries of Spitfires flown in from USS *Wasp*, the dockyards became untenable and the submarine base had to be closed down. Italian convoys were crossing the Mediterranean virtually unscathed. The Axis C-in-C, Field Marshal Kesselring, reported Malta neutralised and transferred much of his air force to Libya.

Even as he was doing so, however, Malta's ability to survive was being restored by the arrival of 60 Spitfires from USS *Wasp* and HMS *Eagle* on May 9 to bring about a sudden, dramatic transformation in the aerial situation. The worst of Malta's ordeal by bomb had passed but the problem of supplying her remained critical. It was decided that a convoy must be attempted in June—simultaneously from east and west on this occasion.

The convoy from Alexandria (Operation 'Vigorous') eleven freighters escorted by all that was left of the Mediterranean Fleet under the tactical command of Admiral Vian, was set upon by a swarm of German dive-bombers. It had had two freighters sunk (two others had been sent back to harbour) when, on the evening of June 14, it became clear that at daybreak it must encounter the Italian battle-fleet in full force if it continued on course. While efforts to halt the latter were made by submarines, by torpedo planes from Malta and by torpedo planes and high-bombing American Liberators from Egypt, the convoy 'marched and counter-marched' indecisively, being attacked after dark by German E-boats which sank the destroyer *Hasty* and damaged the cruiser *Newcastle*. The air attacks failed to deter the Italian fleet, though the cruiser *Trento* was torpedoed and immobilised, later to be sunk by the submarine *Umbra*. With anti-aircraft ammunition running low the convoy was ordered to retire. During its return journey it suffered the loss of the cruiser *Hermione* torpedoed by *U205* and of the destroyers *Nestor* and *Airdale* to dive-bomber attacks.

Meanwhile Convoy 'Harpoon' was coming from the west, five freighters and a tanker. Westward of the Narrows a handful of Sea Hurricanes and Fulmars in the old *Eagle* were able to keep the achievements of enemy air attacks from Sardinia and Sicily down to one freighter sunk and the cruiser *Liverpool* damaged. But the covering force had then to retire, leaving only the little A/A cruiser *Cairo* (Captain C. C. Hardy) and nine destroyers to escort onwards to Malta.

Convoy to stop starvation

At dawn the next morning an Italian force of two cruisers and five destroyers came on the scene. While Captain Hardy's escort was coping with this threat, Stuka dive-bombers attacked unopposed to sink another freighter and disable the tanker. The simultaneous attack by air and sea sank two more freighters, the tanker and the destroyer *Bedouin*. Fortunately the Italian Admiral la Zara failed to follow up his advantages and the last two freighters reached Malta with 15,000 tons of cargo to keep the garrison and civil population meagrely fed for another two months. Although British fortunes elsewhere were reaching their lowest ebb with Rommel's armies at El Alamein only 160 miles from Alexandria—causing the British naval C-in-C Admiral Harwood to evacuate the base and disperse his fleet between Haifa, Port Said and Beirut—Malta was rising from the ashes. A renewed attempt to neutralise it by air attack was defeated by the strong force of Spitfires now based there, the submarine base was re-opened and once again Rommel's supplies became scanty and unreliable.

On the other hand, by August the island was facing early starvation unless a proportion at least of the convoy (Operation 'Pedestal') which passed Gibraltar on the 10th could be fought through. It comprised freighters and one large tanker, *Ohio*. On this occasion the task force escorting it as far as the Narrows was to be particularly power-

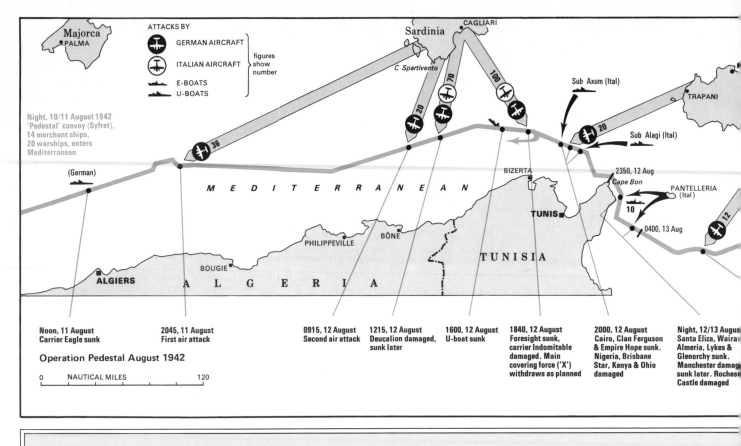

ATTACKS BY

- **GERMAN AIRCRAFT**
- **ITALIAN AIRCRAFT** — figures show number
- **E-BOATS**
- **U-BOATS**

Majorca
PALMA

Sardinia
CAGLIARI
C Spartivento

Sub Axum (Ital)

TRAPANI

Night, 10/11 August 1942
'Pedestal' convoy (Syfret),
14 merchant ships,
20 warships, enters
Mediterranean

(German)

M E D I T E R R A N E A N

Sub Alagi (Ital)

2350, 12 Aug
Cape Bon

PANTELLERIA
(Ital)

BIZERTA

0400, 13 Aug

TUNIS

PHILIPPEVILLE   BÔNE

TUNISIA

BOUGIE

ALGIERS   A L G E R I A

Noon, 11 August	2045, 11 August	0915, 12 August	1215, 12 August	1600, 12 August	1840, 12 August	2000, 12 August	Night, 12/13 August
Carrier Eagle sunk	First air attack	Second air attack	Deucalion damaged, sunk later	U-boat sunk	Foresight sunk, carrier Indomitable damaged. Main covering force ('X') withdraws as planned	Cairo, Clan Ferguson & Empire Hope sunk. Nigeria, Brisbane Star, Kenya & Ohio damaged	Santa Eliza, Waira Almeria, Lykes & Glenorchy sunk. Manchester damag sunk later. Roches Castle damaged

Operation Pedestal August 1942

0   NAUTICAL MILES   120

HMS Manchester

The *Southampton* Class cruisers were built in reply to
Japanese cruisers and marked a return to the large
cruiser. They were the first RN cruisers to adopt a
triple gun-mounting and the first designed to carry
aircraft on board. The *Manchester* is depicted as she
was when she sailed with the 'Pedestal' convoy to
Malta in August 1942. She is unusual in having an
ex-Army 40-mm Bofors gun on 'B' turret.

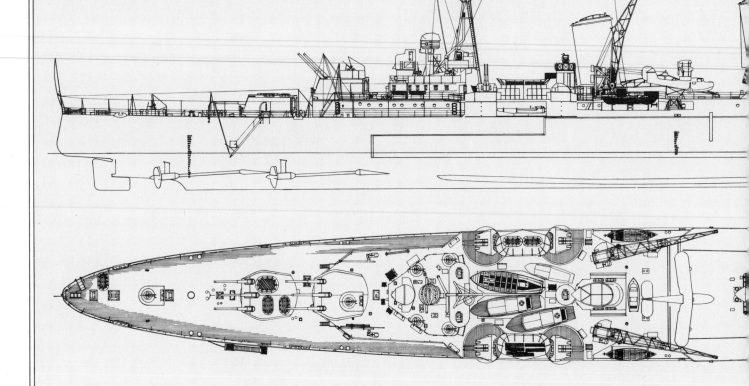

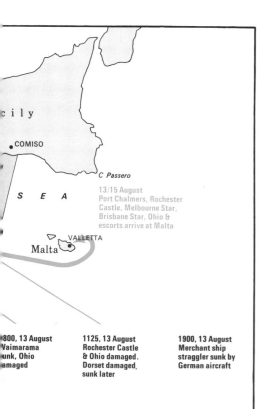

13/15 August
Port Chalmers, Rochester
Castle, Melbourne Star,
Brisbane Star, Ohio &
escorts arrive at Malta

COMISO

Sicily

C Passero

SEA

Malta

VALLETTA

800, 13 August
Waimarama
sunk, Ohio
damaged

1125, 13 August
Rochester Castle
& Ohio damaged.
Dorset damaged,
sunk later

1900, 13 August
Merchant ship
straggler sunk by
German aircraft

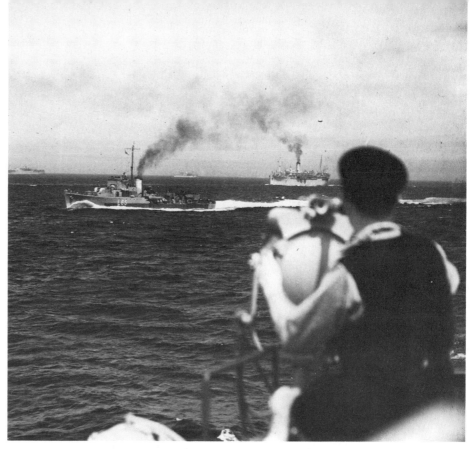

*A convoy in the Mediterranean, with the
Greek destroyer* Pindos *steaming between
the lines of merchantmen.*

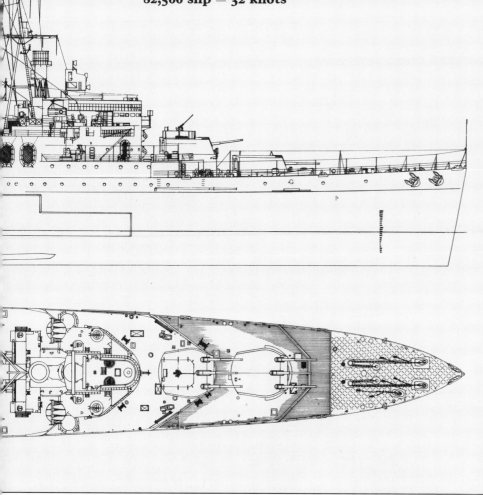

**Displacement: 9,400 tons
Armament: Twelve 6-inch guns, eight 4-in AA,
six 21-in TT
Machinery: Four-shaft geared turbines,
82,500 shp = 32 knots**

ful with the *Nelson* (flagship of Vice Admiral
E. N. Syfret) and *Rodney*, two new carriers,
Victorious and *Indomitable* and the old *Eagle*,
three cruisers, three anti-aircraft carriers and
24 destroyers. As usual, most of these went
no further than the Narrows, after which
only the three cruisers and 12 destroyers
remained as escort.

In opposition the Axis powers put out
their maximum effort. German submarines
met the force on the 11th, sinking the *Eagle*.
That evening and throughout the next day
massed air attacks were kept up from Sardinia
and Sicily. The majority were beaten off, but
one freighter was sunk, the *Indomitable*'s
flight deck was put out of action and the
destroyer *Foresight* torpedoed. Italian
U-boats encountered during the 12th
achieved nothing, the submarine *Cobalto*
being destroyed and the *Emo* damaged.

Epic struggle of the *Ohio*

Admiral Syfret's covering force had to turn
back when the convoy reached the entrance
of the Skerki Channel at nightfall. And at
dusk in those restricted waters more Italian
submarines attacked simultaneously with
dive-bombers and torpedo planes. The A/A
cruiser *Cairo* and two freighters were sunk,
the cruisers *Nigeria* and *Kenya* were torpedoed and damaged, as was the tanker *Ohio*.
But, stopped and on fire, the *Ohio* began an
epic struggle, against repeated air attacks and
mounting damage, which was to get her
finally to Malta under tow and in a sinking
condition.

Then, about midnight, Italian E-boats
took up the attack. The cruiser *Manchester*
was torpedoed and immobilised to be finally
abandoned and scuttled the following day.
Four freighters were sunk and a fifth, the
Rochester Castle, was torpedoed but was kept

131

going. Dawn on August 13 discovered her leading the undamaged *Waimarama* and *Melbourne Star*, followed at a little distance by the *Ohio* now making 16 knots, and finally Convoy Commodore Venables' flagship *Port Chalmers* and the *Dorset*. One other damaged ship, the *Brisbane Star*, was solitarily following her own route, hugging the Tunisian coast.

The convoy's ordeal was far from over at daybreak, although it was now coming within range of Spitfire air-cover from Malta. Dive-bombers blew up the *Waimarama* and the *Dorset* was crippled. She was later to be again bombed and sunk. The *Ohio*, favourite target for every attack, was further damaged; efforts now began to get her in tow of a destroyer, but early in the afternoon she was temporarily abandoned to await darkness and further help in the shape of mine-sweepers which arrived from Malta. While they struggled, between intermittent air attacks, to get her under way, the *Port Chalmers*, *Rochester Castle* and *Melbourne Star* were receiving well-deserved heroes' welcomes as they entered the Grand Harbour.

The *Ohio* had another day of painful progress to make but, as the distance from Malta decreased and the Spitfire effort grew, the air attacks petered out. Early on the 15th the tanker finally reached harbour, shortly after the enterprising *Brisbane Star*.

At a grievous loss of ships and lives Malta had been given a new lease of life which, in the event, was to prove just sufficient to save her. Even this costly success must have eluded British efforts if the Italian Navy had intervened, as with the 'Harpoon' convoy, in

HMS Illustrious

The *Illustrious* launched the strikes against Taranto in November 1940 but just two months later the Luftwaffe took its revenge when Stuka dive-bombers of *Fliegerkorps X* hit her with three 1,000 Kg bombs. She was saved by her armoured flight deck and the very high standard of fire precautions built into her design.
The *Illustrious* is depicted as she was after rebuilding, with the camouflage scheme worn at the Salerno landings in September 1943.

1 5   3 3   5 2   6 9   7 7

A, D: Admiralty Disruptive camouflage scheme – March 1942–January 1943

A

B: Admiralty Disruptive scheme – May 1943–August 1944

B

the Narrows. But an inter-service disagreement which denied air cover to the squadron of six Italian cruisers assembled for the purpose caused them to be recalled. They were intercepted as they steered for Messina early on August 13 by the submarine *Unbroken* (Lieutenant Alastair Mars) and the heavy cruiser *Bolzano* and the light cruiser *Attendolo* were both torpedoed and put out of action for the rest of the war.

Navy wins a tank battle

From Malta's airfields and submarine base, as well as from the airfields of Egypt and the submarine base at Haifa, the steady attrition of Rommel's supplies could now go on. The relative situation of the German and British armies facing one another across the Alamein line was thus that the former's supplies of every category were shrinking critically whereas the latter, their 14,000 miles of supply route round the Cape of Good Hope made secure by Allied seapower, needed only time to build up an overwhelming superiority. Realising this, Rommel, his health breaking down under the frustrations of his situation, was forced to launch an early offensive on the night August 30–31.

In the Battle of Alam el Halfa which followed, the early exhaustion of fuel reserves for Rommel's armour played an important part in his defeat. And so the stalemate on land set in during which, with the October casualty rate of ships sunk or damaged on

The tanker Ohio *battles her way through to Malta with the 'Pedestal' convoy.*

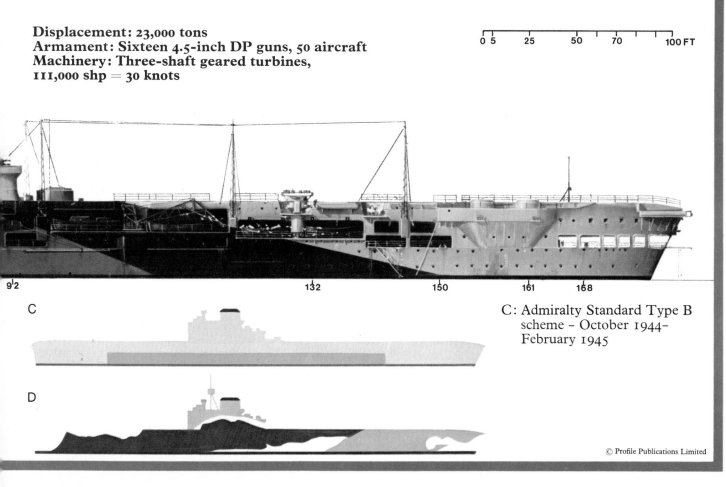

Displacement: 23,000 tons
Armament: Sixteen 4.5-inch DP guns, 50 aircraft
Machinery: Three-shaft geared turbines,
111,000 shp = 30 knots

0 5   25   50   70   100 FT

9 2   132   150   161   168

C

D

C: Admiralty Standard Type B scheme – October 1944– February 1945

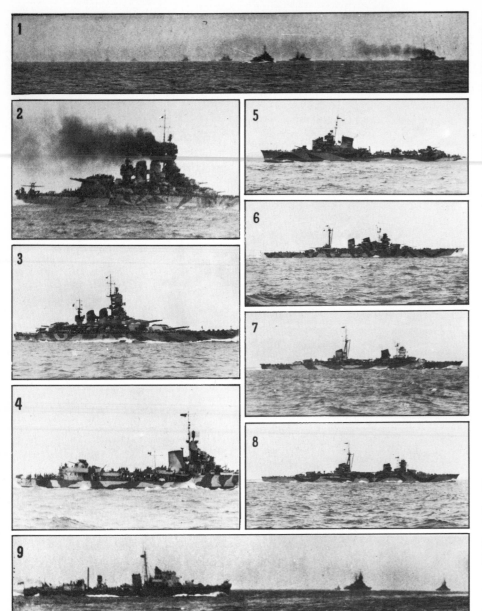

Above : British LCTs lying off Anzio. These were the first specialized amphibious craft of the war.

Right : US Army Sherman tanks disembark from an LST on the Anzio beaches, part of the Allies' enormous amphibious force.

Below : British infantry march up the beach while an American LST disgorges its load of vehicles over the bow ramp.

1 *The Italian Fleet surrenders at Malta on September 10, 1943.*

2 *The battleship* Italia *(formerly the* Littorio*), completed in 1940.*

3 *The* Vittorio Veneto, *sistership of the* Italia, *escaped destruction at Matapan.*

4 *The destroyer* Artigliere *which made 39 knots on trial.*

5 *The destroyer* Granatiere, *a sister of the* Artigliere, *completed in 1939.*

6 *The 6-inch gunned cruiser* Giuseppe Garibaldi *entered service in 1938.*

7 *The cruiser* Eugenio di Savoia, *given to Greece as war reparations.*

8 *The* Emanuele Filiberto Duca d'Aosta, *a sister of the* Eugenio di Savoia.

9 *A Hunt Class destroyer escorts the Italian Fleet to Malta.*

the route to Libya standing at 40 per cent while the British Eighth Army steadily built up a superiority of 2½ to 1 in tanks over the Axis Panzer Army and stockpiled a lavish supply of ammunition and fuel, sea power provided General Montgomery with the favourable odds he demanded before opening the Battle of El Alamein on October 23, 1942.

As the Axis armies in North Africa were driven westwards the Cyrenaican airfields fell again into British hands, enabling a replenishment convoy to be run through to Malta, arriving on November 20 without loss to the transports. The island's ordeal was at last over.

Meanwhile, through the submarine infested Atlantic, the greatest convoy operation in history up to that time had been in progress since October 2 when the first convoy of Operation 'Torch', the Anglo-American invasion of French North Africa, had sailed from the Clyde for Gibraltar. Between that date and November 8, when simultaneous landings were made in French Morocco by an all-American force, at Oran by American troops and at Algiers an Anglo-American force, both escorted by the British navy, no less than 16 large convoys from the United States and Britain made their way unmolested, partly because many of Dönitz's U-boats had been concentrated upon a trade convoy from Sierra Leone.

Even when the invasion fleets for Oran and Algiers were reported in the Straits of Gibraltar, the German Naval Staff, 'outwitted in the intelligence game' as they were subsequently to admit, did not guess their destination. Not until the 8th did any air attack upon them develop and it was the 11th before Hitler gave orders for a German army to be transported to Tunisia.

Sacrificial gallantry

In this first large-scale amphibious assault mounted by the Allies there were miscalculations and mishaps but in general the landings were successful. The most difficult and dangerous were the triple landings on the surf-pounded Moroccan coast where, apart from the natural hazards, the French coastal defences and naval forces including the battleship *Jean Bart* and the heavy cruiser *Primauget* were on the alert.

Faulty landfalls on the flat, featureless coastline and the heavy surf combined to cause much confusion and the loss of a high proportion of the landing craft. Fortunately no opposition was encountered at the beaches

A transport loads a truck into an LCT. Apart from their assault role LCTs were essential to keep the army supplied.

or confusion must have led to disaster. The French navy, reacting with sacrificial gallantry to the superior naval force opposing it, had the *Primauget* and two destroyer leaders driven ashore heavily damaged, four destroyers and seven submarines sunk and the *Jean Bart* and a number of smaller ships damaged by gunfire. On the 10th, U-boats arrived to sink four Allied transports and damage a destroyer and a tanker. But this did not affect the issue and French resistance on shore ceased at midnight on November 10/11 on orders from their C-in-C, Admiral Darlan.

At Algiers and Oran the landings on beaches along the coast on either side of the two ports were also subject to some confusion and delay; but it was during the operations to force the harbours from seaward before the facilities were destroyed that the worst casualties were suffered. At Algiers the old British destroyers *Broke* and *Malcolm*, carrying three companies of US infantry and trying unsuccessfully in the dark to find the harbour entrance, came under fire from the forts. The *Malcolm* was hit and forced to withdraw; the *Broke* finally forced her way through the boom after daybreak but, having landed her soldiers, she was was also forced by accumulating shell damage to put to sea where she foundered the next day in heavy weather.

At Oran the two lightly armed and very

vulnerable ex-American coastguard cutters, HMS *Walney* and *Hartland*, having broken the boom, were met by an overwhelming fire which destroyed them and most of their crews.

To add to the bitter wounds inflicted on each other by former Allies, French warships put to sea to engage the naval covering forces. During the two days before Oran finally capitulated, they lost one flotilla leader, three destroyers, a corvette, six submarines, three armed trawlers and five minesweepers—tragically sacrificed 'for the honour of the flag'.

Surprise landing in Sicily

With a Force 'K' of British cruisers and destroyers now operating out of Malta and a similar Force 'Q' based on Algiers, the central Mediterranean passed under Allied sea and air domination from the end of November. In spite of dogged courage by Italian seamen in continuing to run supply convoys through to Tunisia and Tripolitania in the face of daunting losses, the Axis forces were doomed to defeat. And when that came at the beginning of May 1943 there was to be no 'miracle of Dunkirk' for them. A quarter of a million prisoners fell into Allied hands.

Meanwhile, at the Casablanca Conference in January 1943 it had been decided that the next Allied objective should be Sicily. Once again a complicated organisation of convoys starting from widely separated points—in this case Egypt, Tunisia, Algiers, Oran and Britain, organised in an Eastern (mainly British and Canadian) Task Force under Vice Admiral Sir Bertram Ramsay and a Western (mainly American) Task Force under Vice-Admiral H. K. Hewitt, US Navy —came together on July 10 to land on beaches on either side of Cape Passero, Sicily's southern tip. Except for four ships out of this huge array sunk by U-boats, the Task Forces arrived unscathed and on time to achieve surprise and rapid success. By August 17 the whole of Sicily was in Allied hands.

Naval losses by the Allies in assaulting the coast of the strongly-held island in the face of powerful land-based air forces and numerous submarines were inevitable, but they were less than could have been expected. Submarine attack accounted for four merchant ships and two Tank Landing Ships (LST) sunk, two cruisers and three merchantmen damaged. In reply three German and nine Italian U-boats were destroyed. Air attack sank seven transports, two LST, a destroyer and a minesweeper, and damaged the carrier *Indomitable*, a monitor, two destroyers and several transports and landing craft.

On September 3, 1943, the Allied armies crossed the Straits of Messina under cover of a massive bombardment by the 15-inch guns of the British monitors *Abercrombie*, *Roberts* and *Erebus*, and the smaller guns of two cruisers, six destroyers and two gunboats as well as the British Eighth Army's own artillery. As the armies began their advance up the Italian peninsula, plans were made for a classic employment of sea-power in landing an army far behind the enemy's line. The position chosen was the Gulf of Salerno whence it was intended to capture the vital port of Naples. Salerno was just within extreme range of air cover by fighters from Sicily, but at that distance those aircraft could remain over the battle area only for a few minutes. It was decided, therefore, to include in the mainly British naval covering force a squadron under Vice-Admiral Sir Philip Vian of five escort carriers operating Seafires, naval adaptations of Spitfires, which would reinforce the air cover until a landing ground on shore could be secured. These ships in turn were to be given fighter cover from the carriers *Illustrious* and *Formidable* of Force 'H' operating further to seaward.

Sinking by guided bomb

D-day for the operation was September 9. As the assault convoys were approaching on the evening of the 8th, news of an Italian capitulation was broadcast; on the following morning the main body of the Italian fleet, the battleships *Roma*, *Vittorio Veneto* and *Italia* (ex-*Littorio*) with six cruisers and eight destroyers sailed from Spezia to surrender. A squadron of German bombers armed with a new weapon, the FX1400 guided bomb, were unopposed when they attacked, sinking the *Roma*. The remainder arrived at Malta, where they were joined by the rest of the Italian fleet on the 11th—a triumphant moment for Sir Andrew Cunningham who, after an interval during which he had been

the Allied Naval Commander of the Expeditional Force for 'Torch', had resumed the title of C-in-C Mediterranean, now however under the supreme command of General Eisenhower.

At Salerno, the assault convoys reached their objectives on time having met little opposition *en route*. But on this occasion surprise was not achieved and stiff fighting was necessary on shore with disaster at some points narrowly averted by timely gunfire support by the battleships *Valiant* and *Warspite*, US Cruisers *Savannah* and *Philadelphia*, the 15-inch monitors and numerous destroyers.

Capture of the airfield was held up and so the fighter cover from the escort carriers, intended only for D-day, was maintained until the 12th when the surviving Seafires were flown ashore to a landing strip which had been prepared at Paestum. There they continued to operate until the 15th when the airfield at Montecorvino was finally overrun by the advancing Allied troops. By the 17th the assault phase was over and on October 1 the Allies entered Naples.

During the Salerno operations casualties amongst major naval units were restricted to the US destroyer *Rowan*, sunk by a motor torpedo boat, the *Savannah*, HMS *Warspite* and *Uganda* hit by FX guided bombs and put out of action. This was far from insupportable considering the great strategic success achieved.

When the Allies' naval superiority was next put to use strategically in support of the land campaign in Italy, it was to put the Allied VI Corps ashore at Anzio on January 22, 1944.

Heavy losses to air attack

The delivery and landing of the troops with their tanks and artillery achieved perfect surprise and by the end of D-day 36,000 men with 3,609 vehicles and a large quantity of stores had been safely landed with trifling casualties. Had the troops exploited this success and moved quickly inland they could have advanced to the Alban Hills overlooking Rome and thereby cut the supply route of the German Tenth Army and perhaps occupied the capital itself. Instead there was hesitation and delay during which the Germans were able to deploy forces sufficient to pin the Allied expedition to their beach-head for four months.

A British destroyer lays a smokescreen in a Mediterranean action, using funnel smoke (black) and chemical smoke apparatus (white).

During all that time the naval supporting forces and the supply ships were exposed to intensive air attack including glider bombs and torpedoes, to E-boat and U-boat attack, and to the gunfire of enemy artillery on shore. Glider bombs sank the British light-cruiser *Spartan* and the destroyer *Inglefield*, with heavy loss of life, as well as two transports, and damaged the destroyer *Jervis*. Her sister-ship *Janus* was sunk by a torpedo plane, the USS *Mayo* was mined, and the cruiser *Penelope* and two LST's were sunk by U-boats.

The next and final major naval operation of the war in the Mediterranean was the invasion of the South of France on August 15, 1944. Mounted under the overall command of Vice-Admiral H. K. Hewitt, USN, an Anglo-American-Free French Western Naval Task Force was to land Lieutenant General A. M. Patch's Seventh US Army and the Free French II Corps under General de Lattre de Tassigny on a number of beaches on the Rivièra extending from the Baie de Cavalaire to Calanque d'Anthéor.

In support of the landings, five battleships —three US, one British and one French— and three US heavy cruisers were employed besides the usual destroyers and gunboats for close-in gun support. Aerial cover was supplied by fighters from nine escort-carriers —five British under Rear Admiral Tom Troubridge and four US under Rear Admiral Durgin.

Thorough training and exhaustive rehearsals ensured the faultless execution of the assault. By the end of D-day, 56,390 troops and 8,240 vehicles had been landed and the Germans were in full retreat. Toulon and Marseilles surrendered on August 28, 1944.

This was the last full-scale naval operation of the war in the Mediterranean although many more minor ones were to engage Allied naval forces in the Adriatic and the Aegean as scattered German garrisons fought stubbornly against their inevitable ejection from the islands.

The 15th Cruiser Squadron at the Battle of Sirte in March 1942. They bravely fought off a battleship and heavy cruisers.

The end of German naval power

The sinking of the battleship *Scharn-* *horst* at the Battle of the North Cape marked the end of Germany's surface challenge of Allied sea power. The *Tirpitz,* under constant air attack, was finally eliminated in November 1944. But in June of that year the Allies mounted their last great naval enterprise of the war in European waters —the invasion of Normandy. Frantic German naval resistance was crushed. U-boats kept up their attacks on convoys but German naval power had been eliminated.

As the Autumn equinox of 1943 drew near with the prospect in the Arctic of short, grey stormy days and long, dark nights, plans were made to re-start the convoys carrying desperately needed war supplies to the Russian armies through Murmansk. To avoid any repetition of the debacle of PQ17, the elimination of that immensely powerful unit, the *Tirpitz,* was essential.

Efforts by the RAF to do so had been made on several occasions during 1942 without success. In October of that year a gallant but unsuccessful attempt had been made to damage her as she lay refitting at Trondheim by the use of 'human torpedoes' or 'chariots', transported across the North Sea lashed under the bottom of a Norwegian fishing boat commanded by Lief Larson, the famous resistance fighter. In March 1943 the *Tirpitz* had rejoined the *Scharnhorst* and *Lützow* in Kaafiord near the North Cape. During the summer she lay idle except for a brief sortie with the *Scharnhorst* to turn their big guns on the huts of the Norwegian weather-reporting station on Spitzbergen. Meanwhile, in a remote Scottish loch, a little band of men were being trained to operate midget submarines. These little 'X' craft, each with a crew of three, were fitted to carry a two-ton charge of high-explosive on either side which they would lay on the bottom underneath their moored target.

Six of them were towed across the Norwegian Sea by conventional submarines. Two were lost on passage; another broke down and had to give up; but *X5*, *6* and *7* pressed on up the fifty miles of fiord to the battleship's anchorage. *X6*, under the command of Lieutenant Donald Cameron, and *X7*, commanded by Lieutenant Godfrey Place, and possibly *X5*, commanded by Lieutenant Henty-Creer, succeeded in penetrating the patrols and net defences to place their charges under the *Tirpitz*'s hull. The resultant explosions caused heavy damage to the battleship which was to keep her out of action throughout the coming winter. With the *Lützow* back in Germany for a refit, only the *Scharnhorst* and six destroyers were left effective in the north. Resumption of the Arctic convoys could go ahead.

Mastery over the U-boats

And through November and the first half of December 1943 they ran unmolested even by U-boats. The mastery established by the escorts over the U-boats left the surface ships as the only means of attacking the convoys during the dark mid-winter months. On Christmas Day, therefore, accompanied by five destroyers, the *Scharnhorst*, flying the flag of Rear Admiral Bey, left Altenfiord and steered north into the wild westerly gale that was tormenting the men of Convoy JW55B and its escorts in the Barents Sea.

Bey's plan, in accordance with the strict instructions given him, was for the battle-cruiser to annihilate the convoy with her powerful armament, but if any heavy enemy ships came on the scene the *Scharnhorst* would retire at once, leaving the destroyers to fight a rear-guard action. Nevertheless from Dönitz, now head of the German Navy, had come signalled exhortations 'to exploit tactical situations with skill and daring and not end the battle with half a victory.' The Grand-Admiral assured Bey of his 'faith in your spirit of attack.'

Bey signalled that, in the heavy weather prevailing, his destroyers would have little fighting value and asked if the operation should proceed. The High Command was torn with indecision finally brought to an end by Dönitz's decree that only the man on the spot could decide. The German squadron drove on into the Arctic night. But Bey's signals, intercepted by Allied direction-finding stations, had alerted the C-in-C Home Fleet, Admiral Sir Bruce Fraser, hovering 200 miles to the westward in his flagship, the battleship *Duke of York*, accompanied by the cruiser *Jamaica* and four destroyers. Fraser steered at once to cut the Germans off from their base. He had previously followed a hunch that the convoy might be threatened and had ordered four destroyers of the escort of the homeward-bound convoy RA55A under Commander R. L. Fisher to reinforce the escort of JW55B under Captain James McCoy. Another force which was approaching the convoy from the eastward was Vice-Admiral Bob Burnett's of three cruisers, *Belfast* (flagship), *Norfolk* and *Sheffield*.

Bey was aware of none of this owing to the grounding of all reconnaissance aircraft. It was still dark when, at 0930, without any warning from the *Scharnhorst*'s two radar sets, Bey found himself illuminated by star-shells bursting overhead. They had come from the *Belfast* to the eastward and were followed by salvos of 8-inch shells, one of which burst against the *Scharnhorst*'s fore-top, wrecking her forward radar, and another on her forecastle.

Unable to see his enemy, Bey increased to full speed and swung away to the south. Had he at once given up and steered for his base, he would have got clean away. But as he drew out of range he decided to use his superior speed in the heavy sea running to circle round to eastward of the British cruisers, hoping to achieve a new thrust at the convoy. A breakdown in communications with his destroyers at this time caused them to get so far detached that they were to play no further part in the events which followed. Meanwhile Burnett, now in company with Fisher's four destroyers, sensing Bey's intentions, steered to intercept him again and at 1205 the *Belfast*'s radar detected the *Scharnhorst* approaching from the east. As the guns on either side roared out, Bey finally gave up hope of breaking through to the convoy and at his best speed shaped course for base.

He was too late: Fraser's squadron could now intercept him, aided by the information coming from Burnett's shadowing cruisers. And at 1615 radar contact was established at 23 miles. At 1650 the *Scharnhorst*, all unaware of the trap she was in, was illuminated by star-shells from the *Belfast*; at the same moment the *Duke of York*'s 14-inch guns opened fire, obtaining a hit abreast the battlecruiser's foremost turret almost at once. A minute later another plunged on to her quarter deck. The *Scharnhorst* fled eastward. The *Duke of York* careering along in chase

The surrendered German heavy cruiser Prinz Eugen is escorted by her British opposite number HMS Devonshire on her way from Norway. She ended her career at Bikini.

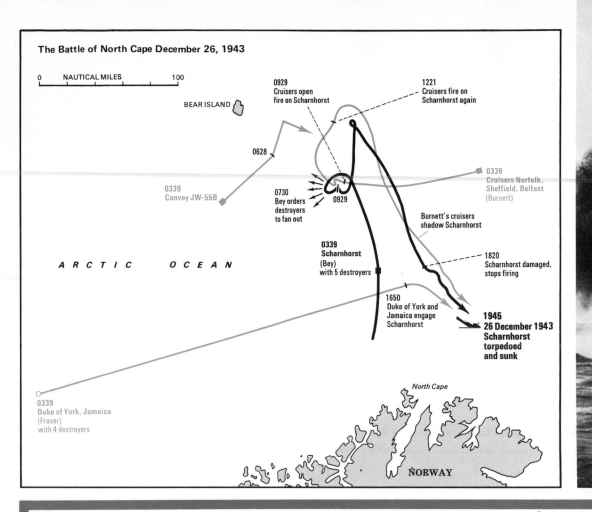

The Battle of North Cape December 26, 1943

0 NAUTICAL MILES 100

BEAR ISLAND

0929
Cruisers open
fire on Scharnhorst

1221
Cruisers fire on
Scharnhorst again

0628

0339
Convoy JW-55B

0730
Bey orders
destroyers
to fan out

0929

0339
Cruisers Norfolk,
Sheffield, Belfast
(Burnett)

Burnett's cruisers
shadow Scharnhorst

0339
Scharnhorst
(Bey)
with 5 destroyers

1820
Scharnhorst damaged,
stops firing

A R C T I C   O C E A N

1650
Duke of York and
Jamaica engage
Scharnhorst

1945
26 December 1943
Scharnhorst
torpedoed
and sunk

0339
Duke of York, Jamaica
(Fraser)
with 4 destroyers

North Cape

NORWAY

Scharnhorst

After a lucky career with her sister *Gneisenau* this 32,000-ton battle-cruiser was finally sunk in the last major surface action in European waters. The *Scharnhorst* sank the carrier HMS *Glorious* off Norway in 1940, carried out successful raids in the Atlantic and steamed in broad daylight through the English Channel. In all this she was accompanied by her sister ship but once they parted company their luck ran out. On December 26, 1943 HMS *Duke of York* and a force of cruisers and destroyers caught her trying to attack a convoy to North Russia. The resulting Battle of North Cape was fought almost entirely by radar and the *Scharnhorst* went down in the Arctic night with most of her crew.

was making no more hits and unable to match the *Scharnhorst*'s speed. At 1715 her two pairs of destroyers were sent on at their best speed to attack with torpedoes. In the heavy following sea they gained very slowly.

Then suddenly the situation was changed as a 14-inch shell hit and penetrated the battlecruiser causing her speed to fall rapidly off. By 1840 the destroyers were exchanging gunfire with her; and soon afterwards, attacking in pairs, as she swung round, apparently turning at bay, they fired a total of 28 torpedoes, scoring probably four hits. At the same time the *Scharnhorst* was being battered to a wreck by the guns of the *Duke of York* and *Jamaica* from one direction and of the *Belfast* from another. Then the *Duke of York*'s guns fell silent as the *Belfast* and *Jamaica* closed to fire torpedoes, obtaining two more hits and being followed by Fisher's four destroyers which delivered the *coup-de-grâce* with six more. At 1945 a heavy underwater explosion and the disappearance of the glowing centre of a smoke cloud which was the doomed *Scharnhorst* marked her end.

Sad end for *Tirpitz*

It was the end of Germany's efforts to challenge Allied sea-power with her few surviving

The battleship Duke of York, *instrumental in* Scharnhorst's *destruction, fires her 14-inch guns as heavy seas break over her.*

surface units. The *Tirpitz*, when she finally completed repairs in March 1944, was promptly put out of action again by a carrier-borne air attack. On April 3, from the flight decks of the *Victorious* and *Furious*, a striking force of 42 Fairey Barracuda dive-bombers took off at dawn. They were escorted by a swarm of fighters—Grumman Wildcats and Hellcats and Vought Corsairs, which the Royal Navy was now obtaining from America —which took off from the escort carriers *Emperor*, *Searcher*, *Fencer* and *Pursuer*.

Covering the 120 miles to the target at wave-top level to avoid radar detection, they achieved complete surprise. With fourteen bomb hits they put the *Tirpitz* once again out of action with damage from which she never fully recovered. Eventually moored at Tromsö to act as a coastal defence battery, she was destroyed by the RAF's expert block-buster squadron with 12,000-pound bombs.

The remaining major German surface units, the cruisers *Prinz Eugen and Hipper* the light cruisers *Nürnberg* and *Leipzig* and the pocket battleships *Lützow* and *Scheer*, had by this time been deployed in the Baltic where, until the end of the war, they were employed giving support to the German armies.

Meanwhile the Arctic convoys continued to run until the end of the war menaced during the mid-winter months by U-boats only. Equipped with the *schnorchel* and the acoustic torpedo, they were deployed in the inshore

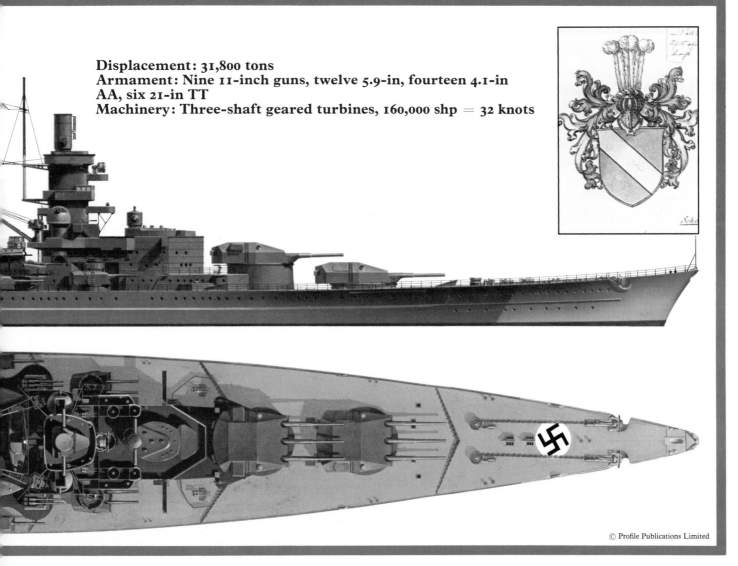

Displacement: 31,800 tons
Armament: Nine 11-inch guns, twelve 5.9-in, fourteen 4.1-in AA, six 21-in TT
Machinery: Three-shaft geared turbines, 160,000 shp = 32 knots

Above: The Tirpitz *fires her 15-inch guns during battle practice.*

Above: German torpedo-boats in line ahead.

approaches to Murmansk where they were more difficult to counter than in the open sea. They caused a number of losses amongst the escorts but very few of the merchantmen suffered. When increasing hours of daylight enabled the German Air Force to join the U-boat effort, their bombers had no success and were made to pay heavily by fighters from the escort carriers.

One last, great naval enterprise remained to the Allies in the war against Germany—the delivery on the beaches of Normandy of two American, two British and one Canadian Army Divisions on June 6, 1944 and the follow-up troops and supplies. It was to comprise the biggest convoy operation and the biggest amphibious assault in history. Its

scale may be gauged from the statistics: the initial landings employed 1,213 warships and 4,126 landing ships and craft of 23 different types.

Bombardment surprise

Two Naval Task Forces were formed: a Western (American) Task Force under Rear-Admiral A. G. Kirk, USN was responsible for landing and supporting the US First Army on beaches off Varreville ('Utah') on the Cotentin Peninsula and St Laurent ('Omaha'); a British (Eastern) Task Force under Rear Admiral Sir Philip Vian for the British Second Army on beaches off Asnelles ('Gold'), Courseulles ('Juno') and Ouistreham ('Sword'). The Supreme Naval Commander was Admiral Sir Bertram Ramsay, while General Eisenhower was in Supreme Command of the whole Allied Expeditionary Force. Unlike other amphibi-

ous operations of the war, it was possible to provide entirely land-based air cover by 171 squadrons of fighters which had, indeed, achieved absolute air supremacy long before D-day.

The five assault forces embarked in their landing craft and ships at various ports between Plymouth and Newhaven and sailed in time to converge during the night of June 5/6 on a junction area south of the Isle of Wight, known as 'Piccadilly Circus'. From there they turned south to follow the ten channels, one for each of the groups in which the assault forces were organised, which had been swept and marked by the minesweepers. Time for touchdown of the first assault craft (H-hour) depended upon the time at which the beach obstacles became uncovered to allow the clearance teams to get to work on them. It was, therefore, 0630 in the American sector, 0730 in the British. A bombardment force consisting of the American battleships *Arkansas*, *Nevada* and *Texas*, the British *Warspite* and *Ramillies*, 21 cruisers (14 British, 2 US, 2 Dutch, 2 French and 1 Polish) and 58 destroyers (33 British, 17 US, 3 Norwegian, 2 Polish, 2 Canadian and 1 Free French) had opened at 0530 a vast two-hour cannonade with guns of all sizes between 15-inch and 4-inch. So well had the time and place of the assault been kept hidden from the Germans that this shattering hail of shells was the first intimation they received of it.

At four of the beaches—Utah, Juno, Gold and Sword—the landings were brilliantly successful. At Omaha, a combination of rough sea conditions, a lowering position too far out for the assault landing craft and a failure of the amphibious tanks, led to great confusion, much delay and a cruel casualty list.

Nevertheless, by the end of D-day the

The D-Day Landings (Bombarding Ships), 1944

Great Britain			
Battleships			
Warspite	Ramillies	Rodney	Nelson
Cruisers			
Black Prince	Glasgow	Orion	Arethusa
Hawkins	Argonaut	Belfast	Danae
Enterprise	Emerald	Mauritius	Scylla
Monitors			
Erebus	Roberts		
U.S.A.			
Battleships			
Nevada	Texas	Arkansas	
Carriers			
Augusta	Tuscaloosa	Quincy	
Allies			
Gunboat			
Soemba (Dutch)			
Cruiser			
Georges Leygues (French)			

'impregnable' defences of Hitler's 'Fortress Europe' had been breached. At the low cost of some 4,300 British and 6,000 American casualties, 132,715 Allied soldiers had been put ashore and were advancing inland. To consolidate their bridgehead, however, and then to expand the assault into a full-scale invasion, an immense and constant flow of reinforcements, supplies, vehicles and ammunition had to be established.

This started with the 'follow-up' troop convoys from the Thames, Plymouth, Falmouth and Harwich and with the 'build-up' convoys from the Bristol Channel and the Thames. Until proper ports were captured and put into operation, two artificial harbours, known as 'Mulberries' were established, the arms of which reached out about half-a-mile from the shore to an outer breakwater three and a half miles long composed of concrete caissons towed across the Channel and sunk in position. Inside this enclosed area were floating jetties, connected by floating piers to the shore at which coasters, barges and LST's could unload. As shelters for small craft close inshore, three other smaller areas were enclosed by sunken blockships and known as 'Gooseberries'.

The construction of these artificial harbours proceeded with admirable smoothness and within a week the two Mulberries were working at a capacity worthy of regular ports. The chief hazard to the transports and their escorts was the mine, at first the magnetic and acoustic types which laid off the beaches with various sorts of delay action partially defeating the efforts of the sweepers. They claimed a number of victims. Later there were the newly-developed 'oyster' mines which, strewn in large numbers by enemy aircraft over the sea bottom in the assault area, were actuated by the water pressure

Left: HMS Nelson *in early March 1945 shortly before her transfer to the Far East, where she finished the war.*

Above: A Landing Craft Rocket hurls her cargo at the Normandy defences.

wave of a ship passing over them.

The German Air Force made its first appearance on the night of June 7/8 and during the following days had some success with the fast Dornier 217 aircraft operating glider bombs. But the overwhelming Allied air power kept the enemy's efforts within negligible proportions.

Smallcraft action by night

The available surface units of the German Navy were mainly confined to three large Z-class destroyers and a smaller one, *T24*, which left Brest for Cherbourg on June 6, and a large number of E-boats at Le Havre and Boulogne. The destroyers were intercepted west of Cherbourg by a mixed flotilla of British, Canadian and Polish destroyers during the night June 8/9 and, after a confused battle, the *ZH1* and *Z32* were sunk; *Z24* and *T24*, the former badly damaged, escaped back to Brest.

The E-boats from Le Havre came into action at dawn on D-day to sink the Norwegian destroyer *Svenner*. Thereafter they were out almost nightly, being met by Allied MGB's which prevented them having much success as they tried to get at the convoys making for the invasion anchorage. On June 14 a raid by 325 Lancaster bombers on Le Havre destroyed 14 of them as well as 40 other small craft. The next day Boulogne was given the same treatment.

Something which was to achieve more damage to the invasion shipping organisation than all the enemy's efforts now occurred. At midnight on June 18/19 there began a summer storm of extraordinary severity which blew from the north-east until the 22nd. It demolished the Mulberry off the American beaches and nearly succeeded in doing the same to the other one as well as the Gooseberries and piers. More than 800 craft of all types were stranded between June 16 and 19 as compared to 64 lost by enemy action and 30 by stress of weather during the first six critical days of the assault. The whole great military enterprise came near to foundering through the interruption of supplies. Before the normal flow was resumed on the 22nd it

had become necessary to ration ammunition among the troops ashore.

In spite of the aerial pounding given to Le Havre, the Germans transported more E-boats there by rail and they now began to threaten the eastern flank of the invasion anchorage with these and with the ingenious, unorthodox weapons they had devised.

These included 'human torpedoes', other

torpedoes which, fired into the invasion anchorage from well outside it, circled amongst the shipping, and explosive motor boats. The first of these achieved a few minor successes at first; but in spite of the gallantry with which all types were operated, they were soon mastered by the Support Squadron Eastern Flank specially formed to deal with them.

HMS Belfast

The *Belfast* and her sister *Edinburgh* were completed in 1939 as *Edinburgh* Class cruisers, improved editions of the *Southampton* Class. Less than three months after the beginning of World War II the *Belfast* was badly damaged by a magnetic mine. Her back was broken, and to repair her required major ship-surgery which took two-and-a-half years. She is depicted here, as at the Battle of North Cape in December 1943, with all the alterations and additions carried out during her rebuilding. After service in the Korean War *Belfast* was again rebuilt, with lattice masts in place of her tripods.

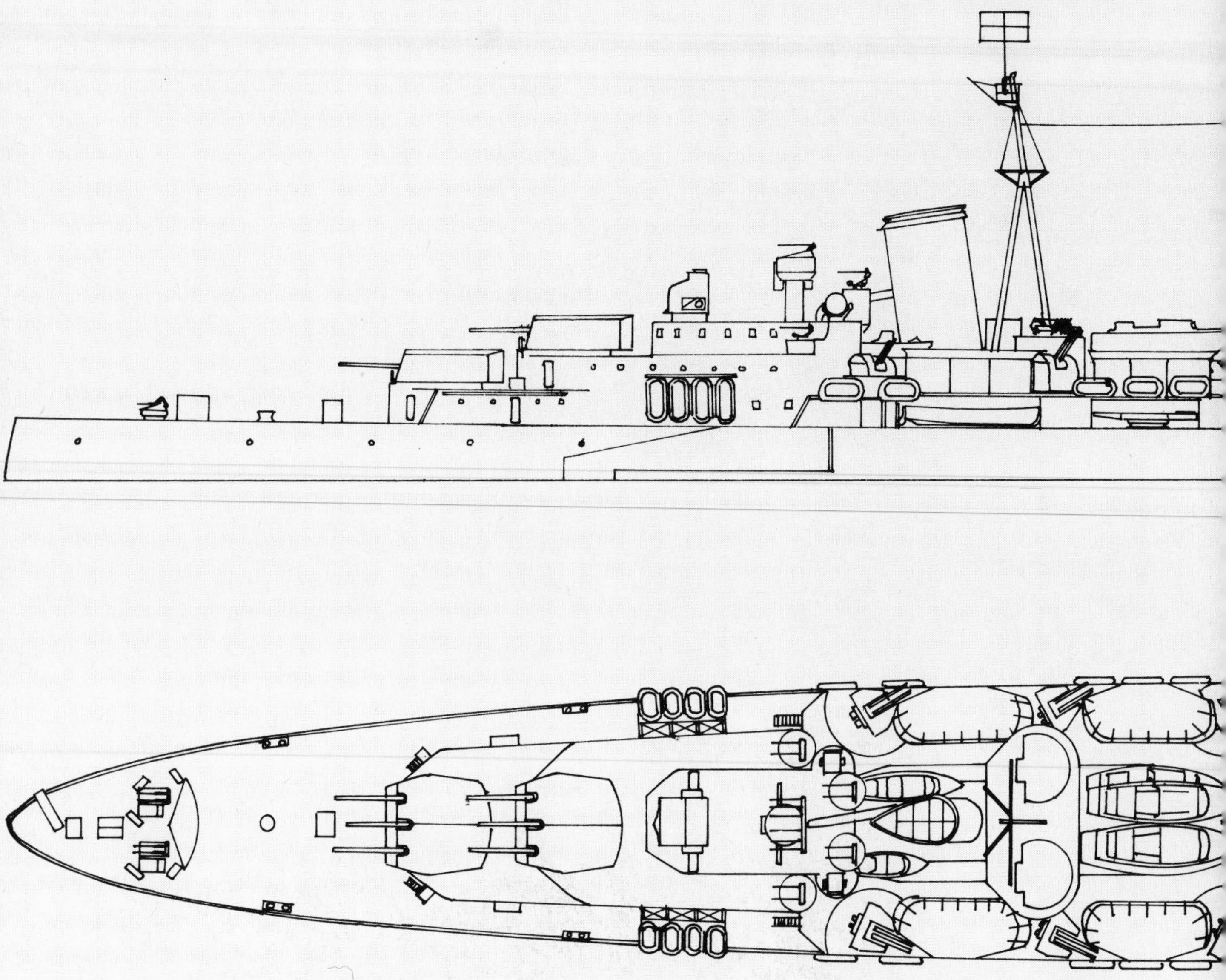

Finally there were the U-boats of which there were some 36 in Brest on D-day, only about half of which were *schnorchel*-fitted. Fifteen boats were immediately ordered up-Channel to attack the invasion convoys; they found the approaches patrolled by escort groups and by so wide and dense a round-the-clock air patrol area that the non-*schnorchel* boats could not cross it without surfacing or without being detected when they did so. These defences were decisively effective. In the first three days five U-boats were sunk, seven more were forced back to harbour, damaged. Eight more were sunk by escorts or aircraft before the end of the month.

By August 23, when U-boats finally abandoned efforts to operate in the Channel, 13 of them had been destroyed to sink three escorts and one empty troopship and damage four supply ships.

U-boats based in Norway and Germany continued to operate in small numbers in the Atlantic, in the coastal waters of Britain and in the approaches to Murmansk, but they never became more than a harassment. Germany's naval power was at an end.

Displacement: 11,260 tons
Armament: Twelve 6-inch guns, eight 4-in AA, six 21-in TT
Machinery: Four-shaft geared turbines,
80,000 shp = $31\frac{1}{4}$ knots

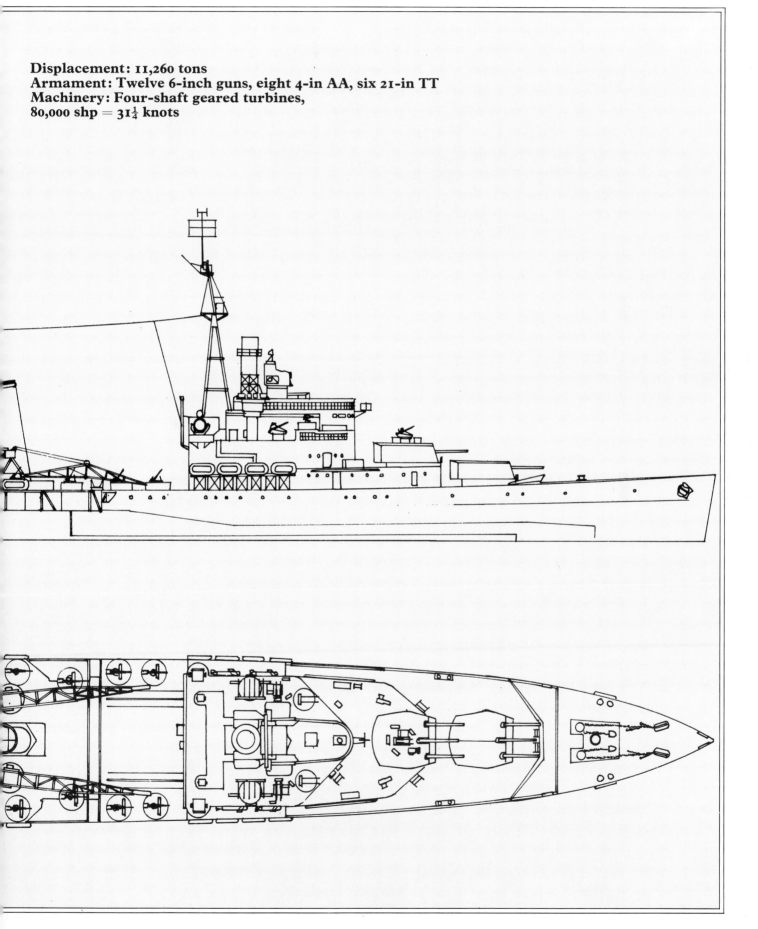

Strike and counterstrike
Pearl Harbor to Midway

At the outbreak of war in the Pacific the Japanese held all the advantages. Britain's naval presence did not amount to much and America's Pacific Fleet was outnumbered in every type of ship and aircraft by the Japanese who possessed the largest carrier-based airforce in the world. The Japanese believed that to win at all they must win quickly and they struck a crippling opening blow at Pearl Harbor. But the Americans, incredibly, hit back, first in the Coral Sea and then at Midway. The Japanese successes were not entirely stemmed, they went on to virtually destroy the Royal Navy as a force in Asian waters, but the decisive victory at Midway, won within months of Pearl Harbor, gained parity for America in the Pacific.

In July 1941 the Japanese took control of Indo China from the French who, beaten a year earlier by Germany, were unable to resist. The Americans, British, and Dutch responded by halting trade with Japan. Since the latter depended on such trade for her oil, which came from the Dutch East Indies, as well as for almost all the other materials needed by an industrial nation, she would soon be brought to her knees unless she complied with President Roosevelt's demand that she withdraw not only from the French colonies but from China itself. Diplomatic maneuvering that summer and fall led nowhere. All that was left was war. That came on December 8 which, on the Eastern side of the International Date Line, was December 7.

The US Pacific Fleet had been moved in the spring of 1940 from its bases on the California coast to Pearl Harbor in the hope that it would deter the Japanese from attacking the Western colonies in Asia. But by late 1941 it was so reduced by the needs of the Atlantic that it was in all respects inferior to the Japanese Combined Fleet.

Under the grandiose title, US Asiatic Fleet, the Americans had long maintained a small naval force in the Far East. In December 1941 this force, based on Manila, consisted of three cruisers, 13 old destroyers and 32 sea-based patrol planes. There were also 23 new submarines, (about half the country's total strength in modern ships of that type) and six old ones. After two years of war elsewhere, Britain had few warships left in East Asian waters, only three elderly cruisers and, including a pair at Hong Kong, seven destroyers. There were no carriers, no battleships, and no submarines. The Netherlands' three cruisers, seven destroyers and 13 submarines were obsolete in design, if not in years.

The Americans were inexperienced in war. They had developed skill in daylight gunnery,

Her crew at flight deck parade, the new aircraft carrier Hornet stands out from Pearl Harbor in the spring of 1942. Escorting her are two 77-foot motor torpedo boats.

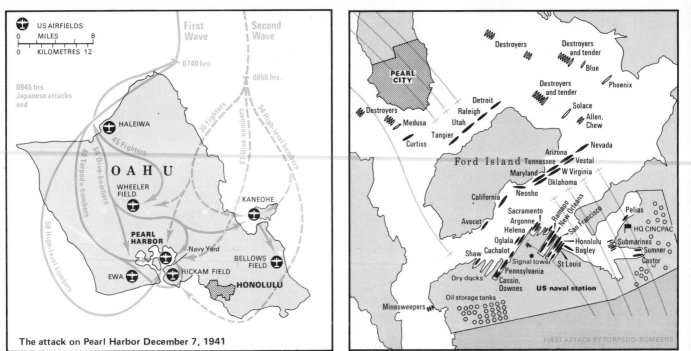

The attack on Pearl Harbor December 7, 1941

FIRST ATTACK BY TORPEDO-BOMBERS

and tactics and had developed naval aviation highly. But they weren't very good at night fighting, submarine warfare, or anti-submarine warfare, and were just developing an expertise in amphibious warfare. Their big guns were good, but not their light weapons. Their torpedoes were bad, though nobody knew it. Their ships were good, even though shaped for battles of a kind they were seldom to fight. Their aircraft, too, were more than adequate and better ones were on the way.

The British were adept at surface action both by day and by night and, with two years of hard experience, particularly good at anti-submarine warfare. Their submariners were also a potent force, but the British had no important experience, or any doctrine, of amphibious warfare and, while their carrier aviators were brave and skilled, they lacked satisfactory aircraft. The ships of the Royal Navy generally were more seaworthy but less battle worthy than those of other major navies. Their officers and men had learned how to endure.

The Japanese also knew how to endure. They knew their purpose, and they were well equipped. Their ships were powerful and battle worthy. They had good guns and superb torpedoes. Their naval aircraft were as good as, or better than, any other airplanes in the sky, especially their Zero fighters. Like the British, they were skilled at night fighting and, at first, they were better than anyone in carrier warfare. In addition to possessing the world's largest carrier-based air force, they also had a large shore-based naval air force. They were the world's most experienced in amphibious warfare, and had a powerful submarine fleet. But they were uninterested in anti-submarine warfare and the protection of shipping. Their merchant marine, on which the weight of their newly-acquired empire was to rest, was not big enough for its task and, more important, not valued highly enough by the fighting navy.

The instruments used on either side were rather more modern than were the concepts of most of the admirals wielding them. But the concepts quickly caught up with, and eventually led, the instruments. At first the Japanese admirals were the most advanced

Above : The Shaw *blows up. Both she and the* Nevada *were salvaged and fought again.*

Left : The battleship Nevada *makes a brave attempt to get to sea. The destroyer* Shaw *blazes fiercely.*

Below : On the morning of Thursday, October 30, 1941, the carrier Enterprise, *five old battleships and many other ships, lie quietly in Pearl Harbor.*

conceptually, but the Americans soon outdistanced them.

Admirals and politicians

Though the strategic insight of Isoroku Yamamoto, Commander in Chief of the Japanese Combined Fleet, was defective, the ideas of most of the principal admirals were sound, particularly that of the Americans and Britons. But the Americans and Britons had to contend with political leaders, Roosevelt and Churchill, whose strategic thinking was not always of a quality to match their power to deploy fleets and armies across the globe. The Japanese had to contend with generals hypnotized by the idea of war on the Asian mainland.

Admiral Yamamoto felt the need to protect his country's drive to the south from interference by the US Pacific Fleet at Pearl Harbor. He appreciated the industrial might of the United States and feared, correctly, that, if Japan did not win within the first 18 months, she would not win at all. Indeed, in common with the opposing admirals at Singapore, Pearl Harbor, and Manila, he wished for no war at all. But the decision on that matter was taken at a higher level.

Admiral Yamamoto had an exaggerated opinion of the strength of the Pacific Fleet. True, the Americans had six large carriers and a small one, and a seventh large carrier had been commissioned just a few weeks before, but only three of these were in the Pacific. He had six large carriers, too, all in the Pacific, as well as four smaller ones. In every type of ship and aircraft his fleet outnumbered the Pacific Fleet. Moreover, his ships were nearer their objectives than were the Americans' and his government was motivated both by a common arrogance and a common desperation, while the Americans were divided as to purpose.

Yamamoto sent off his six best carriers—the *Kaga* and *Akagi*, *Hiryu* and *Soryu*, *Shokaku* and *Zuikaku*—bearing on their decks over 400 aircraft, to attack the American fleet at Pearl Harbor. Most of his cruisers, almost half of his destroyers, and the bulk of his shore-based aircraft took part in the attacks to the south under command of Vice Admiral Nobutake Kondo.

The first devastating blow

When about 200 miles north of Pearl Harbor at dawn December 8 (December 7, local time), Vice Admiral Chuichi Nagumo, commander of the Japanese task force, launched his aircraft. Just before eight o'clock the first Japanese airplanes attacked the unsuspecting Americans. Luckily not one of the American carriers was at Pearl Harbor, but eight of the Pacific Fleet's nine old battleships were, and a substantial number of cruisers, destroyers, submarines, and auxiliaries. There were also hundreds of shore-based aircraft, the majority of them belonging to the Army. At a cost of 55 men and 30 airplanes, Nagumo's force slaughtered over 2,000 sailors and soldiers, destroyed 188 aircraft, and sank two old battleships, the *Arizona* and *Oklahoma*, and an old auxiliary. Over a thousand men were wounded and scores of aircraft damaged. Three other battleships, the *Nevada*, *California*, and *West Virginia*, were so badly damaged as to be out of the war for a year or two, and a dozen other ships suffered some damage. Nagumo withdrew and sailed for home, but on the way he detached the *Hiryu* and *Soryu* to help take the island of Wake whose Marine defenders had proved harder to subdue than anticipated. The island was taken on December 23 while an American relief task force bumbled about getting refueled 500 miles to the east.

Guam fell on December 10, the Gilbert Islands the same day, and Hong Kong on December 25.

The main attack on the Philippines began with a noon air raid by Kondo's shore-based aircraft of the 11th Air Fleet, which destroyed half of the US Army's modern bombers and a third of the fighters on their fields near

Hit by six torpedoes, the battleship West Virginia *settles and burns. The* Tennessee *lies inboard.*

USS Hornet

Her career lasted little more than a year from commissioning to sinking but the *Hornet* covered herself with glory. She was still on her shakedown cruise at the time of Pearl Harbor, and she was chosen to launch the famous Mitchell bomber raid on Tokyo under Lt. Col. James Doolittle. *Hornet* is shown with Doolittle's own Mitchell B-25B on the white lines painted as wheel guides for the B-25s. She was finally sunk by air attack in October 1942.

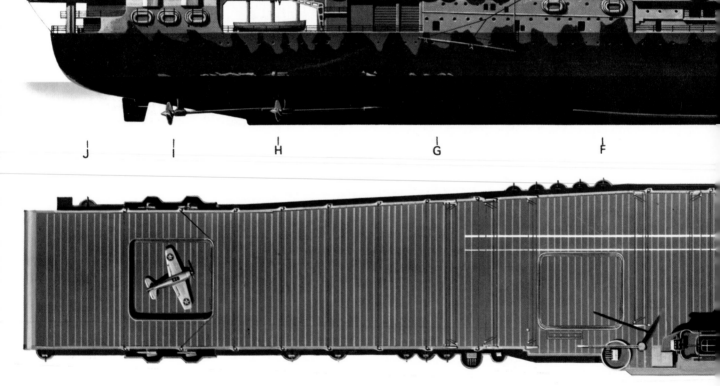

J   I   H   G   F

SBD-3 Dauntless scout/dive bomber

TBF-1 Grumman Avenger torpedo bomber

Manila. The success of this attack, and the superiority of the Zero naval fighter over the US Army Air Force's P–40, meant that the skies over the Philippines were open to Japan. Most of the Asiatic Fleet's cruisers and destroyers had earlier been sent south to join the Dutch at Java and the rest soon followed. The submarines stayed based on Manila, deploying to frustrate Japanese invasion attempts. But it was the submarines that were frustrated. Their torpedoes were so bad as to be useless, and they accomplished almost nothing. Meanwhile Japanese aircraft destroyed the navy yard and dominated Manila Bay by day. Soon the submarines followed the surface ships to Java.

Japanese land unhindered

The Japanese landed over a multitude of beaches, unhindered by either aircraft or submarines. The main landing came on December 22 at Lingayen Gulf on Luzon's western coast. General Douglas MacArthur's Filipinos and a few Americans, attempted to meet the Japanese at the beaches. But the defenders were brushed aside everywhere and quickly they fell back to the Bataan Peninsula at the entrance to Manila Bay.

From the beginning the defenders were on short rations and, shortly after, they fell sick. Nonetheless, they held out till April 9, while others on the fortified islands which commanded the entrance to Manila Bay lasted till May 6. In March, MacArthur, at the order of President Roosevelt, left the Philippines by motor torpedo boat and bomber. Australia was his destination, where he was first to lead the defense of that continent and then prepare for the recovery of the Philippines.

Meanwhile, an hour or so before the air-craft attacked Pearl Harbor, 5,500 Japanese soldiers were landed in the dark on the Malayan beaches at Kota Bharu. The main force for the invasion of Malaya landed in Thailand and pushed across the border and then down the western side of the narrow peninsula toward Singapore. Despite the misgivings of the Royal Navy, Prime Minister Churchill had sent the new battleship *Prince of Wales* and the 25-year-old battle-cruiser *Repulse* to Singapore and, screened by four destroyers, they arrived just before the Japanese attacked.

They sailed in search of the Japanese troop transports, failed to find them, but were themselves found by the twin-engined bombers of the 11th Air Fleet, based at Saigon in French Indo China. The 84 aircraft, armed mainly with torpedoes, sank both ships mid-day on December 10 at almost no cost to themselves. The Royal Air Force,

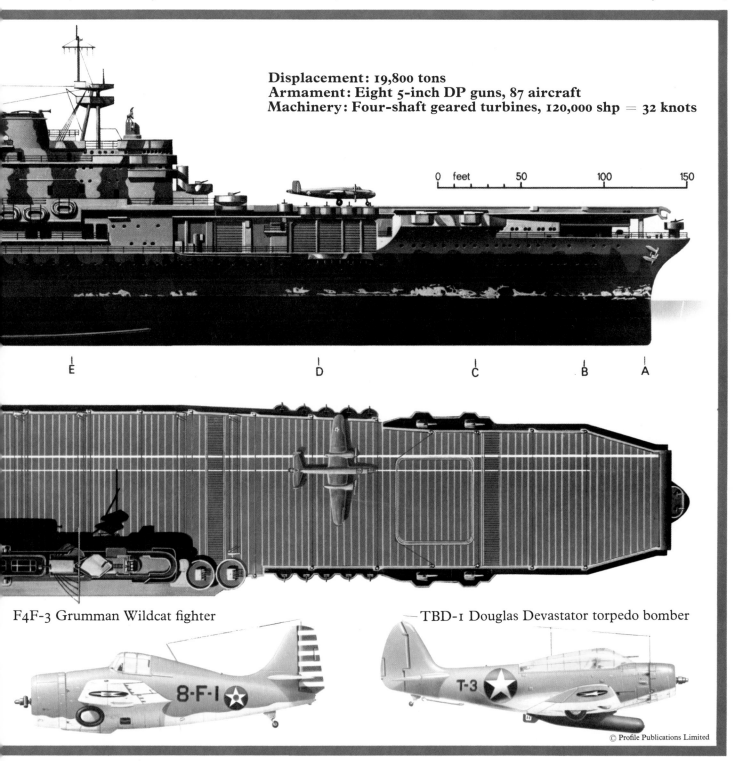

Displacement: 19,800 tons
Armament: Eight 5-inch DP guns, 87 aircraft
Machinery: Four-shaft geared turbines, 120,000 shp = 32 knots

0 feet 50 100 150

E   D   C   B   A

F4F-3 Grumman Wildcat fighter

8-F-1

TBD-1 Douglas Devastator torpedo bomber

T-3

© Profile Publications Limited

151

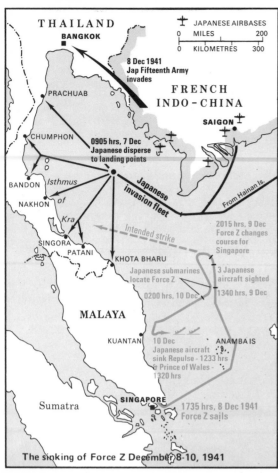

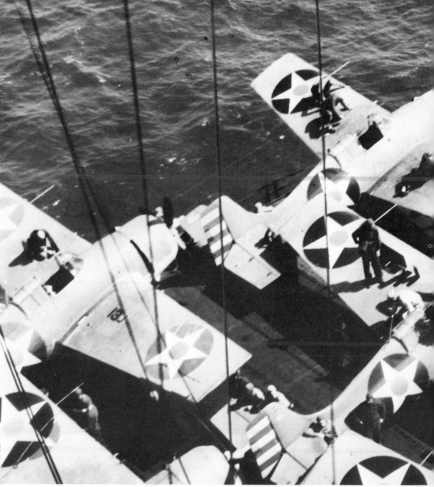

The sinking of Force Z December 8-10, 1941

JAPANESE AIRBASES

THAILAND
BANGKOK

8 Dec 1941
Jap Fifteenth Army
invades

FRENCH
INDO-CHINA

SAIGON

PRACHUAB

0905 hrs, 7 Dec
Japanese disperse
to landing points

CHUMPHON

Japanese
invasion
fleet

From Hainan Is.

BANDON

Isthmus
of

NAKHON

Kra

SINGORA
PATANI

KHOTA BHARU

2015 hrs, 9 Dec
Force Z changes
course for
Singapore

3 Japanese
aircraft sighted
1340 hrs, 9 Dec

Japanese submarines
locate Force Z

0200 hrs, 10 Dec

MALAYA

KUANTAN

ANAMBA IS

Intended strike

10 Dec
Japanese aircraft
sink Repulse - 1233 hrs
& Prince of Wales -
1320 hrs

Sumatra

SINGAPORE

1735 hrs, 8 Dec 1941
Force Z sails

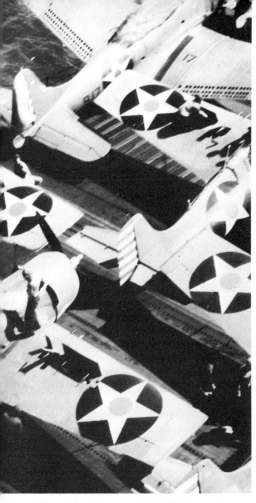

Above left: Grumman F4F Wildcats are rearmed aboard the Enterprise *after a raid on Marcus Island.*

Left: Six Douglas TBD Devastator torpedo planes fly over their carrier while the task force speeds to a new course.

already overwhelmed and ignorant of the ships' position or their need for help, got some fighters to the scene after the ships had been sunk.

A brave effort in vain

At Singapore the Japanese continually outflanked the defenders, sometimes using captured boats for this purpose, unhampered either by the RAF, which had largely been destroyed, or by the Royal Navy which had no small fighting ships with which to oppose them. But the Royal and Dutch navies did escort safely to Singapore and nearby ports ships laden with 45,000 troops and about 100 Hurricane fighters. It was in vain. General Tomoyuki Yamashita's troops swiftly drove their enemies onto Singapore Island itself. They crossed the strait to the island on February 7 and on the 15th the island surrendered.

Not content with the conquest of Malaya and the Philippines, Admiral Kondo also invaded Borneo, where he made the first of seven landings on December 16; Celebes (first landing of three on January 11); and Amboina, on January 31. For the last-named Kondo had the assistance of the carriers *Hiryu* and *Soryu*. The only effective Allied response was a night torpedo attack by four

American destroyers against the invasion ships anchored off Balikpapan, Borneo, on January 24. The destroyers sank four transports and an escort ship, but they did not stop the invasion.

Meantime, far to the east Admiral Nagumo with four of his carriers struck at the small British and Australian garrisons at Rabaul, New Britain; Kavieng, New Ireland; and Lae and Salamaua, New Guinea. The aircraft were followed by troops who quickly secured their new holdings.

On February 5 a combined Dutch and American force of cruisers and destroyers under the Dutch Rear Admiral Karel Doorman headed for another Japanese invasion force reported near the southern end of Makassar Strait. Doorman's ships were attacked by 37 twin-engine bombers of the 11th Air Fleet flying from a captured field on Celebes. All three cruisers were damaged; one, the USS *Marblehead*, almost fatally, and so Doorman retired.

On February 14, the day before Singapore surrendered, the Japanese dropped paratroops on Palembang, the capital of Sumatra. That attack failed. But the next morning Japanese amphibious ships were at the approaches to Palembang. On hearing that an Allied naval force was approaching, the invasion force put about, while the light carrier *Ryujo* attacked Doorman's mixed force of five cruisers and ten destroyers representing four navies. The *Ryujo*'s attack sank none of the ships but it was enough to frustrate Doorman's purpose. The invasion took place on the 16th and soon the whole island was in Japanese hands.

Darwin is abandoned

The same day, over a thousand miles to the east a small convoy carrying American and

Above: The heavy cruiser Salt Lake City *fires her ten 8-inch guns on the Marshall Islands, February 1, 1942.*

Australian troops from Darwin to Timor came under a fierce but unsuccessful attack by 46 Japanese land-based aircraft. But, because of the known presence of Nagumo's carriers to the north, the convoy was ordered back to Darwin. The day after their arrival there Admiral Nagumo attacked with 190 aircraft from four carriers. They sank nearly everything that floated and destroyed nearly everything that didn't. What was left of Darwin was abandoned.

While Nagumo's aviators were attacking Darwin, Kondo was landing troops on Bali and the next day he did the same thing at Timor. Nothing could now be done about Timor and Admiral Doorman's attempt in a night action at Badoeng Strait to break up the landing at Bali cost the Dutch a destroyer and did the Japanese no great harm.

All that was left now for Kondo to take was Java. He sent Rear Admiral Jisaburo Ozawa with 56 transports in from the west and Rear Admiral Shoji Nishimura in from the east with 41. On the afternoon of February 27 Admiral Doorman sailed to attack Nishimura's transports. Once again, Doorman's force consisted of five cruisers and ten destroyers from four navies. The Japanese had four cruisers—*Nachi*, *Haguro*, *Naka*, and *Jintsu*—and 14 destroyers, commanded by Rear Admiral Takeo Takagi. In a long action that began in the afternoon and ended at night the Japanese lost no ships. The Allies lost the Dutch light cruisers *De Ruyter* and *Java* (the former with Doorman on board) and three destroyers.

The other Allied ships, including the severely damaged British heavy cruiser *Exeter*, were sent off to make good their escape. Some went east and some went west. Those who went east, four American destroyers who slid through a shallow strait between Java and Bali, made their way to Australia. None of those who went west made it. The American heavy cruiser *Houston* and the Australian light cruiser *Perth*, heading for Sunda Strait, ran into Ozawa's invasion force. They fired until their magazines were empty and then, engaged by the heavy cruisers *Mogami* and *Mikuma*, the light cruiser *Natori*, and ten destroyers, they perished. The next morning the *Exeter* and two destroyers were sunk by the fire of four Japanese heavy cruisers and aircraft from the *Ryujo*.

Japanese push on to Rangoon

Meantime Nagumo with his carriers and Kondo with a pair of battleships were south of Java where they caught and sank two American destroyers and an assortment of minor warships, auxiliaries, and merchant ships seeking the safety of Australia. So ended the Dutch empire in the East Indies.

While these enormous events were taking place in the waters surrounding the islands of Asia, Japanese troops pushed through Thailand into Burma. They reached the only big city, Rangoon, on March 8. Before the end of the month the Andaman and Nicobar Islands in the Bay of Bengal were in Japanese hands and, hampered more by the jungle and the monsoons than by anything else, before long the Japanese were on the border of India.

The tale of Japanese triumph was not over. To secure their conquests in the Bay of Bengal and the seaborne supply of their forces in Burma, Admiral Kondo sent Nagumo into the Indian Ocean with five large carriers (all the Pearl Harbor ships except the *Kaga*) to attack the British. This he did with a raid on Colombo, Ceylon, on April 5, by 180 aircraft and again four days later on Trincomalee by a similar-sized force.

Both times the carrier planes brushed aside defending interceptors and attacked ships, port facilities, and airfields. Chance sightings led to the destruction by Nagumo's planes of the small British carrier *Hermes* (which had no planes aboard), the heavy cruisers *Cornwall* and *Dorsetshire*, and a destroyer. Meanwhile Admiral Ozawa with the *Ryujo*, six cruisers, and four destroyers cruised off India's east coast, sinking 23 merchant ships in five days.

Though they had 300 planes on the island, the only British response was an attack on Nagumo's fleet by nine Blenheim bombers from Ceylon on the 9th. They got no hits and five were shot down. Admiral Sir James Somerville, Commander-in-Chief, Eastern Fleet, had two carriers, the *Indomitable* and *Formidable*, with between them about 80 aircraft. Not only did his fleet have only a quarter the number of aircraft his enemy had, but they were also inferior aircraft.

Britain's navy withdraws

Somerville sought opportunities for a night strike against his powerful foe, but that never came to pass. Then, while Nagumo and Ozawa left the Indian Ocean through the Malacca Strait, never to return, Somerville

The Yorktown *steams slowly into the wind as she launches aircraft during the Battle of the Coral Sea.*

sent some of his ships to Kilindini on the East African coast to provide protection to ships supplying the Eighth Army in Egypt. He took his remaining ships to Bombay where he could dominate the Arabian Sea.

On May 5 British forces from home, guarded by the carriers *Illustrious* and *Indomitable*, made an amphibious descent upon the huge French island of Madagascar which lies off the south-eastern coast of Africa. Their intention was to deny to the Japanese the use of the harbour at Diego Suarez at the island's northern end. By the end of May 7 this had been accomplished with little loss.

In June and July, before the British could base sufficient anti-submarine forces in the area, Japanese submarines sank 20 merchant ships in waters near Madagascar. But by then naval activity in the Indian Ocean was slackening. By the end of August Somerville was down to one carrier, the *Illustrious*, and in January 1943 even she was taken from him for use elsewhere. It would not be until late in 1944 that powerful naval forces would re-enter that ocean.

The attack on Pearl Harbor led to a desire for revenge on the part of Americans that did not end until Japan lay in ruins in 1945. It led to a change in naval leadership, with Admiral Ernest J. King taking control in Washington as both Commander-in-Chief US Fleet and Chief of Naval Operations and Admiral Chester W. Nimitz doing the same at Pearl Harbor where he became both Commander-in-Chief Pacific Fleet and, shortly, Commander-in-Chief Pacific Ocean Area. Thus, Nimitz ruled all Allied forces in the Pacific except those in General MacArthur's corner.

America strikes back

Pearl Harbor also permitted the Pacific Fleet to pursue a strategy which, even had there been no attack, would have been the best possible. This was to hold the line between the US West Coast and Hawaii and a thousand miles beyond, to Midway; and to maintain communications with Australia. This meant landing strong garrisons at Samoa and the other islands on the route to Australia. It also meant that the Philippines and Dutch East Indies were acknowledged as lost.

Meantime, some ships which earlier had been transferred to the Atlantic were recalled to the Pacific. Chief of these was the carrier *Yorktown*. But her arrival was balanced by the torpedoing of the carrier *Saratoga* by a Japanese submarine in January which put the ship out of the war for five months. Be that as it may, the flow of modern high class

Far left: The Lexington *defends herself against attacking Japanese aircraft in the Coral Sea.*

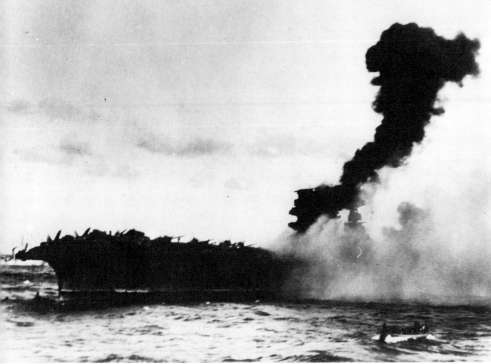

Left: Explosions wrack the Lexington *as she blazes uncontrollably. Boats from other ships pick her men from the water.*

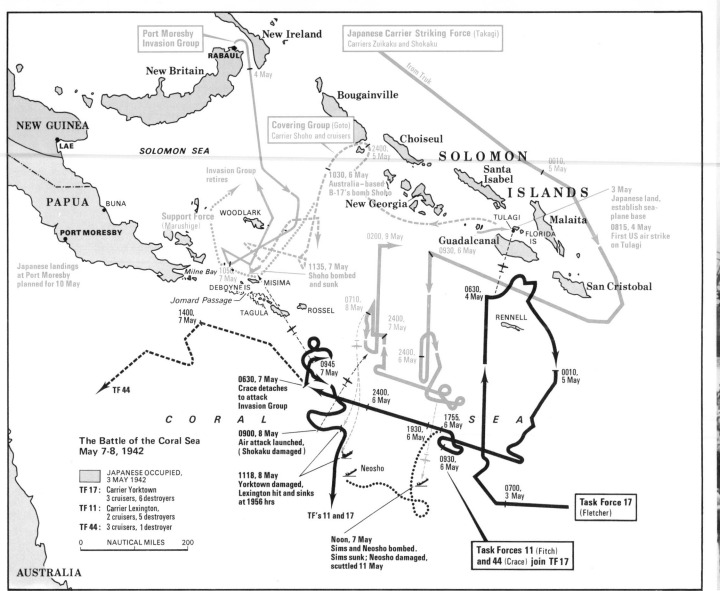

Japanese Carrier Striking Force (Takagi)
Carriers Zuikaku and Shokaku

Port Moresby
Invasion Group

New Ireland

RABAUL

4 May

from Truk

New Britain

NEW GUINEA

LAE

SOLOMON SEA

Bougainville

Covering Group (Goto)
Carrier Shoho and cruisers

2400,
5 May

Choiseul

SOLOMON

**Santa
Isabel**

0010,
5 May

3 May
Japanese land,
establish sea-
plane base

0815, 4 May
First US air strike
on Tulagi

Invasion Group
retires

1030, 6 May
Australia–based
B-17's bomb Shoho

New Georgia

ISLANDS

PAPUA

BUNA

Support Force
(Marushige)

WOODLARK

TULAGI

FLORIDA
IS

Malaita

PORT MORESBY

0200, 9 May

Guadalcanal

0930, 6 May

San Cristobal

Japanese landings
at Port Moresby
planned for 10 May

Milne Bay

1050,
7 May

MISIMA

1135, 7 May
Shoho bombed
and sunk

0710,
8 May

0630,
4 May

DEBOYNE IS

0010,
5 May

Jomard Passage

TAGULA

ROSSEL

RENNELL

1400,
7 May

2400,
7 May

2400,
6 May

TF 44

0945
7 May

C O R A L

S E A

1755,
6 May

0630, 7 May
Crace detaches
to attack
Invasion Group

2400,
6 May

1930,
6 May

**The Battle of the Coral Sea
May 7-8, 1942**

0900, 8 May
Air attack launched,
(Shokaku damaged)

0930,
6 May

0700,
3 May

JAPANESE OCCUPIED,
3 MAY 1942

TF 17: Carrier Yorktown
3 cruisers, 6 destroyers

1118, 8 May
Yorktown damaged,
Lexington hit and sinks
at 1956 hrs

Neosho

TF 11: Carrier Lexington,
2 cruisers, 5 destroyers

TF 44: 3 cruisers, 1 destroyer

TF's 11 and 17

Task Force 17
(Fletcher)

0   NAUTICAL MILES   200

Noon, 7 May
Sims and Neosho bombed.
Sims sunk; Neosho damaged,
scuttled 11 May

Task Forces 11 (Fitch)
and 44 (Crace) join TF 17

AUSTRALIA

ships, once out from the Pacific into the Atlantic, was reversed.

Those things done, Nimitz organized raids upon the Japanese-held islands. The first of these, against Wake, had to be called off when the task force's oiler was sunk by a submarine. But then came a series of small successes as Vice Admiral William F. Halsey and Rear Admiral Frank Jack Fletcher with the *Enterprise* and *Yorktown* raided the Marshall Islands, Wake, and Marcus Island. The latter is less than a thousand miles from Tokyo. An attack by Vice Admiral Wilson Brown with the *Lexington* against Rabaul was called off after the Japanese discovered the task force but, when Brown was rein-

forced by the *Yorktown* another raid, against Lae and Salamaua, New Guinea, succeeded.

Though they did little damage, these raids had an impact on the most important place possible, the mind of Admiral Yamamoto. When, after their great successes the Japanese high command were trying to decide what to do next Yamamoto, concerned about the resurgent Pacific Fleet, persuaded the others that they should move east, toward Hawaii. An air raid on Tokyo in April by sixteen US Army Air Force B–25 bombers launched from the new carrier *Hornet* strengthened Yamamoto's hand. East it would be.

But first there would be a couple of minor ventures to the south. A seaplane base was

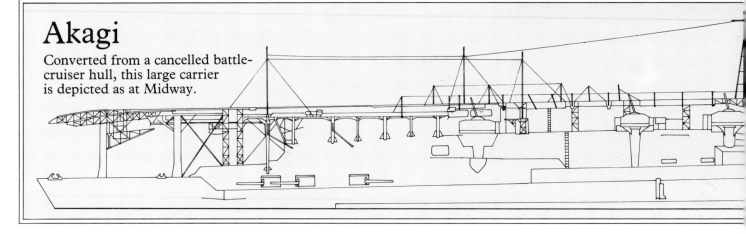

Akagi

Converted from a cancelled battlecruiser hull, this large carrier
is depicted as at Midway.

Above : Between the battles of the Coral Sea and Midway the Yorktown *is repaired at Pearl Harbor.*

Left : The Japanese carrier Shoho *under American attack in the Coral Sea. She was sunk.*

Right : The only survivor of six Grumman TBF torpedo planes which attacked Nagumo's carriers off Midway in June, 1942.

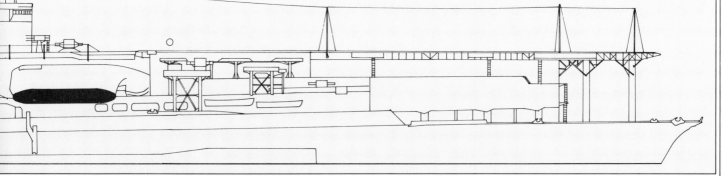

Displacement: 36,500 tons. Armament: Six 7.9-inch guns, twelve 4.7-in AA guns, 91 aircraft
Machinery: Four-shaft geared turbines, 133,000 shp = 31 knots

The situation in the Pacific December 1941

JAPANESE EMPIRE, 1933
OCCUPIED BY JAPAN, JULY 1937/DECEMBER 1941
MILITARY BASES ESTABLISHED BY JAPAN, SEPTEMBER 1940
ABDA (American, British, Dutch, and Australian) COMMAND

MERCATOR'S PROJECTION

set up at Tulagi in the Southern Solomons. And troopships were loaded at Rabaul for a run to Port Moresby, the main Australian outpost remaining on New Guinea. Tulagi and Port Moresby were wanted not only to screen Rabaul but also to support attacks on the islands which guarded the American supply route to Australia.

On May 3 ships of Vice Admiral Shigeyoshi Inouye's Fourth Fleet landed troops at Tulagi. The next day other transports left Rabaul for Port Moresby under the protection of Rear Admiral Aritomo Goto, who had the light carrier *Shoho* bearing 21 planes, four heavy cruisers, and a destroyer. Mean-

while Vice Admiral Takeo Takagi with the *Shokaku* and *Zuikaku*, 63 planes each, sailing from Truk, entered the Coral Sea from the east.

With their excellent intelligence, the Americans anticipated the Japanese moves and had two carrier task forces on hand, Rear Admiral Fletcher's, built around the *Yorktown*, with 72 planes, and Rear Admiral Aubrey W. Fitch's, centered on the *Lexington*, 71 planes. Halsey, with the *Enterprise* and *Hornet*, was racing down from Pearl Harbor. The *Yorktown* had hit the Japanese at Tulagi but accomplished little. On May 7 the Americans discovered what

they thought was Takagi's force and attacked. It turned out only to be Goto's. Nonetheless the American mistake cost the Japanese the *Shoho*. The same morning a similar mistake by Takagi's pilots cost the Americans an oiler and a destroyer.

The next day, May 8, the two carrier groups, which now knew each other's position, exchanged blows. The *Lexington*, *Yorktown*, and *Shokaku* were hit; *Zuikaku*, taking cover in a rain squall, came through

The Yorktown *is hit by aircraft from the* Hiryu *at Midway, June 4, 1942.*

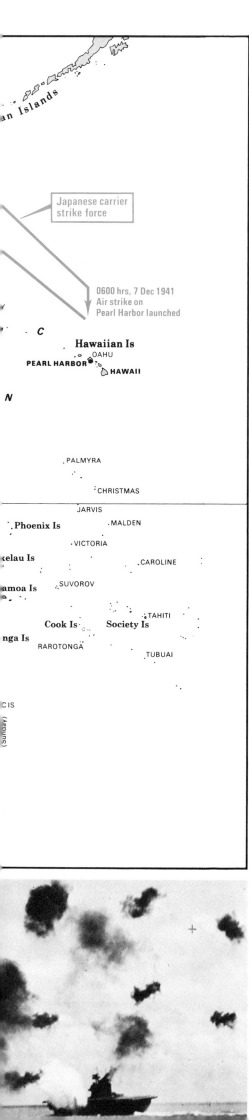

Hit by two torpedoes and three bombs the Yorktown *lies abandoned by all but a salvage crew. Later a Japanese submarine found and sank her.*

unscathed. The opposing carrier forces headed for home and repair, but not before the *Lexington* sank. More importantly Inouye, who had turned around his transports until the issue was cleared up, postponed his invasion of Port Moresby. That summer invasion was attempted overland across the Owen Stanley Mountains and was beaten back at the last minute by Australian and American infantry.

Toward the end of May the Japanese began to sail for Midway. Their plan was to attack with planes from Admiral Nagumo's carriers and then, with the American air defenses wiped out and ground defenses damaged, assault the island with 5,000 troops carried in twelve transports guarded by Vice Admiral Kondo's powerful force built around the light carrier *Zuiho*, 24 planes, two battleships, and eight heavy cruisers.

A secondary attack was planned to strike the American base at Dutch Harbor in the eastern Aleutians from the air and to capture the islands of Kiska and Attu in the west. Central to the force striking Dutch Harbor were the light carriers *Ryujo*, 37 planes, and *Junyo*, 45.

Vice Admiral Nagumo departed from his anchorage in the Inland Sea on May 27. He had four carriers: the *Akagi*, 54 planes; *Kaga*, 63; *Hiryu*, 54; and *Soryu*, 56. Neither the *Shokaku*, still under repair for her Coral Sea damage, nor the *Zuikaku*, short of pilots, accompanied them. Nagumo's screen consisted of two battleships, three cruisers, and eleven destroyers.

Far astern sailed Yamamoto himself in the giant new battleship *Yamato*, accompanied by the small training carrier *Hosho*, which bore only eight aircraft, six old battleships, and some cruisers and destroyers.

Sixteen submarines were sent on ahead to form a barrier between Midway and the American base at Pearl Harbor. Yamamoto believed the American carriers were still in the Coral Sea. But if any of them were at Pearl Harbor, the submarines should either deal with them or provide warning of their presence.

Through his intelligence, Nimitz knew Yamamoto's plans and timing. His ships were no longer in the Coral Sea and the navy yard workmen at Pearl Harbor repaired the

Yorktown's damage, estimated to require ninety days, in three. He moved his three carriers, *Yorktown* (75 planes), *Enterprise* (79), and *Hornet* (79), to sea and west of the Japanese submarine barrier before the submarines arrived. He also set up his own barrier of twelve submarines north and west of Midway.

An American disaster

The Americans made contact with the Japanese when a patrol plane spotted some of Kondo's ships 700 miles southwest of Midway on June 3. Next morning Nagumo, who was approaching the island from the north-west, launched 108 aircraft just before dawn while still about 240 miles distant. The Americans had about 100 planes on the island but the majority were bombers or patrol planes and almost all were obsolete. Despite warning that the Japanese were on their way, the Americans couldn't stop them and the island and its defending airplanes were devastated. A simultaneous attack on Nagumo's carriers by ten planes from Midway resulted in disaster for the Americans. They accomplished nothing and lost seven of their number. Later attacks by shore-based bombers yielded similar results.

The Japanese aircraft returned to their ships and prepared for a second attack on the island when word came to Nagumo from a scout plane that an American carrier was not far distant. Nagumo turned his ships north and began to rearm his planes with torpedoes with which to attack the American carrier. He was too late.

Rear Admiral Raymond A. Spruance, who replaced an ailing Halsey in command of the *Enterprise* and *Hornet* task force, launched aircraft shortly after 0700, before Nagumo knew of his presence. An hour and a half later Admiral Fletcher in the *Yorktown* did the same. It took Spruance's torpedo planes a while to find the enemy so the *Yorktown*'s planes almost caught up. One after the other the three torpedo squadrons, 41 planes in all, attacked Nagumo's carriers. They bored bravely in through defending Zeros and anti-aircraft fire only to achieve no hits and to lose all but four of their number. No sooner had the torpedo attack on Nagumo ended when the dive bombing attack began. Three squadrons, 50 planes total, attacked, each squadron picking one carrier. They destroyed *Kaga*, *Akagi*, and *Soryu*.

Nagumo, his flagship ablaze, was out of the fight, so Rear Admiral Tamon Yamaguchi in the *Hiryu* took over. His

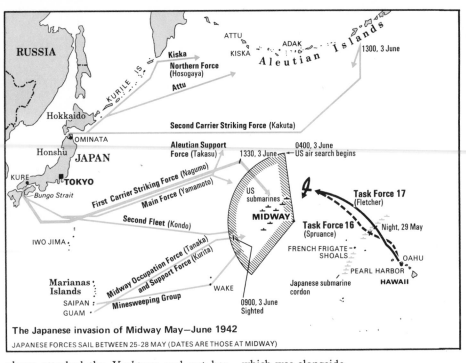

The Japanese invasion of Midway May–June 1942

JAPANESE FORCES SAIL BETWEEN 25-28 MAY (DATES ARE THOSE AT MIDWAY)

planes attacked the *Yorktown* and put her out of action. Admiral Fletcher, in that carrier, passed control of all US carrier operations to Admiral Spruance. The latter responded with an attack on the *Hiryu* which destroyed that ship shortly after the *Hiryu*'s pilots had made a second successful attack on the *Yorktown*.

Parity is won

During the night Yamamoto cancelled the Midway operation and withdrew to Japan. But two of Kondo's cruisers, the *Mogami* and *Mikuma,* collided while attempting to avoid an American submarine. Attacks by shore-based American planes the next day did them little harm. But on June 6 aircraft from the *Enterprise* and *Hornet* sank the *Mikuma* and so damaged the *Mogami* that she was out of the war for two years. Meanwhile the Japanese submarine *I168* found the *Yorktown* under tow of a minesweeper and sank both the carrier and a destroyer which was alongside.

Far to the north on June 3, pilots from the *Ryujo* and *Junyo* struggled through the fog to hit Dutch Harbor and made an unsuccessful attempt to find some American destroyers nearby. Next day the carriers made another attack on Dutch Harbor and then, receiving orders from Admiral Yamamoto, sailed south to join the remainder of the Midway fleet, which shortly headed for home. Kiska and Attu were taken without opposition.

And so, while Japan's advances had not been completely halted, the Americans had, in the space of only six months and against enormous odds, fought back from the brink of total eclipse in the Pacific to win at least parity in the Pacific. It was a splendid achievement.

Above : Before finally having to leave her, the Yorktown's *men find walking difficult because of the heavy list to port.*
Right : The Japanese heavy cruiser Mikuma *before she sank on June 6.*

The Battle of Midway, 1942

U.S.A.		Japan	
Carriers		**Carriers**	
Enterprise	Yorktown	Junyo	Hiryu
Hornet		Ryujo	Soryu
Cruisers		Akagi	Hosho
Astoria	Vincennes	Kaga	
Portland	Northampton	**Battleships**	
New Orleans	Pensacola	Haruna	Yamashiro
Minneapolis	Atlanta	Kirishima	Nagato
		Yamato	Mutsu
		Ise	Hiei
		Fuso	Kongo
		Hyuga	
		Cruisers	
		Sendai	Myoko
		Kumano	Yura
		Suzuya	Kitakami
		Mikuma	Oi
		Mogami	Chikuma
		Atago	Tone
		Chokai	Nagara
		Haguro	

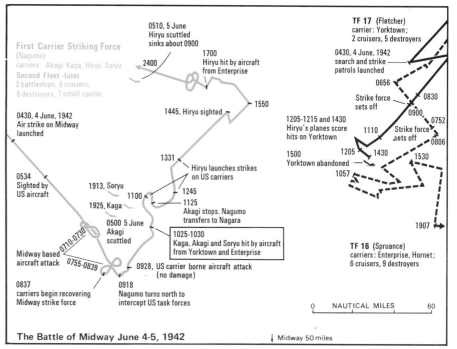

First Carrier Striking Force
(Nagumo)
carriers: Akagi, Kaga, Hiryu, Soryu.
Second Fleet -later
2 battleships, 5 cruisers,
8 destroyers, 1 small carrier.

0510, 5 June
Hiryu scuttled
sinks about 0900

1700
Hiryu hit by aircraft
from Enterprise

2400

1550

1445, Hiryu sighted

0430, 4 June, 1942
Air strike on Midway
launched

0534
Sighted by
US aircraft

1331

Hiryu launches strikes
on US carriers

1913, Soryu

1245

1100

1925, Kaga

1125

0500 5 June
Akagi
scuttled

Akagi stops. Nagumo
transfers to Nagara

0710-0730

1025-1030
Kaga, Akagi and Soryu hit by aircraft
from Yorktown and Enterprise

Midway based
aircraft attack

0755-0839

0928, US carrier borne aircraft attack
(no damage)

0837
carriers begin recovering
Midway strike force

0918
Nagumo turns north to
intercept US task forces

TF 17 (Fletcher)
carrier: Yorktown;
2 cruisers, 5 destroyers

0430, 4 June, 1942
search and strike
patrols launched

0656

0830

Strike force
sets off

0900

0752

1110

1205

0806

1205-1215 and 1430
Hiryu's planes score
hits on Yorktown

Strike force
sets off

1500
Yorktown abandoned

1205

1430

1530

1057

1907

TF 16 (Spruance)
carriers: Enterprise, Hornet;
6 cruisers, 9 destroyers

0   NAUTICAL MILES   60

The Battle of Midway June 4-5, 1942   ↓ Midway 50 miles

Onto the offensive
Guadalcanal to the Admiralties

In an attempt to consolidate the equality hard-won at Midway the Americans went onto the offensive at Guadalcanal. The punishing naval battle for the island lasted over three months with the Americans in control during the day and the Japanese at night, Tanaka's destroyer force, the Tokyo Express, being a particularly potent weapon. Throughout 1943 the battle raged on from Alaska to Australia. Carriers and heavy units of both fleets were involved in many sharp and bloody confrontations. In a vital contribution American submarines sank almost two million tons of Japanese shipping. By the end of the year the Allied advance had acquired an irresistible momentum.

Admiral King, anxious to take advantage of the American success at Midway, persuaded the rest of the American Joint Chiefs of Staff that a small offensive should be undertaken in the Pacific. The Japanese seaplane base at Tulagi in the Solomons and a newly discovered airfield being built on nearby Guadalcanal, were the objectives, for if left alone aircraft flying from them could threaten the supply routes to Australia. As seen from Tokyo they would also provide a shield to the forthcoming overland drive against Port Moresby.

MacArthur and Nimitz each felt he should command the operation; Nimitz was chosen. Under him Vice Admiral Robert L. Ghormley commanded the Allied forces in the South Pacific. The expedition was commanded by Rear Admiral Frank Jack Fletcher in the carrier *Saratoga*.

On August 7 Rear Admiral Richmond Kelly Turner's amphibious ships began landing 19,000 of Major General Alexander A. Vandegrift's Marines on Tulagi and Guadalcanal. It required a few days of tough fighting to take Tulagi. Guadalcanal was easier at first and the unfinished air base, renamed Henderson Field, was soon in the hands of the Marines who quickly put it to use. But it was a long time before the Marines controlled much more of that big island than the air field.

On the second day Rear Admiral Fletcher, anxious about fighter plane losses and the fuel state of his destroyers, unexpectedly announced he was going to withdraw his carriers. While the other Allied leaders were conferring about this in Admiral Turner's flagship, Vice Admiral Guneichi Mikawa was hastening south from Rabaul in the big heavy cruiser *Chokai*, accompanied by the smaller heavy cruisers *Aoba*, *Kako*, *Kinugasa*, and *Furataka*, the small old light cruisers *Tenryu* and *Yubari*, and a destroyer.

Near Savo Island in the darkness of the night of August 9 they pounced on the unprepared cruisers supposedly guarding Turner's transports and cargo ships. In little more than half an hour Mikawa's cruisers had mortally wounded four heavy cruisers—the Australian *Canberra* and the American *Astoria*, *Quincy*, and *Vincennes*, and severely damaged another, the *Chicago*. Then, scarcely touched by return fire, they roared back north to Rabaul. However, before they got there the old American submarine *S44* sank the *Kako*.

Desperate defensive fight

Turner, with most of his cruisers sunk and his air cover gone, pulled his cargo ships and transports south to safety. The Marines were on the beach, but more than half their weapons, food, and supplies were still in the ships. For more than three months they would be hungry, sick, and involved in a desperate defensive fight to hold Henderson Field. Fortunately for the Marines the Japanese underestimated the size of the American force and continually sent in small detachments which attacked and just as continually were destroyed.

From Henderson Field the Americans were able to dominate the local air and therefore controlled the local sea by day. The Japanese cruisers and destroyers, on the other hand, dominated the same waters by night. The Americans had to get reinforcements and supplies to their men on

Her bow blown off by a Japanese Long Lance torpedo at the Battle of Tassafaronga, the heavy cruiser Minneapolis *lies under camouflage netting in Tulagi Harbor.*

The battered Japanese heavy cruiser Aoba *after the Battle of Cape Esperance, October 11–12, 1942.*

Guadalcanal in by daylight, but at nightfall their ships had to leave. The Japanese had to do the same things in the darkness and leave well before dawn. The burden of the Japanese supply effort fell on Rear Admiral Raizo Tanaka and his destroyer squadron. Tanaka's ships shepherded troop-laden transports and cargo ships through the dangerous waters and, often enough, carried the troops and cargoes themselves. Both sides raced to build up ashore and finally, on November 12, the Japanese outnumbered the Americans.

It was these reinforcement efforts, and Japanese naval bombardments of Henderson Field, which led to the fierce sea fights in Ironbottom Sound and the waters nearby.

On August 24 Vice Admiral Kondo, covering a small reinforcement run by Tanaka who had 1,300 troops embarked, clashed in the Battle of the Eastern Solomons with Rear Admiral Fletcher. Admiral Kondo had the *Shokaku* (59 aircraft) and *Zuikaku* (72), both under Vice Admiral Nagumo and, under Rear Admiral Tadaichi Hara, the *Ryujo* (37). Fletcher had the *Saratoga* (88) and *Enterprise* (88). Early in the afternoon the *Saratoga* launched 38 dive bombers and torpedo planes. They found the *Ryujo*, which Kondo had sent ahead as bait, and sank her just as she was about to launch aircraft.

Meanwhile Nagumo launched the squadrons from his two big carriers. They failed to attack the *Saratoga* but got three hits on the *Enterprise*. That hard-working ship soon had her damage under control. Several more attacks were on their way from the American carriers but they never found Nagumo's ships and accomplished little. Then the two opponents steamed out of flying range and the fight was over. Tanaka's 'Tokyo Express' did not finish its run that day.

Action in Ironbottom Sound

The Japanese submarines, used for fleet work rather than against shipping as were Dönitz's U-boats, reached their peak of success soon after. On August 31 the *I26* torpedoed the *Saratoga* and, for the second time, that big carrier was out of the war, this time for three months. Two weeks later the carrier *Wasp*, escorting a troop convoy to Guadalcanal, was sunk by the *I19* while the battleship *North Carolina* and a destroyer were damaged by the *I15*. The destroyer eventually sank.

An American troop convoy from Noumea, New Caledonia, with 3,000 soldiers aboard and a Japanese convoy from Rabaul with 700 troops embarked led to the next big clash, on the surface of Ironbottom Sound. During the night of October 11–12 the American escort force under Rear Admiral Norman Scott met a Japanese force under Rear Admiral Aritomo Goto who had come down with the convoy, intent on shelling the Marines ashore. Goto's force, the cruisers *Aoba, Kinugasa,* and *Furataka,* along with two destroyers, were surprised off Cape Esperance when, just before midnight, Scott's cruisers *San Francisco, Boise, Salt Lake City,* and *Helena* crossed their 'T' and opened fire. After a minute Scott, fearing he was shoot-

Above: The severely damaged American cruiser San Francisco *after the Battle of Guadalcanal, November 12–13.*

Right: The Enterprise *in the Battle of Santa Cruz, October 26.*

ing into some of his own destroyers, ceased firing. At the same time Goto, just before he was killed, believing he was being shot at by another Japanese force, ordered course reversed. Fire quickly was resumed by the Americans. When it was all over the *Furataka* and one destroyer on each side were gone, while *Aoba* and *Boise* were severely damaged. Bombardment plans forgotten, the surviving Japanese hastened north. Both convoys unloaded their men and supplies undisturbed.

Two nights later a pair of swift old battleships, the *Kongo* and *Haruna,* commanded by Vice Admiral Takeo Kurita, spent an hour-and-a-half bombarding Henderson Field. They destroyed 48 airplanes and most of the defenders' aviation

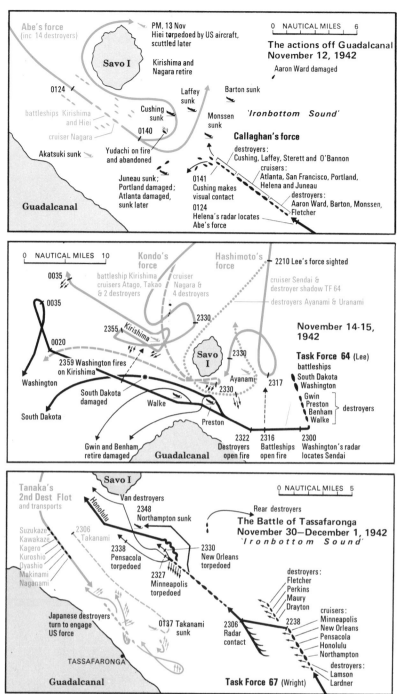

The actions off Guadalcanal November 12, 1942

Abe's force (inc 14 destroyers)

PM, 13 Nov Hiei torpedoed by US aircraft, scuttled later

0 NAUTICAL MILES 6

Savo I

Kirishima and Nagara retire

Aaron Ward damaged

0124

battleships Kirishima and Hiei

cruiser Nagara

Laffey sunk

Barton sunk

Cushing sunk

Monssen sunk

'Ironbottom Sound'

Callaghan's force

0140

Akatsuki sunk

Yudachi on fire and abandoned

Juneau sunk; Portland damaged; Atlanta damaged, sunk later

0141 Cushing makes visual contact

0124 Helena's radar locates Abe's force

Guadalcanal

destroyers: Cushing, Laffey, Sterett and O'Bannon
cruisers: Atlanta, San Francisco, Portland, Helena and Juneau
destroyers: Aaron Ward, Barton, Monssen, Fletcher

---

0 NAUTICAL MILES 10

Kondo's force

Hashimoto's force

2210 Lee's force sighted

battleship Kirishima cruisers Atago, Takao & 2 destroyers

cruiser Nagara & 4 destroyers

cruiser Sendai & destroyer shadow TF 64

0035

destroyers Ayanami & Uranami

0035

2355 Kirishima

2330

November 14–15, 1942

0020

Savo I

2330

Task Force 64 (Lee)
battleships
South Dakota
Washington

2359 Washington fires on Kirishima

Ayanami

2317

Washington

South Dakota damaged

Walke

2330

Gwin
Preston
Benham
Walke } destroyers

South Dakota

Preston

Gwin and Benham retire damaged

Guadalcanal

2322 Destroyers open fire

2316 Battleships open fire

2300 Washington's radar locates Sendai

Tanaka's 2nd Dest Flot and transports

Savo I

Van destroyers

0 NAUTICAL MILES 5

2348 Northampton sunk

Rear destroyers

Honolulu

The Battle of Tassafaronga November 30–December 1, 1942 'Ironbottom Sound'

Suzukaze
Kawakaze
Kagero
Kuroshio
Oyashio
Makinami
Naganami

2306 Takanami

2338 Pensacola torpedoed

2330 New Orleans torpedoed

2327 Minneapolis torpedoed

destroyers: Fletcher, Perkins, Maury, Drayton

cruisers: Minneapolis, New Orleans, Pensacola, Honolulu, Northampton

Japanese destroyers turn to engage US force

0137 Takanami sunk

2306 Radar contact

2238

destroyers: Lamson, Lardner

TASSAFARONGA

Guadalcanal

Task Force 67 (Wright)

Above: The wreck of a Japanese transport lies off the Guadalcanal shore after the actions of November 14–15.

gasoline. The next night the heavy cruisers *Chokai* and *Kinugasa* repeated the bombardment, although on a smaller scale. In the morning the Marines could see six Japanese transports unloading troops and supplies. Enough fuel was found to permit the Americans to fly the short distance to the Japanese ships and sink three of them. That night the heavy cruisers *Myoko* and *Maya* shelled Henderson Field. The same day an American supply convoy was sighted by a Japanese plane and turned back, with the loss of a destroyer to the *Zuikaku's* pilots.

Another major battle

It was now that Vice Admiral William F. Halsey reappeared, after several months'

illness. On October 19 he took command in the South Pacific. His arrival brought cheers from the hard-pressed Americans. But American bad fortune did not end. The next day submarine *I176* found an American task force and torpedoed the heavy cruiser *Chester*, which had to go to the East Coast for repairs.

On October 23 the Japanese Army began a major drive to capture Henderson Field. After three days of savage fighting they acknowledged failure. Meanwhile, Marine dive bombers sank the light cruiser *Yura* which had intended to bombard the Americans.

Some two hundred miles to the eastward a major sea battle was shaping up near the Santa Cruz Islands. The Japanese commander-in-chief, Admiral Isoroku Yamamoto, was directing affairs on his side from his flagship anchored at Truk. Halsey was doing the same thing from headquarters in Noumea. Each fleet was aware of the other's presence, but neither knew exactly where the enemy was or how powerful he was. Just before dawn on October 26 Admiral Halsey

ordered his commander at sea, Rear Admiral Thomas C. Kinkaid, to 'Attack-Repeat-Attack.'

Kinkaid was in the *Enterprise* (83 aircraft) screened by the battleship *South Dakota*, two cruisers, and eight destroyers. A second task force consisted of the *Hornet* (88), screened by four cruisers and six destroyers.

Vice Admiral Kondo was Yamamoto's man on the spot. He had the *Junyo* (55), two battleships, five cruisers, and 14 destroyers. Commanding Kondo's main striking force was Nagumo, with the *Shokaku* (61), *Zuikaku* (72), and *Zuiho* (24), accompanied by two battleships, five cruisers, and 15 destroyers. A dozen submarines were posted about the expected battle area. Scouts from the opposing fleets found their enemies, about 200 miles apart.

Two American scouts found the *Zuiho*, attacked her, and got two hits, temporarily putting her out of business. But Nagumo's three carriers already had a 65-plane strike in the air. They passed 73 American planes from the *Hornet* and *Enterprise* going the other way. For the most part the opponents ignored each other.

With the *Enterprise* hidden by a rain squall the Japanese concentrated on the *Hornet*. Time and again they hit the carrier with torpedoes and bombs (and a couple of suicide aircraft) and left her dead in the water. The Americans did much the same to the *Shokaku* except that as she had not been hit by torpedoes (or suicide planes), she could still steam. Soon thereafter the submarine *I21* sank one of Kinkaid's destroyers.

A second Japanese air strike found the *Enterprise* and hit her with three bombs, while a torpedo plane crashed into the destroyer *Smith's* forecastle. The *Smith's* skipper put her bow into the high wake of the nearby battleship *South Dakota* and quenched the flames. The *South Dakota*, struck by one bomb, was credited with shooting down 26 Japanese aircraft. Afternoon strikes by the *Junyo* got more torpedo hits on the *Hornet* and frustrated American efforts at salvage. The flaming carrier was

Kongo

Kongo started life as a British-built battlecruiser in 1913, but was completely reconstructed as a fast battleship before World War II. The *Kongo* was finally sunk in 1944, and she is depicted as she appeared then. On the catapult is a 'Jake' floatplane, used for reconnaissance.

Displacement: 31,720 tons
Armament: Eight 14-inch guns, fourteen 6-in, eight 5-in AA
Machinery: Four-shaft geared turbines,
136,000 shp = 30½ knots

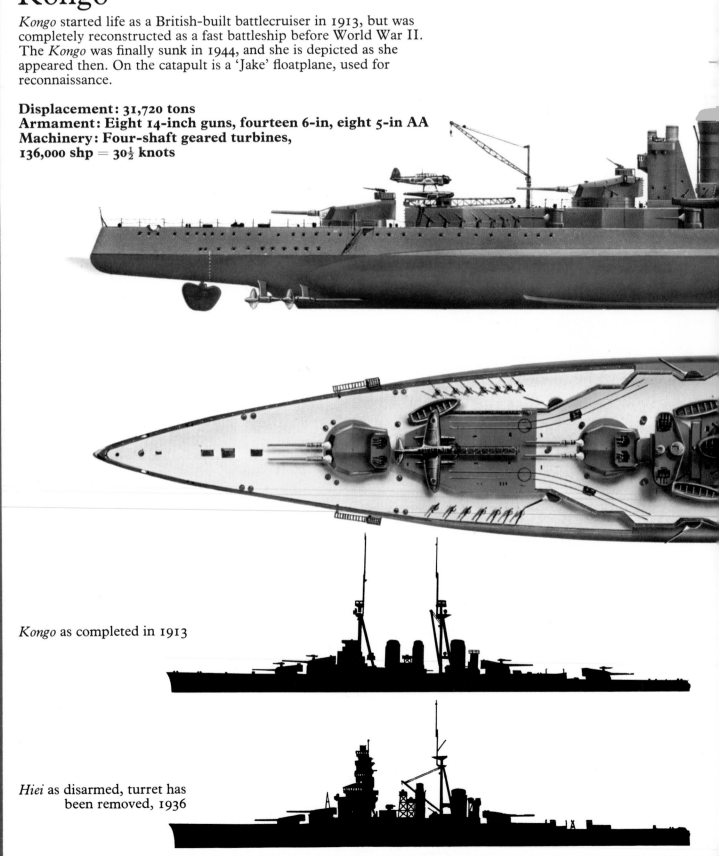

Kongo as completed in 1913

Hiei as disarmed, turret has been removed, 1936

abandoned, and Kinkaid took the rest of his ships south. Kondo sent his damaged carriers north. With the rest of his fleet he pursued the Americans, without success, though they did come upon and sink the floating wreckage that was once the *Hornet*.

The *Enterprise* now was the only American carrier left in the Pacific and she was full of bomb holes. The forward elevator was jammed, fortunately in the up position so the flight deck could still be used.

Both sides continued to send convoys to Guadalcanal laden with troops and arms. The Japanese then planned another battleship bombardment of Henderson Field for the night of November 12–13, to be followed by Tanaka whose eleven destroyers would escort an equal number of transports crammed with 13,500 troops and their arms and supplies.

The bombardment force under Vice Admiral Hiroaki Abe, consisting of the battleships *Hiei* and *Kirishima*, the light cruiser *Nagara*, and 14 destroyers, had just passed

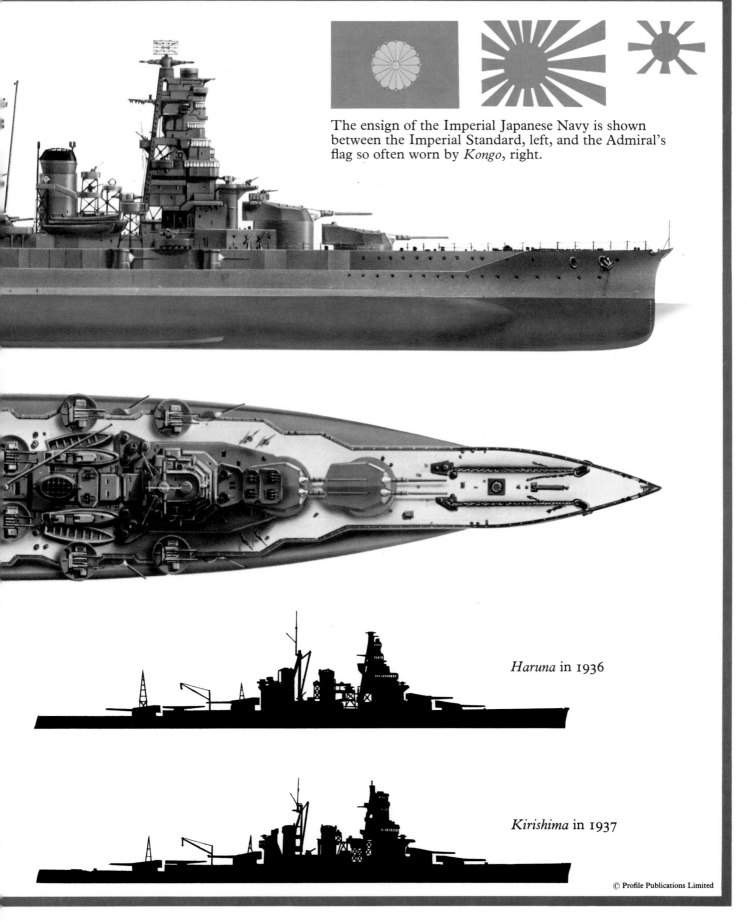

The ensign of the Imperial Japanese Navy is shown between the Imperial Standard, left, and the Admiral's flag so often worn by *Kongo*, right.

Haruna in 1936

Kirishima in 1937

© Profile Publications Limited

The Battles around Guadalcanal, 1943

U.S.A.		Japan	
Carrier		**Carriers**	
Enterprise		Junyo	Hiyo
Battleships		**Battleships**	
South Dakota	Washington	Hiei	Haruna
Cruisers		Kirishima	Kongo
Pensacola	Helena	**Cruisers**	
Portland	Juneau	Nagara	Kinugasa
Atlanta	Northampton	Maya	Atago
San Francisco	San Diego	Suzuya	Takao
		Tenryu	Tone
		Chokai	Sendai
		Isuzu	

Savo Island at 0141 on November 13 when contact was made with an American force sent out to prevent the bombardment. The Americans, under Rear Admiral Daniel J. Callaghan, consisted of a column of five cruisers and eight destroyers—first four destroyers, then the *Atlanta* (with Rear Admiral Norman Scott embarked), *San Francisco* (Callaghan's flagship), *Portland*, *Helena*, *Juneau*, and then four more destroyers.

The Americans headed into the midst of the oncoming Japanese formation. A Japanese destroyer's searchlight illuminated the *Atlanta*. Before the offending light could be extinguished by the little cruiser's 5-inch guns the Japanese concentrated on her, first with gunfire, which killed Admiral Scott among others, then with torpedoes. She went dead in the water only to be struck by two salvoes of 8-inch from the *San Francisco*. The *San Francisco* then fired several salvoes into the *Hiei*, and the *Kirishima* in turn hit the cruiser with 14-inch, killing Admiral Callaghan and nearly everyone else on the bridge. The *Juneau* was torpedoed. The *Portland*, also torpedoed and circling without steering control, fired into the *Hiei* with her 8-inch at only two miles. Of the American cruisers only the *Helena* came through unharmed; and of the destroyers, four were sunk and two damaged. Of the Japanese, two destroyers were gone while *Hiei* and one destroyer were severely damaged. The whole affair was over in little more than 20 minutes. The surviving Americans retired south-ward, the Japanese northward. There was no bombardment of Henderson Field.

Seven out of eleven are sunk

When dawn came the crippled ships picked on one another but soon found self-salvage a more pressing matter. The *Atlanta* was beyond help and the *Juneau*, torpedoed by the *I26*, blew up with the loss of all but ten of her people. But the *Portland* and *San Francisco* survived. The *Hiei*, attacked all day by planes from the *Enterprise* and from Henderson Field, finally sank early in the evening. During the night the heavy cruisers *Suzuya* and *Maya* shelled Henderson Field, destroying 18 aircraft.

The next morning, that of the 14th, aircraft from the *Enterprise* and Henderson Field sank one cruiser, the *Kinugasa*, and damaged several others. But more important work was the destruction of the oncoming troop transports which were screened by Tanaka's destroyers and Zeros from the carrier *Hiyo*. Despite Tanaka and the Zeros, the Americans sank seven of the eleven transports. But the other four, plus four destroyers, continued south to Guadalcanal. They arrived during darkness. Before dawn of November 15 the transports beached themselves, 2,000 troops went ashore, and the destroyers raced back to safety.

On the night of November 14 Kondo himself went south with the old *Kirishima*, the heavy cruisers *Atago* (flag) and *Takao*, the light cruisers *Nagara* and *Sendai*, and nine destroyers. Their purpose was the bombardment of Henderson Field.

At 2316 the *Sendai* and a destroyer came under battleship gunfire as they were steaming east of Savo Island. They hastened away under cover of smoke. A few minutes later the *Nagara* and four destroyers engaged four American destroyers, sinking three and severely damaging the fourth. The battleships which had chased off the *Sendai* and her companion were the new *Washington* and *South Dakota*, with Rear Admiral Willis A. Lee embarked in the former. They next fired on the *Nagara* force without result. The Japanese, in turn, fired 34 24-inch Long Lance torpedoes, also without result. At this point Kondo with the *Atago*, *Takao*, *Kirishima*, and two destroyers entered the fight. A destroyer illuminated the *South Dakota* and Kondo's ships fired on her with Long Lance torpedoes and guns. The torpedoes missed but the guns did not and the *South Dakota* was seriously damaged. Then the *Washington* opened fire. The range was 8,400 yards and the target was the *Kirishima*. Inside of seven minutes that ship, hit by nine 16-inch and forty 5-inch shells, was reduced to a flaming wreck. Aside from another unsuccessful torpedo attack, this time by a pair of Tanaka's destroyers which were screening the transports, the battle was over. The *Kirishima*, and a damaged Japanese destroyer were scuttled. While Kondo retired north, his bombardment plans cancelled, Lee and his surviving ships steamed south.

Tokyo Express in reverse

At dawn the only ships in sight were the four transports which had just beached themselves. Marine and Army gunners ashore, pilots from the *Enterprise* and Henderson Field, and a destroyer combined to destroy them where they lay. The Naval Battle of Guadalcanal was over.

Thereafter no more Japanese heavy ships approached that island, and no more large reinforcement convoys carrying Japanese soldiers sailed for that island. Indeed, though the Japanese Army wished to hold on to Guadalcanal, the Navy no longer did. The resulting compromise was an attempt to maintain what they had on the island while building new defenses further up the

Maya

Ostensibly within the terms of the Washington Treaty, the Japanese built a series of powerful heavy cruisers and their heavy armament and high speed amazed foreign observers. However, they had considerably exceeded the treaty's 10,000-ton limit. *Maya* and two sisters were sunk in the Battle of Leyte Gulf.

Above: Torpedoed by the submarine
Nautilus, *the Japanese destroyer* Yamakaze
sinks off Tokyo Bay, June 25, 1942.

*Left: Burdened with supplies for troops
struggling for control of New Georgia in
mid-1943, one LST follows another up a
narrow channel.*

Solomons chain.

The maintenance effort meant more trips
by Tanaka's Tokyo Express, but with destroyers only. Those swift ships would dart
in at night, push off supplies in drums for the
defenders near Tassafaronga, and be gone
long before dawn. The first of these efforts,
on November 30, found Tanaka and eight
destroyers between Savo Island and Guadalcanal just before midnight. There Tanaka,
steaming at 12 knots, was surprised by an
American force consisting of the cruisers
*Minneapolis, New Orleans, Pensacola,
Honolulu,* and *Northampton,* and eight
destroyers. The Americans fired first, both
with torpedoes and with shells, and over-

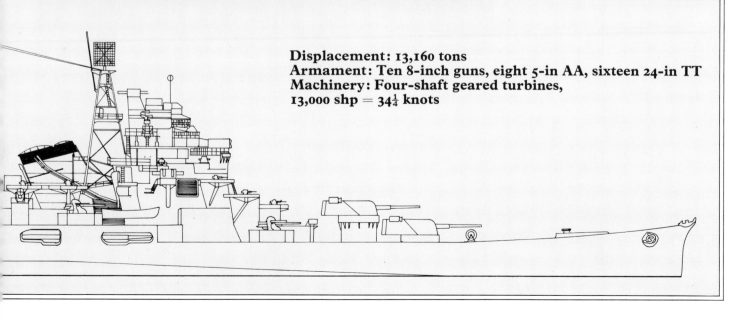

Displacement: 13,160 tons
Armament: Ten 8-inch guns, eight 5-in AA, sixteen 24-in TT
Machinery: Four-shaft geared turbines,
13,000 shp = 34¼ knots

USS Cushing

The *Mahan* Class were similar in layout and size to their British contemporaries. They were better armed, with the excellent 5-inch dual-purpose gun, but suffered from a cumbersome arrangement of sided torpedo-tubes, which gave them no increase in the number of torpedoes which could be fired on either broadside. The *Cushing* is depicted with early wartime modifications, principally the removal of a fifth 5-inch gun on the after deckhouse and the provision of 20-mm anti-aircraft guns. Note also the early radar aerial at the masthead. She was sunk by gunfire from Japanese destroyers off Savo Island in 1942.

whelmed one of the Japanese destroyers. Surprised but not unprepared, Tanaka responded with his Long Lance torpedoes. In a few minutes he had sunk the *Northampton*, blown the bows off the *Minneapolis* and *New Orleans*, and severely damaged the *Pensacola*. Tanaka then made it safely back to base.

While the Japanese had chosen merely to hold onto their position on Guadalcanal, the Americans managed both to reinforce and to relieve the exhausted defenders of Henderson Field. On January 4 the Japanese decided to evacuate the island. The Tokyo Express reversed itself and, unbeknown to the Americans, by February 7 the Japanese Navy had quietly removed every Japanese soldier still alive.

Meanwhile it was Halsey's ships, not Yamamoto's, which were bombarding their enemies ashore, at the next big island in the Solomons chain, New Georgia. But the Japanese won the last major success of the Guadalcanal campaign when on January 30 torpedo planes based on New Georgia sank the cruiser *Chicago*, which had just been repaired following the damage sustained at Savo Island in August.

Sickness claims more than war

During the summer of 1942 each side was anxious to occupy both the spacious harbor of Milne Bay, at the eastern end of New Guinea, and Buna, a native village and air

Far left: The torpedo-twisted bow of the cruiser St. Louis *after the Battle of Kolombangara, July 12–13, 1943.*

Left: Oil-covered survivors of the cruiser Helena, *sunk at Kula Gulf on July 6, 1943, muster on the deck of a rescue ship.*

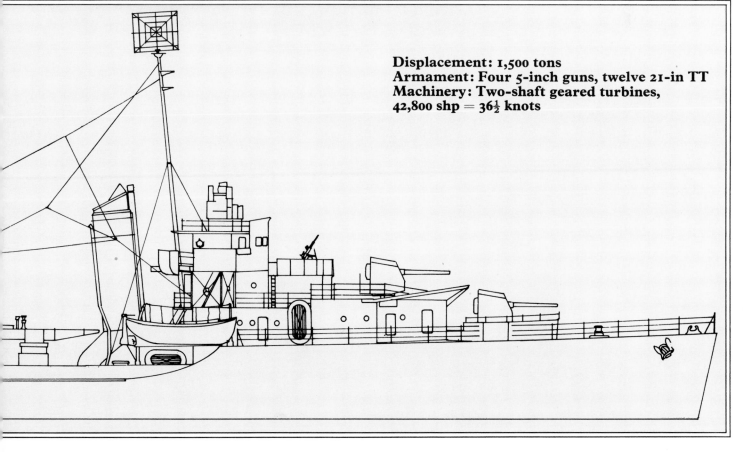

Displacement: 1,500 tons
Armament: Four 5-inch guns, twelve 21-in TT
Machinery: Two-shaft geared turbines,
42,800 shp = 36½ knots

strip about 150 miles to the northwest of Milne Bay on the northern shore of New Guinea's Papuan Peninsula, The Americans and Australians were first at Milne Bay, in June; the Japanese first at Buna, in July. By the time the Japanese were able to land 2,000 troops at Milne Bay beginning on August 25, the Australians and Americans had nearly 10,000 there to greet them. After a couple of week's fierce fighting the Japanese re-embarked their surviving troops and left the place to their enemies.

Then, late in September, Australian troops halted the Japanese overland drive on Port Moresby only 30 miles from its destination. Anxious to get to Buna but unwilling to risk their few ships in the reef-strewn, uncharted Solomon Sea (over which the Japanese, in any event, maintained control), MacArthur's planners had to push their troops over the high mountains which had so impeded the Japanese and then down into the malarial swamps along the north coast. About half the supply and reinforcements went by air, the remainder in coastal freighters and fishing craft which were under hazard of Japanese air attack once they cleared Milne Bay. MacArthur's 30,000 men began their attack on Buna and a couple of neighbouring villages on November 19; they ended it on January 22, 1943, when they finally crushed the 12,000 Japanese defenders. Allied casualties from battle were 8,500, from sickness three times as much.

During most of 1942 Japan's strong submarine force was quite successful in fleet warfare against the Americans, especially in the Solomons. But toward the end of the year the submarines fell under the influence of the Army, which used them as clandestine supply boats for troops isolated at Guadalcanal and elsewhere. Consequently those

The 6-inch guns of the cruiser Columbia *fire at night near Bougainville, November 1, 1943.*

USS Alabama

The *South Dakota* Class was the second class of new battleships begun under the USA's rearmament programme. They were shorter but better protected than the previous *North Carolina* Class, and were roughly comparable to the British *King George V* Class.
A noticeable feature of the *Alabama's* layout is the compact superstructure crowded with anti-aircraft guns. This was possible because in American battleships and cruisers the spotting aircraft and catapults were sited on the quarterdeck.

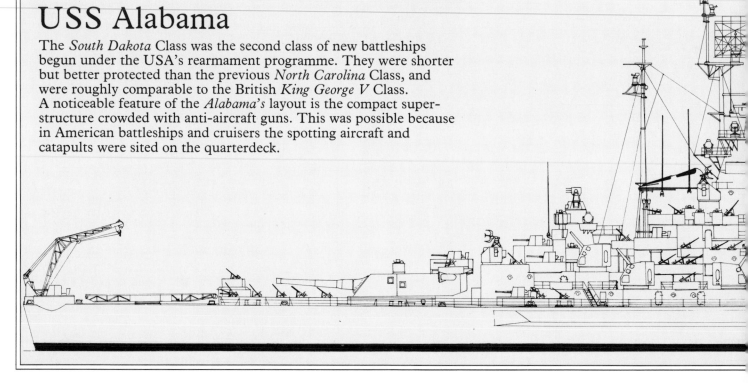

The flight deck of the Saratoga *after her attack on Rabaul, November 5, 1943. The aircraft are Douglas SBD Dauntless dive bombers.*

submarines seldom took an effective part in the later fighting. During 1943 they were to lose 23 of their number. They sank only one important American ship, the escort carrier *Liscombe Bay*, during the Gilbert Islands invasion.

Underwater successes

The American submarines, however, which had been unable to defend the Philippines early in the war, and which were seldom deployed with the rest of the fleet, ended the year with a small success north of New Guinea when in December the new *Albacore* sank the old Japanese light cruiser *Tenryu*. All told during the year the American submarines sank two cruisers, four destroyers, and six submarines, results that did not match those of the Japanese.

But more importantly, US submarines sank 23 Japanese supply ships during the Guadalcanal campaign. And in the shipping war in general, which the Japanese largely eschewed, American submarines made about 500 attacks in 1942. These resulted in 140 ships of over half a million tons sunk, quite an achievement against an enemy who started the war with only six million tons, especially in view of the insufficient number and abysmal quality of torpedoes with which the Americans had supplied themselves. Eight American submarines were lost that year, but only three of them to Japanese attack; thirty-five new ones were added.

While in 1942 the US Navy's submarines contributed merely to the war effort, in 1943

This beached and wrecked torpedo boat was, along with large numbers of other small craft, involved in the struggle in the Solomons.

Displacement: 38,000 tons
Armament: Nine 16-inch guns, twenty 5-in DP
Machinery: Four-shaft geared turbines, 130,000 shp = 28 knots

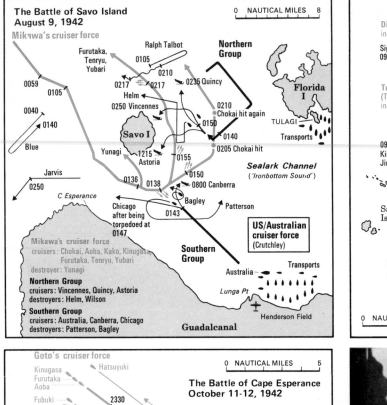

The Battle of Savo Island
August 9, 1942

0 NAUTICAL MILES 8

Mikawa's cruiser force

Furutaka, Tenryu, Yubari
Ralph Talbot
0105
0059
0105
0210
0217
0217
0235 Quincy
0040
0140
Helm
0210
Chokai hit again
0250 Vincennes
0150
0140
Blue
Savo I
0205 Chokai hit
Yunagi
1215
Astoria
0155
0136
0138
0150
0800 Canberra
Jarvis
0250
C Esperance
Bagley
Chicago after being torpedoed at 0147
0143
Patterson

Northern Group

Florida I

TULAGI

Transports

Sealark Channel ('Ironbottom Sound')

US/Australian cruiser force (Crutchley)

Southern Group

Transports

Australia
Lunga Pt
Henderson Field

Guadalcanal

Mikawa's cruiser force
cruisers: Chokai, Aoba, Kako, Kinugasa, Furutaka, Tenryu, Yubari
destroyer: Yunagi

Northern Group
cruisers: Vincennes, Quincy, Astoria
destroyers: Helm, Wilson

Southern Group
cruisers: Australia, Canberra, Chicago
destroyers: Patterson, Bagley

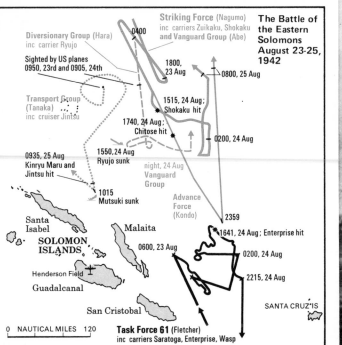

The Battle of the Eastern Solomons
August 23-25, 1942

Striking Force (Nagumo)
inc carriers Zuikaku, Shokaku and Vanguard Group (Abe)

Diversionary Group (Hara)
inc carrier Ryujo

Sighted by US planes 0950, 23rd and 0905, 24th

Transport Group (Tanaka)
inc cruiser Jintsu

0400
1800, 23 Aug
0800, 25 Aug
1515, 24 Aug; Shokaku hit
1740, 24 Aug; Chitose hit
0200, 24 Aug
0935, 25 Aug Kinryu Maru and Jintsu hit
1550, 24 Aug Ryujo sunk
night, 24 Aug Vanguard Group
Advance Force (Kondo)
1015 Mutsuki sunk
2359
1641, 24 Aug; Enterprise hit
0600, 23 Aug
0200, 24 Aug
2215, 24 Aug

Santa Isabel
Malaita
SOLOMON ISLANDS
Henderson Field
Guadalcanal
San Cristobal
SANTA CRUZ IS

0 NAUTICAL MILES 120

Task Force 61 (Fletcher)
inc carriers Saratoga, Enterprise, Wasp

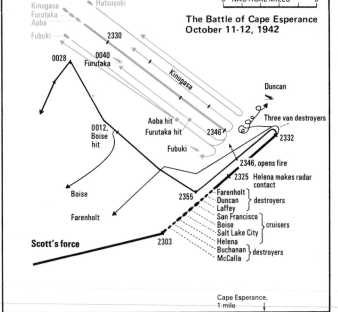

The Battle of Cape Esperance
October 11-12, 1942

0 NAUTICAL MILES 5

Goto's cruiser force

Kinugasa
Furutaka
Aoba
Hatsuyuki
Fubuki
2330
0028
0040 Furutaka
0012, Boise hit
Kinugasa
Aoba hit
Furutaka hit
2346
Fubuki
Duncan
Three van destroyers
2332
2346, opens fire
2325 Helena makes radar contact
Boise
Farenholt
2355

Farenholt
Duncan } destroyers
Laffey
San Francisco
Boise } cruisers
Salt Lake City
Helena
Buchanan } destroyers
McCalla

Scott's force
2303

Cape Esperance, 1 mile

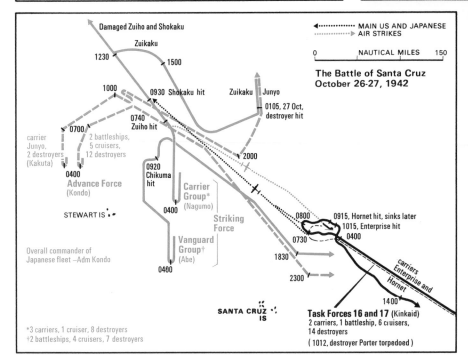

The Battle of Santa Cruz
October 26-27, 1942

MAIN US AND JAPANESE
AIR STRIKES

0 NAUTICAL MILES 150

Damaged Zuiho and Shokaku
Zuikaku
1230
1500
1000
0930 Shokaku hit
Zuikaku
Junyo
0105, 27 Oct, destroyer hit
0700
0740 Zuiho hit
0300 Zuiho hit
carrier Junyo, 2 destroyers (Kakuta)
2 battleships, 5 cruisers, 12 destroyers
0920 Chikuma hit
2000
Advance Force (Kondo)
0400
Carrier Group* (Nagumo)
Striking Force
0800
0915, Hornet hit, sinks later
1015, Enterprise hit
STEWART IS
0400
0730
0400
Vanguard Group† (Abe)
Overall commander of Japanese fleet – Adm Kondo
0400
1830
carriers Enterprise and Hornet
2300
SANTA CRUZ IS
1400

Task Forces 16 and 17 (Kinkaid)
2 carriers, 1 battleship, 6 cruisers, 14 destroyers
(1012, destroyer Porter torpedoed)

*3 carriers, 1 cruiser, 8 destroyers
†2 battleships, 4 cruisers, 7 destroyers

patrol boats.

Though most of the forces in both fleets were sucked south into the Solomons (southeastward for Yamamoto's forces, southwestward for Nimitz's), each fleet also had responsibilities across the broad face of the Pacific. The Americans, resenting the Japanese occupation of two worthless islands in the Aleutians, planned to eject the invaders. Air bases were set up on other islands from which the Japanese on Kiska and Attu could be bombed despite the almost continual foul weather; submarines patrolled through long depressing fogs; cruisers and destroyers blockaded, and occasionally shelled, the enemy garrisons. On March 26 a Japanese attempt to get two transports through to Attu was frustrated by a small American task force.

Duel at long range

Rear Admiral Charles H. McMorris in the old light cruiser *Richmond*, accompanied by the heavy cruiser *Salt Lake City* and four destroyers, sighted masts to the north while they were on patrol near the Soviet Union's Komandorski Islands. They hastened to make contact. The masts belonged not only to the transports, but also to Vice Admiral Boshiro Hosogaya's escort, which consisted of the heavy cruisers *Nachi* and *Maya*, the light cruisers *Tama* and *Abukuma*, and four destroyers. All morning was spent in a long-range gunnery duel. McMorris' attempt to sink the transports was frustrated, but so was Hosogaya's attempt to get them to Attu. The Japanese admiral, with his transports, retired to his base in the Kuriles. The Japanese did not again try to bring in reinforcements or supplies to the islands.

In May the Americans landed and re-took Attu after much fighting ashore. In August, after a heavy naval bombardment they landed on Kiska. Nobody was there. Three weeks earlier the Japanese had crept through the fog and quietly evacuated their whole garrison.

The year-long Japanese sojourn in the Aleutians was poorly conceived but in the end they had led the Americans to commit not only large naval and air forces, but also 100,000 ground troops to an inconsequential campaign. Tactically the Americans were the victors; strategically the Japanese were.

In April 1943 Admiral Yamamoto denuded the decks of his four operational carriers—the *Zuikaku*, *Zuiho*, *Junyo*, and *Hiyo*, sending the 170-odd aircraft to join a similar number of shore-based planes of the 11th Air Fleet at Rabaul and nearby fields. They made a series of heavy raids on Allied shipping, first at Guadalcanal and then at Oro Bay, Port Moresby, and Milne Bay, New Guinea. They sank few ships, shot down few airplanes and lost few of their number. Then Yamamoto halted his offensive and sent the carrier planes back to their ships. He himself was killed on April 18 when a bomber in which he was riding was shot down in the Northern Solomons by a US Army Air Force P-38. He was succeeded

warships not needed for escort work could be used for other purposes.

The million-ton setback

American submarines, sometimes acting in packs of three or four but more often singly, made over a thousand attacks during the year. They launched 4,000 torpedoes and sank 300 ships of 1,800,000 tons. Since Japan built only 800,000 tons of new ships, this effectively put that country back by a million tons.

Fifty-two of those ships sunk were in the South and South West Pacific, where most of the year's naval activity was centred, and this had enormous impact on Japan's ability to withstand the American offensive there. Additionally, the submarines sank 17 destroyers and smaller escort vessels in various parts of the Pacific, as well as the escort carrier *Chuyo*.

In February 1943 the Japanese became anxious to take the Australian outpost at Wau, well inland in New Guinea. Lacking the necessary troops on the island, the Japanese had to import them. Nearly 7,000 were embarked in eight transports at Rabaul. Accompanied by eight destroyers under Rear Admiral Masatomi Kimura, they departed on February 28 en route to Lae, a coastal village in New Guinea.

At first weather shielded the convoy, but it was found eventually. In attacks on March 2 and 3 Major General George C. Kenney's V US Army Air Force, consisting largely of twin-engined B-25 and A-20 light bombers, sank all the transports and half the destroyers in the Bismarck Sea. Japanese shore-based air cover was unable to cope with Kenney's low-flying bombers and his P-38 fighters. The brave Japanese destroyers saved nearly half those whose ships were sunk. The rest died in the sinkings or in the strafings they suffered from MacArthur's airplanes and

and thereafter they played such a dominant part that the achievements of all the other Allied forces have to be seen against a backdrop of submarine accomplishments. Both the supply and the quality of their torpedoes improved and so did the number of their excellent Fleet-type submarines, 66 of which were added, while losses amounted to 15.

Japanese merchant ships, which once had moved independently, now were formed into convoys. These were small—four or five ships, escorted by two or three destroyers or patrol craft. A 'Grand Escort Fleet,' created early in 1943 with 40 escorts had more than three times that number by the year's end. Meanwhile the Americans, in contrast, were able to abandon convoys. Merchant ships were routed independently, which is the most efficient way to do it. Destroyers and other as Commander-in-Chief Combined Fleet by Admiral Mineichi Koga.

In pursuit of air strips

At the end of June 1943 both Halsey and MacArthur moved forward once again, the former up the Solomons to New Georgia Island, the latter into the Trobriand Islands and Nassau Bay, New Guinea. For more than half a year the two would advance similar, but not large, distances, with the aim first of taking and then, more wisely, of neutralizing the great Japanese base at Rabaul at the north-eastern tip of New Britain. The general purpose of each invasion was to seize air strips in order to deny them to the Japanese, to use them for support of future advances. and to use them for raids on Rabaul. Because Halsey's advance was the more dangerous, it was the one which the Japanese opposed with the greater force.

The assault on Munda, New Georgia, led to the night battle of Kula Gulf on July 6, the first in a series in which the reactivated Tokyo Express collided with American forces sent to stop them. Rear Admiral Teruo Akiyama, with seven destroyers in column, met Rear Admiral Walden L. Ainsworth who had the big light cruisers *Honolulu*, *Helena*, and *St. Louis* and four destroyers. The battle opened at little more than three miles' range. Akiyama's Long Lance torpedoes bested Ainsworth's 6-inch guns, for while Akiyama was killed and his flagship sunk, so too was the *Helena* lost. Another Japanese destroyer was wrecked on a reef, but the Tokyo Express landed its troops.

Six nights later, off Kolombangara, it was the Tokyo Express against Ainsworth again. Rear Admiral Shunji Izaki in the old light cruiser *Jintsu* and five destroyers met Ainsworth with the *Honolulu*, *St. Louis,* the New Zealand light cruiser *Leander*, and ten destroyers. The battle opened at five miles. The *Jintsu* and Admiral Izaki were lost. An

American destroyer was sunk and all of Ainsworth's cruisers were severely damaged by torpedoes. Again, the Tokyo Express landed its troops

On the night of August 6–7 Commander Frederick Moosbrugger with six destroyers encountered the Tokyo Express in Vella Gulf. By using his torpedoes rather than his guns Moosbrugger sank three out of four Japanese destroyers at no cost to his force.

Carrier strike in response

The next landing was at Vella Lavella, in August. This intensified the fierce fighting which had been going on in the confined waters of the Solomons among island-based aircraft, destroyers, motor torpedo boats, troop-carring barges, assorted small warships, and occasional submarines. The Japanese decision to evacuate Vella Lavella led to a night action between nine Japanese and three American destroyers. One of the Americans was sunk, the others damaged, and the evacuation was completed.

On November 1 the Americans invaded the northernmost island in the Solomons, Bougainville. The defenders ashore expected the Americans to attempt to take the whole big island. But all the invaders wanted was space for an air strip so fighters could escort bombers over Rabaul. While the Japanese Army found itself frustrated, the Navy reacted quickly. Rear Admiral Sentaro Omori set out from Rabaul to destroy the American transports in Empress Augusta Bay with the heavy cruisers *Myoko* and *Haguro*, the small light cruisers *Agano* and *Sendai*, and six destroyers. In the darkness of November 2, he was intercepted by Rear Admiral Aaron S. Merrill with the large light cruisers *Montpelier, Cleveland, Columbia*, and *Denver,* and eight destroyers. With small loss to themselves Merrill's ships sank the old *Sendai* and a destroyer, and Omori retired. The next morning over 100 aircraft from Rabaul attacked Merrill's ships, again with-

out success.

Koga, alarmed by the landing at Bougainville, sent seven heavy cruisers and some lesser vessels from Truk to Rabaul. Halsey's response came in a form unused for a year, a carrier strike. The *Saratoga* and the new light carrier *Princeton* launched 97 planes on the morning of November 5 from the same waters where Merrill had just won his victory. They caught Rabaul by surprise and damaged four heavy cruisers, two light cruisers, and a pair of destroyers. Six days later the two carriers attacked Rabaul again and were followed by a strike of about 185 aircraft from the new *Essex, Bunker Hill*, and *Independence*. Most of the Japanese ships were gone but one destroyer was sunk.

A beleaguered fortress

The Japanese retaliated, attacking the *Essex* task force with over 100 aircraft. The attackers lost a third of their number and got no hits. The survivors were sent back to the carriers from which they had been drawn. And soon, no more big ships, naval or merchant, anchored at Rabaul until the war's end. That place, once an advanced base from which offensives could be launched, had now become a beleaguered fortress.

But the Tokyo Express still had a few runs to make. On the night of November 25 the

Sailors aboard the old battleship Pennsylvania *enjoy a quiet moment in northern waters before the attack on Attu in May, 1943. At the time of her completion in 1916 the* Pennsylvania *was in theory the most advanced design afloat, but she was sadly dated by the time of World War II. While in dry dock she was slightly damaged in the attack on Pearl Harbor but she was repaired and modernized for service in the Pacific. She survived the war only to be used as a target for atomic bombs at Bikini.*

USS Atlanta

In common with the British, the US Navy developed the idea of the anti-aircraft cruiser, a ship specially designed to provide air defence for a fleet. The *Atlanta* was the first of a series of eleven cruisers armed only with the 5-inch dual-purpose gun and torpedoes which allowed them to function with destroyers. Although designed for very high speeds indeed, 38 knots being quoted, they proved no faster than other American cruisers because of additional weight, and they lacked endurance. In spite of this they played an important part in the fighting around Guadalcanal in 1942, when *Atlanta* was sunk.

Express, taking about as many soldiers out of Bougainville as it had brought in, encountered Captain Arleigh Burke's Destroyer Squadron 23 near Cape St. George, New Ireland. Each had five destroyers. Burke sank two Japanese destroyers with torpedoes and one with gunfire. He had no losses.

Rabaul was now under constant air attack, both from the Solomons and from New Guinea. Occasionally destroyers shelled installations ashore. Halsey, with plenty of force to employ, seized the unoccupied Green Islands, north of Bougainville in February 1944 and, in March he took Emirau, north of Rabaul.

Though largely unopposed by the Japanese Navy, MacArthur was also barely assisted directly by the US Navy. Yet, it was under cover of Halsey's advances that MacArthur operated. In any event, by September 1943 that general had enough amphibious ships to make a combined airborne, overland, and amphibious descent upon Lae at the head of the Huon Gulf. The next month by amphibious means he took Finschafen at the north-western end of the Solomon Sea. In December he landed troops first at Arawe on New Britain's southern coast and then at Cape Gloucester, near that island's western tip. He was now in control of the Vitiaz and Dampier straits which led out of the confined waters of the Solomon Sea and he could proceed westward back to the Philippines.

In January 1944 he captured Saidor and Sio, both on the New Guinea side of Vitiaz Strait. In February he made a daring attack across the Bismarck Sea into the Admiralties. His force was too small and it was touch and go for a while. But eventually he had those islands and there the United States soon developed the great naval base of Manus.

The campaign which may properly be said to have begun in the Coral Sea in May 1942 was now finished.

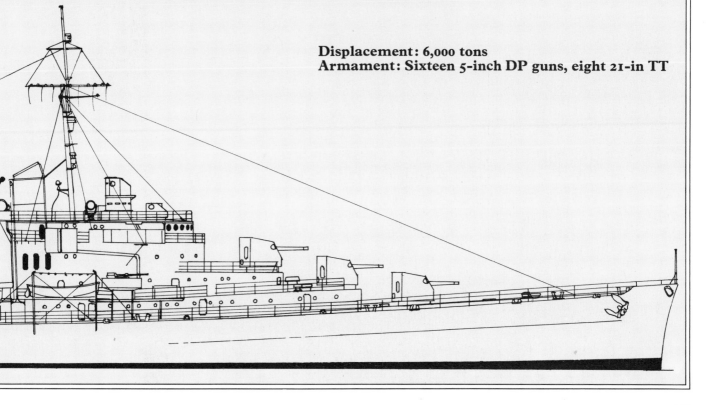

Displacement: 6,000 tons
Armament: Sixteen 5-inch DP guns, eight 21-in TT

The big leap
The Gilberts to Guam

In 1944 Japan lost four million tons of ships, the bulk to submarine attack, leaving her unable to maintain civil life, far less wage a war. She was also losing on the ground and in the air. In one brief battle alone 219 out of 326 attacking aircraft were lost. By August MacArthur had reached the western end of New Guinea; Nimitz had taken the Gilberts and pushed on to Saipan and Guam. The Americans now had an airfield from which the B29s could bomb Japan and the Allies had a base from which to launch the last part of their drive on Japan.

At the beginning of 1944 there were 123 American submarines in the Pacific. They had solved their torpedo problems and they had excellent radar, which was especially useful for night work on the surface. About half the time they worked in wolf packs. During the year they sank over 500 ships totalling 2,500,000 tons. This, combined with the work of both ship- and shore-based aircraft, which sank another, 1,500,000 tons left Japan at the year's and with much less than the three million tons of shipping she needed merely to continue her civil life.

Of course, military needs took precedence

over the needs of both civil life and industry. People had too little to eat. Airplane manufacturing and shipbuilding slumped—no surprise when 1944's imports of iron ore were only a third those of 1941. Oil was scarce for everyone. Because of the oil shortage the Japanese fleet moved first to Tawi Tawi, near Borneo's oil fields, and then to Lingga Roads, near the Sumatra fields. Even so, ships steamed too infrequently to keep up their training and pilots flew too seldom to gain and hold their skills.

In addition, submarines sank a substantial part of the Japanese fighting fleet. Off Truk in February the *Skate* sank the new light cruiser *Agano*; in March the *Sandlance* sank the old light cruiser *Tatsuta*; in April the *Bluegill* sank the *Yubari*, another old cruiser, and the *Flasher* sank the cruiser *Oi* in July. The escort carrier *Taiyo* fell victim to the *Rasher* in August and that same month the light cruisers *Nagara* and *Natori* were sunk by the *Croaker* and *Hardhead*. In September the escort carrier *Unyo* was sunk by the *Barb*. In October on the fringes of the Battle for Leyte Gulf the *Jallao* sank the already damaged light cruiser *Tama* while the *Bream* damaged the *Aoba*, though that heavy cruiser made it back to Japan.

In November the *Archerfish*, lurking in Japan's Inland Sea, sank the world's largest aircraft carrier, the *Shinano*, just a few miles from where she was built, while the *Spadefish* sank the escort carrier *Shinyo* and the *Sealion* destroyed the old battleship *Kongo*. The heavy cruiser *Myoko* was so badly damaged by the *Bergall* that she never sailed again, while the *Kumano*, ambushed by a wolf pack of four, was beached and the wreck destroyed by air attack. In December the large carrier *Junyo* was severely damaged by the *Sea Devil* and *Redfish* and barely made port; that same month the *Redfish* sank the *Unryu*, another large carrier. Thirty destroyers were sunk during the year by American submarines four of them by the *Harder* alone, though that submarine did not long survive her successes. Moreover, American submarines were also able to play a major part in the great naval battles of that year.

Nimitz thrusts straight on

Their considerable successes cost the Americans 19 submarines, including six lost through accidents. By the year's end they had 156 submarines in the Pacific. In contrast, the Japanese, who lost 57 submarines that year, accomplished nothing.

Meanwhile, British submarines working out of Ceylon and later, out of Fremantle, Australia, and helped by aircraft, closed Japan's supply route through the Malacca Strait to her forces in Burma. One submarine, the *Tally Ho*, sank the light cruiser *Kuma*, and another damaged the light cruiser *Kitakami*.

General Douglas MacArthur had tried to get his New Guinea campaign, aimed at returning to the Philippines, approved as the main American line of advance. But the Combined Chiefs of Staff, while not disapproving his campaign, also approved Admiral Chester Nimitz's proposal to thrust directly across the Central Pacific with his now powerful Marine divisions and amphibious force, protected by his new carriers.

Nimitz opened in November 1943 with an amphibious assault on the Gilbert Islands. Marines landed at Tarawa, soldiers at Makin Island, on November 20. Makin was not difficult, but Tarawa was. The Japanese defenders were numerous, tough and in excellent fortifications. To compound the Marines' difficulties, an unexpected low tide forced them to wade 600 yards between a

On July 21, 1944 the Americans returned to Guam, which had been under Japanese rule since December, 1941. The destroyer Farragut *lies inshore to give gunfire support to the Marines. A white phosphorus shell explodes beyond her.*

Shooting at nearly zero elevation, the 16-inch guns of the battleship Maryland *fire at the defenses of Tarawa. The fire was more impressive than effective.*

coral reef and the beach through a heavy fire. Preparatory bombing and naval gunfire support from many ships, most notably the old battleships, was heavy. But the gunners and aviators tended to believe the impressiveness of their fire was matched by the results at their targets. It wasn't, and the Marines fought a bloody battle before overcoming their foe.

The Americans learned their lessons at Tarawa and applied them in the Marshall Islands, their next objective, which were invaded on January 31, 1944. The main targets, undefended Majuro and heavily defended Kwajalein, quickly passed into the competent hands of the Marines. On February 22 the Marines were landed 300 miles farther west, at Eniwetok Atoll, after a heavy bombardment, and they soon won control.

Two days to sink 200,000 tons

The seizure of these atolls provided the Americans with anchorages, air strips, and

USS Reuben James

When the USA entered World War II the grave shortage of anti-submarine escort vessels was immediately apparent. But fortunately a diesel-electric escort was already under construction for the Royal Navy under Lend-Lease. This design was immediately adopted for mass-production but it had to be lengthened to accommodate turbo-electric machinery. The *Reuben James* was one of this "long-hulled" group, two hundred of which were under construction by early 1942. The gun armament was heavier than in contemporary British escorts, but one British feature, the open bridge was adopted for the first time. Ships of this class, many of them in the Royal Navy, served in both the Pacific and Atlantic theatres.

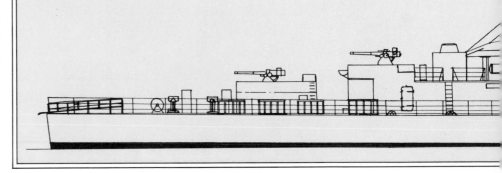

staging areas to be used for further advances. Simultaneously they denied these same assets to Japan.

While the amphibious force, Marines, and soldiers were occupied with the issue at Eniwetok, nine carriers under Rear Admiral Marc Mitscher attacked the Japanese naval base at Truk in the Carolines, some 700 miles from both Eniwetok and Rabaul. Admiral Koga had withdrawn his fleet, but in two days and a night, Mitscher's aviators sank 200,000 tons of shipping and destroyed 275 aircraft. A similar raid on Palau at the end of March led to the sinking of another 130,000 tons of shipping.

All these operations in the Central Pacific were conducted by the Fifth Fleet under Vice Admiral Raymond A. Spruance. Later, when Admiral William F. Halsey took his turn at command, the force would be called the Third Fleet. But the ships and the men were the same, no matter what the label. 'MacArthur's Navy', the Seventh Fleet, under Vice Admiral Thomas C. Kinkaid, consisted of different ships and men.

Now, while Spruance's men paused, Kinkaid's moved ahead. After MacArthur's aviators, under Major General George C. Kenney, had gained control of the air, on April 22 Kinkaid's amphibious sailors landed troops at Hollandia, New Guinea, 200 miles to the westward of the Japanese Army's now by-passed fortress at Wewak. On May 17 MacArthur's men invaded Wakde and then, in order to get a site suitable for a heavy bomber base, they landed on Biak Island, 350 miles beyond Hollandia, on May 27.

Admiral Koga had recently been killed in an airplane crash. His successor, Admiral Soemu Toyoda, responded to the Biak in-

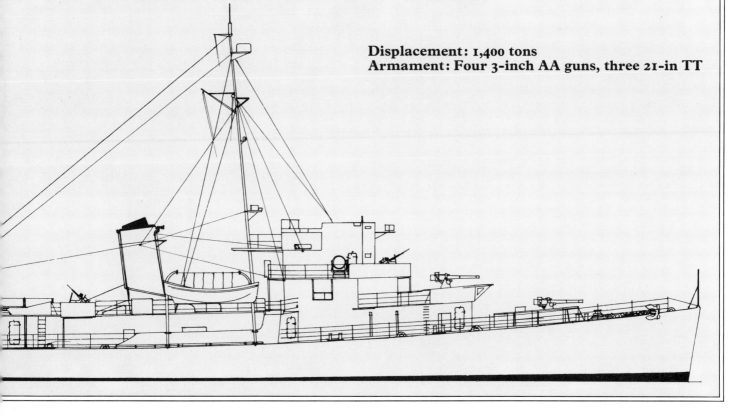

Displacement: 1,400 tons
Armament: Four 3-inch AA guns, three 21-in TT

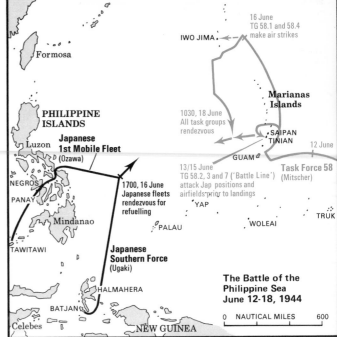

The Battle of the
Philippine Sea
June 12-18, 1944

0 NAUTICAL MILES 600

Anxiety in their eyes, American soldiers heading for the beach at Hollandia, New Guinea, watch Navy planes overhead.

vasion with an attempt to reinforce that island with troops from the Philippines. Frustrated in two attempts, first by a false report of a US carrier and then by the presence of a superior Allied cruiser and destroyer force, Toyoda decided to send a force built around the huge battleships *Yamato* and *Musashi*. But before those ships could get to Biak, Spruance began his attack on Saipan. To meet the greater threat from the Central Pacific, Toyoda called off the Biak operation.

On July 2 MacArthur, still looking for airfield sites, landed at the island of Noemfoor and then, on July 30, he occupied Sansapor at the western end of New Guinea. It had taken him a year-and-a-half to get out of the Solomon Sea; but then he had reached the other end of New Guinea in only half a year more.

England sinks six submarines

The Japanese planners had anticipated an attack by Nimitz's forces. In the hope, as much as in the belief, that it would be aimed at Palau, in May they placed a strong barrier of submarines north of the Admiralties. And, to make use of their multitude of island air bases, by early June they had deployed 540 aircraft into those islands, with the majority of them to the south.

When news came to Toyoda of Spruance's preliminary bombardment of Saipan he sent his main force, the First Mobile Fleet under Vice Admiral Jisaburo Ozawa, to unite with the island-based aircraft to destroy the US Pacific Fleet. Ozawa's command, most of it at Tawi Tawi, consisted of five carriers and four light carriers, with 430 planes on their decks, as well as an assortment of battleships, cruisers, and destroyers. He set sail on June 13, met up with the ships of the aborted Biak expedition on the 16th well to the east of the Philippines, and continued north-east. Unbeknownst to him he had been sighted and reported several times by well-placed

American submarines and his opponents were expecting him.

That was not all the bad news for Japan. The Americans had found most of the Japanese barrier submarines as well as a number of those on supply missions to nearly forgotten garrisons, and of the 25 submarines at sea had sunk ten. Six of these fell victim to one small ship, the destroyer escort *England*. Seven more would be sunk within the next few days. The submarines themselves accomplished nothing for Japan. At the same time Task Force 58, Spruance's fast carriers under Vice Admiral Mitscher, were busy destroying the Japanese aircraft on their island bases In consequence, Ozawa was to be left largely on his own.

On June 15 Spruance's amphibious commander, Vice Admiral Richmond Kelly Turner, began to land Marines and soldiers on Saipan. Turner had seven battleships and seven escort carriers, as well as many cruisers and destroyers to support the men going ashore.

Seeing the task of Mitscher's nine carriers and six light carriers (with 891 aircraft embarked) to be mainly the protection of Turner's transports, Spruance kept his carrier admiral on a short stay. In contrast to Ozawa's pilots, who were inexperienced, Mitscher's were largely veterans. So Mitscher, tied to the transports, had the advantages of numbers and experience. Ozawa had the advantages of the offensive, of having a choice of objectives, and of having longer-ranged planes which enabled him to find and strike his enemy before the latter even knew where he was. And he had the advantage of the wind, which blew from the east. Mitscher had to turn around in order to launch or recover his aircraft; Ozawa simply kept going, for east was where he was headed.

219 planes lost out of 326

On June 19 Ozawa launched his strikes, four in all, against the American carriers, who still had failed to find him. They did see his planes coming, though. Of the first raid's 69 aircraft 42 were shot down by the defending Hellcat fighters. The second raid, of 128

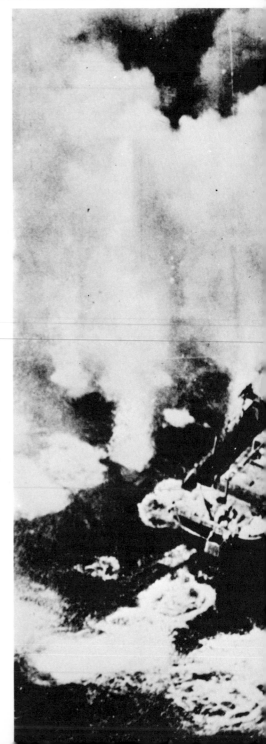

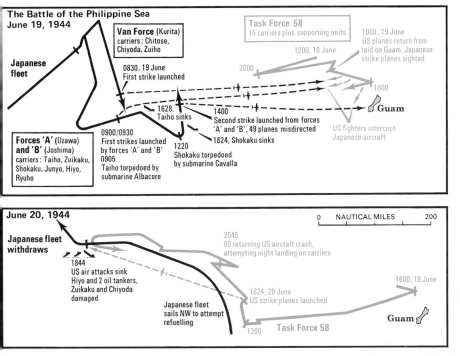

The Battle of the Philippine Sea
June 19, 1944

Japanese fleet

Van Force (Kurita)
carriers: Chitose, Chiyoda, Zuiho

Task Force 58
15 carriers plus supporting units

1200, 18 June

1000, 19 June
US planes return from raid on Guam. Japanese strike planes sighted

2000

0830, 19 June
First strike launched

1600

Guam

1628,
Taiho sinks

1400
Second strike launched from forces 'A' and 'B', 49 planes misdirected

US fighters intercept Japanese aircraft

Forces 'A' (Ozawa) and 'B' (Joshima)
carriers: Taiho, Zuikaku, Shokaku, Junyo, Hiyo, Ryuho

0900/0930
First strikes launched by forces 'A' and 'B'
0905
Taiho torpedoed by submarine Albacore

1220
Shokaku torpedoed by submarine Cavalla

1624, Shokaku sinks

June 20, 1944

Japanese fleet withdraws

2045
80 returning US aircraft crash, attempting night landing on carriers

0   NAUTICAL MILES   200

1844
US air attacks sink Hiyo and 2 oil tankers, Zuikaku and Chiyoda damaged

Japanese fleet sails NW to attempt refuelling

1624, 20 June
US strike planes launched

1600, 19 June

1200

Task Force 58

Guam

Bearing a torpedo beneath its fuselage, a Japanese airplane races through heavy American fire. A moment later it was shot down.

A small Japanese freighter, far from home, is smothered by fire from US carrier-based planes in the Marshall Islands in February, 1944.

planes, lost 97 of their number. The third, of 47 planes, lost only seven. The fourth raid, 82 planes, lost 73 of its number. Most of these 219 planes were shot down by the carriers' fighters. In return the Japanese did little, obtaining a hit of no consequence on the battleship *South Dakota*. While Mitscher's fighters were defending the task force, his bombers were attacking the island air bases again, destroying about 50 more aircraft, so Ozawa could get no use out of them. All this activity cost the Americans 29 aircraft.

Meanwhile, Ozawa's fleet ran right into the submarine *Albacore*, which torpedoed and sank his flagship, the big carrier *Taiho*. Sixty miles beyond that they encountered the submarine *Cavalla*, which torpedoed and sank the carrier *Shokaku*. Both submarines escaped unharmed.

Despite the submarines' reports, the American carriers did not find Ozawa's remaining ships until mid-afternoon of the next day by which time they were a considerable distance away. Mitscher, knowing that his planes were going too far and would come back in the dark, launched anyway. Some 216 planes went out. They sank the large carrier *Hiyo* and a couple of oilers, and damaged the carriers *Zuikaku* and *Chiyoda*. Ozawa was now down to 35 planes on his surviving flight decks. He headed for Okinawa.

Mitscher turned on all his ships' lights to help his pilots find their way home. Most of them did, though not necessarily to the right ship. About 80 planes ditched or crashed on deck but almost all of the pilots and crews were saved. So ended the battle.

With the sea battle over, full attention was paid to Saipan, where fighting lasted well into July. Among the thousands of Japanese dead was Vice Admiral Chuichi Nagumo, Ozawa's predecessor in command of the carrier force, who had been sent to an inconsequential post with headquarters on that island.

A base for mainland raids

Guam and Tinian were invaded almost simultaneously, on July 21 and July 24. Tinian fell quickly. The recovery of Guam was tougher but in three weeks that island was safely back in American hands. As soon as possible Admiral Nimitz moved his headquarters there from Pearl Harbor.

Far beyond Singapore, in the Indian Ocean, peace reigned. Neither Japan nor, because of her Atlantic and European campaigns, Britain, could find the ships with which to make war effectively, even though in Burma massive armies glowered, and occasionally clawed at each other through the jungle.

In April and May 1944 the American carrier *Saratoga* while briefly in the Indian Ocean combined with the British *Illustrious* to attack oil targets at Sabang and Surabaya in the Dutch East Indies. In July the *Illustrious* and *Victorious* carried out a similar mission at Sabang while gunnery ships, notably the French battleship *Richelieu*, shelled targets ashore.

All this offensive activity on the part of the Allies had led, by August 1944, to the establishment of a base from which to launch the last part of the drive to the Japanese mainland. The taking of Saipan and Guam in the Marianas put the B29 bombers within range of Japan and the raids on the mainland could begin in earnest.

Return engagement the Philippines and Leyte Gulf

Throughout 1944 MacArthur fought a bitter campaign to achieve his cherished goal—victory in the Philippines. This involved the navy in a massive and decisive battle in Leyte Gulf which all but finished off the Imperial Japanese Navy. But the Allied navies had to suffer the onslaught of one more fearsome weapon—the fanatical, suicidal Kamikazes. The war was clearly nearing an end but the bloodshed was very far from being over.

The Philippines, MacArthur's goal, were the next target. But first a number of preliminary air strikes and landings would have to be made. Admiral Halsey had relieved Spruance and the fleet was now called the Third Fleet; Mitscher's carriers were Task Force 38. In September Halsey struck at the Philippines, destroying 200 Japanese planes at a cost of only eight of his own. He saw that it would be possible to drop many preliminary operations and land directly at Leyte in the Central Philippines. President

Rockets streak for the shore from converted landing craft during the invasion of Peleliu in September, 1944.

Roosevelt, Prime Minister Churchill, and the combined Chiefs of Staff, meeting in Quebec, concurred, as did Nimitz and MacArthur. Leyte would be invaded in mid-October.

In the meantime, without difficulty, MacArthur took Morotai, a small island south of the Philippines wanted for an air strip site, while Nimitz's Marines and soldiers landed at Peleliu and Angaur in the Palau Islands east of the Philippines. This was a difficult proposition and took a while. More usefully, Ulithi, an undefended atoll in the Northern Carolines, was seized and its lagoon put immediately to use by the fleet. Halsey sailed from there early in October and struck Japanese air bases successively on Okinawa, Luzon, and Formosa, destroying some 350 Japanese planes in the process at a cost to his force of 89 planes down and no ships sunk. Two cruisers were damaged by Japanese aerial torpedoes, and offered to Toyoda as bait. The latter sent airplanes, including his partly-trained carrier air groups, but no ships, and the crippled cruisers made it to safety.

MacArthur returned to the Philippines on October 20 and by the end of that day more than 60,000 American troops were ashore on Leyte.

The Japanese response was powerful. It consisted of four separate squadrons, each under a vice admiral. Vice Admiral Ozawa was in nominal command but in practise each of the commanders ran his force with little reference to the others. The Japanese carriers were in home waters, the battleships and cruisers in Southeast Asian waters. American seizure of the Philippines threatened to perpetuate the split and deny both oil to the ships in the north and ammunition and supplies to those in the south.

Ozawa's decoy carriers

Ozawa had four carriers but, with only 116 aircraft for their decks, manned by inexperienced aviators, he could serve merely as a decoy to draw off the American carriers while the unmolested battleships and cruisers destroyed MacArthur's transports in Leyte Gulf. In the event, most of the transports had disembarked their troops, discharged their cargo, and gone before the Japanese could bring off their attack.

In addition to his carriers Ozawa had two old battleships, three light cruisers, and nine destroyers. They departed the Inland Sea on the evening of the 20th. Two days later Takeo Kurita left Brunei Bay, Borneo, with five battleships, ten heavy cruisers, two light cruisers, and 15 destroyers. Shoji Nishimura left Brunei Bay the same day as Kurita with a pair of old battleships, a heavy cruiser, and four destroyers. Kiyohide Shima was coming down from the Ryukyus with two heavy cruisers, a light cruiser, and four destroyers. In all, 64 ships. There were also 300 airplanes, those on Ozawa's decks as well as those based on Luzon and Formosa.

While Ozawa came down north-east of the Philippines, making himself as conspicuous as possible, the others approached through the South China Sea. Nishimura, with Shima in his wake, sailed through the Sulu Sea towards Surigao Strait, the southern entrance to Leyte Gulf. Kurita sailed west of Palawan, en route to San Bernardino Strait, whence he could plunge south outside Samar and then into Leyte Gulf.

Four separate sighting reports were made on Ozawa's progress by submarines, and two on Shima's. While Kurita was west of Palawan on October 23, the Dace sank his flagship, the heavy cruiser Atago, and damaged a sister, the Takao. The Darter sank another sister, the Maya, though she herself was soon wrecked on a reef. The Dace rescued her people. So the American command had a good idea of what was coming.

Vice Admiral Thomas C. Kinkaid, commanding the Seventh Fleet, had not only the hundreds of amphibious ships needed to land MacArthur's army, but also the scores of warships needed to escort them and then provide the troops with gunfire and close air support. The warships included six old battleships, as well as escort carriers, heavy and light cruisers, destroyers and destroyer escorts.

No fighter cover for Kurita

Admiral Halsey, commanding the Third Fleet, which at this time consisted almost solely of Mitscher's Task Force 38, was responsible for protecting the invasion force

Above: The Japanese battleship Nagato *racing for safety after the defeat by the escort carriers off Samar Island on October 25, 1944.*

Right: Sailors of the cruiser Birmingham *prepare to help the carrier* Princeton *just before the latter blew up in the Battle of Leyte Gulf, October 24, 1944.*

Above: A Japanese bomb explodes near the carrier Hancock *during the October, 1944, attack on Formosa.*

from naval attack and for destroying as much of the enemy fleet as possible. Halsey had eight carriers and eight light carriers, with about 800 aircraft on deck, as well as six battleships and a substantial number of cruisers and destroyers. His ships were in four task groups, one under Vice Admiral John S. McCain and the others under Rear Admirals Frederick C. Sherman, Gerald F. Bogan, and Ralph E. Davison. All had worked hard and McCain's group, which included three carriers and two light carriers, was on its way back to Ulithi for rest, repair, and replenishment. The other task groups were deployed east of Luzon and Samar, Sherman in the north, Davison in the south, Bogan in between.

The next morning, October 24, Japanese planes from Luzon attacked Sherman's group. Most of the planes were shot down but one hit the light carrier *Princeton*. That ship was so badly damaged that eventually she blew up and had to be sunk. The explosion caused hundreds of casualties aboard the cruiser *Birmingham*, which was about to take the *Princeton* in tow. A destroyer was also damaged. Ozawa, too, launched a strike on Sherman's ships, but lost most of his planes and got no hits.

Meanwhile, the *Enterprise* of Davison's southern group found and attacked Nishimura's force, without much result, while 42 planes from the *Intrepid* and *Cabot* of Bogan's group made the first of the day's attacks on Kurita in the Sibuyan Sea, between Mindoro and Luzon. The latter had hoped for fighter cover from fields in the Philippines but it never materialized. The *Intrepid* made a second attack, with 35 planes. In the afternoon the new *Lexington* and *Essex* of Sherman's force attacked with 68 planes. A smaller attack was made later by those same two ships and then one each by the *Enterprise* and *Franklin* of Davison's group and *Intrepid* and *Cabot* from Bogan's. As a result of all these efforts the huge battleship *Musashi* was sunk, the heavy

Yukikaze

The *Kagero* class ships are typical of the large destroyers built by the Japanese in the 1920s and 1930s to outclass any foreign destroyer afloat. The *Yukikaze* was involved in almost every Pacific sea battle, but survived the war without receiving a single hit.

Displacement: 2,033 tons
**Armament: Six 5-inch DP guns,
eight 24-in TT**
**Machinery: Two-shaft geared
turbines, 52,000 shp = $35\frac{1}{2}$ knots**

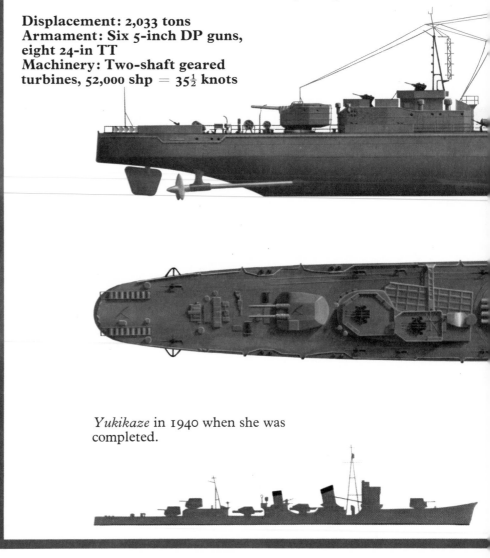

Yukikaze in 1940 when she was completed.

cruiser *Myoko* was so damaged she had to be sent back to Singapore, and a number of other ships were hit. Most importantly, Kurita was seen to have turned back to a westerly course.

Halsey commits all his ships

Just at this time Ozawa's decoy carriers were sighted. They were what Halsey had been waiting for. He ordered all three task groups, plus McCain's, which had not yet reached Ulithi, to head north for Ozawa. They would strike as soon as possible the next morning. Nothing was left behind to guard San Bernardo Strait. But, unbeknownst to Halsey, when no more air attacks came, Kurita again turned eastward toward the strait. Night scouts from the *Independence* provided some warning of this, but the reports were discounted by Halsey. Kurita passed through San Bernardino Strait at midnight. Not a single American was there to notice.

Meanwhile, Nishimura was pushing up Surigao Strait. Thirty-nine motor torpedo boats in groups of three successively

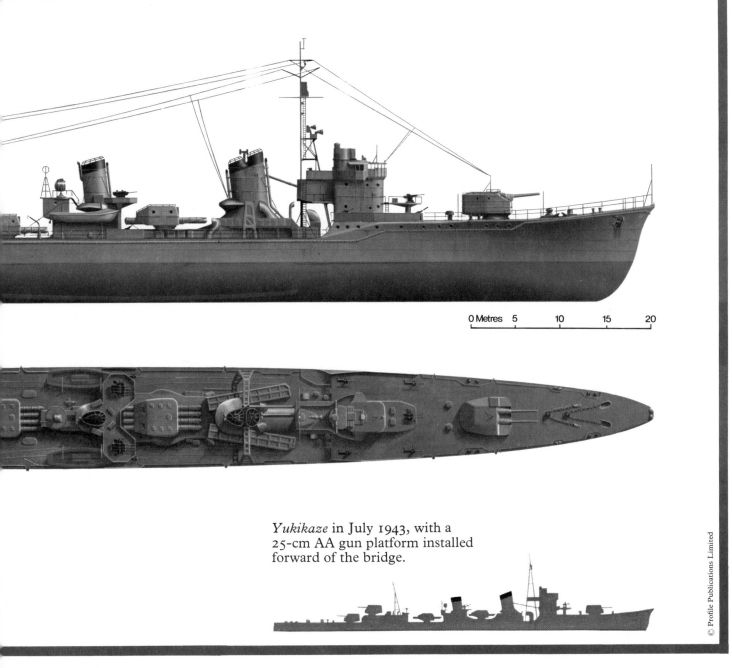

Yukikaze in July 1943, with a 25-cm AA gun platform installed forward of the bridge.

POSITIONS OF US CARRIER TASK GROUPS, 0600, 24 OCTOBER
TIMES ARE THOSE FOR 24 OCTOBER UNLESS OTHERWISE INDICATED

0   NAUTICAL MILES   300

The First Battle of Leyte Gulf
October 22-25, 1944

C. Engaño

Carrier 'Decoy'
Force (Ozawa)   0100

0000, 25th

1140   0600, 25th

Group 'A'
(Matsuda)

Luzon

2000

2241   0822, 25th

Task Force 38 (Halsey's
Third Fleet) steams north
to engage Ozawa's force

Second Striking Force
(Shima)

Clark
Field

TG 38.3
(Sherman)

0935 Carrier Princeton hit,
sinks at 1630

Princeton

2345

PHILIPPINE
ISLANDS

MANILA

2000

TG 38.2
(Bogan)

1200, 23 Oct

Mindoro

Sibuyan

1026/1530
US air strikes. Battleship Musashi
sinks at 1935, cruiser Myoko
retires damaged

Sea

2330

San Bernardino Str

1000

Masbate

0600, 25th

CALAMIAN
GROUP

Samar

TG 38.4
(Davison)

Panay

0400,
25th

1200, 23 Oct

Leyte

US Seventh Fleet
(Kinkaid)

0632, 23 Oct
US Submarines sink
cruisers Atago and Maya,
Takao retires damaged

1000

Negros

Cebu

Bohol

Palawan

Surigao Str

Force 'A'
(Kurita)

2000

2330

TG 38.1 (McCain)
to Ulithi

0918   1000

Force 'C'
(Nishimura)

1200, 23 Oct

Mindanao

Sulu   Sea

First Striking
Force (Kurita)

**BRITISH
NORTH BORNEO**

Sails 22 Oct

BRUNEI

The Battles around Leyte Gulf, 1944

U.S.A.		Japan	
Carriers		**Carriers**	
Lexington	Franklin	Zuikaku	Chiyoda
Essex	Fanshaw Bay	Zuiho	Chitose
Princeton	Sangamon	**Battleship/carriers**	
Wasp	Santee	Yamato	Haruna
Hornet	Suwanee	Musashi	Fuso
Hancock	Enterprise	Magato	Yamashiro
Cowpens	San Jacinto	**Cruisers**	
Langley	St. Lo	Mogami	Tone
Intrepid	Kalinin Bay	Atago	Nachi
Cabot	Kitkum Bay	Takao	Ashigara
Monterey	Belleau Wood	Chokai	Abukuma
Independence	White Plains	Maya	Aoba
Battleships		Myoko	Kinu
West Virginia	Pennsylvania	Haguro	Isuzu
California	Iowa	Kumano	Tama
Tennessee	Massachusetts	Suzuya	Oyodo
Maryland	Indiana	Chikuma	Noshiro
Mississippi			
Cruisers			
Birmingham	Chester		
Boise	Pensacola		
Phoenix	Salt Lake City		
Denver	Boston		
Australia	San Diego		
Shropshire	Oakland		
Columbia	Santa Fe		
Minneapolis	Mobile		
Portland	New Orleans		
Louisville	Honolulu		

Hit by a Kamikaze during the Mindoro invasion in December, 1944, an LST is reduced to a flaming hulk.

reported his progress and attacked him, but got no hits. Nishimura was in column— four destroyers, battleships *Yamashiro* and *Fuso*, and heavy cruiser *Mogami*. The flag was in the *Yamashiro*. At 0300 it was moonless, dark, and calm. Then five US destroyers launched torpedoes which blew the *Fuso* in two, sank one of Nishimura's destroyers, and damaged the *Yamashiro* and two other destroyers. Six more destroyers attacked, hit the *Yamashiro* again, and finished off one of the crippled destroyers. The flagship, the *Mogami*, and a destroyer plodded on. Ahead of them were six old American battleships, eight cruisers, and nine destroyers, all under Vice Admiral Jesse B. Oldendorf, who commanded all the US forces in the strait that night. They were armed mainly with shells suitable for support of troops ashore, not for engaging armored ships. But the Japanese had only two armoured ships, one of them severely damaged, when the American ships opened fire on them at 0351. The *Yamashiro* was

The heavy cruiser Nachi *under attack in Manila Bay by Admiral Halsey's planes, November 5, 1944. Eventually the ship was sunk.*

blazing from end to end, the *Mogami* was badly hurt, when the remaining US destroyers launched their torpedoes. The *Yamashiro* went down with her admiral; the other ships escaped southward.

Admiral Shima, 60 miles astern of Nishimura, encountered the motor torpedo boats and his light cruiser, the old *Abukuma*, was badly hurt by one of their torpedoes. He sailed on, saw the gunfire and blazing hulks ahead and, after launching torpedoes at long range, retired. One of his cruisers, the *Nachi*, collided with the flaming *Mogami* but was little damaged. Indeed, except for the *Abukuma*, his ships suffered no more damage as they made their way to safety. The crippled *Abukuma* was sunk the next day by Army B-24 bombers.

Carriers hide in the rain

Oldendorf sent cruisers down the strait. They finished off a destroyer, hit the *Mogami* again, and then were recalled. The battered Japanese cruiser was then attacked by planes from Rear Admiral T. L. Sprague's escort carriers. Her crew was taken off by other ships before she sank.

As the sun rose on October 25 six American escort carriers, screened by three destroyers and four destroyer escorts, were

steering north, fifty miles east of Samar. They were the northernmost of three similar task groups intended to support troops and protect amphibious ships from air and submarine attack. Commanding these ships was Rear Admiral C. A. F. Sprague in the *Fanshaw Bay*. The others were the *Saint Lo, White Plains, Kalinin Bay, Kitkun Bay*, and *Gambier Bay*. These ships had barely half the speed of a fleet carrier and had only about a third the number of airplanes. Some of their planes were in the air when Kurita's force appeared dead ahead.

Sprague immediately turned eastward into the wind to launch aircraft, and ordered his ships to make as much speed as they could and make smoke to hide themselves. They hid in every patch of rain they could. While their airplanes were roaring off the decks, armed with whatever was available, the escorts, the destroyers *Hoel, Heerman*, and *Johnston*, and the destroyer escorts *Dennis, John C. Butler, Raymond*, and *Samuel B. Roberts*, attacked the foe.

Kurita, in the huge battleship *Yamato*, ordered a general attack. His ships, the battleships *Nagato, Kongo*, and *Haruna*, eight cruisers, and eleven destroyers, forged ahead, believing they were attacking one of Halsey's task groups of big carriers and cruisers. They reached past Sprague and forced him to run south, away from the wind. Splashes from their huge shells towered over the small carriers, and occasionally a shell bit deep into a target.

Taken aback by the fierce attack of Sprague's pilots, who used bombs, torpedoes, rockets, and machine guns, and when their weapons were gone made dry runs; confused by the charge of the escorting destroyers which launched torpedoes in profusion and

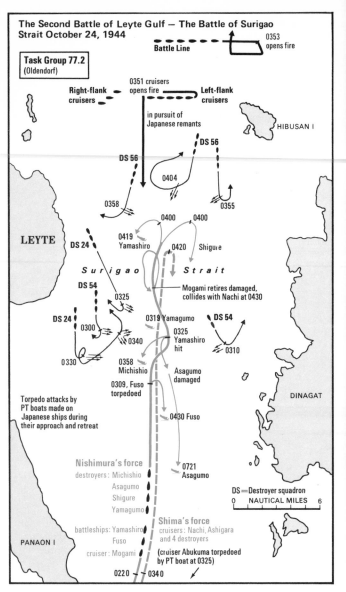

The Second Battle of Leyte Gulf — The Battle of Surigao Strait October 24, 1944

0353 opens fire

Battle Line

Task Group 77.2 (Oldendorf)

0351 cruisers opens fire

Right-flank cruisers

Left-flank cruisers

in pursuit of Japanese remants

HIBUSAN I

DS 56

DS 56

0404

0358

0355

LEYTE

DS 24

0419 Yamashiro

0400 0400

0420 Shigure

S u r i g a o   *S t r a i t*

Mogami retires damaged, collides with Nachi at 0430

DS 54

0325

0319 Yamagumo

DS 54

0325 Yamashiro hit

0310

DS 24

0300

0340

0330

0358 Michishio

Asagumo damaged

0309, Fuso torpedoed

DINAGAT

0430 Fuso

Torpedo attacks by PT boats made on Japanese ships during their approach and retreat

0721 Asagumo

Nishimura's force

destroyers: Michishio
Asagumo
Shigure
Yamagumo

battleships: Yamashiro
Fuso

cruiser: Mogami

DS = Destroyer squadron

0 NAUTICAL MILES 6

Shima's force

cruisers: Nachi, Ashigara and 4 destroyers

(cruiser Abukuma torpedoed by PT boat at 0325)

PANAON I

0220 — 0340

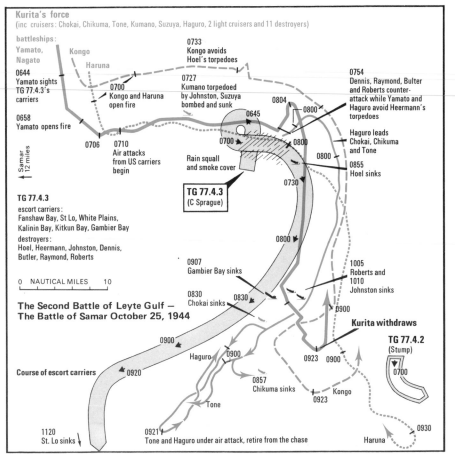

Kurita's force
(inc cruisers: Chokai, Chikuma, Tone, Kumano, Suzuya, Haguro, 2 light cruisers and 11 destroyers)

battleships:
Yamato,
Nagato

Kongo

Haruna

0733 Kongo avoids Hoel's torpedoes

0644 Yamato sights TG 77.4.3's carriers

0700 Kongo and Haruna open fire

0727 Kumano torpedoed by Johnston, Suzuya bombed and sunk

0754 Dennis, Raymond, Bulter and Roberts counter-attack while Yamato and Haguro avoid Heermann's torpedoes

0804

0800

0658 Yamato opens fire

0645

Haguro leads Chokai, Chikuma and Tone

0706

0700

0800

Samar 12 miles

0710 Air attacks from US carriers begin

Rain squall and smoke cover

0800

TG 77.4.3 (C Sprague)

0800

0855 Hoel sinks

0730

TG 77.4.3

escort carriers:
Fanshaw Bay, St Lo, White Plains,
Kalinin Bay, Kitkun Bay, Gambier Bay

destroyers:
Hoel, Heermann, Johnston, Dennis,
Butler, Raymond, Roberts

0800

0907 Gambier Bay sinks

1005 Roberts and 1010 Johnston sinks

0 NAUTICAL MILES 10

0830 Chokai sinks

0830

0900

The Second Battle of Leyte Gulf — The Battle of Samar October 25, 1944

Kurita withdraws

TG 77.4.2 (Stump)

0900

0923 0900

0700

0900

Haguro 0900

0920

Course of escort carriers

0857 Chikuma sinks

Kongo

0923

Tone

Haruna

0930

1120 St. Lo sinks

0921 Tone and Haguro under air attack, retire from the chase

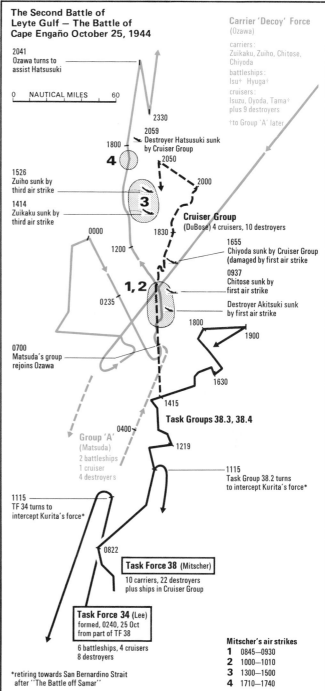

The Second Battle of
Leyte Gulf — The Battle of
Cape Engaño October 25, 1944

2041
Ozawa turns to
assist Hatsusuki

0   NAUTICAL MILES   60

2330

2059
Destroyer Hatsusuki sunk
by Cruiser Group

1800

4

2050

2000

1526
Zuiho sunk by
third air strike

3

1414
Zuikaku sunk by
third air strike

1830

Cruiser Group
(DuBose) 4 cruisers, 10 destroyers

0000

1200

1655
Chiyoda sunk by Cruiser Group
(damaged by first air strike

0937
Chitose sunk by
first air strike

0235

1, 2

Destroyer Akitsuki sunk
by first air strike

1800

1900

0700
Matsuda's group
rejoins Ozawa

1630

1415

1219

Task Groups 38.3, 38.4

0400

1115
Task Group 38.2 turns
to intercept Kurita's force*

Group 'A'
(Matsuda)
2 battleships
1 cruiser
4 destroyers

1115
TF 34 turns to
intercept Kurita's force*

0822

Task Force 38 (Mitscher)

10 carriers, 22 destroyers
plus ships in Cruiser Group

Task Force 34 (Lee)
formed, 0240, 25 Oct
from part of TF 38

6 battleships, 4 cruisers
8 destroyers

*retiring towards San Bernardino Strait
after ''The Battle off Samar''

Carrier 'Decoy' Force
(Ozawa)

carriers:
Zuikaku, Zuiho, Chitose,
Chiyoda
battleships:
Isu† Hyuga†
cruisers:
Isuzu, Oyoda, Tama†
plus 9 destroyers

†to Group 'A' later

Mitscher's air strikes
1   0845—0930
2   1000—1010
3   1300—1500
4   1710—1740

*Above: Two ships go alongside to help an
LST conquer the flames caused by a
Kamikaze hit.*

Left: The escort carrier Ommaney Bay
aflame in the Sulu Sea.

Below: The West Virginia *sails to support
the landing at Lingayen Gulf.*

fired their guns at anything visible; Kurita's
ships failed to close their targets. Soon help
came to Sprague's beleaguered ships from
airplanes of the other two escort carrier
groups.

Where are the battleships?

After nearly three hours of this Kurita
suddenly reversed course and, eventually,
headed back to San Bernardino Strait. He
had lost the heavy cruisers *Chokai* and
Chikuma, and soon, the *Suzuya*, while the
Kumano was damaged. This was a high
price to pay for sinking the *Gambier Bay*,
Johnston, *Hoel*, and *Samuel B. Roberts*.
There were wounded ships on both sides.

The battle did not end when the opposing
sides lost sight of each other. American
carrier-based planes continued to attack
Kurita's ships. Japanese shore-based planes
attacked the American ships. And now the
Japanese introduced the most fearsome
weapon of the naval war—the suicide plane,
or *Kamikaze*. One destroyed the *Saint Lo*.

ship do so. The once formidable cruisers and destroyers were reduced to a remnant—only four of the original 18 heavy cruisers, for example, were still afloat and battle worthy. The submarines long had been beaten. Only the Kamikazes, based ashore where their lack of flying skill would not be an insuperable flaw, remained to the Imperial Japanese Navy.

Because they had a hard time building airfields, General Kenney's shore-based aviators could not take over responsibility for gaining control of the Philippine air, or of supporting the troops and supply ships. So Halsey's and Kinkaid's carrier pilots had to do those things. Early in November Halsey attacked Luzon's airfields and harbors, sank the heavy cruiser *Nachi* in Manila Bay, and destroyed over 400 aircraft.

Meanwhile the Japanese resurrected the Tokyo Express to bring troops to Ormoc Bay. Airplanes, motor torpedo boats, small gunboats, and destroyers engaged in the American effort to stop this traffic. Halsey's carriers destroyed one convoy of five transports and four destroyers with 10,000 troops aboard. Another strike sank the light cruiser *Kiso* and five destroyers. Many Japanese aircraft were destroyed, but the carriers *Intrepid, Cabot, Lexington, Franklin,* and *Belleau Wood* had all been hit by Kamikazes and needed repair.

Japanese can do nothing

On December 7 Kinkaid landed troops at Ormoc Bay and, for a time, both sides were bringing in reinforcements side by side. Eight days later the Americans invaded the island of Mindoro in order to get airfields to support the next landing, at Lingayen Gulf.

Lingayen Gulf, which placed MacArthur's army on the road to Manila Bay, took place on January 9 1945. It was grim. By January 13, when all the Kamikazes had been used, 44 ships had been hit, though only two, including the escort carrier *Ommaney Bay,* had been lost. The Australian heavy cruiser *Australia* was hit five times, with 116 casualties.

The rest of the Philippines, and parts of Borneo, were invaded and liberated without further serious loss to the US Navy.

In December a typhoon sank three of Halsey's destroyers and destroyed 146 aircraft. Task Force 38, now under Vice Admiral McCain, with its flight decks almost totally filled with fighter aircraft, entered the South China Sea on January 10 after giving Formosa a good cuff. The task force, and its oilers, spent ten days in that sea surrounded by Japanese-held land. Losing not a ship of its own, it sank 300,000 tons of Japan's shipping and destroyed 600 Japanese airplanes. With her navy utterly defeated, the end was clearly in sight for Japan.

The carrier Hancock *and the flagship* New Jersey *plough through heavy seas.*

Others damaged the *Kalinin Bay* and *Kitkun Bay.* The southern group of escort carriers was hit by Kamikazes, too, with severe damage to the *Suwanee* and *Santee.* The latter was also torpedoed by a lurking submarine, the *I56,* but she survived.

At this moment Halsey, racing north, was nearing Ozawa off Cape Engaño, the northeastern point of Luzon. Night search planes had kept track of the Japanese, who were also steering north, and at dawn Halsey's ten carriers launched 180 aircraft. They sank the light carrier *Chitose* and a destroyer. A second raid damaged the light carrier *Chiyoda* and the old light cruiser *Tama.* By this time Halsey was getting calls for help from Sprague and Kinkaid, but he pressed on. He did, however, send McCain's five carriers, who were still far to the southeast, to Kinkaid's assistance. Ninety-eight of McCain's pilots, launched from 340 miles— too far away— attacked Kurita's ships, which by then were retiring. With their light bomb loads they did little damage and a second strike by 53 planes did no more.

Admiral Nimitz, reading the message traffic at Pearl Harbor, then asked Halsey where the fast battleships that everyone had assumed to be guarding San Bernardino Strait were. Halsey, with Ozawa's ships only 42 miles distant, turned his six battleships around and headed south with them, along with Bogan's three carriers. By the time they got to San Bernardino Strait, it was too late. Kurita had gone through.

Mitscher, left behind with seven carriers, continued north. He launched 160 planes and sank the big *Zuikaku.* Another strike finished the smaller *Zuiho.* After a final strike accomplished nothing he sent some cruisers ahead and sank the damaged *Chiyoda* and a destroyer. The *Tama* later fell victim to a submarine, but the rest of Ozawa's ships got home.

Kamikazes—all that is left

The next morning, October 26, Kurita's ships, now back in the Sibuyan Sea, were still barely within range of Bogan's and McCain's planes. The latter hit hard and sank the light cruiser *Noshiro* and a destroyer. A Japanese transport group, carrying 2,000 troops to Ormoc Bay, on Leyte's west coast, was hit by the escort carriers, which sank the old light cruiser *Kinu* and another destroyer. The Japanese Kamikazes hit the *Suwanee* again, but she refused to be sunk.

The Battle for Leyte Gulf was over. The Americans were at sea, ready for more fighting. The Japanese were beaten and fleeing. The cost to the Americans in ships sunk was seven—a light carrier, two escort carriers, a submarine, two destroyers, and a destroyer escort. The Japanese lost 26 ships —two large and two light carriers, three battleships, six heavy and four light cruisers, and nine destroyers. Never again would a Japanese carrier go to sea on a combat mission, and only once more would a battle-

The drive for victory
Rangoon to Hiroshima

As 1944 came to an end the oil shortage had become crucial for the Japanese. American submarines continued their successes against merchant and navy shipping. The Royal Navy re-established itself in Asian waters and the tough island-hopping offensive and the drive overland towards Japan continued relentlessly. Desperate Kamikaze attacks claimed many ships and lives and the giant *Yamato* made her celebrated last ride in vain. The Japanese navy was finally eliminated as a force in devastating attacks on ships at Kure and Kobe. Then the atomic bomb forced Japan's surrender, appropriately signed on the battleship *Missouri*, in September.

While Marines roar by in landing craft the old battleship Tennessee, *a veteran of Pearl Harbor, fires her twelve 14-inch guns into the Japanese defenses at Iwo Jima, February 19, 1945.*

In February 1945 the Japanese government began efforts to end the war. They worked through the Soviet Union, which was still neutral. But the Japanese did not know how to end the war and the Soviets did not help. So the war went on, reaching its peak of death and destruction with Japanese Kamikaze attacks on US and Allied ships and American fire raids on Japanese cities.

By January 1945 the American submarines had sunk most of Japan's deep-water merchant ships. In the months remaining they passed on more and more of their work to shore-based and carrier-based aircraft which could strike at shipping in harbours and the shallow places that submarines could not reach. But, mainly as a result of their work, no oil reached Japan after March. Japanese traffic still ran on domestic routes and across the Sea of Japan to Korea. So in June nine submarines braved thick minefields to enter that sea. They lost one of their number but sank 28 ships. Other submarines took on reconnaissance and life-guard tasks; in the latter role they rescued 380 aviators whose damaged B–29s could not return to their fields after bombing targets in Japan.

At the end of March the B–29s took on, as a side job, the mining of Japanese coastal waters and straits, thus aiding the effort of the submarines in strangling the empire without causing death or destruction ashore.

The submarines continued their work against what was left of the Japanese Navy, too. In April the *Charr* and *Gabilan* sank the *Isuzu*, one of the last of Japan's light cruisers, south of Borneo. Submarines also sank a couple of destroyers and about 40 escort ships in 1945. In June the British submarine *Trenchant* sank the heavy cruiser *Ashigara* near Sumatra, and at the end of July the British got a couple of their midget submarines into Singapore harbour where they immobilized the already damaged heavy cruiser *Takao*.

Japan's submarine fleet made a final offensive in July and one of their ships, the *I58*, sank the heavy cruiser *Indianapolis* on July 29. The latter, which perished with 800 of her people, was the last major warship to be sunk on either side during World War II.

The fight for Iwo Jima

In the Indian Ocean theatre, there were two worthwhile objectives for the Allies' South East Asia Command, Rangoon and Singapore. Both could best be taken by amphibious assault. Happily for the Allies, from mid-1943 on their supreme commander in the theater was Admiral Lord Louis Mountbatten, Britain's outstanding amphibious leader. But though he had an enormous army and supporting air force in India and Burma,

he had little in the way of a fleet. Eventually a substantial fleet was assembled, but its big carriers were soon taken away for operations in the Pacific and the promised amphibious ships never got there.

To keep his powerful forces occupied Mountbatten began an overland campaign through Burma's appalling terrain and climate. In May 1945, after months of fierce jungle fighting, they drove the Japanese out of Rangoon. The East Indies Fleet, commanded by Admiral Sir Arthur John Power, supported operations along the coast, destroyed what Japanese shipping remained in the Andaman Sea, and shelled Japanese outposts in the Andaman and Nicobar islands. On May 16 the heavy cruiser *Haguro* and a destroyer were ambushed deep in the Malacca Strait by five British destroyers under Captain M. L. Power and, though the destroyer escaped, the cruiser was sunk.

Meanwhile the Americans had continued to make territorial advances.

About halfway between the Marianas, where the B–29 bombers were based, and their targets in Japan there was an air strip, on the tiny island of Iwo Jima. Japanese fighters flying from the strip harassed the bombers. That strip was wanted by the Americans, not only to deny it to the Japanese but also for their own use, to base fighters with which to escort the bombers and for the bombers to use in an emergency. The island, a four-and-a-half mile long pile of volcanic ash inhabited only by 23,000 Japanese soldiers, was subjected to a prolonged bombing by the US Army Air Force, supplemented by shelling from the sea.

On February 19, after three days of intensive shelling—the Marines had hoped for ten days—30,000 Marines were put ashore. Many more were to follow. Thus began one

of the hardest fights in the Marines' history. Only on March 16 was the island declared secured, and even so, fighting lasted till May. It was of the Marines on this island that Admiral Nimitz said, 'uncommon valor was a common virtue.'

800 die in the bombed *Franklin*

The US Navy's part in this struggle was to put the Marines ashore, to keep them supplied with ammunition, food, and replacements, and to provide close air and gunfire support. In the latter role the old battleship *Nevada*, a veteran of Pearl Harbor and Normandy, shone brightly. The Japanese attempted unsuccessfully to break up the assault with Kamikaze attacks. They damaged severely the Japanese Navy's favourite target, the *Saratoga*, and sank the escort carrier *Bismarck Sea*. But that was about it.

The Japanese lost all 23,000 in the defence of the island. In taking it the Americans, of course, aided their bombing effort over Japan, and saved hundreds of airmen in crippled airplanes. Whether that was worth the 7,000 dead and 22,000 wounded is worth asking. Be that as it may, the battle went on much longer than expected. Before it was over the next invasion, that of Okinawa, had begun.

But first, the fast carrier task force under Admiral Spruance and Vice Admiral Mitscher made several raids on Japan, both in February and in March. The March attacks, on the airfields of Kyushu, Japan's southernmost island, cost the Americans heavily, for Japanese bombers damaged the *Enterprise* and the new *Yorktown* and *Wasp*. One bomber got two hits on the *Franklin* while that carrier was launching her planes. The damage which resulted killed more than 800 of the *Franklin*'s men. But, despite wounds more severe than those suffered by any other ship which survived World War

After winning their gunfight with an armed trawler, men of the submarine Tambor *rescue the crew of their vanquished foe.*

Right : Covered by low cloud, a fleet type submarine surfaces off the shore of Kyushu to rescue a shot-down US Army Air Force fighter pilot (circled).

Above : Marines lift supplies up the black sands of Iwo Jima.

Above : On the sunlit waters of the Western Pacific a destroyer under Kamikaze attack fights for her life.

Right : Fire hoses snake across the Saratoga's *deck as her people fight the flames caused by seven Kamikaze and bomb hits off Iwo Jima on February 21, 1945.*

II, that ship was brought to safety by her officers and men. Because West Coast shipyards were full of damaged ships, she had to go to New York for repair.

Air strikes by Task Force 58 began on Okinawa on March 23 and gunfire strikes the next day. An anchorage was seized in the Kerama Retto, a small group of islands fifteen miles west of the main island on March 26. The invasion of Okinawa itself began on April 1. The whole invasion force, under Vice Admiral Richmond Kelly Turner, included 1,300 ships and craft and 182,000 Marines and soldiers, with over 100,000 follow-up troops.

The landings went easily, for the Japanese had learned not to contest an invasion on the beaches against the power of naval gunfire and close air support. But the operation turned soon enough into a difficult campaign which lasted until the end of June.

The Yamato's last ride

It was at Okinawa that the British Pacific Fleet, built around the Royal Navy's heavy carriers, joined the US Pacific Fleet. This British fleet was commanded by Admiral Sir Bruce Fraser, who was mainly at Sydney, Australia, or Guam. Commanding at sea was Vice Admiral Sir Bernard Rawlings in the battleship *King George V,* and commanding the aircraft carrier squadron was Admiral Sir Philip Vian. That squadron consisted of the new carrier *Indefatigable* and the veterans *Illustrious, Victorious,* and *Indomitable,* with about 60 planes each on deck. These ships had made several attacks on Japanese oil targets in Sumatra before going into the Pacific where, operating first under Admiral Spruance they were known as Task Force 57 and then, under Admiral Halsey, as Task Force 37.

During the Okinawa campaign they were to keep the Japanese air forces on Formosa from supporting their army on Okinawa.

This they did through the continued bombing and strafing of airfields on some islands in between Formosa and Okinawa, though at great cost to their own air groups. Moreover, each of the carriers was damaged more or less severely by Kamikazes. After about two weeks the *Illustrious,* which had painful wounds from earlier campaigns, was replaced by the *Formidable* and in June the *Implacable* joined the fleet. In July and August these ships joined in the attacks on Japan proper.

Aside from the efforts of the 100,000 troops on the island, the Japanese response to the attack on Okinawa was almost entirely a matter of suicide attacks on the US fleet from the air. There was however, one suicide effort from the surface, when the battleship *Yamato,* the light cruiser *Yahagi,* and eight destroyers sailed on April 6 for Okinawa. In their fuel tanks was almost all the oil remaining to the Japanese Navy, yet it was enough for only a one-way voyage. At Okinawa they were to beach themselves and fight until destroyed. But they were seen and reported by submarines. The next day, when halfway to their destination they were set upon by Mitscher's carriers. The *Yamato, Yahagi,* and four destroyers were sunk. The rest returned to Japan with survivors.

Constant threat of death

The Kamikazes made ten main attacks in April, May, and June, as well as many minor attacks. Over 1,400 suicide planes took part in the main attacks alone, and they were accompanied by a similar number of bombers. They damaged Spruance's flagship, the *Indianapolis,* on March 30, so the admiral transferred his flag to the old battleship *New Mexico.* That ship, in turn, was hit by a Kamikaze on May 12, but she stayed on station for two weeks more. On April 6 and 7 some 355 Kamikazes and 341 other aircraft attacked the fleet. They sank three destroyers, an LST, and two ammunition-laden freighters, and damaged seventeen other ships, some so badly they were scrapped as soon as the war was over.

Though no other Kamikaze attack at Okinawa was so damaging as the first one,

Yamato

The *Yamato*, shown here as she appeared in 1944 during the Battle of Leyte Gulf, and the *Musashi* were the largest battleships ever built. They carried nine 18-inch guns and displaced 64,170 tons. Both were sunk by heavy air attacks without proving themselves in battle.

21	20	19	18	17	16	15	14	13	12

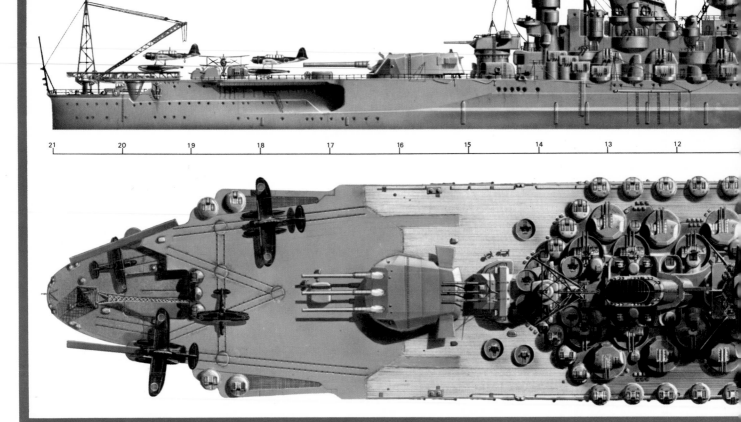

by the end of June 21 ships had been sunk by them, mostly in Okinawan waters, and 66 others severely damaged. No big combatants were among those sunk, but there were plenty of them among those damaged.

British and Japanese sailors had proved that they could endure. It was at Okinawa, and especially on the radar picket stations, that the American sailors showed that they, too, could endure. And for three months endure is what they did. The threat of death was always there; the action, when it came, was intense. For example, in a period of an hour and twenty minutes one picket destroyer, the *Laffey*, came under 22 separate attacks. She shot down eight of her attackers. But six more crashed into the destroyer, and four bombs hit her. More than a third of her men were casualties. But they brought the ship home and she served for many years afterwards.

The pickets were at their exposed stations around the island to give warning of air attacks headed for the ships gathered at Okinawa. The ships were there to support the army intent on conquering the island. And the conquest of the island was sought in order to provide airfields, harbours, supply

Left: Her bridge smashed by a Kamikaze, her captain and 76 others of her crew dead, the destroyer Hazelwood *paid a price for the safety of the amphibious ships, far left, anchored off Okinawa in April, 1945.*

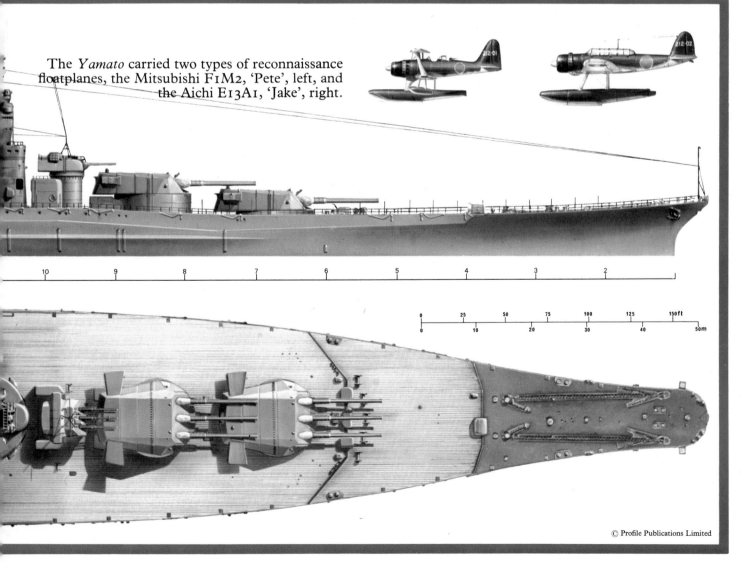

The *Yamato* carried two types of reconnaissance floatplanes, the Mitsubishi F1M2, 'Pete', left, and the Aichi E13A1, 'Jake', right.

Hyuga

Stunned by the losses of carriers at Midway the
Japanese Navy converted two old battleships to hybrid
battleship carriers. A hangar, flight deck and two
catapults replaced two after 14-inch gun turrets, and
22 seaplanes could be carried. Both ships took part in
the Battle of Leyte Gulf and were finally sunk in harbour
in 1945.

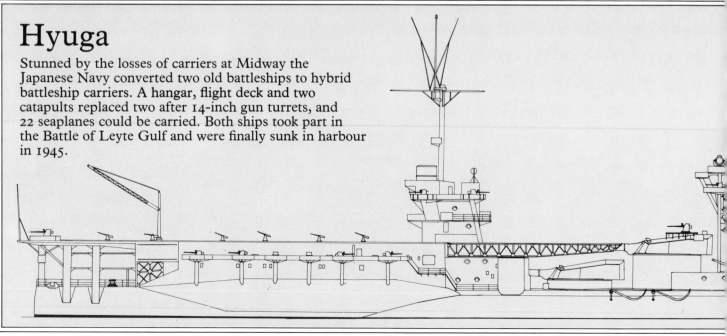

Above : The war is over. The Japanese surrender delegation is met on the deck of the Missouri *by a representative of General MacArthur.*

Left : The heavy cruiser Tone *under attack by Admiral Halsey's carrier planes in Kure harbor, July 24, 1945.*

dumps, and staging areas for the anticipated invasion of Japan.

Final battleship surrender

By the end of June Okinawa was in American hands. The fleet, now under Admiral Halsey, and centred on fifteen carriers, put to sea from Leyte Gulf on July 1. Ten days later came the first of a series of air raids (and, beginning four days after that, shore bombardments) on Japan. Partly they were to supplement (or to rival) the B-29s' attacks on industrial targets and partly to sink coastal shipping and surviving Japanese warships. On July 16 the British, with three carriers, joined the attacks.

Immobile for the lack of fuel and their crews largely disbanded, Japan's surviving warships were moored in shallow water. On July 24, those ships at Kure and Kobe on the Inland Sea came under attack by Task Force 38, which launched 1,747 sorties. The new carrier *Amagi*, the old battleships *Haruna*,

Ise, and *Hyuga*, the heavy cruiser *Aoba*, and the light cruiser *Oyodo* were all destroyed or damaged so severely they settled to the bottom, much as had the US ships at Pearl Harbor in December 1941. Other warships were damaged and fifteen merchant ships and auxiliaries were sunk. On July 28 the heavy cruiser *Tone* and eight auxiliary ships were sunk.

On August 6 an atomic bomb was exploded over Hiroshima. Another one was exploded on August 9, over Nagasaki. That same day the Soviet Union declared war on Japan. Aircraft and motor torpedo boats of the Soviet Pacific Fleet attacked Japanese shipping in Korean waters, while amphibious landings were carried out on the northeastern coast of Korea in support of the advancing Soviet army.

Meantime, task forces 37 and 38 continued strikes on Japanese shipping and airfields until August 15 when Fleet Admiral Nimitz ordered them to cease hostilities. However, for another ten days Soviet naval forces launched amphibious attacks on southern Sakhalin and on the Kurile Islands, all of which were successful despite, in some cases, strong opposition.

On September 3 the war which had begun six years earlier on the Polish plain formally came to an end on the deck of the American battleship *Missouri* anchored in Tokyo Bay. Neither the Kaiser nor Napoleon would have been surprised at such an ending.

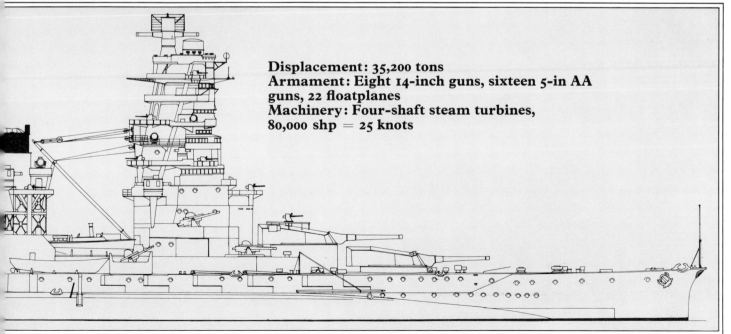

Displacement: 35,200 tons
Armament: Eight 14-inch guns, sixteen 5-in AA guns, 22 floatplanes
Machinery: Four-shaft steam turbines, 80,000 shp = 25 knots

The world-wide role of sea power

The years since World War II have seen the confrontation and conflict of two idealogies. In thòse years the navies of the Western Alliance have found important roles to play throughout the world. They have taken part in humanitarian operations, in the routine defence of national interests, in peace-keeping duties and in armed conflict. In the seas around Cuba in 1962 they ably demonstrated the key role of sea power in world affairs. But, despite a continuing need for naval forces, economies have severely restricted the size of the navies of the Western Powers, while that of Russia has been steadily expanded.

The ending of World War II saw a massive run-down of the strength of the two principal navies—those of the United States and Britain. By 1946, between them they had scrapped, sold to foreign navies or commercial interests or, in some cases, returned to pre-war commercial owners some 3,000 named warships and auxiliaries— a total which did not include thousands of landing ships and craft, patrol boats, minesweepers, small auxiliaries and so on which had been known only by numbers.

Obsolescence; the rundown in wartime manpower as civilian industry demanded labour for the work of reconstruction; the need for economy in military spending and the need also to help smaller nations make good the losses their navies had suffered in the war all meant drastic reductions in the number of commissioned ships in the American and British navies. But also there was no appreciable threat in sight to challenge the Anglo-American command of the seas.

Yet even before the conflict had ceased in the Far East it became evident that a new factor was emerging on the world scene to fill the vacuum created by the defeat of Nazism and Japanese Imperialism —international Communism. The first signs were seen in Greece where there was a bitter civil war between the Communists and their opponents. As a consequence of

Two British Leander *Class frigates manoeuvre in company. Anti-submarine escorts such as these are the most numerous warship type in modern navies, replacing the destroyer as the maid-of-all-work.*

this the United States, in the late 1940s, began forming what was to become the Sixth Fleet in the Mediterranean to help ensure the survival of the frail flower of democracy in Greece.

Until then the eastern Mediterranean had been largely a British responsibility with large British forces in Egypt, Libya, Greece and Malta. Thus the British Navy was to suffer first from Communist hostility when two British destroyers ran into an unmarked minefield in 1946 in the Corfu Channel between that island and the mainland in the southern Adriatic. One ship, the *Saumarez*, had to be scrapped and there was severe loss of life. Eventually, Britain's claim for compensation from the Albanian government, whose craft had laid the field, was upheld by the International Court at The Hague—though no compensation has ever been paid.

Soviet 'War of Proxy'

The Corfu Channel incident marked the start of what might be termed a 'war of proxy' by the Soviet Union against the West. By providing arms and money to nationalist movements the Kremlin saw a way by which, at little cost to itself and without the political involvement that would arise if Russian servicemen were employed, it could extend its empire and influence to the discomfort of the Western powers.

For the Communists the increasing nationalism around the world was an ideal vehicle and often little prompting was needed for nationalists to confront one or more of the Western powers—usually to the embarrassment of the latter who were cast in the role of the villain in the United Nations and elsewhere.

In Central America Britain faced for several years a series of demands from Guatemala that the colonial territory of British Honduras be handed over to that state and these resulted in the cruiser and frigates on the West Indies station having to move small numbers of troops into the colony from time to time. British frigates in the late 1940s were also being called upon to help maintain law and order in West African colonies and later to prevent a Communist-backed take-over in British Guiana.

The Mediterranean, however, remained the principal trouble spot. The wartime trickle of Jewish refugees to Palestine became a flood when Hitler's victims, or those who had survived the concentration camps, began seeking a new life. But, in order to integrate these new settlers in what was still a state with a considerable Arab population, the British insisted on controlling this flow and thus the British Navy had the unpleasant task of watching for and turning back to Cyprus and elsewhere illegal immigrant ships.

By 1948 the dam had broken and the emergence of the new state of Israel precipitated what the British had feared—a war between the Arab powers and the Israelis. Britain's action in relinquishing responsibility for Palestine was to arouse hatred of the West among the Arabs and lead to further troubles of direct importance to the West's sea communications. But by 1949 the world focus was on the Far East while in China the Nationalists were fighting—and clearly losing—a civil war with the Communists.

Amethyst's dramatic run

Western merchant ships attempting to run the Nationalist blockade into Communist-held ports such as Shanghai, Canton and Swatow were bombed, shelled and sometimes seized by the Nationalists and British and American warships had to provide escorts for merchantmen on occasion. In April 1949 the British frigate *Amethyst* on her way up the Yang-tse river to take over as guard and communications ship for the foreign community at Nanking was shelled and severely damaged by the Chinese Communists. Three months later she made a dramatic escape at night down the river to safety but the incident made it apparent that Western warships no longer had a role to play up the rivers of China—a task they had regularly performed for more than 50 years, except during the Japanese occupation.

By 1950 the civil war in China was over and the Communists were in complete control. Back in the Mediterranean the resentment against Britain over the new state of Israel spilled over in 1951 with demands by Egypt for the removal of all British forces from the Suez Canal Zone. Frequent strikes and riots meant that the British Navy had the task of keeping the great international waterway open. Further east in Iran the government of Dr. Mossadeq seized Western oil interests and here, too, the British Navy had the task of safeguarding the lives of Westerners and eventually evacuating them to safety.

In 1949 Russia had demonstrated that she had the atomic bomb. This, together with the first intimations of the Kremlin's growing fleet of submarines and the appearance of the first of their new post-war built cruisers, brought about among other things the drawing together of the United States, Canada and most of the Western European powers in the North Atlantic Treaty Organisation. Massive naval exercises rapidly became a well publicised feature of the Organisation's activities.

Massive naval rearmament

The confrontation resulting from Russia's new policy of threatened aggression and support of insurrection became known as 'the Cold War'. This, and the overt aggression in Korea, caused both Britain and America to bring large numbers of warships out of mothballs in which they had lain for some five years. In 1951 some 150 British warships were commissioned from reserve and the number in the United States was even larger. The same year the British introduced a massive naval rearmament programme under which some 300 ships—mainly minesweepers—were ordered.

The ending of the war in Korea brought about some slackening in the pace of naval rearmament though there were still many problem areas around the world. In Malaya British forces fought a five year campaign against Chinese Communist terrorists and in this naval forces played their part,

Above: The enormous navies of the victorious Allies in 1945 quickly shrank as old ships were scrapped and newer ships decommissioned to release manpower. These are 'mothballed' ships in the US Navy's Pacific Fleet Reserve.

mainly on bombardment duties and in running supplies to remote areas. The first British military helicopters, manned and operated by the Navy and bought with funds from the United States under the Mutual Defence Aid Programme, were used in Malaya, though in 1952 the Australian Navy became the first to follow the lead of the United States Navy and make use of helicopters at sea from a carrier. The fighting in Malaya also involved ships of both the Australian and New Zealand navies.

By 1954 the British forces had left the Suez Canal Zone in Egypt and two years later President Nasser seized the Canal as an Egyptian national asset. Britain and France responded with heavy carrier-launched air attacks followed by an amphibious assault. Despite the subsequent political repercussions the military side of the operation was a complete success and within a few days British troops had reached Ismailia halfway down the Canal towards the Red Sea. The United States, fearing this could lead to a more general

conflict, brought considerable pressure to bear both economically and politically and the operation was halted. A massive salvage operation under American control was then undertaken to clear the Canal of blockships sunk by the Egyptians. In the Red Sea there was one surface action when an Egyptian frigate was sunk by the British cruiser *Newfoundland*, but chiefly the operation on the naval side demonstrated the invaluability of helicopters for assault and the ability of naval airpower to provide virtually all the air support required for a major amphibious assault.

Trial of strength off China

While 1956 was a year of trouble for Britain and France it was to be America's turn two years later. In 1958 the Chinese Communists captured some Nationalist-held off-shore islands and forced Washington to order massive reinforcement of the Seventh Fleet to ensure the safety of Formosa. In the Middle East American Marines were landed to ensure the safety of Lebanon from a take-over by the newly formed United Arab Republic of Egypt and Syria, and British

The Royal Navy had the unhappy task of turning back illegal Jewish refugees trying to enter Palestine in 1947–48.

205

In response to a request from the President of the Lebanon, US Marines landed peacefully in 1958 to forestall a coup.

naval forces put troops ashore at Aqaba to boost the government in Jordan.

In the North Atlantic Iceland increased her fishery limits and in the resulting dispute with British trawlers the British Navy had to keep destroyers and frigates constantly on patrol to stop the arrest of the trawlers by Icelandic gunboats.

By the early 1960s a new phenomenon was becoming evident in the Atlantic. This was the increasing use by Russia of intelligence-gathering trawlers to shadow Western warships on exercises. At much the same time Russian espionage, particularly in naval fields of research and development, was stepped up and resulted in a number of sensational spy trials, in Britain particularly. Western naval aviation and anti-submarine techniques, being two areas in which they were clearly far behind, were the principal targets of the Communists' intelligence effort.

The commissioning of the first American Polaris nuclear missile submarine in 1960 captured public imagination in Britain as well as in America and the missile was seen as the 'ultimate weapon' by politicians.

Though missiles were extremely costly to develop, the politicians believed, they would, in the long-term, be cheaper as they would, it was hoped, enable conventional manpower hungry (and therefore costly) forces to be reduced to a token level.

In 1961 the need for conventional forces was once again demonstrated when the vitally important oil-producing state of Kuwait in the Persian Gulf appealed for British assistance to repel a threatened invasion by Communist-backed Iraq. The British carrier *Victorious* and the helicopter carrier *Bulwark* were available to provide assistance long before air-lifted ground forces could be made available and positioned. *Victorious* initially provided all the radar early warning and air control for both her own and RAF aircraft.

Uncertainty in total war

But though in 1957, in the light of the failure of the Suez Canal operation, the British Defence Minister, Mr. Duncan Sandys, was 'uncertain' about the future role of naval forces in total war there were no such doubts in either America or Russia. The former's carriers in the Sixth Fleet particularly formed an important part of the deterrent with their 2,000 mile range aircraft able to carry nuclear weapons while the Russians responded with the continuing build-up of a massive submarine fleet, largely to counter the American carriers.

Though the 'War of the Running Dogs', as the Communists termed their terrorist activity in Malaya, had virtually collapsed by the late 1950s a new threat appeared with growing opposition by Indonesia to the merger of Malaya with Singapore and parts of Borneo in a new independent state within the British Commonwealth. Fortunately British naval forces had not been so drastically run-down in the Far East after the Korean war as they had been in 1945–46, partly because of the need to stop piracy—a problem also encountered in the Persian Gulf and Arabian Sea.

Naval helicopters were used extensively in Borneo to lift troops and supplies. Frigates and minesweepers kept watch off Singapore for terrorists attempting to infiltrate into the city from sampans while in Borneo a force of assault landing craft and naval stores lighters armed with machine guns was formed for coastal patrols.

Gannet radar early warning aircraft from the carrier *Victorious* were used to watch for Indonesian transport planes attempting to drop paratroops in the Malayan jungle. No comparable RAF aircraft was available to carry out the Gannet's task.

The Australian and New Zealand navies played a big part in these operations and the latter took over, at short notice, the manning of two of the minesweepers for patrol work.

Could war have been averted?

An incident, now largely forgotten, occurred early in the campaign against Indonesian confrontation when the carrier *Victorious* was returning in a hurry to Singapore from Australia. It was known by the Indonesians that she was at sea but where they had no means of telling. Consequently, when she was eventually sighted off some Indonesian-owned islands panic broke out in the Indonesian capital of Djarkarta with thousands of people fleeing to the jungle in anticipation of air attacks. Had some low-level passes been made over the city by naval aircraft it might well have been

that the Indonesian government would have crumpled in chaos and a war that was to drag on for two more years might have been averted—but the carrier was ordered by the politicians in London to keep well clear of the principal Indonesian islands to avoid 'exacerbating the situation'.

The ending of hostilities between Indonesia and Malaysia in 1964 was overshadowed by the rapidly worsening situation in Vietnam and particularly the Tonkin Gulf incidents in which North Vietnamese torpedo boats attempted to attack patrolling American destroyers. But, in 1962, there occurred what was probably the classic example of the use of seapower for the preservation of peace. This was the establishment by the US Navy of a blockade of Cuba to prevent Russian freighters bringing in nuclear missiles to threaten North America's 'soft underbelly' along the Gulf of Mexico. The frustration of the Kremlin's aims by the use of American seapower undoubtedly gave further impetus to the build-up of Soviet naval power.

Increasingly, the Russians demonstrated their growing strength at sea and in 1970 conducted an impressive world-wide exercise code-named 'Okean'. In that same year harrassment of Western warships on exercises resulted in a spectacular collision in the Mediterranean between a Russian destroyer and the British carrier *Ark Royal* although there had been a similar incident earlier between Russian and American warships in the Sea of Japan.

Irony of discarding carriers

In 1966 Britain had decided to discard carriers yet, practically while this was being written into government policy, the British carrier *Eagle* was once again demonstrating the use of seaborne airpower off East Africa where patrols were conducted to watch for blockade runners attempting to take oil to Rhodesia through Portuguese ports in Mozambique. It took five weeks to bring in and start operating land-based fighters from Zambia. Ironically, some five years earlier a British carrier had put Marines ashore and supported them with fighters in East Africa at the request of African governments there who were threatened by army mutinies.

But though Britain was getting rid of her carriers the lesson of seaborne airpower was not lost on the Kremlin and today her carriers are adding a new dimension to Russia's ability to back up her policies overseas. The Vietnam war also reinforced the case for big carriers in the United States.

In the 1970s the use of naval forces to further political aims has been demonstrated by the Anglo-American clearance of mines and explosives from the Suez Canal. Another facet of the use of seapower was the evacuation of civilians, including Russians, from war-torn Cyprus in 1974 by British and American warships, a task that could have been achieved in no other way since the principal airport was the scene of heavy fighting.

The humanitarian role of naval forces has for some years also been demonstrated in the West Indies where US Coastguard cutters and British warships frequently

rescue refugees from Cuba, escaping on occasion on mattress rafts!

In 1973 a further 'fish war' erupted between Britain and Iceland over the latter's increase in the national fishing grounds. Once again British warships had the task of preventing the arrest of trawlers by Icelandic gunboats. In the fight against terrorism in Northern Ireland British minesweepers were called upon as early as 1969 to carry out patrols to stop gun-running and the navy has provided support in the shape of three large tenders for the Army to use as barracks and depots. Warships also play a significant part in preserving Australian fishing grounds. Over the years there have been numbers of arrests of foreign poachers, notably Japanese.

Soviet 'buzzing' wakes Britain

Although essentially a task for unarmed naval vessels ocean research and hydrographic surveying is carried out around the world by several navies—principally those of the United States, Britain, France and the Soviet Union. For the British Navy especially this is a role of increasing importance in connection with the development of under-sea oil resources in the North Sea and elsewhere around the British Isles. Indeed, totally new responsibilities in the defence of North Sea oil operations, and the vessels to carry them out, feature in the British Navy's plans for the 1970s and 1980s to an extent that few people even as recently as 1970 would have appreciated. Ironically, it was a Russian intelligence gathering trawler which, in June 1974, made the British government look afresh at the security of this new source of national wealth. For two years the Naval Staff had been emphasising the need for action but with little effect. The Russian trawler, by 'buzzing' some drilling rigs at a distance of 30 yards at last awoke public and political thinking.

Since 1945, for the Western nations particularly, there seems, too often, to have been a lack of awareness of the role that naval forces can play in averting dangerous confrontations which could lead to open conflict. Rather, naval forces have been used to react to a situation already dangerous.

The Russians, 'land animals' as they were always considered by the West, on the other hand have been under no such misapprehension. Unless there is a swift and rapid reawakening in the West to the role that seapower can play in preventing war the day may not be far off when the Russian Navy will be able to inhibit the West's policy options as much as the US Navy was able to do to the Kremlin off Cuba in the early 1960s.

Korea and Vietnam – sea power in action

United States control of the sea prevented the quick loss of South Korea to invading communist forces. Much of the subsequent air war was fought from carriers but the NATO navies also laid down bombardments, landed raiding parties, swept mines and kept isolated units supplied. The helicopter first came into its own in combat situations in Korea but it was in Vietnam that tactics and techniques were perfected. The Vietnam War saw the deployment of naval forces in the same conventional roles they had occupied in the Korean War, but it also led to the creation of specialist forces, such as riverine units, which made use of unconventional vessels, including hovercraft.

The USS Missouri fires her forward 16-inch guns against North Korean communications at Chong Jin in 1950. Battleships carried out many shore bombardments in the Korean War and their pinpoint accuracy proved cheaper and more valuable than aerial bombardment.

Thwarted after World War II by prompt American assistance for Western Europe, first in the form of Marshall Aid and then by the signing of the North Atlantic Treaty, the Soviet leaders looked elsewhere for territorial and political advantages to be gained at the free world's expense. In South Korea the country itself was recovering from years of Japanese occupation and government at best was shaky. American forces had by June 1949 been reduced to instructors and advisers with the Republic's forces. To the Kremlin and its allies South Korea looked like an over-ripe plum which would fall with the mildest breeze. Yet, surprisingly, the West had had some warning for a tremendous propaganda barrage had been going on against South Korea for some months from Russia and North Korea.

Such warnings were ignored and military intelligence seems to have been faulty because the North Korean offensive launched in June 1950 took both South Korea and the Americans completely by surprise. Within

a few weeks almost the whole of South Korea had been over-run except for an area around the port of Pusan in the far south.

Fortunately this was held and a massive American build-up by air and sea began. There can be no doubt that had the United States not had control of the sea South Korea would have been lost.

British and American carrier aircraft and US Air Force heavy bombers from Japan were in action immediately but ground forces were also needed to boost South Korea's flagging defences. Some attempt was made by the North Koreans to interfere with the

support given by British and American warships and five of their motor torpedo boats were sunk in an action with surface forces. The North Koreans also made a number of amphibious assaults along the east coast as well as supplying their forces in the South by small craft using coastal routes.

In July 1950 the escort carrier *Sicily* left San Diego carrying large quantities of aircraft for the Korean campaign and the attack carrier *Philippine Sea* was among early reinforcements. In the highest American military and political circles the need for close tactical air support, which could be provided only by carriers since the land situation was still far too insecure to permit the building of large air bases, did not pass unnoticed—somewhat to the discomfort of the Air Force who had largely won their battle to stop construction of the new carrier *United States*. The same lesson was not learnt in Britain, though the carrier *Triumph* was available at the start of the conflict and almost the entire British contribution in the air to the UN forces in Korea was provided throughout the war by the Navy.

Battleships from reserve

By August 1950 British naval forces off Korea included a carrier, an aircraft maintenance ship, three cruisers, seven destroyers, eight frigates and a hospital ship. Australia was providing a destroyer and a frigate,

The US Navy transport Begor, *lies off Hungnam as UN forces blow up dock installations on their withdrawal from North Korea.*

Canada three destroyers and New Zealand two frigates. In America work began on taking three Essex class carriers from reserve. Although America, Britain and the Commonwealth countries were the principal nations involved in Korea, the Netherlands, Denmark, Thailand, South Africa and Turkey were among early contributors to the UN forces.

The reassessment of defence requirements as a result of the war was well under way by the autumn of 1950 in a number of free world countries. In America it was decided to commission another battleship from reserve—*Missouri* was soon to be engaged on bombardment duties off Korea and was later replaced in turn by her sister ships *Iowa* and *New Jersey*. Canada planned to modernise 12 destroyers to improve their anti-submarine capabilities.

In the war zone itself two destroyers were damaged in October 1950 by floating mines while the British cruiser *Jamaica* was hit by enemy coastal batteries and the destroyer *Comus* suffered fairly severe damage and casualties as a result of air attacks. A major amphibious assault at Inchon, not far south of the 38th parallel which divides North and South Korea, helped to relieve pressure on the UN forces in the south although subsequently the intervention by the Chinese Communists forced the UN forces to restrict the fighting, principally to a broad front running across the country from coast to coast.

But throughout the war warships landed raiding parties, carried out bombardment duties, swept mines and helped supply isolated units and civilian communities. A particular example of the last was carried out by the Australian destroyer *Warramunga* which supplied rice and other food to lighthouse-keepers and other islanders off South Korea.

Her sister ship *Bataan* spent some time escorting the American light attack carrier of the same name. After a refit in Australia in 1951 *Bataan* and *Warramunga* returned to Korean waters, only for *Bataan* to be hit by an enemy coastal battery shell. But *Bataan* established a very considerable reputation among UN naval forces and became known as 'The Grey Ghost of the West Coast', or on occasion 'Brace's Circus' after her captain.

Life-saving helicopters

By early 1951 the plan to bring a large number of US warships out of reserve was underway with the battleship *New Jersey*; the carriers *Princeton, Monterey, Cape Esperance, Sitkoh Bay, Bairoko*; the cruiser *Macon* and numbers of destroyers and auxiliaries all scheduled to rejoin the fleet in 1951–52. The American minesweeping forces lost three minesweepers in the first six months of the war and more casualties were to follow.

But in one field at least losses were appreciably smaller than in previous conflicts. The US Navy was now using helicopters to rescue crews of aircraft which had crashed—often far behind enemy lines. This technique was to reach an almost incredible degree of efficiency in the Vietnam War some 15 years later.

Early 1951 saw a particularly remarkable exploit when the Australian destroyers *Warramunga* and *Bataan*; the American *Forrest Royal*; and the Canadian *Athabaskan, Cayuga* and *Sioux* navigated in a snowstorm for 30 miles up the shallow unlit channel in a minefield in the Daido Ko estuary to cover the withdrawal of civilians and wounded and non-essential military personnel from the Pyongyang area. Meanwhile the British carrier *Theseus*, which had relieved the *Triumph*, carried out air attacks on enemy communications and supplies at an intensity not previously equalled by any British carrier.

In February 1951 a nice, but perhaps unconscious, bit of irony occurred when the US patrol frigates *Rockford* and *Muskogee* were handed over to the South Korean Navy following the ships' return with 13 others from the Russian Navy to whom they had been lent in World War II. Two months later the Thai corvette *Prase* of some 900 tons ran aground off Wonsan and became a total loss—the largest UN ship lost in the war.

The British Navy brought forward 60 ships from reserve in spring 1951 as part of the immediate rearmament plan while in Australia the government stepped in to stop the sale of two minesweepers to Chinese allegedly 'commercial' interests. A number of other partially disarmed warships sold by Western navies after World War II had reappeared as warships in the Chinese Communist Navy.

Duel at point-blank range

The constant patrolling to stop supplies reaching the Communist forces by sea and the provision of bombardment support for the troops ashore resulted in some impressive times being spent at sea by warships with the UN. The Canadian destroyer *Athabaskan*, nicknamed the 'Little Mo', had steamed 60,000 miles, much of the time escorting USS *Missouri*, when she returned home in

A South Korean minesweeper blows up in Wonsan harbour. The Korean War alerted Western navies to the effectiveness of the latest Russian mines.

Corsair fighter-bombers warm up before taking off from an aircraft carrier during the Korean War.

summer 1951, while the New Zealand frigate *Tutira* was continuously at sea for 46 days on one occasion. The British cruiser *Kenya* in twelve months steamed 63,000 miles and fired 3,000 6-inch, 2,242 4-inch and 14,240 40 mm shells. The American carrier *Bataan* and the British carrier *Glory* working in company in summer 1951 were flying 100 missions a day with the British carrier frequently using RATO—Rocket-Assisted Take-Off for her aircraft. *Glory* was relieved by the Australian carrier *Sydney*, late in 1951, at about the same time that the Australian frigate *Murchison* with other UN ships was involved in a vicious gun duel with Communist field guns in the Han river at almost point blank range.

By January 1952 *Sydney*'s aircraft had completed 270 missions, mainly against enemy industry and rail communications. She also provided spotter aircraft for a number of ships on bombardment duties, including the Australian destroyer *Tobruk*.

A particularly remarkable engagement was that in August 1952 when four 390-knot piston engined Sea Fury fighters from the British carrier *Ocean* were engaged by eight Communist 650-knot MiG-15 jet fighters. They shot down one MiG and damaged another without loss to themselves. In November 1952 *Ocean* achieved a record for a British carrier by flying 123 missions in a single day.

While the Korean War demonstrated that control of the seas remained vital if an enemy potentially vastly superior on the ground was to be held in check, in one respect it produced a dangerous conclusion. Both the United

Above: An American built amphibious vehicle is used by French troops in Indo China.

US Marines land at Da Nang in 1965. The United States made good use of sea power in the Vietnam War by landing troops at selected points on the coastline and by providing gunfire support and carrier airstrikes for hard-pressed ground forces.

States and Britain brought large numbers of ships from reserve and it was the swiftness and ease with which this was accomplished which led to considerable complacency in political circles. So long as large numbers of ships remained in mothballs, the politicians maintained, it was not necessary to build much more than token numbers of costly new warships. Only after the ending of the Vietnam War in 1973 did it become widely apparent in the United States that a reserve of ships built 25–30 years before would be of little relevance in a future conflict.

The need for specialist units

In Britain the war did push the government of the day into building some 300 new ships. Had the war in Korea been averted it seems most unlikely such a programme would ever have been started and it is a sobering thought that at least some 80 ships in service in the British Navy in the mid-1970s were ordered under the 1951–52 emergency programme.

But while America and Britain were involved in the conflict in Korea, France was heavily engaged in her Indo-China colony where she was faced by a Communist-backed 'army of liberation' fighting for independence from French rule. Though basically a land war it did involve naval units up the Mekong and other rivers and larger units off-shore on support duties or ferrying men and supplies from France. On occasion the battleship *Richelieu*, all the surviving pre-war built cruisers, a former British and two

former American light attack carriers and many minor vessels, including some received from Italy as war reparations, were involved.

But the biggest problem undoubtedly was the creation of special riverine units. Small landing craft were brought in by the old carrier *Bearn* from the British base at Singapore and these, together with junks and other native craft once used by the Japanese, were converted by, for example, arming them with turrets from tanks as well as a wide array of 40 mm, 20 mm and other light automatic guns.

The collapse of the French forces in Indo-China in 1954 and the emergence of the four separate states of North and South Vietnam, Laos and Cambodia did not mark the end of the fighting. The Communists in North Vietnam struggled to take over the South and guerilla movements elsewhere, notably in Laos, sought to impose Communist style rule. By the early 1960s the United States was becoming increasingly involved as more and more 'advisers' were made available, particularly to the South Vietnamese forces.

In 1964 North Vietnamese torpedo boats attempted to attack American destroyers

Right: An armed Iroquois helicopter co-operates with two river patrol boats in a sweep up the Bassac River to flush out Vietcong emplacements. The rivers of Vietnam were a major battleground of their own and special techniques of river-fighting were developed by the French and the Americans.

Le Fantasque

The six ships of this class, some of which served in Indo-China post-war, formed the fastest destroyer squadrons in the world. On trials they averaged 40 knots and could steam continuously at high speed. *Le Fantasque* is depicted after her refit in the USA in 1943–44, with a new outfit of anti-aircraft guns and reduced torpedo armament.

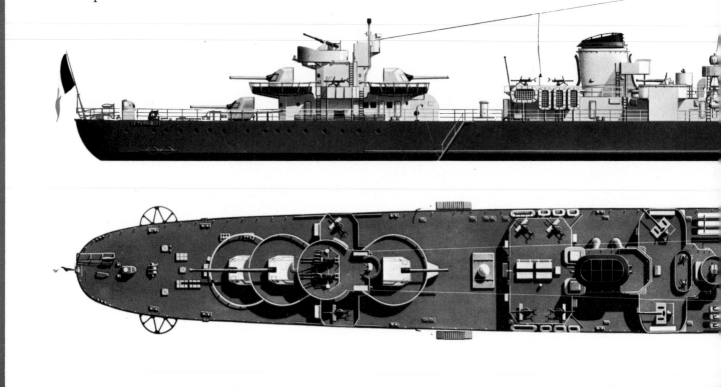

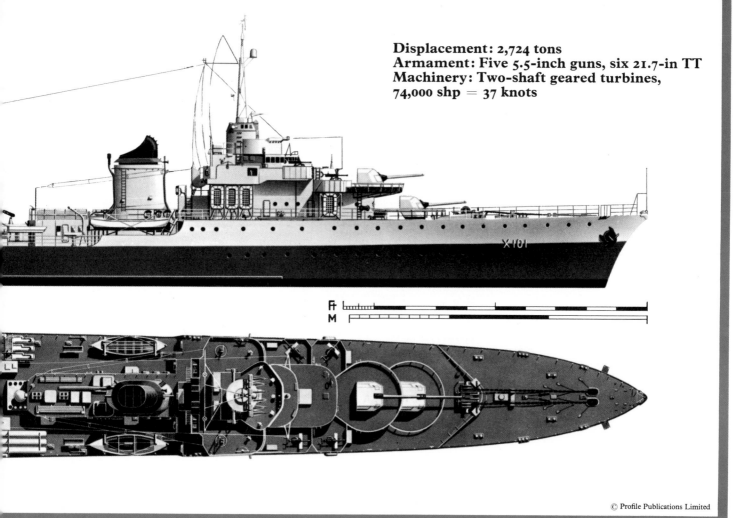

Displacement: 2,724 tons
Armament: Five 5.5-inch guns, six 21.7-in TT
Machinery: Two-shaft geared turbines,
74,000 shp = 37 knots

Ft
M

patrolling off the coast at night. This resulted in attacks on the boats' bases by carrier aircraft from the Seventh Fleet and a gradual escalation of the war to a point where there was full American involvement in the air, on land and along the coasts and up the rivers.

Russian mines cast loose

By 1965 it was clear that the North Vietnamese supply route along the coast would have to be stopped and that this would necessitate the use of better trained forces than were then available to the small navy of South Vietnam. Accordingly numbers of US Coastguard-manned 82 foot patrol craft were employed with a considerable degree of success—several fierce engagements being fought with well-armed enemy trawlers and coastal freighters. A number of radar picket destroyer escorts and larger Coastguard cutters reinforced the inshore line of craft in the operation known as 'Market Time'.

The main supply port for the vast flow of war material into South Vietnam was Saigon, lying some 30 miles up an easily mined river from whose banks it would also be easy for the enemy to ambush passing ships with anti-tank rifles and other weapons. A wide variety of crude mines as well as more sophisticated types of Russian origin, usually cast loose to drift down river, were used by the Viet Cong.

Besides a range of minesweeping craft, riverine warfare on a large scale produced a considerable number of sometimes rather strange craft. There were 'monitors', usually fitted with tank turrets; command and control craft, usually adapted landing craft which sometimes had even a helicopter landing platform; eight-ton river patrol boats and the somewhat larger 22.5 ton 'Swift' type inshore patrol craft; armoured troop carriers; swimmer support craft designed to back up SEAL diver teams whose task was intelligence-gathering, sabotage, surveying and various other clandestine tasks in enemy-held territory; and hospital craft. To support these various craft—some 500 of the eight-ton river patrol boats alone were built— numbers of tank landing ships (LST) were taken out of reserve and some of these had been adapted in World War II as mobile barrack ships.

Hovercraft were also employed for patrol duties and naval tugs were used to move barges in some river and coastal areas. The larger type Coast-guard cutters supplemented naval off-shore patrols in the 'Market Time' operation while inshore fire support vessels (converted landing ships); destroyer-escorts; destroyers; cruisers and even the battleship *New Jersey*, which was taken out of mothballs, were used to bombard the enemy, sometimes from as much as 25–30 miles from the coast. The Seventh Fleet maintained at least three attack carriers on station at all times to provide strikes against enemy targets in the North and to support friendly forces in the South.

Flushing out snipers

But these massive American forces, supported by South Vietnam's growing navy, which included numbers of converted armed junks and at least one Australian missile destroyer at all times, were by no means unopposed. On

Above: The USS Inchon *lies off Haiphong during operations to re-open the port after the ceasefire in 1973. Her helicopters were used in minesweeping duties, a task that the US Navy relies largely on helicopters to perform.*

The hovercraft with its air-cushion and flexible skirts was ideally suited to operate in the rivers and paddy-fields of Vietnam and the war offered the first opportunity to test the military potential of this revolutionary amphibious craft.

several occasions ships on bombardment duties were hit by Communist shore batteries while in 1972 the destroyer *Higbee* was hit by a MiG-17 fighter. The nuclear powered cruiser *Long Beach* and the guided missile destroyer *Sterett* were both credited with shooting down Communist aircraft with their missiles, the former using her Talos missiles in 1968 and the latter using Terrier missiles in 1972.

At the other end of the weapon scale, while *Long Beach* was believed to be the first warship to shoot down aircraft with missiles in war, some armoured troop carriers used in

Right: Wing tip vortices appear around the rotor blades of a US Marine Corps Sea Stallion helicopter sweeping for magnetic mines off Hon Gay, in North Vietnam, during Operation End Sweep in March 1973. In a strategy that was instrumental in obtaining the final ceasefire the US Navy used its most advanced mines to block North Vietnamese harbours and after the peace treaty was signed it was naturally anxious to be responsible for sweeping them.

the Mekong Delta were probably the first warships fitted with high pressure water guns which could literally 'flush' snipers from along the river banks!

In 1972, to the surprise of political observers, President Nixon ordered a mine blockade, to be laid by Seventh Fleet aircraft, of North Vietnamese ports. Though, for obvious reasons, few details were given of the mines used they included a timed self-destructing device in their mechanism and were also believed to combine two or more detonating systems such as acoustic and magnetic. In this way the enemy could not be certain whether, for example, steel ships which had been 'degaussed' by running a weak electric current round their hulls to counter their natural magnetism, would be safe and, equally, if ships towing underwater noise-makers would also be safe.

The mine blockade was evidently highly successful in that ships seen by air reconnaissance in North Vietnamese harbours like Haiphong just before the mines were laid were still there when, following the peace agreement, American surface and helicopter minesweepers arrived in North Vietnamese waters to clear the mines in 1973.

The problem of the skill factor

From the mid-1960s the Americans turned over an increasing number of smaller warships and river patrol craft to the South Vietnamese Navy. By 1970 it was, purely in terms of numbers of hulls, the ninth largest Navy in the world. In all a total of some 850 ships and craft were transferred by the United States, including, rather curiously, one former Coastguard lightship. Her task is to serve as a floating radar station to supplement naval-manned shore stations which watch for craft infiltrating from the North.

One of the biggest problems facing the South Vietnamese Navy today is the shortage of skilled personnel for maintenance and repair work. This factor alone is likely to keep the number of ships and craft that are operational at any one time well below the overall total.

Although no longer directly involved in the fighting, the US Navy's leaders have had the foresight to retain at least a nucleus of the huge riverine and coastal forces built up for the war in Vietnam so that the techniques of this kind of warfare are not totally lost. Some prototype craft of new designs are also being produced

The Vietnam War has reiterated the lesson first taught in Korea—without the ability to bring in vast quantities of stores of all kinds by sea America could never have sustained her own effort nor that of South Vietnam for more than a few months. Admittedly, the creation of new ports, such as Camranh Bay, helped to speed the flow of stores and to ensure that at least they arrived intact on the dockside but such a vast new port would have been useless if North Vietnam and her allies had been able to interrupt the flow of shipping from America. For reasons of geography and politics the Western powers, in deterring—and if need be defeating—Communist aggression outside central Europe, must always rely on the seas and therefore must be ready to maintain the unrestricted right to use them. This is a lesson they neglect at their peril.

Technology takes over at sea

After the dramatic U-boat successes of World War II the submarine was viewed as the main threat to survival in the future, forcing rapid strides to be taken in the fields of detection and destruction of submarines. The menace of air attacks, too, had to be countered, leading to the research and development of missiles of all types; first to combat aerial attack and then to fight surface actions at increasingly longer ranges. The rapidly changing nature of war at sea led to a radical re-think in ship design, construction materials and propulsion and, inevitably, to a growing reliance on technology.

The submarine, as in World War I, had by 1942–43 come so near once again to defeating the Allied powers that it was not surprisingly seen by post-war naval leaders as the main threat in the future. This fear was amply justified by the alarming increase in Soviet submarine construction which became apparent in the late 1940s.

In the latter part of the war ahead-throwing weapons had been developed. Firing explosive weapons ahead of a ship allowed Sonar contact to be maintained with the target during the attack. The British and US Navies relied first on the 'Hedgehog' which fired numbers of small bombs in large patterns, but which only exploded on contact.

Later, the British developed 'Squid'— a triple-barrelled mortar, firing very much larger bombs than 'Hedgehog' which could be pre-set to explode at the depth at which Sonar indicated the submarine to be. A near-miss by a 'Squid' bomb could be sufficient to cripple or even sink a submarine.

By the late 1940s the British had developed the Mortar Mark X, or 'Limbo'. This offered an advantage over 'Squid' in that it could be trained through a reasonably wide arc. It has a range of about 1,000 yards and the latest version has proximity fusing.

Though the US Navy continued to rely on 'Hedgehog' for many years, both it and the British Navy pushed ahead with improving the range of 'active' Sonar and with the detection capabilities of 'passive' Sonar. The former requires a ship to emit sound waves which, upon striking a submarine, produce an 'echo'. A series of such echoes gives the submarine's course and speed as well as its bearing from the transmitting ship and its depth.

But the disadvantage with active Sonar is that it can quickly betray the presence of the hunting ship to an alert submarine. Its range is also limited.

Passive Sonar, on the other hand, being basically a hydrophone or underwater listening device, has a very much greater range. While its use does not give away the presence of the hunting ship it is obviously much more difficult to obtain an accurate indication of the submarine's range, bearing and depth.

Embarrassing DASH

In the United States this problem was met more by concentrating on ways to improve the response time so that a submarine detected with active Sonar could be attacked more quickly than would be possible by steaming the hunting ship, possibly for some distance, along the Sonar bearing until the submarine was within range of its

Two Westland Wasp helicopters exercise with a Leander Class frigate. The Wasp was specially developed by the Royal Navy for anti-submarine work from frigates. The shipborne helicopter, with its speed far in excess of any submarine but combined with superb manoeuvrability, proved an important countermeasure to the nuclear submarine.

anti-submarine weapons—a matter of a few hundred yards.

Increasing underwater speeds of submarines made it essential to be able to attack them at or near the limit of Sonar detection range. One such method was DASH, the Drone Anti-Submarine Helicopter. A number of American war-built destroyers were modified with the addition of a hangar and flight deck for two small, radio-controlled, unmanned helicopters, each carrying two homing torpedoes.

But despite long and intensive trials the system did not prove reliable. There were a number of reasons, one of which was that the DASH, once airborne, was susceptible to jamming of its radio command system—either deliberate or accidental. An example of the latter occurred when on one occasion the helicopter responded to directions for manned aircraft from a carrier— to the embarrassment of both the carrier and her pilots!

Consequently, in the 1960s the US Navy followed the example of the British and began introducing LAMPS—Light Airborne Multi-Purpose System—or manned helicopters. The first British manned anti-submarine helicopter to be part of a ship's integral weapon system went to sea in the frigate *Ashanti* in 1961. The aircraft used, the Wasp, is purely a weapon carrier armed with two anti-submarine homing torpedoes. It has no detection capability of its own, apart from visual observations by pilot and observer, and simply extends the range of the ship's weapons. Wasps are now fitted in 42 British as well as New Zealand, Dutch, Chilean, Indian and South African frigates.

Another American solution to the problem of attacking fast submarines as quickly as possible after Sonar detection was the missile carrying a homing torpedo. Such a weapon, known as ASROC—Anti-Submarine Rocket—is now widely in service in the US Navy and is also fitted in some West German, Italian, Japanese and Canadian warships.

Ikara and ASROC

Homing torpedoes, whether missile, helicopter or ship launched, may be fitted with conventional explosive or nuclear warheads. They seek out their target by the noise made by a submarine's propellers.

But ASROC has one disadvantage in that it follows a ballistic flight path and cannot be directed once launched. In the British Navy this was seen as a basic drawback and consequently a weapon with greater accuracy as well as an improvement in range over the six mile maximum of ASROC was sought.

The answer was the Australian Ikara. This weapon is a solid-propellant missile carrying an American type Mark 44 anti-submarine torpedo. Data on the submarine's changes in course, speed and depth are fed from the launching ship to the missile in flight. Such information may also be relayed from helicopters or other ships or even submarines to the launching ship for processing by computers and transmission to the missile. Once in close proximity to the target the missile breaks up and releases the torpedo on a parachute. Ikara

is already fitted or is in the process of being fitted in nine Australian destroyers and frigates and in one British destroyer and eight frigates.

While light helicopters and missiles could clearly improve the range of a surface ship's offensive capability against a submarine, they could add nothing to its detection capability. On the other hand a larger type of helicopter could combine both the weapon-carrying and detection functions. Undoubtedly the most successful helicopter so far developed that combines these roles is the American SH-3. Designed originally for operating from carriers it is also used by the Canadian Navy in frigates and by the British Navy in two cruisers partially converted for an anti-submarine and troop-carrying role.

Besides being able to carry four homing torpedoes the SH-3 (or Sea King as it is known in the Australian, West German, Indian, Pakistan, Egyptian and British navies, all of which have a British-made version built under licence) has a dipping Sonar to detect submarines. This is lowered as required into the water on a cable attached to an automatic winch in the aircraft. The Italian Navy has the aircraft built under licence in Italy and these may be carried in two missile destroyers; the Spanish Navy has the American-built version in its helicopter carrier *Dedalo*; and the Brazilian Navy in its carrier *Minas Gerais*.

Defeating the thermals

The British Sea Kings are fitted with a computer which can take over control of the aircraft so that it follows a submarine once it has been detected by Sonar. This leaves the pilot free to concentrate on when to launch his weapons and to guide other anti-submarine forces.

In the Canadian Navy particularly, which has long specialised in anti-submarine warfare, promising developments were achieved in the field of VDS—Variable Depth Sonar. Similar development work was also carried out by America, Britain and France but Britain eventually purchased the Canadian system.

It had long been recognised that one of the biggest problems facing a surface anti-submarine ship was its inability to overcome thermal layers. These layers of warmer water, whose extent, seasonal variations and depth have been and still are the subject of considerable research by several navies and by NATO itself, tend to diffuse Sonar waves so that a submarine beneath them can escape detection. By lowering a Sonar transducer on a cable over the stern of a surface ship it is possible largely to overcome the protection these layers afford a submarine. Considerable research was necessary to produce a hydrodynamic form which, when towed, did not itself create so much underwater disturbance that it became useless. It was also necessary to find a design which could maintain the required depth for long periods.

In the late 1940s and early 1950s, before the advent of VDS and helicopters in anti-submarine warfare, it was increasingly recognised by many navies that the 15-18

A Kamov Ka-25 "Hormone" anti-submarine helicopter on the flight deck of the Russian helicopter-cruiser Moskva. *The Russian Navy uses helicopters for anti-submarine duties and troop-landings.*

knot World War II escort was becoming an anachronism. Even if it could just keep up with a submarine the underwater disturbance around its Sonar dome when travelling at maximum speed made it virtually impossible to keep track of a submarine.

The American, British, Australian and South African navies therefore embarked on a programme of modernising existing destroyers. This meant reducing their gun armament in favour of more anti-submarine mortars. In the US Navy these modifications did not alter the ships' basic design, but alterations made in British and Australian war-built destroyers were much more drastic.

'Limbo' extends ships' lives

Twenty-three British and four Australian destroyers had their complete superstructures stripped and their forecastles extended aft almost to the stern. Their gun armament of four 4.7-inch and smaller guns was cut to a twin 4-inch and two smaller guns; torpedo tubes were removed and fully enclosed bridges were fitted. In some cases these alterations resulted in increasing the ships' effective lives from the normal 20 years to 30. Their anti-submarine weapons were two triple 'Limbo' Mark X mortars.

While anti-submarine warfare has, since 1945, occupied the attention of many navies the Soviet Navy has, until recently, been the one major exception. Possibly because the national economy does not rely to the extent of some Western powers on shipping, the Russians for many years after the war tended to neglect anti-submarine weapons. But in the latest Kresta and Kara class cruisers particularly a helicopter is now carried, although whether its basic role is anti-submarine or surface-to-surface missile mid-course guidance is not clear. On the other hand the helicopters carried in the cruisers *Moskva* and *Leningrad* are definitely

Above : An aerial view of a Russian helicopter-cruiser of the Moskva *Class.*

Left : A Royal Navy Sea King helicopter from the carrier HMS Ark Royal *using a dipping sonar to search for submarines.*

for anti-submarine work and these ships also carry VDS. Little is known of the capabilities of Russian ship-borne anti-submarine weapons except that they now favour multi-barrelled rocket launchers of types which appear to be much improved versions of 'Hedgehog'.

Second only to the anti-submarine problem for many navies is that of air attack, particularly since some Russian long-range aircraft have missiles with an air-to-surface range of 150 miles. Against piston-engined aircraft the high-angled gun ranging from 5-inch down to 20 mm was reasonably effective enough in a concentrated barrage. But high speed jet aircraft posed a problem that even the most sophisticated gunnery fire control systems could not fully meet.

The first two missile ships to become fully operational were the American heavy cruisers *Canberra* and *Boston* which re-entered service in 1956 armed with two twin Terrier SAM launchers in place of their after triple 8-inch gun turret. The same year the Canadian-built freighter *Girdle Ness*, which was taken over by the British Navy during construction in 1944 for service as a tender, completed a major conversion to test the Seaslug SAM system. This weapon first became operational in 1962 in the new destroyer *Devonshire*.

Terriers and Seaslugs

But both Terrier and Seaslug required considerable magazine space and thus were unsuitable for smaller ships. Consequently, in America the smaller Tartar missile was developed and began going to sea in 1960 on board the *Charles F. Adams* class missile destroyers. Ships of this design are in service in the Australian and West German navies while Tartar is also fitted in some American cruisers; the Dutch cruiser *De Zeven Provincien*; four French, a Japanese and two Italian destroyers. Apart from American warships, Terrier is fitted in three Italian missile cruisers.

These early SAM systems have a range of around 10 nautical miles in the case of the two American weapons while Seaslug has been officially credited with a 90 per cent accuracy rating against targets at 50,000 feet. The later Terrier design has a range of about 20 nautical miles while Seaslug has been developed to give it a surface-to-surface capability out to radar horizon, or about 9-12 miles. But all three missile systems required extensive modifications to any ships not originally designed to carry them.

In Britain the first tests at sea began in 1958 with Seacat. This is a short-range missile controlled with a joystick by an operator using a visual sight. More recently,

A hovercraft of the Iranian navy at speed.

the system has been modified so that the operator follows a light 'blob' on a screen and it has also proved possible to use existing gunnery control radars in conjunction with the missile. Seacat is now in service with the British, Australian, New Zealand, Chilean, Indian, Dutch, Swedish, Malaysian, Thai, Iranian, Brazilian, Argentinian, Libyan and Venezuelan navies and is fitted in ships ranging from helicopter carriers (LPH) to small destroyers. Under development are a version using closed-circuit television and a surface-to-surface version.

In the United States the problem of fitting existing ships with some close range or 'point' defence is being overcome with Sea Sparrow. This is now being fitted in carriers and LPHs and a NATO version

is under development in which America, Canada, Norway, Denmark, Italy, The Netherlands and Belgium are involved.

To provide longer range or 'area' defence against air attacks the 60 nautical mile range Talos was developed in America and is now fitted in a number of cruisers. The nuclear powered cruiser *Long Beach* is credited with having destroyed with her Talos missiles two Russian-built MiG fighters at around 60 miles range off North Vietnam in 1968.

In Britain the Sea Dart missile fulfils a similar role and, like Talos, has a limited

Right : The frigate USS England *fires a Terrier beam-riding AA missile.*

HMS Cavalier

Represents the final evolution of the single-funnelled type of destroyer developed by the Royal Navy from the *Kelly* and her sisters. She is depicted after her post-war modernisation, with new fire-control, heavier anti-submarine armament and a Seacat close-range guided missile defence. The *Cavalier* served in the Far East and elsewhere from 1957 to 1972.

Displacement: 2,053 tons
Armament: Three 4.5-inch guns, one missile launcher
Machinery: Two-shaft geared turbines, 40,000 shp = 34 knots

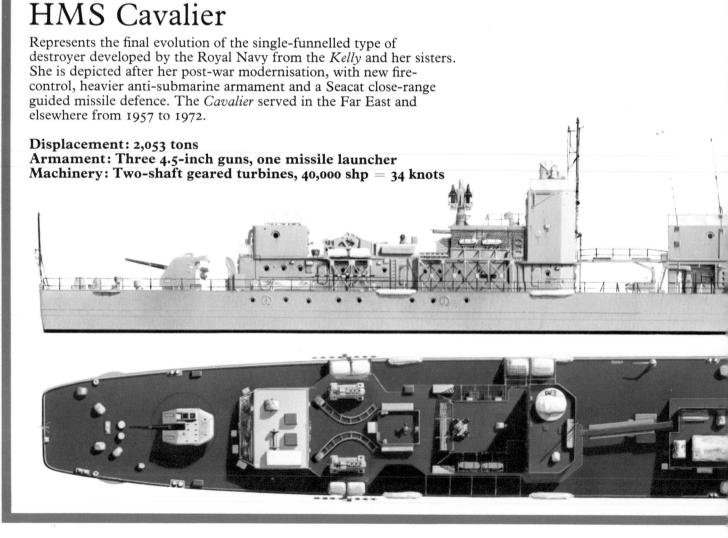

surface-to-surface capability. The missile has been at sea since 1972 in the missile destroyer *Bristol* and is to be fitted in seven other ships now building. As a replacement for Seacat the British are now developing Seawolf and this is expected to be in service in the late 1970s. Though light enough to be handled manually it is capable, like Sea Dart, of destroying approaching air-to-surface and surface-to-surface missiles.

The US Navy is concentrating increasingly on missiles which can be launched from existing launchers. Thus the Standard SAM system is a replacement for Tartar and Terrier in older destroyers and other ships while the new Aegis coming into service in the latter part of the decade will be launched from ASROC launchers.

Despite the purchase of American Tartar missiles for four destroyers the French Navy is leading the Western World in some areas with the development of naval missiles. They already have the Malafon 9.5 mile range Sonar directed anti-submarine missile in service and the 25 mile range Exocet surface-to-surface missile. This is already in service or planned for 23 British destroyers and frigates as well as in ships of the Chilean, West German, Greek, Pakistani, Malaysian and, probably, Singaporean navies. The standard French naval SAM system is the 21 nautical mile range Masurca. Though the radar beam-riding version has proved entirely successful a modified version which uses an active homing system in the missile has had problems.

As a joint venture the French and Italians are introducing the Otomat 32.43 nautical mile range surface-to-surface missile while Italy has the 13 nautical mile range Sea Killer missile and is developing an advanced version with a range of over 24 nautical miles.

Russia develops her missiles

In the Soviet Union the first SAM system, with the NATO code name Goa, came into service about 1961. It has a range of about 15 miles. The 22 mile range Guideline appears to have come into service about 1957 and seems to have been fitted in only one converted cruiser. The latest SAM, Goblet, is fitted in the newest Russian warships and has a arnge of 20 miles but is otherwise an improved version of Goa. A further SAM system, which has a novel feature in that it is housed in silos reminiscent of those used on a much larger scale for the land-based Minuteman ICBMs in America, is also at sea in ships ranging from cruisers to small escorts.

The most important Soviet missile development has, however, been in the field of surface-to-surface missiles. The first of these, with a range of 130 nautical miles (which, being a distance greater than the launching ship's radar horizon, required mid-course guidance), came into service in 1958.

In 1960 numbers of small high speed craft of two designs armed with the 23 nautical mile range Styx surface-to-surface missile began to enter service. Vessels of these types are now in service with the Algerian, Yugoslav, Chinese, Cuban, Indian, Indonesian, Syrian, Egyptian and several Warsaw Pact navies. In 1967 some of these craft at least nominally of the

Above: The Israeli Gabriel surface-to-surface missile was developed for fast patrol boats in reply to the Russian-supplied Styx missile of the Egyptian and Syrian navies. The shorter range Gabriel proved lethal in the Yom Kippur War.

Above right: The Anglo-Australian Ikara, guided from a ship's sonar, is basically a pilotless aircraft with a homing torpedo.

Egyptian Navy sank the war-built Israeli destroyer *Eilath* and others of the Indian Navy were responsible for sinking several ships in the war with Pakistan in 1971.

A modified version with a greater range is believed to be in service. For a time Russian surface-to-surface missiles went on increasing in range up to about 300 nautical miles. But the latest versions are down to under 30 miles range thus obviating the vulnerable mid-course guidance needed for long range missiles.

Such is the relative simplicity of surface-to-surface missiles that these are no longer the prerogative only of the larger navies. Norway has a powerful force of 26 fast patrol boats fitted with the 10.15 nautical mile range Penguin missile which is also fitted in five American designed escorts. The Norwegians also have their own rocket powered depth charge, the Terne.

The 'Vengeance of Gabriel'

In October 1973 Iarael first demonstrated her Gabriel 11-nautical mile range surface-to-surface missile in action when a number of Egyptian Styx-armed missile boats were sunk, even though the Russian weapon has twice the range.

The supersonic air-to-surface; surface-to-surface or sub-surface-to-surface missile represents a considerable threat to conventional surface ships. Against radar beam riders it may be possible to jam the guidance system if the enemy's frequency can be found in time. It may also be possible electronically to change the 'range gate' so that the approaching missile is made to believe that the target is nearer than is the case. The British and Dutch navies have adopted the use of rocket-launchers to fire strips of metal foil, or 'chaff' into the air to confuse the missile's radar.

In the United States modern versions of the Gatling gun are being developed which will put an almost solid barrage of 20 mm. shells into the air around the target while both the latest American and British SAM systems have an anti-missile capability.

The naval gun, despite the development

of surface-to-surface missiles, can still prove of great value. As a result of having to deal with very small craft during Indonesia's 'confrontation' campaign against Malaysia in the early 1960s, most British destroyers and frigates are now equipped with 20 mm guns, the semi-automatic twin 4.5-inch guns with which most are fitted being too large and the missiles impracticable against very small targets.

The latest British and Iranian destroyers and frigates now have a fully automatic single 4.5-inch gun while partially automatic guns up to 8-inch have been available in the US Navy since 1945. In Vietnam it was found possible to give such guns a range of over 39 miles using a rocket attachment fitted to the shells.

All-seeing 'data link'

In the late 1950s the 3-inch guns fitted in the three British Tiger class cruisers had to have their rate of fire cut from 120 to 90 rounds a minute as the magazine capacity would otherwise have been inadequate. The same type of gun is fitted in a number of Canadian escorts.

The performance of all types of weapons has been vastly improved with the introduction of computer systems. The American Naval Tactical Data System and the British Action Data Automation allow for simultaneous tracking of all air, surface and sub-surface targets and the automatic passing

Commissioned in 1961, the world's first nuclear-powered warship. The 14,000-ton cruiser USS Long Beach is armed with Talos and Terrier missiles, an ASROC anti-submarine weapon system and two guns.

of information to ships fitted with a 'data link'. These systems have been modified to permit their installation in ships of destroyer size and smaller. But the Americans have also developed two special command ships, the *Mount Whitney* and *Blue Ridge*, to provide complete command and control facilities of sea, air and land forces for amphibious force commanders.

To provide widespread radar coverage and direction of friendly aircraft both navies also developed a new type of ship—the radar picket and aircraft direction destroyer or frigate. Destroyers were first employed on radar picket duties in the Pacific in the closing stages of the war to give long range warning of the approach of Kamikaze suicide planes.

While in the 1950s nuclear power was considered in the US Navy to be the propulsion system of the future, in Britain propulsion development centred on the marine gas turbine. The first two American nuclear powered surface ships were the carrier *Enterprise* and the missile cruiser *Long Beach*, both completed in 1961. They were followed in 1962 by the missile frigate *Bainbridge*.

The British Navy after testing gas turbines in a number of fast patrol boats produced its first major gas turbine warship, the former steam turbine powered frigate *Exmouth*, in 1968. But seven years earlier gas turbines were at sea in frigates as part of their power plants. Apart from providing additional boost for steam turbines, gas turbines can be started from cold without the need for waiting several hours to raise steam. They are also more easily replaced, take up less space and need fewer crewmen.

Plastic ships to hunt mines

Future British warships will all be gas gas turbine powered except probably for a new class of mine warfare vessels built of glass reinforced plastic. The world's largest ship made of this material, the British Navy's 500 ton mine-hunter *Wilton*, was completed in 1973. Mine-hunting was first developed by the British in 1962 and involves the use of a Sonar to detect mines and other explosives on the seabed. Mine-hunters are now in service in several NATO navies as well as those of Argentina and Australia.

Air cushion vehicles (hovercraft) are in service mainly as patrol craft with the Iranian Navy although the British Navy has been trying them out as minesweepers and the US Marines are testing them for amphibious warfare. In Italy the first hull has been produced of what it is hoped will be the prototype for a standard NATO hydrofoil gunboat. Various types of hydrofoil have been under evaluation in the US Navy for several years and one, *High Point*, has been used to test the new Harpoon surface-to-surface missile at sea.

In the field of amphibious warfare the large assault ship in service with the US, British and French navies has to some degree replaced the more conventional landing ship. With its built-in dock for landing craft it can allow troops and vehicles to be loaded in sea conditions which would make loading from a conventional transport into craft alongside impossible.

Carriers supreme

World War II confirmed the carrier as the capital ship. Steam catapults, angled flight-decks, the mirror landing sight and nuclear power kept the conventional carrier viable, and new smaller types ensured its versatility and continued supremacy.

World War II firmly established the carrier as the capital ship, in place of the battleship, in both the American and British navies. But the same message was also received by several smaller navies, notably those of Canada, Australia, The Netherlands and, somewhat later, Argentina and Brazil, which had previously not possessed such ships.

Early Japanese Kamikaze attacks on American and British carriers in the Pacific had shown that making the flight deck the 'strength' deck might reduce aircraft capacity but greatly enhanced the chance of a carrier remaining operational after a hit by a bomb or suicide plane on the flight deck.

The British armoured deck carrier *Formidable*, for example, was hit by a Kamikaze on May 4, 1945. The plane was carrying a 500 lb bomb, part of which penetrated the deck and came to rest in a fuel tank after fracturing a main steam pipe which filled one boiler room with steam. The bridge windows were shattered and radar and radio aerials on the 'island'

superstructure were damaged. There was a hole in the flight deck; all aircraft tractors and eight aircraft were destroyed by fire; and two officers and six ratings were killed. The attack took place mid-morning. By five o'clock that afternoon the carrier was landing on aircraft again.

The attack on the *Formidable* was in contrast to one on the American carrier *Franklin*, of similar size and age, which burned for days and despite being repaired, never again became fully operational. This was because the 24 American Essex class carriers had their hangar decks as their strength decks while the flight deck was of planks laid over a light steel frame. The reason for this was that American designers reasoned that putting a heavy weight such as an armoured flight deck so high up would tend to make the ship top-heavy, particularly if a fire in the hangar resulted in quantities of water accumulating thus adding to the ship's top weight.

However, in the light of the survival of some of the British armoured deck carriers despite tremendous damage, three new American carriers with armoured flight decks were put in hand. However, the *Midway*, *Franklin D. Roosevelt* and *Coral Sea* were commissioned too late for war service.

Carrier under sail

As completed in 1945–47 they had a maximum capacity of 158 aircraft compared to

the 109 of the Essex class. But they were also considerably larger having an original designed displacement of 45,000 tons against 27,100 tons for the Essex class. But in one other important design aspect they were the same as the Essex class in that, unlike contemporary British carriers, they had 'open' bows—that is to say the forward end of the flight deck was supported on pillars on top of a conventional forecastle.

In heavy seas when travelling at speed to launch aircraft the forecastle deck could easily become unusable. The British carriers all had the gap between the flight deck and the forecastle plated in—a feature known in the US Navy as a 'hurricane bow'. During particularly fierce North Atlantic storms there had been cases of escort carriers, which were usually merchantmen converted by the replacement of their upperworks by a wooden flight deck with a hangar beneath, having the forward ends of their flight decks rolled back in much the same way that sardine tins are opened.

But for one American Essex class carrier, the *Intrepid*, the open forecastle proved a blessing. The ship had been torpedoed aft which jammed the rudder and put both propellers on one side out of action. In order to keep the ship on approximately a straight course as she limped back across the Pacific every stitch of canvas on board was used to provide a monster wind deflector at an angle across the forecastle. This helped to counter the ship's tendency to swing to one side because of the propellers' thrust on the opposite side. For years after it was the crew's proud boast that theirs was the only aircraft carrier ever to have been underway under sail!

The first British carriers joined the American fleet in the Pacific in 1944 and it was quickly apparent that their aircraft capacity suffered because of their armoured flight decks. The first three of the six large carriers completed during World War II had only one hangar, though a second,

This view of the flight deck of the USS Saratoga *shows how the 'super-carriers' of the US Navy can operate large numbers of aircraft. These 60,000-ton ships are superbly equipped to maintain these aircraft and to provide comprehensive radar and communications.*

lower hangar was installed in the fourth, fifth and sixth ships. Their tonnage was, unofficially, slightly greater than that of the Essex class, but they carried only some 50 aircraft. Another reason for the much smaller number of aircraft was that the American practice of parking aircraft on the flight deck while using the hangar mainly for repairs and maintenance was not adopted in European waters as it was felt this could lead to aircraft being damaged in heavy seas and suffering corrosion from salt spray. However in the Pacific US Navy techniques were readily adopted.

The first jet lands on

To overcome these drawbacks design work was put in hand on three large 50,000-ton carriers, *Gibraltar*, *Malta* and *New Zealand*. But only *Malta* had been laid down by the end of 1944 and construction of all three was halted when Japan surrendered. Two smaller 33,000-ton carriers, *Eagle* and *Africa*, were also cancelled at this time but work on two more, *Ark Royal* and *Audacious* (later renamed *Eagle*) went ahead slowly.

Meanwhile both the British and American navies developed more quickly built alternatives to the larger carriers which exceeded battleships in complexity. In the US Navy a number of Cleveland class light cruisers were converted during construction into light carriers with a capacity of up to 45 aircraft. In Britain, since no hulls were available for conversion, a number of light fleet carriers were built whose construction was to Lloyds' specifications up to main deck level. The idea was that after the war they could be converted into fast freighters— a role never taken up as they proved too useful in peacetime requiring fewer men than the larger carriers.

In December 1945 one of these British light fleet carriers, the *Ocean*, landed an adapted Vampire jet fighter on her flight deck, but it was not until the early 1950s that significant numbers of jets became operational in British carriers.

As a kind of 'half way house' between the larger carriers and the light type, the British also planned eight 18,000 tonners which would be somewhat faster than the 26 knot light type but being longer would have a larger hangar. Four were cancelled at the end of the war.

Numbers of escort carriers were retained, mostly in reserve, in the US Navy while some 30 obtained by Britain under the Lend-Lease agreement were handed back to the United States. One British-designed escort carrier was lent to The Netherlands but was soon replaced by a light fleet carrier. France also acquired a British light fleet carrier in addition to a former British, American-built, escort carrier.

By the late 1940s naval aviation in both Britain and the United States was in the doldrums. In July 1946 a McDonnell Phantom I jet fighter had landed on the *Franklin D. Roosevelt* and the first operational US Navy jet squadron was formed in 1948.

Carrier politics

In 1950, just before the outbreak of the Korean War, the American operational carrier force had been cut to 15 ships of which four were escort carriers. In Britain, among the politicians and retired senior officers, who still hankered after the battleship as *the* capital ship, there was near consternation when the Home Fleet flag was moved in 1949 from a battleship to a carrier.

This was also an important year for the Australian Navy as it marked commissioning of the first true aircraft carrier, the *Sydney*, which had been laid down during the war as the *Terrible* for the British Navy. She was equipped initially with Sea Fury fighters and Firefly strike reconnaissance planes—both piston-engined types. *Sydney's* commissioning had an even greater significance since it marked the acceptance by the politicians of the impossibility of providing sufficient shore-based aircraft and bases not only to give the Australian continent a comprehensive air defence system but also to defend shipping. The vast distances to be covered made provision of carrier aircraft imperative.

The eve of the Korean war saw the British Navy with five carriers fully operational; one in use as a transport; one as a flying training carrier and one as a training ship. This last ship, the fleet carrier *Indefatigable*, spent much of her time training young seamen while swinging round a buoy in Portland harbour, Dorset, where she was the object of much interest for holidaymakers on afternoon cruises from the nearby holiday resort. Many must have been puzzled as to how she could operate her one Seafire fighter (a naval adaptation of the famous Spitfire fighter) since a large deckhouse stood firmly at one end of the flight deck! In fact the Seafire had no engine, being simply a reminder to raw recruits that their ship had been a carrier, and the deckhouse contained oars and boats' sailing gear.

One further light carrier, the *Warrior*, was also in commission for special trials. It was recognised that the increasing weight of naval aircraft and the much higher landing speeds involved in the operation of jets made it imperative to find a safer way of landing aircraft. Even piston-engined aircraft missing all the arrestor wires on the deck could be severely damaged if the safety barrier had to be elevated and there was also the risk of this proving insufficient

to stop an aircraft. Such an accident occurred in the early 1950s in one British light carrier and resulted in nine aircraft being destroyed as the 'bolter' ploughed into the temporary aircraft parking area at the forward end of the flight deck.

Wheels-up landing tried

One solution which was tried out in the *Warrior* was to fit a rubber mat along about a third of the flight deck. The idea was that a jet fighter should land with its wheels up and 'bounce' along the deck. This idea proved, perhaps not surprisingly, to be a failure.

The Korean War once again showed the value of carriers and indeed the British air effort in the war was provided almost entirely by planes from the light carriers *Triumph*, *Glory*, *Ocean* and *Theseus* working in rotation along with Australia's *Sydney*. That she was able to play a major part in the war so soon after the re-creation of naval aviation in Australia was very creditable.

In the United States the huge 75,000 ton carrier *United States* was laid down in 1949. It was the intention that she should carry some two dozen very large aircraft which would be capable of delivering nuclear weapons halfway round the world. This idea was given impetus by the 5,000 mile flight to San Francisco of a normally land-based P2V Neptune long range maritime patrol aircraft from the carrier *Coral Sea* off Florida.

But the laying down of the *United States* caused intense political and inter-service controversy with the Air Force who saw large carrier-borne strategic bombers as a threat to their own plans for strategic bombers. Eventually they won and the carrier was cancelled.

In Britain the Korean War gave a considerable filip to naval construction and work on the 33,000 ton carriers *Eagle* and *Ark Royal* as well as on the 18,000

Below : A-1 Skyraiders are prepared for take-off aboard USS Coral Sea. *Skyraiders were amongst the most effective of the many types of aircraft used in Vietnam.*

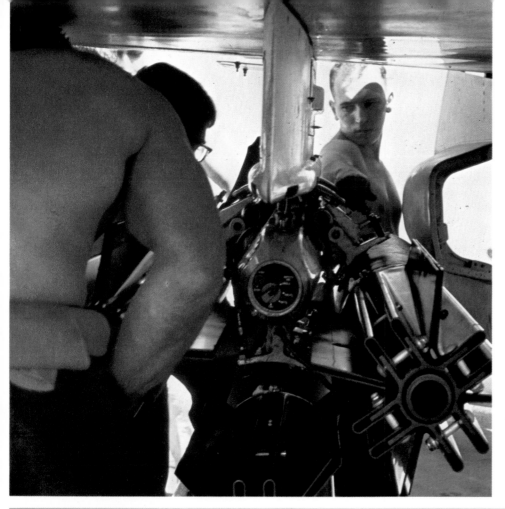

tonners, *Hermes*, *Centaur*, *Albion* and *Bulwark* was speeded. The war also demonstrated the value of a type of carrier unique to the British Navy. This was the maintenance carrier.

One, *Unicorn*, had been built during World War II and was a small conventional carrier in external design but she had extensive workshops. Taken out of reserve in 1949 this ship gave invaluable support to whatever carrier was operational off Korea. Two light carriers had also been converted for a similar role during the course of their construction in the latter part of World War II.

It was one of these, the *Perseus*, which was used to try out a new British invention:

Left: US Navy personnel arm a strike aircraft with missiles aboard the carrier USS Coral Sea, *which saw extensive action off Vietnam.*

Below: A-4 Skyhawks prepare for take-off from USS Saratoga. *This* Forrestal *Class attack carrier, completed in 1956, operates some eighty aircraft comprising two fighter squadrons, three light attack squadrons, a reconnaissance heavy attack squadron, a helicopter detachment and a number of airborne early warning aircraft.*

the steam catapult. It was realised that the compressed air catapults used to launch aircraft were becoming increasingly inadequate as heavier aircraft came into service. In order to prove the power of a steam catapult the *Perseus*, whose catapult had been built on a slightly inclined ramp fitted at the forward end of the flight deck, was tied up alongside a jetty in Rosyth, Scotland, naval yard. An elderly twin-engined naval bomber was launched, unmanned, with the controls jammed and, it was calculated, just enough fuel to take her down the river Forth and out to sea where she could crash harmlessly. But as a result of some miscalculation, although she was launched successfully, she flew in a circle for several minutes over

The nuclear-powered attack carrier USS Enterprise *under way with aircraft ranged on her flight deck. Because she has no funnel her island is square.*

USS Enterprise

The world's largest warship when built, 1,123 feet long, she was also the first nuclear-powered aircraft carrier. In 1964 the *Enterprise* and two other nuclear-powered warships circumnavigated the world in two months without refuelling. She carries about 95 aircraft, including bombers armed with nuclear weapons, but is armed only with two close-range missile launchers.

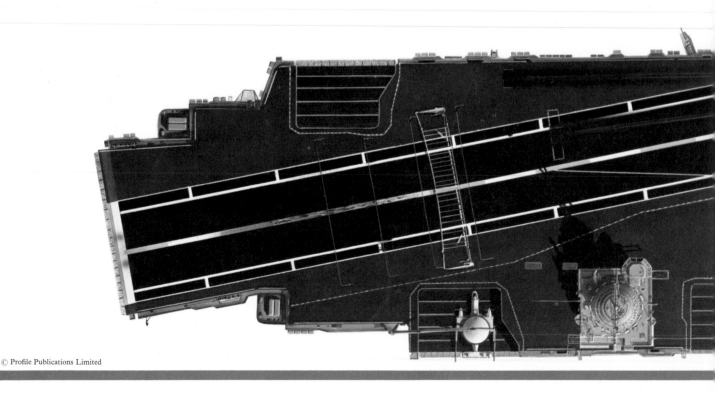

Edinburgh before, luckily, crashing into the river!

New angle on landing

Yet if the problem of launching heavier aircraft was solved with the invention of the steam catapult there remained that of landing heavy and fast aircraft. The solution to this, found in 1952, was the angled deck. Instead of aircraft landing along the centre-line of the ship they approached from the starboard side over the round-down at the stern. Sufficient length of deck could be found for the arrestor wires by extending the flight deck on a sponson over the port side. Thus if an aircraft missed all the arrestor wires the pilot could accelerate and fly off over the port side of the flight deck for another try. In this way there was no risk of his crashing into the island superstructure or aircraft parked at the forward end of the flight deck.

The first carrier to have a full angled deck

A Corsair II is ready for launching from the steam catapult on board USS Constellation *during operations in the Gulf of Tonkin. Modern aircraft are too heavy to take off without catapult assistance.*

of eight degrees was the USS *Antietam* while in 1954 the new 18,000 tons British carrier *Centaur,* which had been completed the previous year, was given a 5½ degree angled deck.

Another British improvement for carrier operations was the mirror landing sight.

Clearly the high approach speed of jet aircraft, which had come into squadron service in the British Navy in 1951, meant that it was no longer safe to rely on the human reactions of a 'batsman', or landing control officer, particularly at night. The idea of the landing sight was first tried out by the inventor, a senior serving naval officer, getting his girl secretary to put a blob of lipstick in the centre of her compact mirror propped up against a book on a desk top. Provided the girl kept her eyes firmly fixed on the lipstick blob no matter from what height she moved her head towards the table her chin always came to rest in the same spot! The sight, basically a mirror with a red light reflected into the centre and white

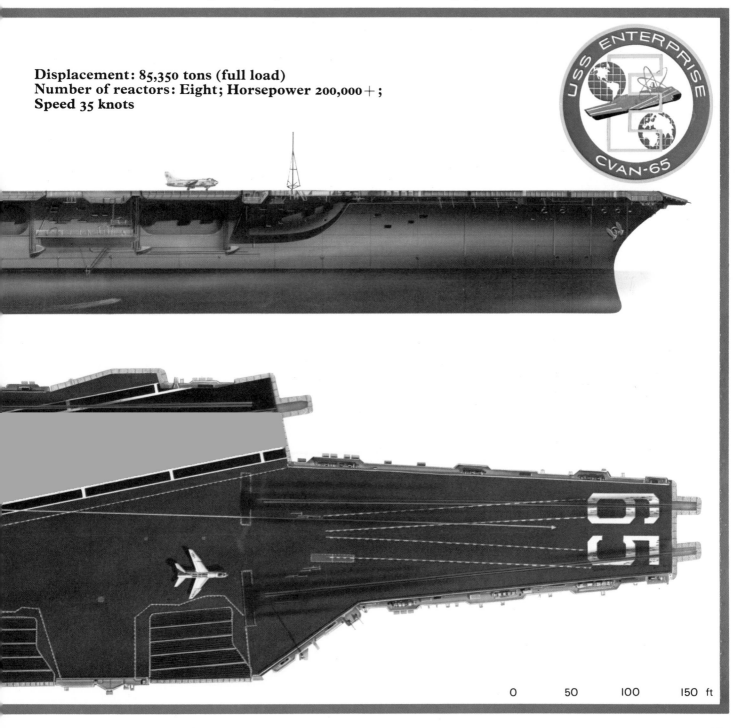

Displacement: 85,350 tons (full load)
Number of reactors: Eight; Horsepower 200,000+;
Speed 35 knots

USS ENTERPRISE
CVAN-65

0   50   100   150 ft

A-3 Skywarriors and F-3 Demons on the flight deck of USS Saratoga. *Four steam catapults, two on the angled flight deck and two forward, enable* Saratoga *to launch four aircraft every 30 seconds.*

lights on either side to provide a datum line, showed a pilot well away from the ship if he was too high, in which case the red light appeared below the white datum line and, conversely, above it if he was too low. Later, the system was refined but the basic principle is still employed.

US Nuclear breakthrough

All these inventions were incorporated in the *Forrestal*, the first of a new class of giant American carriers. Completed in 1955, her designed displacement is just short of 60,000 tons but her full load displacement is 78,000 tons, or more than half as big again as that of the largest British carrier, the *Ark Royal*, completed in the same year. The 'Ark' as she is affectionately known in the British Navy, was the first British carrier to have a side lift but this was removed in 1959 when her 'interim' angled deck was extended to the full eight degrees.

The *Forrestal* was followed over the next four years by three sister ships, each with an aircraft capacity of about 85 planes. Then in 1961 came the world's first major nuclear powered surface warship, the carrier USS *Enterprise*. She cost over \$450 million and is powered by eight nuclear reactors. She was built in the astonishingly short time of three-and-a-half years.

This was something of a contrast to the time taken to reconstruct the 1941 completed British carrier *Victorious*. Work on rebuilding her began in 1950 and was not completed until eight years later. But she emerged from the yard with a new Comprehensive Display System radar which gave both air and surface targets on the same display screen. Later the system was to be coupled with a battery of computers, known as ADA or Action Data Automation, in the 1951 completed carrier *Eagle* which was rebuilt in the mid-1960s.

The last carrier to be completed in Britain was the *Vikrant* for India in 1961. She had started life as a light carrier during World

War II and after many years lying partially finished she was modified and completed for the Indian Navy. She once again vindicated the use of carriers with several successful attacks against Pakistani warships in the war with that country in 1971.

The early 1960s saw the completion of two 27,000 ton carriers, *Foch* and *Clemenceau*, for France while Australia added a second carrier to her fleet, the *Melbourne*, in 1955. This ship was laid down during World War II as the *Majestic* for the British Navy. Unlike the *Sydney*, she has a steam catapult, angled deck and mirror landing aid.

But mounting costs of both ships and aircraft began having their effect on the carrier forces of most navies equipped with these ships. In America, in the face of fierce controversy, the next two large carriers completed after the *Enterprise*, the *America* in 1965 and the *John F. Kennedy* in 1968, reverted to conventional steam turbine propulsion which cut their costs compared to *Enterprise* by some \$200 million and \$180 million respectively.

Change to helicopters

In Australia *Sydney* was not modified to bring her up to *Melbourne's* standards and in 1962 she completed a conversion to a fast transport. In Britain the two 18,000 ton carriers *Bulwark* and *Albion* were converted to carry some 850 Royal Marine Commandos and, eventually, up to about 20 Wessex V troop-carrying helicopters in place of their fixed-wing aircraft. This conversion resulted from the highly successful 'vertical assault' carried out by helicopters flying from the light carriers *Theseus* and *Ocean* during the 1956 Anglo-French attack on Egypt. This was the first fully operational use of helicopters, apart from rescue missions, to be staged in modern warfare.

Of the smaller, light type, British carriers one was converted into a heavy repair ship and three were scrapped. One, *Vengeance*, which had been lent to Australia in 1953, was sold outright to Brazil three years later and was commissioned by that nation's navy in 1961 after extensive modernisation. *Warrior*, after serving as a support ship for British hydrogen bomb tests in the Pacific, was sold to Argentina in 1958 but

ten years later she was replaced by her modernised sister ship *Venerable*. This ship had been transferred to the Netherlands in 1948 and later, as the *Karel Doorman*, was sold, again to Argentina.

Canada in 1970 discarded as an economy measure the last of three carriers she had had (the first two were on loan from Britain) since World War II. It was for reasons of economy, too, that in 1966 the British government cancelled plans to build a new 50,000 ton carrier code-named *CVA-01* and at the same time decreed that the remaining carriers *Eagle*, *Ark Royal* and *Hermes* (an 18,000 ton design modified while building to provide an angled deck, steam catapults, deck-edge lift, mirror landing sights and Comprehensive Display System radar and completed in 1959) would be phased out in the mid-1970s by which time the RAF American-built F.111 aircraft flying from shore bases would replace the carrier aircraft. As part of the case for switching to shore-based aircraft the RAF, in presenting its arguments, 'moved' Australia 400 miles westwards across the Indian Ocean in order to make the F.111's range viable from the likely bases!

British date of execution

In 1968 the further economies following sterling's devaluation put forward the British carriers' phase out date to the end of 1972. Meanwhile American Phantom II fighters had been bought for *Ark Royal* and *Eagle* but only the former was to get them and although she was reprieved by the government in 1970 *Eagle* was paid off and, in 1973, *Hermes* became a combined anti-submarine and Commando carrier. While the British carriers were being given their date of execution the US Navy was able, in 1968, to order its second nuclear powered carrier, the *Nimitz*. Two more sister ships have since been ordered.

Over a nine year period starting in 1961 the US Navy completed six amphibious assault helicopter carriers and it was one of these, *Guam*, which, in 1972, began operating a number of 'borrowed' Marine Corps British-built Harrier vertical take-off and landing fighters. In Britain, in 1968, plans to replace, in the late 1970s, the cruisers *Tiger* and *Blake*, which had been fitted to carry four anti-submarine helicopters in place of their after twin 6 inch gun turrets, with a new type of cruiser which would carry Harriers and anti-submarine carriers were announced. The first of three such ships, *Invincible*, was laid down in 1973 for completion in 1978.

She will be equipped with the naval version of the Harrier, once the subject of considerable political controversy in Britain. It is expected that *Ark Royal* will be scrapped by 1978 and with her will go the last conventional British aircraft carrier able to operate fixed wing aircraft.

Plans for Harriers for a ship similar to *Invincible* which Iran is considering ordering, for re-equipping India's *Vikrant*, for the American Sea Control Ships, and, on a longer term basis, for equipping a possible successor to Australia's *Melbourne* all awaited the British government's recent decision. Such an order was considered essential in order to put the British Navy's 'seal of

Above: The VTOL/STOL Harrier aircraft carrying out landing trials at sea. A naval version has been ordered by the Royal Navy to provide its future fixed-wing air power.

Left: The flight-deck of the commando-carrier HMS Bulwark *flying off Wessex helicopters.*

approval' on the aircraft.

The $100 million American Sea Control ships are a logical result of the rapidly escalating costs of the new nuclear carriers—estimated to be $1,000 million in the case of the *Nimitz*. But conventional carrier supporters oppose the cheap Harrier and helicopter-equipped Sea Control Ships on the grounds that they will deplete funds available for the big carriers and their aircraft, even though prices will cause an eventual drop in the number of big carriers.

But with the Soviet Union apparently completeing in 1975 the first of two 45,000 ton carriers operating 'Freehand', the Russian answer to the Harrier, the entry of the Soviet Union into the field of seaborne airpower may well have forced the hands of the British government in ordering naval Harriers and could make Congress approve the planned eight Sea Control Ships.

Submarine power

The submarine has been the subject of considerable research and development by the major powers ever since World War II. Major breakthroughs in hull design and methods of propulsion have revolutionized naval warfare. Nuclear capability has drastically altered the world balance of power which continues to be affected by submarine building programmes. New technology continually upsets the delicate balance of supremacy maintained by hunter, now very likely to be another submarine, or hunted. The submarine seems destined to be the most influential and versatile warship of future navies.

During World War II the submarine easily surpassed any other type of naval weapon in its influence upon the course of that war. The Germans in particular developed submarine tactics to a point where they came close to achieving the victory that would have followed the cutting of Britain's sea communications with North America and her other sources of food, fuel and raw materials.

But the gradually increasing success of various countermeasures, notably the aircraft working in conjunction with the surface ship task group, showed that what was needed was the true submarine—that is the vessel which, once submerged, could remain underwater for weeks.

One partial solution was the 'Schnorchel', or breathing tube, which allowed a submarine at periscope depth to use its air-breathing diesel engines to recharge its electric batteries. But this pre-war Dutch invention still made it necessary for a submarine to betray its position by putting the breathing tube above water.

The Germans therefore introduced the Walther submarine. This used turbine propulsion relying on Ingolin and the idea was originally developed by Dr. H. Walther before the war. Ingolin is a highly concentrated form of hydrogen peroxide which by a process of decomposition can be made to give off heat, or, in other words, the oxygen given off, when mixed with a sulphurless fuel, can be used to heat water into steam for passing through a turbine.

Being a closed cycle system such combustion requires no external source of oxygen and therefore a Walther-engined submarine could run for long periods totally submerged. By the war's end the Germans had managed to complete only a few of these submarines although one each became available as war reparations for the British and American navies.

The British Navy pursued experiments with their Walther submarine, renamed *Meteorite*, and in 1955 completed the first of two fast training submarines fitted with a modified form of Walther engine.

But such was the explosive and fire hazard of this fuel that the idea was not pursued further and indeed in the US Navy was not developed beyond the point of conducting trials with the captured German submarine.

German ideas help Russia

Both the British and American navies, later followed by those of France, Portugal and the Scandinavian countries in particular, adopted the German Schnorchel—later to be known as 'Snort' in the British Navy and 'Snorkel' in the US Navy. Not only did this allow batteries to be charged while a submarine was almost submerged but when cruising the submarine could use its diesels, thus conserving the batteries until a more silent approach was needed towards a target.

In the United States numbers of war-built submarines were given what was known as the 'Guppy' conversion. This involved streamlining the superstructure and external surfaces to lessen water resistance or 'drag' and also, incidentally, to reduce underwater noise.

The hulls were also toughened to allow the battery capacity to be doubled. Similar conversions were carried out to the submarines of the British and other European navies.

But if the British and Americans were fairly cool towards the Walther engined

submarine the Russians seem to have been quite enthusiastic—possibly because much of Germany's submarine technology, designers and technicians and numerous completed or half-completed submarines fell into Russian hands in 1945. Nevertheless, there is no evidence that any Walther submarines are still in service in today's Soviet Navy.

By the late 1950s the British Navy had reverted to constructing diesel-electric powered submarines although it was claimed that these were the world's quietest underwater.

In America considerable study was made of underwater forms such as that of the whale and porpoise. This resulted in the 'teardrop' design of the experimental submarine *Albacore* completed in 1953. This basic design was one adopted in both American and British nuclear submarines. One characteristic of this design is the submarine's handling underwater.

Instead of the vessel leaning away from the angle of turn it 'banks' like an aeroplane.

The experimental submarine USS Albacore *introduced radical new concepts of design which enabled the full potential of nuclear power to be exploited. Her 'tear-drop' hull form made her difficult to handle on the surface but gave high speed and great manoeuvrability under water. This type of hull has now been adopted by all navies.*

Another feature even with the diesel-electric powered *Albacore* was the very considerable increase in speed—33 knots submerged compared to 14–16 knots of the latest conventional diesel-electric submarines to be built for the US Navy in the 1950s.

Modern day *Dreadnought*

When surfaced, the *Albacore* design does not handle very easily as the rounded bows tend to push rather than cut through the water. But it is a totally different story underwater since, as one early American nuclear submarine captain once commented: 'About the only thing we haven't done is to loop the loop!'

The world's first nuclear powered submarine was the American *Nautilus*, completed in 1954 and therefore too early to benefit from the *Albacore* design experiments. It is fair to say that *Nautilus* as much revolutionised naval warfare as did the first all-big-gun battleship, the British *Dreadnought*, nearly 50 years earlier.

Here at last was the true submarine able to stay submerged, totally submerged, indefinitely since her endurance is limited only by that of the crew.

The reactor in *Nautilus* relied for its cooling on a pressurised water system. In view of the novelty, and to some extent uncertainty, of nuclear propulsion systems the US Navy also developed a liquid sodium cooled reactor and fitted this in the submarine *Seawolf* which was completed in 1957. But this form of reactor did not prove a complete success and after two years it was removed and replaced by a pressurised water system similar to that in the *Nautilus*. But during that time *Seawolf* set up a record by steaming continuously submerged for 60 days during which time she covered a distance of over 13,000 miles. This record was beaten in 1960 when the then giant nuclear powered submarine *Triton* of nearly 8,000 tons submerged displacement—almost twice the size of *Seawolf* and *Nautilus*—circumnavigated the world, covering some 41,500 miles in 83 days at an average speed of 18 knots.

These early American nuclear submarines dramatically illustrated one important way in which they were revolutionising sea warfare by travelling under the North Pole and often surfacing in the icepack. Here was an area in which they could operate with no opposition apart from another of their kind. In the Soviet Union the first nuclear powered submarine seems to have been completed in 1958. No attempt appears to have been made, somewhat surprisingly, to build a prototype and the first class, the 'Novembers', ran to 13 boats of similar size to *Nautilus*. One of this class, *Leninsky Konsomol*, was photographed in ice allegedly at the North Pole.

Seaborne nuclear missiles

In Britain development work on nuclear propulsion was going on throughout the latter part of the 1950s. But progress was slow and in 1958 agreement was reached to purchase a complete nuclear propulsion reactor from the United States. This was installed in the *Dreadnought*, which was commissioned as the first British nuclear submarine in 1963.

The launch of the Nautilus *on January 21, 1954 at the Electric Boat Yard at Groton, Connecticut, performed by Mrs Eisenhower.*

American legislation severely restricted the availability of information on nuclear propulsion systems to other nations—an exception had been made for Britain—and consequently only three nations for some years possessed nuclear submarines. In 1969 trials began of the French nuclear powered missile submarine *Le Redoutable*. This was a particularly courageous step for the French Navy to take since not only were they pioneering a propulsion system new to them but in the same hull they had fitted a totally new weapon system.

In America growing doubts about the continuing credibility of manned strategic bombers carrying nuclear weapons and of some land-based nuclear missile systems prompted examination of the Jupiter missile for use at sea. Although this missile was not taken up a new weapon was designed. This was the A.1 Polaris.

It was designed to be launched from a totally submerged submarine and it was planned to fit 16 in vertical launching tubes in adapted nuclear powered submarines of the Skipjack class under construction in the late 1950s. One of these, the *Scorpion*, which had been laid down in 1957, was appropriated as the first Polaris ballistic missile submarine and was renamed *George Washington*. Her conversion basically involved the insertion of an additional 130 ft section in her 251 ft long hull to accommodate two rows of eight missile tubes.

In due course the 1,250 mile range A.1 Polaris was replaced by the A.2 with a range of 1,500 miles and, finally, with the A.3 with a range of 2,500 miles. Since the completion of the *George Washington* at the end of 1959 a further 40 Polaris submarines have been built in the United States and ultimately all 31 of these will be fitted with the Poseidon missile. Maintaining the range of the A.3 Polaris, this provides a number of independent warheads in each missile nose which can attack different targets or can serve as decoys for defending anti-missile missiles.

The British Navy, as a result of an agreement reached with the United States in 1962, was given design details and information to construct four (a fifth was cancelled) Polaris submarines of her own. The first of these, *Resolution,* was completed in 1967. Under the Anglo-American agreement only the missile bodies are constructed in the United States together with certain computer control plant for the missiles while the warheads are entirely British built.

Deadly Soviet 'Yankee'

The nuclear missiles in the five French submarines in service or building appear very similar externally to Polaris. They have a range of 1,900 miles.

Russia adopted a somewhat different policy to that of the United States in that her earliest strategic missile submarines were diesel-electric boats which had partially to surface in order to launch their missiles. The missiles' range was only a matter of about 200–300 miles. Development of diesel-electric strategic missile submarines continued in the Soviet Union for some years though the first nuclear powered types were completed in 1958–1961.

Only in 1967, seven years after completion of the *George Washington*, was the first comparable nuclear powered ballistic missile submarine completed in the Soviet Union. This was the 'Yankee' class armed with 16 1,350 mile range underwater launched missiles.

It would seem that the Russians have had some problem adapting these submarines to carry longer range missiles. Consequently, a new class, known as 'Delta', but developed from the 'Yankee' class was announced in 1972. These boats carry 12 missiles with a range of 4,000 miles. It is believed that Russia intends to have at least 45 missile submarines of the two classes.

Above : Le Redoutable *carries out her trials off Cherbourg. When the United States would not supply Polaris missiles the French were not slow to provide their own underwater missile system.*

The A.3 Polaris missile is ejected from a submerged submarine by compressed air or gas, and as soon as it leaves the water the rocket motor starts. The A.3 Polaris has a range of 2,500 miles, making submarine launched missiles a credible part of the West's nuclear deterrent force. The deterrent is maintained by the constant world-wide deployment of Polaris-armed submarines.

Although their high speed and great diving depth compared to diesel-electric submarines make the nuclear powered missile submarines largely immune to attack by surface ships they can be countered by the nuclear powered attack or hunter-killer submarine. This is because the enormous generating capacity of a nuclear reactor allows these submarines to be fitted with a Sonar underwater detection system considerably more powerful than any mounted in surface ships.

In addition, the Sonar waves emitted by a surface ship must inevitably pass through the water at a fairly acute angle. This means that variations in the water temperature at different depths, a phenomenon known as a 'thermal layer', may 'bounce back' Sonar waves allowing a submarine below the thermal layer to escape detection.

Importance of the hunter

But with a submarine-mounted Sonar the beam angle tends more to follow a horizontal path and is less likely to be diffused or distorted by thermal layers. The efficiency of the nuclear hunter-killer submarine as an anti-submarine weapon prompted one early British hunter-killer captain to comment that his boat was as much part of the deterrent against nuclear war as a Polaris missile carrying submarine in that it would be his boat's task to seek out potentially hostile submarines tracking the missile submarines and also to find enemy missile submarines.

Although the Soviet Navy is so far the only major one to make considerable use of submarine tactical missiles, largely as a counter to America's and Britain's aircraft carriers, the idea of putting what are known as 'cruise' missiles in submarines was tried out by the US Navy in the 1950s. The first such missile to become operational was the Regulus I which was a development of the wartime German V.1 flying bomb used against Britain in 1944–45. Regulus had a range of 500 miles and was subsonic. Four diesel-electric submarines and the nuclear powered *Halibut* were equipped with it and it was intended that *Halibut* and the diesel-electric *Grayback* and *Growler* should in due course get the 1,000 mile range transonic Regulus II. But this missile was cancelled in the mid-1960s. Consequently *Halibut* was reclassified as an attack submarine while *Grayback* was fitted out as a submarine troop carrier and *Growler* was decommissioned.

The development of the nuclear powered submarine has not been achieved without cost. Early examples were extremely noisy, partly because of lack of muffling on their reactor pumps, and consequently Britain and France have enjoyed a considerable export market for their much quieter diesel-electric submarines. Although the last of the British Navy's diesel-electric submarines was completed in 1967 boats of this class were being completed for Australia and Chile in 1974–75 and others had previously been delivered also to Australia, Canada and Brazil. France has supplied submarines to South Africa, Pakistan and Portugal; and Spain is building French designed submarines under licence. Outside the Warsaw Pact countries, Russian diesel-electric submarines have been supplied to Egypt, Indonesia, India and Albania—although the Albanian submarines were seized when that country opted out of Russia's orbit and adopted China's brand of Communism.

Unexplained losses

Three nuclear powered submarines are known to have been lost. The first was the American *Thresher*, an attack submarine, which sank in the Atlantic in 1963 with all hands. The reason is thought to have been the failure under pressure of a water pipe joint which caused electrical failures. The second nuclear submarine to be lost was also American. She was the second nuclear submarine to be named *Scorpion*—the first became the Polaris submarine *George Washington*. *Scorpion* sank some 400 miles south-west of the Azores in 1968 but no official explanation has ever been given as to the cause of her loss.

Unlike the *Scorpion*, which went down with all 99 of her crew, it is thought that all the Russian crew of the 'November' class nuclear attack submarine which sank some 150 miles south-west of the British Isles in 1970 were saved. The submarine had evidently suffered some damage, possibly in a collision with a Russian warship, and shortly before she sank was seen to be under tow. In 1972 a Russian 'Hotel' II type nuclear ballistic missile submarine got into difficulties in the North

Atlantic but within 24 hours 19 Russian warships and merchant ships had come to her aid—a remarkable achievement. She is thought eventually to have reached Russia steaming on the surface.

It is little over 20 years since the first submarine got underway on nuclear power and the development that has taken place since is little short of astonishing. In the future we may, perhaps, see much of the world's trade carried in giant submarines and if that happens it will be necessary for most countries' navies to become underwater fleets.

Above : The Polaris missile tubes on board the Fleet ballistic missile submarine USS John Adams. Computers associated with an inertial navigation system update the 16 missiles in each compartment with information on the submarine's position.

Right : Nuclear powered and armed submarines constantly patrol the world's oceans, returning every three months to berth alongside depot ships for maintenance.

Below : An RAF Nimrod anti-submarine aircraft keeps watch on a Russian submarine.

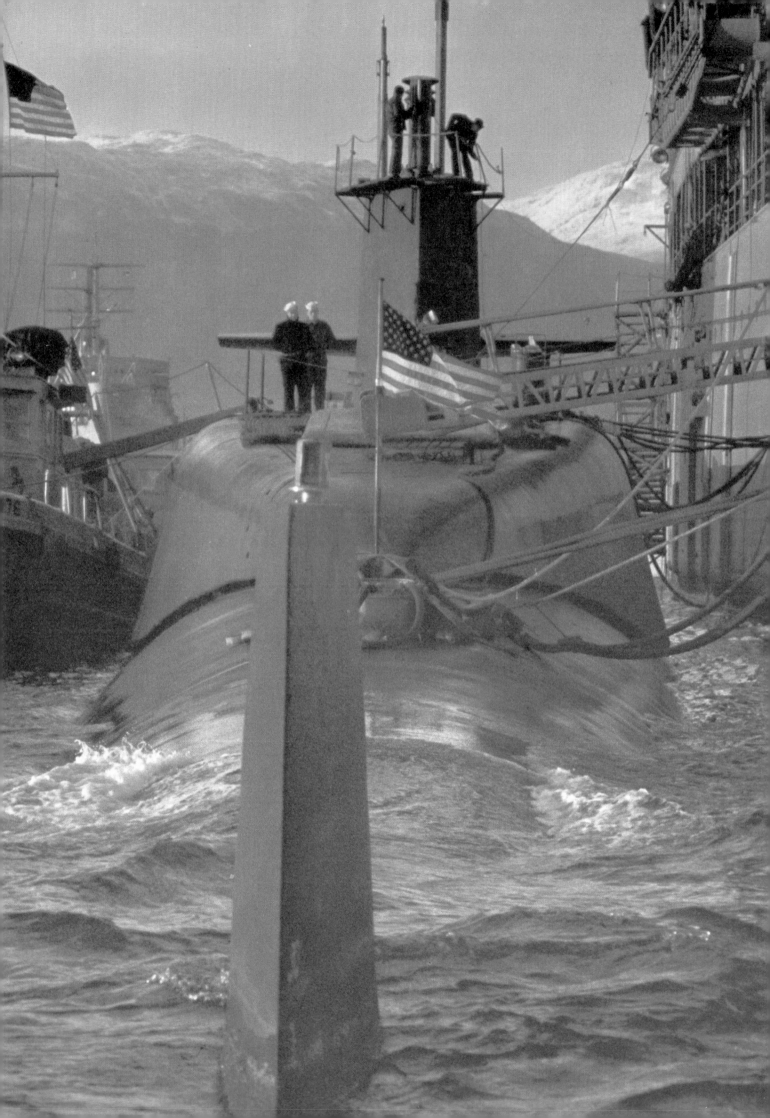

The impact of technology

Developments in the fields of weapons, communications, electronics and propulsion have radically altered the shape and size of the world's navies. They have revolutionized tactics and enormously influenced political strategies. Indeed, so spectacular has been the progress, that technology shows signs of outpacing man's ability to harness it.

The period of gestation of a new major warship design is reckoned today to be a minimum of ten years, of which perhaps only half is taken up with actual construction work. Naval planners today are therefore studying designs of ships which will still be in service in the next century.

Developments over the past 20 years in the fields of propulsion, weapons, communications and electronics have caused some radical changes in tactics, ship design and the provision of skilled technical manpower. The shortage of the last, because of intense competition from industry, is one that is likely to continue to bedevil the plans of navies, at least in the democratic countries, for a long time ahead.

There are a number of areas in which it is possible to make predictions with a reasonable degree of confidence.

Nuclear propulsion for surface ships as well as submarines is certain to become the major system for larger ships but it is doubtful if, in the foreseeable future, it will be possible to reduce the weight of reactor shielding to a point where it will be feasible to install a reactor in a ship much under 8,000 tons displacement without unacceptable sacrifices in other directions.

Thus the gas turbine and the high speed diesel look to have established their future. But within 20 years it may well be possible to use super-conductor motors—that is electric motors operating in a refrigerated environment to cut power loss. Both the American and British navies are experimenting with such motors.

The size of nuclear powered submarines is likely to continue to grow and the ten planned American Trident missile submarines will have a submerged displacement of about 15,000 tons compared to about 8,000 of the existing Polaris-Poseidon missile submarines. Less certain, however, is the validity of such things as the submarine aircraft carrier whose cost would be prohibitive. The Trident submarines are each expected to cost $1,000 million but this may well be exceeded by the time the first is in service in 1979.

With the exception of amphibious ships the size of future surface warships is likely to decrease and in Britain this is already evident in that the new Sheffield class missile destroyers are only just over half the size of the County class completed in the 1960s and early 1970s. In the United States the Sea Control Ship, displacing about 14,000 tons and carrying fixed-wing V/STOL aircraft and helicopters, and subsequent developments of the design seem likely in the long term to replace the large carrier in the 70,000–80,000 ton bracket.

The new American Spruance class destroyers are the largest ever built for the US Navy but if enough escorts are ever to be provided the American patrol frigate design of some 3,400 tons is likely to be a better indication of the size of future escorts.

Landing craft from HMS Intrepid *swarm ashore in a combined forces assault exercise.*

Above : A Royal Navy fast target craft manoeuvres at speed while making smoke.

While the Soviet Navy is building 10,000 ton missile cruisers it has kept the size of missile destroyers fairly rigid at about 5,000–6,000 tons which is about the smallest displacement needed to permit fitting of both SAM and surface-to-surface missile systems while retaining good sea-keeping qualities.

This trend towards keeping down the size of warships is also evident in a number of other navies. The French, for example, are building missile ships in the 3,000–4,000 ton category and Australia is buying two American patrol frigates instead of the planned destroyer-leader type which would have been some 1,000 tons larger.

But hull design forms by the 1990s will start changing radically with the introduction of the ocean-going hydrofoil and possibly the air cushion vehicle (hovercraft). Already the first of a class of 30 NATO hydrofoil missile boats are under construction at Seattle following the development of prototypes by the US Navy and an Italian company with American participation.

The Soviet Union has for some years had small naval hydrofoil patrol boats though there is no indication so far that they are thinking in terms of ocean-going hydrofoil ships. Canada, too, has had an experimental naval hydrofoil but this is now in reserve. Britain, particularly with craft like the Vosper Thornycroft Shipbuilding group's patrol/amphibious hovercraft, has pioneered this field of development. But like so many

The hydrofoil Pegasus, *propelled by water-jets and armed with Harpoon missiles, ready for launching at Boeing's Seattle yard.*

promising British inventions there has been little production follow-up as a result of the stultifying shortsightedness of successive governments in failing to provide funds for further development by placing naval prototype orders.

Weapon systems at sea are causing not only a change in tactical thinking but are also likely to have far-reaching strategic consequences. The lesson of 1967, when some nominally Egyptian missile boats armed with the Russian Styx missile sank the old Israeli destroyer *Eilath* off Alexandria, has been

absorbed by many smaller as well as the major navies.

At least 15 of the smaller navies already have, or are in the process of getting, fast missile boats. Although anything but near calm sea conditions severely inhibit the use of such craft their mere existence must serve to deter would-be aggressors. It would also be possible for a small navy effectively to

blockade a neighbouring country in a way
that would not have been feasible using small
conventionally armed ships.

The answer to the surface-to-surface missile boat is the fixed-wing aircraft or helicopter—and the latter are being equipped
with increasingly more powerful and longer
range air-to-surface missiles. But the delivery
of effective strikes on small, fast-moving
craft requires a degree of pilot training that
by no means all air forces possess—the
sinking of a Turkish destroyer by Turkish
fighters off Cyprus in 1974 illustrates the
problem of using essentially air defence aircraft in an unaccustomed role at sea.

It would, however, be wrong to assume
that the use of surface-to-surface missiles
is confined to the small navies. A number of
American patrol gunboats in the Mediterranean are fitted with the Standard missile
which has a surface-to-surface capability,
and by the 1980s the Harpoon missile is
expected to join the US Fleet.

The British Navy has opted for the French
Exocet surface-to-surface missile in a number of destroyers and frigates and has plans
to develop a submarine-launched missile for
use against surface targets.

But so far neither the US nor British, nor
for that matter the Soviet, navies have

Above: The Red Sea and Gulf of Aden from the Gemini XI spacecraft in 1966. Satellites have simplified naval reconnaissance tasks.

Right: The Russian 'Osa' Type fast patrol boat, armed with four missiles with a range of 25 km, scored its greatest success in 1967 when one in Egyptian hands sank the Israeli destroyer Eilat.

adopted missiles for the defence of submarines against helicopter and surface ship attacks. But one such system, SLAM, which has been developed by private enterprise in Britain, is believed to be fitted in three new British-built diesel-electric submarines of the Brazilian Navy.

The SUBROC tactical nuclear missile has been fitted in American attack submarines for some time but, unlike the Soviet Navy, neither the US or British navies yet have a non-nuclear tactical submarine-launched missile. The US Navy is, however, examin-

The USS Spruance, *completed in 1975, is the first of a controversial class of destroyers. A further 29 units, all to be built by one shipyard using advanced prefabrication methods, are planned for completion by the late 1970s. The* Spruance Class, *displacing 7,800 tons and carrying less armament than previous ships, are the first large warships of the US Navy to be propelled by gas turbines. The weapons carried include two medium-calibre guns, a close-range Sea Sparrow missile system, an ASROC launcher and anti-submarine torpedoes.*

ing the possibility of developing Harpoon for use in submarines—it has already been tested in the ship and aircraft launched roles.

The advent by the 1980s of surface-to-air missile systems, for defence against air-to-surface and surface-to-surface missiles, such as the American Aegis and the British Seawolf now under trials, means that the days of the subsonic tactical cruise missile as an effective weapon against sophisticated modern warships are numbered.

The use of mines in sea warfare off North Vietnam in 1972 and in the Red Sea by Egypt with Russian assistance in 1973 as well as apparently in the Ganges delta by Pakistan in 1971 have prompted a fresh look at this cheap and simple weapon system. In America research is going ahead on a mine which could also become a torpedo. Code-named Captor it would be activated by the Sonar emissions from a passing submarine but would ignore those from surface ships.

In the field of strategic nuclear missiles the US Navy is planning a two-stage development of the new Trident missile. The Trident I, expected to be operational by the 1980s, will have a range of 4,000 nautical miles—500 miles more than the Poseidon and A.3 Polaris now at sea in 41 American and four British nuclear missile submarines. It is intended to deploy all ten Trident submarines in the Pacific leaving the Poseidon submarines in the Atlantic.

Trident I will have a multi-independently targeted re-entry vehicle (MIRV) nose so that each missile will be capable of attacking several targets. A more limited type of MIRV has been fitted to the A.3 Polaris missile for the four British missile submarines.

Longer range for credibility

The fitting of MIRV in Trident I overcomes its slightly shorter range compared to that of the SS-N-8 missile fitted in the latest Soviet Delta type missile submarines. Eventually it is intended to replace Trident I with a later mark which will have a range of 6,000 nautical miles. The increased range will be essential for the maintenance of a credible Western deterrent since it cannot be long before the Russians develop a MIRV system for their submarine-launched strategic nuclear missiles.

Although the navies of America, Britain, China, France and the Soviet Union are concentrating on the development of missiles the gun is not being entirely neglected. Mention has already been made of the US Navy's adaptation of a rocket system to 8-inch shells to give them a vast increase in range. But with the paying off into reserve of the few remaining gun-armed cruisers in the US Navy tests have begun of the Mark 71 light-weight 8-inch gun for fitting in destroyers in order to give them a long range bombardment capability. During shore tests the new gun has developed a rate of fire of 12 rounds a minute while existing American destroyer guns of 5-inch calibre have a rate of fire of 30–35 rounds a minute and the 6-inch guns in the British helicopter-cruisers *Tiger* and *Blake* have a rate of fire of 20 rounds a minute.

The American Mark 71 gun is operated by one man. The new British 4.5-inch Mark 8 gun fitted in seven missile destroyers and eight frigates requires no operator at all in the gun housing.

Another promising American development is the use of a laser control system for 8-inch and other large naval shells. During the final stages of its flight the shell is controlled by four small wing attachments. The wings themselves are controlled by a seeking device in the shell which picks up a laser beam trained on the target.

The use of space satellites for both communications and navigation at sea is already widespread in the US Navy and to a lesser extent in the British Navy—nothing is known of Soviet naval developments in this field. Continuing reliance on high frequency radio systems in NATO exercises is a constant source of problems. The answer lies probably in the acceptance by the European NATO navies of the British SCOT system.

Electronic limitations

This is specially designed for smaller ships where space and weight factors have ruled out the use of large space satellite communications terminals of the type carried in American carriers, command ships and in the British carrier *Ark Royal* and LPH *Hermes*. SCOT is fitted in the British helicopter-cruiser *Blake* and missile destroyer *London*.

Reconnaissance satellites today are a factor which any naval strategist must take into consideration when planning fleet dispositions. But despite the conderable and detailed degree of surveillance of the world's oceans that these satellites have made possible they have little relevance in hunting submarines, for example, and also will never be able to indicate the actual intentions of a group of ships at sea.

It would be a rash political leader or, at a lower level, naval commander who acted entirely on the evidence of a potential enemy's intentions purely from information passed by a space satellite. That, for example, a carrier may be launching aircraft in the direction of a potential enemy's homeland does not prove conclusively that an act of aggression is about to occur nor does the training of missile launchers on a likely target at sea.

In other words, despite the steady increase in computer processing of target information, of the use of space satellites for reconnaissance and global communications and of unmanned weapons, such as a wide variety of missiles, the human element remains vital. Indeed, such is the increase in the range, speed and complexity of warfare at sea over the past few years that the swift decision-making of the human brain in command is more vital than ever if miscalculation and misinterpretation of masses of data, which could lead to catastrophic results, are to be avoided.

Sea power - the critical balance

In an age when even the smallest navy can deal a powerful blow the balance of world sea power stands delicately poised. Leadership has shifted steadily away from the Western Alliance, and Soviet Russia now has the world's largest navy. However, sea power means considerably more than command of the seas. The navies of the major powers control a significant part of the nuclear deterrent with which East and West continually threaten each other. Today, more than at any other time in history, sea power is crucial to our survival.

The most remarkable phenomenon of sea power in the era since 1945 has been the rise of the Soviet Navy as not only a major political and military factor at sea but, to a point where it is the world's largest. Many Western strategists and political thinkers have sought to provide reasons for this phenomenon—some, for example, have declared it to be based upon an abiding suspicion of the West and therefore simply an extension in depth of the defences of 'Mother Russia'.

Yet the truth is simple: under the influence of Admiral Sergei Gorshkov the Soviet leadership has come to see that sea power is essential for the furtherance of the time-honoured, but still utterly valid, aim of achieving the world-wide supremacy of the Communist system.

Where there is room for argument is in what awakened the Soviet leaders to the need for seapower and exactly when this occurred. Various dates have been ascribed and it has been popularly supposed that the American blockade of Cuba in 1962, which forced Khruschev to recall missile-loaded freighters actually on passage across the Atlantic, demonstrated to the Kremlin its inability to further its policies overseas without sea power.

But in fact the impetus was supplied much earlier. Russia's inability to intervene in the 1956 Anglo-French landings in Egypt, following President Nasser's seizure of the Suez Canal, and then to prevent American intervention in Lebanon, to stop a Communist take-over, probably supplied the initial spark.

Yet even these events and the resulting sense of frustration in the Kremlin do not fully supply the answers to the 'when and why' of modern Soviet seapower. A massive naval building programme was underway in 1941 at the time of the German invasion in

British guided missile destroyers and frigates on exercises. The ships in the foreground are County Class DLGs, armed with the Seaslug beam-riding anti-aircraft missile system, with a Leander *Class and a* Tribal *Class to the left.*

which most of the ships were destroyed on the slipways.

New role for Russia's navy

A few ships, mainly cruisers and destroyers, survived and it is significant that the first major Russian warships apparently laid down after 1945, the Sverdlov class cruisers, owe something to pre-war Italian naval architecture and design. Thus the desire to create a sizeable fleet is not a new phenomenon in the Soviet Union. Rather, what is new is the doctrine of sea power in which the Navy is no longer a supporter of the Army's flanks, or even an extension of the homeland's defences, but a means of promoting, in its own right, the aims of the Communist leadership.

The first moves towards extending the Soviet Navy into the deep oceans began in 1961 when exercises were held in the Norwegian Sea. Six years later a permanent naval presence was established in the Mediterranean and the following year a Soviet naval squadron made the first appearance in the Indian Ocean. By 1970 this, too, had become a permanent feature. This was also the year of 'Okean'—the world-wide naval exercise which, judging by the publicity it was given, was intended also to be a major propaganda effort particularly to impress the Third World of uncommitted nations.

The forces carrying out these various deployments have improved as rapidly as has the extension of their activities around the world. Though 1958 saw the completion of the first Russian nuclear powered attack submarine the surface ships for the most part were conventional gun-armed Sverdlov class cruisers; Skory and later Kotlin class destroyers and Riga class escorts—also all conventionally armed.

By the early 1960s the air threat was recognised with the fitting of anti-aircraft missiles (SAM) in Kotlin class ships and at least one Sverdlov. In the late 1950s or early 1960s surface-to-surface missiles were fitted in some converted Kotlin class ships which, when rebuilt, were known as the Kildin class under NATO's system of nomenclature for Soviet warships.

The missiles fitted in these ships are believed to have a range of about 130 nautical miles (166 statute miles). The advent of surface-to-surface missiles in the Soviet fleet caused something of a stir in the West.

Why, it was asked by interested laymen, (and by some politicians and industrialists with vested interests, in electronics and missile production, who should have known better) had the West nothing comparable to these Soviet missiles? Could they not pick off Western warships at will far beyond the range of any gun?

The answer, of course, lay in the different strategic thinking and therefore tactical approach with the weaponry deemed necessary for it by the Western powers. Quite simply this was the reliance by the American, British and French navies particularly on the carrier and its aircraft as the primary naval weapon.

That this thinking was, and still is, correct is clear when the facts are studied. The carrier aircraft can far outrange any missile used tactically at sea even without its own use of air-to-surface missiles. Thus the surprise attack by the missile-armed surface ship would only succeed when the target lacked the benefit of air support.

Moreover, the missile-launching ship has no way of knowing the intentions of its target and in an age of massive nuclear retaliation it would be extremely foolhardy to launch missiles in a pre-emptive attack, unless the aim was to create a highly dangerous incident or to avoid annihilation of one's own forces. But this latter situation would presuppose that the enemy's hostile intentions had been fully demonstrated which might well not be a certainty during a time of international tension.

Thus the manned aircraft has the invaluable advantage over the surface missile ship of the human presence of the pilot. In other words, a human brain can see, assess and report on a situation before an act of war is committed.

One further drawback with the surface ship-launched missile, which was not at once obvious to the uninitiated, is that to achieve a range of 130 miles, or indeed anything much over about 25 miles, it is necessary to have some form of mid-course guidance. This is because at distances over around 20–25 miles the target will be below the missile ship's radar horizon. Therefore some agency —another ship, a helicopter, submarine or aircraft—must provide target co-ordinates so that the missile's flight path can be corrected. Obviously, the presence of some other unit between the launching ship and the target may cancel out the surprise factor and will certainly make it easier for the target to defend itself.

Soviet surface-to-surface missile developments at sea continued apace and a good example is the Kara class cruisers with eight launching tubes. But, significantly, the range has dropped to about 28 miles maximum which indicates that the Soviet Navy's leaders are aware of the vulnerability of a mid-course guidance system. Surface-to-air missiles have also been developed in both accuracy and numbers mounted in ships.

'Charlie' shadows US carriers

But the West was faced with a much greater problem in countering the Soviet development of the tactical missile submarine. Here initial developments began in the 1950s with the conversion of some 'Whisky' class diesel-electric submarines to carry 300-mile range missiles. Apart, again, from the mid-course guidance problem, to launch their missiles the submarines had to surface, albeit briefly, at which point they became very vulnerable.

In 1968 this problem had been fully overcome and 30 mile range missiles which could be fired from totally submerged, nuclear powered, submarines were available. These represented the real challenge to the West's,

and notably America's, carrier fleets for which the Soviet Navy had long been striving.

It is no coincidence that these 'Charlie' class submarines are believed to operate everywhere that American carriers are regularly found. Providing a wartime antidote to the carrier is one thing but no submarine can fulfil all of the many tasks a carrier can perform.

The Soviet Navy has for years, using its AGI—intelligence-gathering—trawlers, as well as conventional warships and submarines, closely studied Western carriers at sea. Now, at last, they have evidently amassed enough information to design their own carriers and the first, *Kiev,* is expected soon to be at sea.

What, then, is the lesson that Western carriers have provided? Basically, it is flexibility. The ability to bring to bear in a situation the minimum, and indeed massive, forces needed—a graduated response. In addition, this response can be provided without the use of shore bases which so often engender political and economic problems.

The carrier in one package provides reconnaissance, strike, fighter protection, anti-submarine defence and rescue facilities—the last a matter of no small importance, as rescue operations by British and American carriers in areas of natural disasters around the world have shown.

That the US Naval leadership is aware of carriers' continuing importance is evident with the construction of three nuclear powered carriers underway in the mid-1970s. These, with ten other carriers (of which one is nuclear powered), will remain the keystone of Western naval policy through the 1980s and probably into the next century.

Making the risk unacceptable

In Britain the carrier force is down to one ship and that, hopefully, will eventually be replaced by V/STOL aircraft flying from a new type of vessel known as the Through-Deck Cruiser. The aim of such a ship would not be to provide on a massive scale for all kinds of air operations that are possible with the large carrier of the American type, but simply to ensure that air or missile ship attacks on Britain's shipping lifelines would be met with a degree of opposition that the would-be aggressor would rate to be unacceptable.

It is for this reason that the ship is more costly and sophisticated than the planned American Sea Control Ship although this would also carry V/STOL aircraft and helicopters. This latter design is intended for the close air support of convoys and of amphibious operations.

The flexibility of the defensive response a carrier can confer has influenced Australia and France to retain one fixed-wing carrier each although the French have a second available and the two are normally used in rotation for anti-submarine helicopter carrying.

If, in saying that the carrier is likely to remain the keystone of Western naval policy it would appear that the nuclear powered ballistic missile armed submarine is a glaring omission, it is as well to put the role of such cruiser-size vessels in their proper perspec-

tive. They are, as indeed was argued by some in the early days of funding of the four-ship British Polaris missile submarine programme, fulfilling a deterrent role that is more of a national political one rather than purely a naval concern. The balance of power at sea would not be altered if every strategic nuclear missile submarine was scrapped tomorrow— the same cannot be said of the carrier or the tactical missile submarine.

Nevertheless, it is the task of America's nearly ninety, Russia's (believed) two dozen, and Britain's dozen nuclear powered attack submarines in service or building to counter as far as possible the threat posed by strategic missile submarines—over forty in the US Navy; four in the British Navy; and at least 45 (plus some conventionally powered types) in the Soviet Navy. Recently, the British Navy has introduced a new tactical technique, known as Group Operating, in which the high speed of these submarines is used to ambush a surface force seeking to attack a similar force. (It should, perhaps, be said that a similar concept was tried out in World War I by the British Navy in which fast steam-driven 'K' class submarines were used. But the concept was a failure owing to the submarines' technical unreliability.)

One ship, many names

Numerically, the most ubiquitous type of ship in all the world's navies of any consequence is that variously described as frigate/destroyer/escort/corvette. Sizes range from over 10,000 down to about 1,000 tons. There is an equally wide range in armament which can include surface-to-surface; surface-to-air; surface-to-sub-surface missiles; guns from 5-inch to 40 mm; various types of mortars for use against submarines; helicopters and anti-missile guidance radar jamming mortars.

The common factor with the majority is that their primary role is against submarines. But air defence, shore bombardment, defence against fast missile boats and even mine-laying are among other roles.

Mine-sweeping forces, once extremely numerous, have somewhat dwindled. Wartime vessels have become obsolete and, often being wooden built, have a limited life in reserve—a category in which many are found since peacetime requirements are limited to training. In the United States Navy the helicopter-minesweeper has almost entirely replaced the surface variety.

In Britain, the Netherlands, Belgium and Australia particularly the mine-hunter now supplements the minesweeper and uses Sonar to detect mines for subsequent destruction by divers.

In the Soviet Navy, and those of several of her European allies as well as those of allies elsewhere and of nations like Albania, Algeria, Egypt and Indonesia, the fast missile boat of Soviet design has become the most important weapon. In calm, confined waters such craft with 15 to 18 mile range Styx surface-to-surface missiles pose a considerable threat to the conventional surface ship.

As a result particularly of French expertise the 25 mile range Exocet surface-to-surface missile is finding a ready market in many navies, including smaller ones such as Malaysia, Chile, Pakistan and Greece. French know-how also probably lies behind Israeli

Above : A truck rumbles down the ramp of the American tank landing ship Saginaw *during exercise 'Agile Jouster' in Puerto Rico in 1973, when units of the British, Canadian and Netherlands navies joined Brazilian and Uruguayan ships.*

Left : A close-up view of the flight deck of a Moskva Class helicopter-cruiser. The two ships of the class so far launched have a heavy armament of guns and missile-launchers forward.

A US Marine Corps AV-8A British-built Harrier VTOL aircraft is readied for a catapult launch from the Interim Sea Control Ship, USS Guam. *Britain is developing a new uprated Pegasus engine to give more power and range.*

developments in this field, something in which South Africa is taking considerable interest.

The large all-gun armed ship of the cruiser type is still to be found in the Indian and several South American navies but elsewhere most conventional cruisers now have at least surface-to-air missiles. In the British Navy two cruisers have been converted, at the expense of more than half their gun armament, to carry four anti-submarine helicopters and Seacat close range surface-to-air missiles. The US Navy alone still boasts four battleships mounting 16-inch guns but since all four are 30 years old their future, except in the reserve fleet is most doubtful.

Is there aggressive intent?

Britain, America, France and Russia all maintain sizeable amphibious forces including ships specially designed to operate large numbers of troop-carrying (or anti-submarine, if required) helicopters. Numerous other powers also maintain landing ships and craft though, for the most part, these are war-built vessels of often doubtful effectiveness.

Fleet support—the underway replenishment of warships with fuel, ammunition, food, stores and spares of all kinds—has been developed to a high degree in the British

and American navies though Russia has now caught up. Most other navies with any sort of role outside their own waters have some replenishment and support ships but in this task particularly the standard of competence very much depends on the amount of seatime performed each year.

So much, then, for the capabilities of some of the world's navies, but what of the tasks they face? The broad aim of the Soviet Navy is generally agreed to be the furtherance of the cause of Kremlin-style Communism around the world. This is, often inextricably, intermingled with the genuine needs of defence of the Soviet homeland. Thus the Baltic, Black Sea and, to some extent, Northern Soviet fleets have essentially defensive tasks. But these sea areas train and provide the ships for the fleets used in the deep ocean areas.

The Mediterranean is an area where the Russians claim the presence of two American carriers in the Sixth Fleet and an unknown number of Polaris missile submarines pose a direct threat to their security. Consequently Russia has some 50 ships in the area most of the time compared to about 40 American, though to these must be added some small British, Italian, Greek and Turkish forces, mainly escorts, which could be spared from their primary role of shipping protection. Soviet Mediterranean forces include missile cruisers and destroyers, nuclear powered

Above : This Fast Patrol Boat of the Federal German Navy is armed with French Exocet surface-to-surface missiles and an Italian 76-mm gun. The Bundesmarine *was formed in 1954 to help defend the exit from the Baltic against Russian naval forces.*

Right : The Leander *Class frigates are armed with two 4.5-inch guns, Seacat missiles, a depth-charge mortar and a Westland Wasp helicopter with homing torpedoes.*

attack submarines, and amphibious forces—the last possessed by the US Sixth Fleet and by the French, Greek, Italian and Turkish navies.

The Sixth Fleet has some shore base support at Athens while the Russians have Latakia in Syria and some residual air facilities in Egypt. Shore-based American maritime patrol aircraft are based in Sicily and there are moorings for support ships for submarines and patrol craft at Naples and in Sardinia. Just outside the area, at Rota in southwest Spain, is an American-Spanish base for US Polaris submarines and a carrier.

NATO's seaborne response

In northern European waters a permanent Soviet naval presence is limited to an intelligence-gathering trawler, often working with a submarine, off Malin Head, the most

northerly point of Ireland, whose task is to monitor the movements of British and American Polaris submarines from their bases on the Clyde. Another Soviet trawler keeps watch on British, Dutch, West German and occasionally other nations' warships undergoing intensive training exercises off Portland in the south-western sector of the English Channel. A submarine rescue ship, the only one of its kind permanently stationed outside Soviet waters, is usually found in the Shetland Islands area to the north of Scotland.

There are frequent movements in the sea areas to the south and east of Britain by a variety of usually British, Dutch, Danish, Belgian, West German and Norwegian warships but there is no permanent force available except the Standing Naval Force Atlantic which spends part of its time cruising in North American waters. This force is usually composed of a destroyer, frigate or other escort, from the US, British, Dutch, Norwegian, West German, Portuguese, Danish and Canadian navies.

Its main task is to deter by convincing the Kremlin that any aggressive moves at sea would at once involve many of the members of the NATO Alliance. A similar force involving minesweepers and hunters has been set up in the NATO Channel area and Britain, Belgium, The Netherlands and West Germany participate.

In the Mediterranean a multi-national 'On Call' force of US, British, Italian, Greek and/or Turkish warships exercise as a single unit at frequent intervals. Because of the age of many of their ships and the size of their navies the Greeks and Turks particularly have not felt able to support a permanent force.

During a higher state of tension the Maritime Contingency Force would be set up by NATO. This consists of British and Dutch ships, if possible including Britain's one carrier *Ark Royal*, and amphibious forces from both countries whose task would be to stand-by off northern Norway to deter a Soviet threat from materialising into open aggression: at which point amphibious forces would be landed and air support provided if sought by the Norwegian government which does not permit foreign forces to be based on its soil in peacetime. This force with the Norwegians would have to 'hold the ring' until the arrival of American reinforcements from across the Atlantic.

Keeping a world-wide balance

In the western Atlantic a number of Soviet intelligence-gathering trawlers are positioned permanently off such areas as the Cape Kennedy missile testing range and elsewhere. The Western presence in the area are ships of the US Atlantic Fleet and the Canadian Navy.

The South Atlantic now is covered by frequent Soviet naval long-range maritime reconnaissance aircraft flights from Conakry, Guinea. In addition, two destroyers are usually stationed off Guinea to prevent any incursion by guerillas. Soviet naval air flights are, of course, a frequent occurrence in the North Atlantic, North and Norwegian Seas and in the Mediterranean.

In the Indian Ocean there remains a small British presence of usually three escorts, supplemented twice yearly by a task force of

A Russian Tu16 Badger maritime reconnaissance aircraft flies over a Moskva Class helicopter-cruiser. The Badger and its successor the Tu-20 Bear provide not only sighting reports but mid-course guidance for surface-to-surface missiles.

a helicopter cruiser or missile destroyer leader, some escorts and a nuclear hunter-killer submarine. The Australian Navy, whose escorts and carrier have the principal task of defending coastal shipping, exercises with US Pacific Fleet ships and both it and the New Zealand Navy provide an escort for the combined British-Australian-New Zealand ANZUK force at Singapore. One British or Australian diesel-electric submarine is assigned to this force.

The US Naval presence in the area has from time to time included a carrier but normally consists of a headquarters ship and two destroyers in the Persian Gulf/Red Sea areas. This is in contrast to the Russian naval forces which number 16–18 ships including a missile cruiser and two missile destroyers in the Aden–Socotra area alone. At least one 'Charlie' class missile submarine and a 'Victor' class nuclear powered attack or hunter-killer submarine have been seen in the Socotra and Malacca Straits areas though it is thought they were in transit rather than permanent units.

SEATO has no standing naval forces nor does CENTO in the Middle East. Both organisations have one major naval exercise annually. The Thai and Filipino navies are large enough only for their own local self-defence though the former has acquired an ocean-going British-built escort.

In the Pacific very little is known of the exact size of the Soviet fleet while the US Seventh Fleet numbers usually three carriers. Its forward bases are in Japan, which herself has a sizeable force of conventional submarines and escorts, and at Subic Bay in the Philippines. This is backed up by the Pacific Fleet with bases on the American Pacific coast and at Pearl Harbor.

The NATO powers today have a total of about 1,000 warships of all types. The Soviet Navy has about 1,500 although these must be divided among the four main fleets of which the Northern and Pacific are easily the largest. But it should not be forgotten that the Soviet Union could survive without sea-power—the Western World could not.

Picture Credits

The publishers wish to thank the following photographers and organisations who have supplied photographs for this book.

Photographs have been credited by page number. Where more than one photograph appears on the page, references are made in the order of the columns across the page and then from top to bottom.

Some references have, for reasons of space, been abbreviated as follows:

The Imperial War Museum, London: **IWM**

The National Maritime Museum, London: **NMM**

US Naval Archives, Washington: **USN**

The Chilean Naval Archives, Santiago: **CNA**

Cover: IWM. Front Flap: Lockheed Corp, California. Front End Paper: Ullstein. Back End Paper: IWM.

1: Barry & Co, London. 3: Robin Adshead. 6: NMM-W. Wyllie. 8: Godfrey Argent. 9: IWM. 10: Science Museum, London. 12: IWM. 13: NMM. 14: IWM. 15: Science Museum/IWM. 16: NMM-W. Wyllie. 18: Science Museum. 19: CNA/JG Moore Collection, London. 20: CNA/CNA/IWM. 21: JG Moore Collection. 23: NMM/CNA. 24: IWM. 26: NMM. 27: Fujifotos, Tokyo/Fujifotos/Fujifotos. 28: IWM. 29: IWM. 30: IWM. 31: IWM/IWM. 34: NMM-A. B. Cull/IWM. 35: IWM/IWM. 36: Ullstein GmbH, Berlin. 37: IWM. 38: IWM/IWM/IWM. 40: NMM-W. Wyllie. 42: Ullstein. 43: IWM/IWM. 44: NMM-W. Wyllie. 46: IWM/IWM. 48: IWM. 50: IWM. 51: IWM. 52: IWM. 52: IWM/IWM. 53: IWM. 54: Ullstein. 56: IWM. 62: IWM. 63: Ullstein. 64: Ullstein. 65: IWM. 66: Ullstein. 68: IWM. 69: Ullstein. 71: IWM/IWM. 72: Ullstein. 73: IWM/IWM. 74: IWM. 76: IWM. 77: IWM/IWM. 78: IWM. 79: IWM. 80: IWM. 82: Bapty. 83: IWM. 84: IWM. 86: Bapty. 87: Blitz Publications, London. 88: IWM. 89: IWM/IWM. 90: Bapty. 91: Blitz. 92: IWM. 94: Blitz. 95: NMM-C.E. Turner. 96: IWM. 97: USN. 99: Blitz. 100: IWM. 103: IWM. 104: IWM/IWM/IWM. 106: Bapty. 107: IWM. 108: IWM. 110: Novosti Press Agency, London. 111: Bapty. 112: USN. 113: IWM. 114: USN/USN. 115: USN. 116: IWM/Bapty. 120: IWM. 121: Blitz. 122: IWM/USN. 124: USN/IWM/Bapty. 127: IWM/IWM. 128: IWM. 131: IWM. 132. NMM-Norman Wilkinson. 134: IWM/IWM/IWM/IWM. 135: IWM. 136: Associated Press, London. 137: NMM-Norman Wilkinson. 138: IWM. 140: IWM. 142: IWM/IWM. 143: IWM/IWM. 146: USN. 148: USN/USN. 149: USN. 150: USN. 152: USN/USN. 153: USN. 154: USN/USN. 156: USN/USN. 157: USN. 158: USN. 159: USN. 160: USN/USN. 162: USN. 164: USN/USN/USN. 165: USN. 169: USN/US Marine Corps, Washington. 170: International News Photos. 171: USN. 172: USN. 173: USN/USN. 174: USN/USN. 175: US Marine Corps. 177: USN. 178: US Coast Guard, Washington. 180: USN. 181: USN. 182: USN/USN. 183: USN. 184: USN. 186: USN/USN. 187: USN. 188: USN/US Coast Guard. 190: US Coast Guard/USN. 191: USN. 192: USN. 193: USN/USN. 194: USN. 196: USN/US Marine Corps/USN. 197: USN/USN. 198: USN. 199: USN. 200: USN. 201: USN. 202: Robin Adshead. 204: USN. 205: AP. 206: USN. 207: Robin Adshead/Camera Press, London. 208: USN. 210: USN. 211: USN/USN. 212: Associated Press/USN. 213: Camera Press. 214: USN/USN. 215: USN. 216: Robin Adshead. 218: Novosti. 219: Ministry Of Defence (RN), London/Ministry Of Defence (RN). 220: British Hovercraft Corporation. 221: USN. 222: Israel Aircraft Industries, Lod. 223: Ministry Of Defence (RN)/USN. 224: Camera Press. 226: Camera Press. 227: Camera Press/Camera Press. 228: USN. 229: USN. 230: Camera Press. 231: Robin Adshead/Robin Adshead. 232: Keystone Press Agency, London. 234: Camera Press. 235: Associated Press/Lockheed. 236: USN/Ministry Of Defence (RN). 237: Camera Press. 238: Robin Adshead. 240: Robin Adshead/USN. 241: Robin Adshead/Robin Adshead. 242: NASA/Novosti. 243: USN. 244: Robin Adshead. 247: USN/Novosti/USN. 248: Robin Adshead. 249: Robin Adshead. 250: Ministry Of Defence (RN). 251: US Coast Guard.